Mary O'Hara-Devereaux
Robert Johansen

GLOBALWORK

Bridging Distance, Culture, and Time

Jossey-Bass Publishers · San Francisco

Substantial discounts on bulk quantities of Jossey-Bass books are available to corporations, professional associations, and other organizations. For details and discount information, contact the special sales department at Jossey-Bass Inc., Publishers. (415) 433-1740; Fax (415) 433-0499.

For international orders, please contact your local Paramount Publishing International office.

TCF Manufactured in the United States of America on Lyons Falls Pathfinder Tradebook. This paper is acid-free and 100 percent totally chlorine-free.

In Chapter Two, Figure 2.3 was adapted from *Going International: How to Make Friends and Deal Effectively in the Global Marketplace,* © 1985, Random House, Lennie Copeland and Lewis Griggs, page 107, produced in conjunction with Griggs Productions' *Going International* video series.

Library of Congress Cataloging-in-Publication Data

O'Hara-Devereaux, Mary.
    Globalwork : bridging distance, culture, and time / Mary O'Hara-Devereaux, Robert Johansen.
        p.   cm. — (The Jossey-Bass management series)
    Includes bibliographical references and index.
    ISBN 1-55542-602-6
    1. International business enterprises—Management.
2. Intercultural communication. 3. Work groups. I. Johansen, Robert. II. Title. III. Series.
HD62.4.O36   1994
658'.049—dc20   94-4431
                                                                      CIP

FIRST EDITION
HB Printing   10 9 8 7 6 5 4 3   *Code 9452*

The Jossey-Bass
Management Series

CONTENTS

ix

PREFACE

The globalization of economic activity is perhaps the defining trend of our time. It is reshaping not only the grand, macro-level aspects of economic life but the personal aspects as well, including where, when, how, and with whom we perform our daily work. At every level, from the personal to the team, corporate, enterprise, and far-flung joint venture, and in every corner of the globe, the new economic order is opening worlds of opportunity by battering down the old barriers and boundaries that divided us from one another and limited our possibilities for interaction, cooperation, and growth.

That, at least, is the ideal—a panoramic vision of the

global economy as a surging, smoothly running, superefficient engine of productivity and prosperity. The reality, unfortunately, is not quite so attractive.

Although we have knocked down our regional and national market boundaries and allowed our aspirations to soar around the globe and into cyberspace—the workplace of the future—in reality, we have only begun to scale the peaks. Working globally is like a journey that traverses many hills and valleys to reach its destination. Despite the leapfrogging capabilities of our new electronic tools, the distances from peak to peak still appear to be vast.

At the same time that we dream of banishing these distances as obstacles to work, we struggle to embrace the human dimension of distance: cultural diversity. For global-work spans not only oceans and continents but the even greater divides between cultures that until recent years have barely even tried seriously to communicate with one another.

How do we make sense out of this? How do we dare do tomorrow—or even today—what just a decade ago was unimaginable? The question is not hyperbolic. Already, every working day, thousands of executives around the world call upon perfectly ordinary people to work on global, regional, or national teams, to communicate and cooperate across radically different cultures, to manage widely dispersed, fragmented organizations, and to hurdle multiple time zones in a single bound. And each working day, millions of managers and line employees struggle with the awkward, frustrating, confounding, down-to-earth questions of the global workplace:

- How do we build trust among team members scattered from Montreal to San Francisco—or from Chicago to Tokyo to Bangkok to Singapore—who have never met and are never likely to?

- How do we implement a strategy for sharing information over half a dozen different national electronic infrastructures ranging from robust to rubbish?

- How do we motivate workers in Brazil and Japan to participate in a collaborative team with an African American manager based in Los Angeles?

- How do we schedule a team conference call among members in Paris, New York, and Jakarta when there is no overlap in our working hours?

- How do we get things done on time when we have different concepts of time and different ideas about what it means to be "done"?

- How do we build and maintain a functioning culture in a strategic alliance or joint venture involving numerous functional, corporate, and national cultures, many of which clash with one another?

- Isn't it lonely out there in cyberspace?

The questions go on and on.

Certainly the recent and accelerating advances in technology have enabled us to confront these questions with some confidence that they can be solved. But we make a classic mistake if we expect technology to do it for us. Technology can help put us in contact with one another — over oceans and over cultures — but it cannot make us understand one another. For that we must still depend on the oldest systems of all: human imagination, tolerance, determination, and the will to learn continuously.

PURPOSE OF THE BOOK

Globalwork is intended to help all the many managers and teams — ourselves included — in large and small businesses, joint ventures, strategic alliances, and government and nonprofit enterprises who are having to come to grips with new ways of working in the global workplace. During our three years of exploratory research it became clear that the shifts in the global economy were of such magnitude that people at nearly every level and every type of work were going to have to change the ways in which they think about and perform their everyday work. Everyone from CEOs to front-end sales, distribution, and service people needs to see the larger, shifting context of their work and then integrate what they see into a new and personal view of a radically changing work environment.

We thus decided to offer as broad a view as possible of the changes, opportunities, and challenges we have witnessed. Others have approached the same landscape from narrower perspectives: the technological promises of groupware, the dynamics of cross-functional and cross-cultural teamwork, the new architecture of the global corporation, and more. All these pieces of the puzzle are complex and challenging in their own right, and many books remain to be written on each and every one. But at this early stage of globalwork, we believe there is a need for a higher-level perspective that pulls together each of the pieces into a working integrated whole. We felt the urgent need for a book that offered not street maps but general, navigational directions to the global workplace for all levels of workers — both the global nomads and those who remain at home to support the pioneers. *Globalwork* is thus written both as a theoretical overview and a practical framework for bridging the chasms represented by cultures, distance, and time.

We also wanted to take some risks — to offer people new, simple, yet robust models for thinking about teams, technology, and culture in the global environment. These models, which we ourselves have been using in our globalwork, are sure to be refined and revised again and again, just as the early maps of a new territory are modified after further and deeper exploration. But if our own experience (and that of many others) is indicative, even these early guideposts provide useful starting points. They often reveal which approach is the wrong way, even if they don't always point out the right way.

Our cultural starting point, as writers from the United States, is U.S. culture. As much as we have endeavored to keep a broad perspective in this book, our root culture will be obvious—and appropriately so, for it would be impossible to transcend our country and culture of origin.

Most of the chapters contain strategies, rules of thumb, and pitfalls drawn from the many organizations, managers, and teams we interviewed during our research. And, being oriented as we are to the future, we have tried to extend our perspectives on challenges and strategies to the challenges and strategies we will meet in the next three to ten years. For tomorrow's workplace will be radically different from that of today.

HOW THIS BOOK
CAN HELP YOU

Although *Globalwork* is not a how-to book, it does attempt to bring together in one accessible format a combination of broad frameworks and specific strategies for meeting the challenges that lie ahead—indeed, confront many of us today. We believe these perspectives and guidelines can help people deal effectively with the following kinds of issues:

- Making confident, informed choices about globalwork as a result of models and metaphors that provide practical frames of reference

- Taking cultural readings in the global business environment and following up with appropriate action

- Using information technology appropriately and avoiding its many pitfalls

- Working more effectively with dispersed teams in every mode from same-place/same-time to different-times/different-places and anytime/anyplace

- Working confidently and collaboratively in "third ways," beyond any single culture

- Supporting continuous cultural learning about oneself and others
- Building a repertoire of cross-cultural and remote management practices appropriate to each situation's specific needs
- Facilitating and managing business processes across distance, time, and culture
- Integrating electronic and human tools and techniques
- Applying the broad lessons of globalization to the more focused realm of regionalization—and vice versa

INFORMATION SOURCES

Much of the information in *Globalwork* emerged from an ongoing research project called the Groupware Outlook Project, a joint venture of the Institute for the Future and the Grove Consultants International (formerly Graphic Guides). The Groupware Outlook Project is supported by more than twenty-five organizations in the United States, Europe, Canada, and Mexico, most of which are global. The purpose of the project, now in its fifth year, is to study the intersection of technology, teams, and organizational change in the near-term future. Our clients include both users and vendors of emerging technologies who are all using team-based, network-style structures and a range of information technologies to support their work.

During the last two years, members of our Groupware Outlook team have worked in many countries: Australia, Canada, Costa Rica, Denmark, France, Germany, Guatemala, India, Japan, Kenya, Mexico, Norway, Panama, Somalia, Sweden, Thailand, the United Kingdom, and most parts of the United States. In our travels we all have interviewed many pioneers of globalwork, and we have watched organizations and teams at work.

Over the life of the project, we have been intrigued by

the number of clients who seemed to be struggling as much with the human issues of globalization as with the technological ones. This was a key impetus for our broad-based response to their needs. Together we talked over the difficulties of working across cultures—where assumptions, work styles, and even views of life are different—and the struggle for electronic connectivity and continuity across the irregular infrastructure of the global workspace. Finally, we explored with them the question of how information technologies might ease the pain of distant and cross-cultural work—or at least not exacerbate it.

We interviewed thousands of pioneers working with diverse teams from more than a hundred different organizations, large and small, to probe for answers to our questions and to single out the key challenges and strategies that seem to work (and not to work). The fieldwork was not meant to be an exhaustive look at any one type of team; rather, we wanted to take a contextual view that would provide a platform for deeper understandings of all types of teamwork. After all, managing across distance, time, and culture will become a high-priority skill for most businesses, whether the business is conducted within national boundaries or across the great expanse of the globe.

The results of our initial study were published in a proprietary report, "Bridging Distance and Diversity," for the Groupware Outlook clients. Over the last year they have used it extensively as a resource for training, orientation, and reference for global managers and teams. Their reactions and their suggestions contributed key insights for our reworking of that material into the present book.

HOW TO USE THE BOOK

Globalwork is intended to provide both practical answers and a broad, theoretical perspective on the issues and trends shaping the globalization of work—specifically, the problems and opportunities of distance and diversity and the strategic implementation of technology and team process. We hope the reader will come away from the book with not only a deeper understanding of why the tectonic shifts in the workplace are occurring but also some useful strategies for responding to them right now in real-world business situations.

Part One of the book (Chapters One to Five) is a broad-brush rendering of our basic perspective on the challenges of working across distances and cultures. We also offer our thoughts on the technological and human tools that we believe will assist practitioners in the field.

Chapter One sets the stage by surveying the forces that govern the world of globalwork. It discusses four drivers of change that we describe as *fault lines*—pressure points where social and technological forces have converged in such a way as to set off earthshaking changes whose effects ripple across the global landscape. These four fault lines are the globalization of consumerism; the transformation of the traditional corporate hierarchy into a multinational or global network; the fragmentation of work and creation of global jobs; and the ascendancy of knowledge as a primary global product. A general appreciation of these forces—and how people and business organizations have responded to them—is vital to understanding the mindshift that is necessary to make globalwork a reality.

Chapters Two to Five present the four competencies we believe are necessary for success in the global world of work: cross-cultural communication, process facilitation, creating and sustaining remote teamwork, and managing information technology. Chapter Two is an acknowledgment of the reality that has been conveyed to us in interviews with hundreds of global workers—the fact that cultural diversity, even more than distance, is perhaps the greatest challenge (and opportunity) of the global workplace. The excitement and allure of globalwork are offset by the shocks of cross-cultural encounters and the physical and mental rigors of working across great distances.

Global workers cannot be expected to come to their tasks

with a full toolkit of anthropological knowledge. And yet we are all being asked to add "cultural filters" and sensitivities to our behavior, both at work and at home in our communities. The expectation is no small matter, for it involves a profound shift of mindsets and the development of specific personal skills. To the initiate in the global workplace, cultures seem impenetrable — there are so many dimensions and so few distinct boundaries. But if one can imagine culture slightly deconstructed, discernible features begin to appear, and they can serve as useful handles and footholds. During our exploration of cultural issues in the workplace, we focused on how cultural differences and similarities can be organized around four centers: the physical, the social, the work-related, and the spiritual manifestations of culture.

In this book we concentrate most of our discussion on the social and work-related aspects of cultures. And to focus even more closely on these dimensions, we have adopted five cultural lenses that represent a kind of taxonomy of culture: language, time, context, power/equality, and information flow. These dimensions have long been observed by many anthropologists as the fundamental ways in which cultures differ; in this book we have adapted these anthropological terms for use in a business context. They can be understood intuitively by anyone and applied to almost any culture. Taken together, they provide a simple but robust framework and common language that any manager and team can apply to the complex and daunting challenges of cross-cultural work. They also serve as a sturdy foundation for further explorations into the mysteries of culture.

Chapter Three examines the ways in which collaborative information technologies are evolving — rapidly but unevenly — to help people leap across the boundaries of distance, time, and culture. Communications and computer networking among North America, Europe, and Japan, for example, are still sometimes tricky but generally quite workable. Good links to Eastern Europe, Africa, and parts of South America, however, are virtually impossible — except in specific cases where leapfrog technologies (like cellular phones and satellites) are changing things overnight. The global electronic infrastructure is definitely improving, although sporadically and often in frustrating ways. It will take hard work just to establish outposts of support, let alone global interconnections. Until then, we are left with some tough questions: Which medium, which types of systems, should we use and when? Out of the increasingly wide variety of electronic and nonelectronic options, what works best in which situations? This chapter offers a general assessment of both the tools that are available and the tools we expect to become available in the near future, and it presents our advice for using the tools in culturally appropriate ways.

Chapter Four explores the issues of global team leadership—the personal characteristics required to manage people and technology in a global setting. It also addresses the need for a new conceptualization of the workforce—one that is populated with nomadic managers, telecommuters, traffic controllers, and the pilots of cyberspace. The discussion concludes with a look at the need for continual learning and a framework for applying the key leadership competency known as *process facilitation*: how to keep teams working together effectively toward a common goal when they span distance, culture, and time.

Chapter Five focuses on global teams by looking at six common challenges facing distributed and cross-cultural teams. We discuss how information technology and key management strategies can be used in developing the new business practices needed to create and sustain global teams.

Part Two of the book, Chapters Six to Eleven, applies the lessons of Part One to the global, regional, and national dimensions of the distributed, cross-cultural workforce, using vignettes drawn from actual situations to illustrate the issues.

Chapters Six and Seven examine the truly global workplace and the "third way" strategies for navigating its challenges. Chapter Six builds on the four critical competencies laid out in the earlier chapters. Using a vignette of a Chinese–U.S. joint venture, we look more closely at the differences in approaches to common business processes as viewed through the five cultural lenses presented in Chapter Two.

In Chapter Seven, we look at "third way" strategies and uses of technology that might have helped the players in the vignette resolve their differences. The chapter concludes with a discussion of the importance of creating global visions as a first step to creating a global corporate culture and a description of a graphic framework used by National Semiconductor Corporation to link their business units around the globe.

In Chapters Eight, Nine, and Ten, we turn our attention to the North American economic region of Mexico, Canada, and the United States—a zone that typifies most of the challenges of globalwork. (The question of U.S. ratification of the North American Free Trade Agreement, which would codify and accelerate the regionalization of the North American economy, was answered by a narrow positive vote by Congress and signed by President Clinton as this book went to press.) These chapters are offered as prototypes for the sort of comprehensive cultural and technological assessment that regional team leaders and corporate managers should perform if they wish to work successfully in the NAFTA environment. Viewing the region from the perspective of each country and through the models developed in the first part of the book, we discuss strategies, rules of thumb, and pitfalls for this special case of globalwork.

Chapter Ten, which focuses on the United States, presents an outside-in view of this country from the global perspective. (It is not intended to be an in-depth treatment of the challenges of domestic cultural diversity, a subject explored in numerous other books.)

Chapter Eleven is a voyage into the mysteries of cyberspace, the work*space* beyond the work*place*. It is meant to raise awareness that, increasingly, workers in distributed teams come to know each other and interact with one another only as virtual teammates: electronic representations in a computer-created world. This dramatic evolution raises a whole new set of questions: What are the rules of work in cyberspace? What are the ethics? Where are the boundaries? We are reminded by John Perry Barlow, president of the Electronic Frontiers Foundation, that the U.S. Bill of Rights is just a local ordinance in cyberspace.

Chapter Twelve provides a personal conclusion reflecting on the changes that have come and those still teasing us from the distant horizon.

March 1994 MARY O'HARA-DEVEREAUX
San Francisco, California

ROBERT JOHANSEN
Menlo Park, California

ACKNOWLEDGMENTS

Although our names appear on the cover, all the members of our Groupware Outlook team and other researchers and staff members at the Institute for the Future and the Grove Consultants International have contributed in significant ways to the ideas, research, and writing of *Globalwork*. The book, therefore, is truly an example of the close and collaborative teamwork we strive to achieve in our work. For us, the book is the result of a successful cross-functional, cross-cultural team collaboration.

Robert Mittman, Tomi Nagai-Rothe, and David Sibbet were our steady consultants and critical readers. All three read and commented constructively on the work in progress, cheerfully meeting our deadlines despite their own heavy workloads. Robert's vast technological competence and his extensive work in France contributed greatly to the ideas expressed throughout the book. David assisted greatly in creating the conceptual models, and he personally drew much of the artwork as well as contributed key ideas to the Chapter Four discussion of process facilitation and the Chapter Seven discussion of "third way" strategies. Tomi worked closely with us in analyzing the results of myriad interviews and case studies and helped develop the vignettes and exploration of culture and distance challenges in Chapters Six and Seven. Her deep cross-cultural competence, particularly her understanding of Asian cultures, was a rich source of support.

Greg Schmid and Andrea Saveri were important contributors to the global trends and fault lines discussed in Chapter One. Andrea was involved in the primary research in Mexico and worked closely with us in the writing of Chapter Eight.

Wendy Cukier, a professor at Ryerson Polytechnical Institute in Ontario, Canada, and a leading telecommunications consultant, conducted much of the primary research in Canada and worked closely with us in preparing Chapter Nine.

Paul Saffo, IFTF's primary explorer of cyberspace, contributed greatly to the ideas and writing of Chapter Eleven.

Richard Dalton and Harvey Lehtman contributed important ideas to the role of information technology in Chapter Three and throughout the rest of the book. Stephanie Bardin made many insightful comments throughout and pulled together the references. Jennifer Wayne helped us with global technology statistics.

In addition to the core team, we collaborated in our research on Mexico with Guadalupe (Lupita) Martínez de León, head of the Department of Organizational Development at the University of Monterrey, Mexico. Lupita worked closely with us to identify a broad range of business leaders and teams to participate in our study. She also conducted interviews and helped us with case studies. Tammy Lowry, a graduate student at Rice University in Houston and with

Texaco's Department of Information Technology, assisted with data collection, interviews, and the case study for Chapter Ten. Ellen Baker, an applied psychologist and groupware expert from the University of Technology, Sydney, Australia, provided an important outside reading of the penultimate draft of the book while on sabbatical at the Institute for the Future.

Our deepest and most profound thanks go to our most recent team member, Jon Stewart—editor, writer, colleague, and new friend—who worked creatively and critically with us through both the report and manuscript phases of this project. Thanks to Jon's extensive knowledge of globalization, as well as his deep appreciation for the impact of these profound changes on workers around the globe, he provided an important review and added many improvements to our synthesis of the research and our own personal globalwork experiences. His collaboration was invaluable in shaping the ideas and improving the manuscript.

Our editors from Jossey-Bass, Bill Hicks and Cedric Crocker, provided extremely useful suggestions, beginning at our first meeting and continuing to the end. They maintained a wonderful balance of contribution, encouragement, and freedom to work on our own. Thanks also to Marcella Friel and Sarah Miller in production and to Terri Welch in marketing.

Robert Pardini, production manager for the Grove Consultants International, managed the multiple electronic versions and revisions that came before the book. He worked tirelessly and cheerfully to bring it to its final form.

The organizations in the Groupware Outlook Project have included 3Com Corporation, American Express, Ameritech, Apple Computer, AT&T, Bell Northern Research, Bellcore, Blue Cross/Blue Shield of Maryland, Coopers and Lybrand, the Defense Systems Management College, EDS, the Federal Aviation Administration, Hewlett-Packard, Intel, Lotus Development Corporation, Metropolitan Life, Philip Morris, National Semiconductor, NCR, Procter & Gamble, Senco, Stentor, Telia (Sweden), Texaco, the U.S. Department of Transportation, and Volpe National Transportation Systems Center. We are grateful for their contributions to this ongoing, applied research effort.

Finally, we thank the many diverse and distributed teams, companies, and individuals who shared their experiences and knowledge with us in interviews and case studies. Their stories and insights are the true life of *Globalwork*. We have learned from many different cultures and will try to share these learnings concisely without stereotyping—a difficult dilemma.

M. O.-D.
R. J.

THE AUTHORS

MARY O'HARA-DEVEREAUX is a global nomad making frequent journeys into the global workspace as director of the Institute for the Future's global work program and vice president of the Grove Consultants International (an organizational consulting firm). Bridging cultures in twenty-four countries in Africa, Asia, Europe, Latin America, and the United States over the past twenty years, she has led global teams, managed global projects, run a small global business, and conducted applied research about large-scale organizational change and what makes collaboration work.

In addition to having held faculty and staff positions at

the University of California and the University of Hawaii (the MEDEX Group), O'Hara-Devereaux is a frequent speaker at national and international forums and is author of many articles and reports that have focused on organizational change and collaborative teamwork in the health system and, more recently, on business teams. In addition, she is lead author of *Eldercare* (1980, with L. H. Andrus and C. Scott) and *Collaborative Practice: A Comprehensive Health Care Model* (1982, with L. H. Andrus). She received her B.S. degree (1964) from the University of Michigan, her M.H.S. degree (1971) and her M.S. degree (1973) in health planning and behavioral sciences from the University of California, Davis, and her Ph.D. degree (1979) from the Fielding Institute in psychology.

O'Hara-Devereaux regularly consults with both private business and government organizations on global management and organizational change programs as well as developing innovative process tools to support collaboration, team productivity, and systems thinking. Through her work around the world, she has gained a deep understanding of how culture works in the workplace and has discovered strategies to build the essential bridges.

ROBERT JOHANSEN is the leader of the Institute for the Future's program on new information technologies. For more than twenty years, he has conducted applied research into the social and business effects of emerging technologies. He is also a research affiliate at the Center for Information Systems Research and the Center for Coordination Science at MIT. A social scientist by training, he received his B.S. degree (1967) from the University of Illinois and his Ph.D. degree (1972) from Northwestern University.

Johansen is author of *Teleconferencing and Beyond: Communications in the Office of the Future* (1984), a synopsis of which was published in the *Harvard Business Review*; and *Groupware: Computer Support for Business Teams* (1988), the first book to explore the use of information technologies to support business teams. He is also lead author of *Electronic Meetings: Technical Alternatives and Social Choices* (1989, with

J. Vallee, K. Spanger, and R. G. Shirts), the first reference work on teleconferencing; and *Leading Business Teams* (1991, with others), a handbook for team leaders. He was one of the first social scientists to explore the human and organizational impacts of new communication and computing innovations.

Johansen is a frequent keynote speaker on emerging information systems and their potential advantages and disadvantages for users. He has been a college professor and has taught both graduate and undergraduate courses at a variety of universities, mostly recently with an emphasis on executive short courses and seminars. Moreover, he is project leader for an ongoing effort to explore the future of new information technologies to assist business teams and flatter, network-style organizations.

O'Hara-Devereaux and Johansen work together in an ongoing research program exploring the present and future of global-work. They can be reached at the Institute for the Future (415-854-6322).

GLOBALWORK

ONE

Introduction:
Fault Lines in the New
Global Business Landscape

A new landscape is emerging across the business world: the old boundaries of national economies and markets are bowing to globalization even as traditional office walls are giving way to new, borderless vistas. The familiar hierarchical structures of corporations — the organizational parallel of the manufacturing economy's "electromechanical" infrastructure — are crumbling and being replaced by the flattened, horizontal networks made possible by the digital infrastructure of the information age. And the single-mold, long-term employer/employee relationship is breaking down as the firm-based workforce itself

fragments into disparate, dynamic new entities that are changing the very meaning of work, employment, and even product.

The managers of the successful global businesses of, say,
the year 2010 will look back on these years of radical transformation at the end of the twentieth century and shake their
heads in amazement. How did we survive it, they will wonder—even as they ponder how to survive the enormous challenges to come in an environment in which change has become the only constant. The old problems may even seem
quaint. The impenetrable cultural walls that once defied
global marketing and global work teams will have been sur-
mounted by the spread of a global supraculture that permits
common visions and understandings above and beyond the
clashes of customs, myths, and civilizations.

The stubborn trade barriers that divided nations will
have finally fallen for much of the world, crushed by the
unrelenting pressures of competition and the need for export-
based growth. And the horrendous communications head-
aches of the past will have been eased by increasingly potent
"groupware" that finally brings to everyday reality the distant
dreams of global teamwork.

Along with these accomplishments, though, old challenges will persist and new ones will arise. While much of the
world will have joined in this robust global economy, some
regions, notably Africa, may still be left out—a source of
continuing instability and lost opportunities. Open trade lanes
will continue to serve as human migration routes so long as
vast gaps of wealth and opportunity persist within and between nations. And even in the richest postindustrial nations,
endemic levels of unemployment will threaten to make a
mockery of the oversold job promises of the global economy.

The working man and woman will be torn between their
need for job security and the countervailing opportunities
(and demands) for flexibility. Constant training, retraining,
job-hopping, and even career-hopping will become the norm.
The demand for stability and sustainability—and for community and continuity—will clash with ever greater repercussions
against the steady, fateful pace of change.

For now, those clashes are a distant, if inevitable, thunder. Surviving and succeeding in the business environment of the 1990s presents its own, more immediate challenges. For earthshaking change confronts us from all directions today.

In the global political arena, yesterday's relatively static (if terrifying) balance of great powers throughout the Cold War era has given way to the elusive possibilities of a "new world order" and the more immediate realities of massive disorder as the centripetal and centrifugal forces of nationalism and internationalism contend for preeminence. Does the future lie with an ascendant United Nations and the global spread of democracy and market economics through multilateral institutions like the General Agreement on Tariffs and Trade (GATT)? Or will the world economy balkanize into regional trade blocs like the European Community, the North American Free Trade Agreement, and an Asian equivalent? Will the former communist world play out the delayed agonies of late-nineteenth-century nationalism while the main axis of global division shifts from East/West to North/South? Or will the logic of free trade and multilateral cooperation overcome an ugly, growth-retarding competition between North and South for resources and economic power? We cannot be sure. We can only place our bets, hedge them, and plan for all contingencies.

Certainly the issue of environmental degradation will continue to unfold as industrial nations, beginning to see the price paid for development, are forced to balance growth with environmental protection. At the same time, industrially developing countries may be willing to exploit the environment to a greater extent in order to get up to speed in the global marketplace. The question is whether the balance of the global economy will parallel the new understanding of the global environment. Will access to profitable, albeit polluting, technologies be a flash point between North and South? Will developing nations be asked to meet expensive and stringent global environmental standards? Will they at the same time be exploited by corporations for their lack of environmental protections? Perhaps the advent of sustainable growth based on biosystemic thinking will create a forum different from the old boundaries.

Similarly, the world of business, which has sometimes led and sometimes followed politics in bridging the national barriers to a global economy, confronts immense uncertainties. The rate of technological and scientific advances—which in certain sectors, such as information technology, have been doubling every six to ten years since the 1960s—has already paved an electronic runway to the future: a future that may leave to history such monuments to the manufacturing era as professional management (as we know it) and the pyramidal corporation itself. Indeed work, as we know it, seems destined for the history books: going, if not yet gone, are the 9–5 workday, lifetime jobs, predictable, hierarchical relationships, corporate-culture security blankets, and, for a large and growing sector of the workforce, the workplace itself (replaced by a cybernetic global "workspace"). Even the products on which the developed world's corporations, skills, and work processes have been based are, if not vanishing into history, at least losing primacy to such intangibles as services, ideas, and manufacturing processes—the "products" of the future.

In the world of business, as in politics, we know pretty well where we have been for most of the past century: change has been constant but relatively predictable, and the central organizing paradigm of the manufacturing economy has held remarkably steady through decades of growth. We even understand where we are today—though part of that understanding includes the knowledge that the sand is shifting beneath our feet in some unpredictable ways. As for the future, the best we can do is catch glimpses of what is to come from the shifts that are already under way and from the experience of those companies and teams that have already pioneered beyond the frontiers of the known world and survived to tell about it.

FOUR EMERGING FAULT LINES

The lessons of such pioneers will provide invaluable guideposts at this historic turning point, and we will take a close look at these lessons in later chapters. But first we should examine some of the key shifts that are rumbling beneath the surface—in some cases erupting in gaping new fault lines—of the economic firmament. The fault lines, as illustrated in Figure 1.1, are the unmistakable signs of change, the points at which innumerable underlying pressures—economic, social, political, technological—have converged and emerged at the surface to change the contours of the world of work, leaving us with new markets, new corporate institutions to serve those markets, and new jobs to produce new goods for the world's new consumers.

The Global Consumer

No single fault line has contributed more to the emerging shape of the new global realities than the explosive expansion of a middle-class consumer market in regions that have previously been beyond the reach of all but strictly local business interests. In vast parts of what used to be called the underdeveloped world, hand-to-mouth existence is finally giving way to the export-led development of a robust middle class with rising consumer demands and the economic means to satisfy them. The Third World, which makes up 80 percent of the world's population, now accounts for as much as 45 percent of the global economy, if one measures economic activity by purchasing-power parity, which compares the cost of a similar basket of goods in different countries (Sesit, 1993).

More than anything else, this dramatic expansion has served as the engine of global economic growth, setting off a competitive scramble throughout the developed world that has forced hungry corporations to reinvent themselves as networks, alliances, and partnerships with a global reach. How these new markets will be organized, integrated, and penetrated remains one of the key questions behind the ongoing debate over free trade. Will the world divide up the new markets into regional blocs dominated by key players? Or will a genuinely global trade regime come about through GATT? If blocs win out, does business follow the same path? Or do the

Figure 1.1. Four Fault Lines in the Global Workspace.

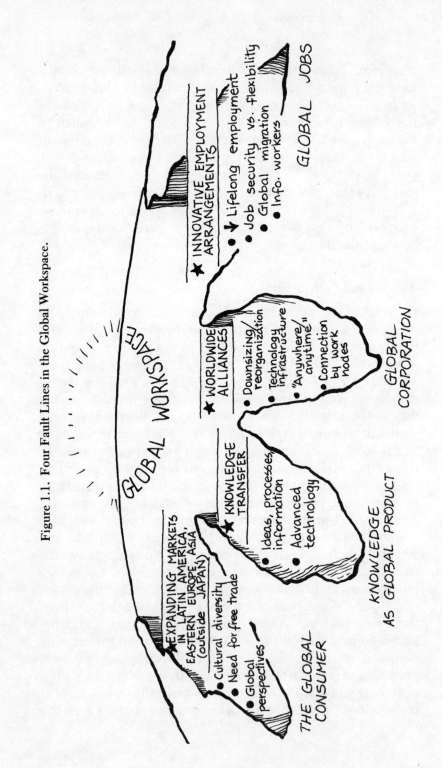

Figure 1.2. The Emergence of New Middle-Class Markets.

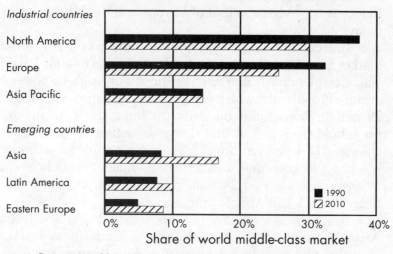

Share of world middle-class market

Source: World Bank, *World Development Indicators,* 1993.

evolving global networks build bridges between blocs as they have between nations? No one know the answers yet. But we do know enough to realize that the global consumer fault line is intricately and dynamically connected to every other major fault line.

We also know that the global impacts of this development can only grow more profound in the decades to come. Although the great majority of middle-class consumers, which we arbitrarily define as households with an income of $25,000 per year, are still in North America, Japan, and Western Europe, the growth of this market over the next two decades will be greatest in Eastern Europe, Asia (excluding Japan) and Latin America, according to World Bank indicators (Institute for the Future, 1993b) (see Figure 1.2). These regions, which today claim around 18 percent of the global consumer class, are projected to increase their share to one-third, or 110 million households, by the year 2010, thanks to an average 5 percent growth rate (compared to an annual growth of about 2 percent for the consumer class in the industrial countries).

Thus the emerging regions will represent a consumer market that is nearly as large as that of Europe and the United States today.

Indeed, the 11 percent share of the world consumer market now claimed by the Asian-Pacific region (mainly Japan) will be tremendously increased by the rest of Asia's 4.5 percent average growth rate, which will produce a consumer market of 29 million households by 2010, up from about 12 million households today. And that does not include China, whose stunning 11.4 percent projected average annual growth rate will boost its consumer market from 3 million households in 1990 to an estimated 26 million, nearly double the size of today's total Latin American market.

In just the six countries of the Association of Southeast Asian Economies (ASEAN), the rise of a consumer market over the past decade has been stunning. With 328 million people, these countries have enjoyed an average annual growth rate of 7 percent for more than a decade, during which they have become the United States' fifth largest export market, following Canada, Japan, the EC, and Mexico. U.S. exports to ASEAN reached $24 billion in 1992, and U.S. direct investment topped $32 billion (about half the level of Japanese investment in the region), according to the *New York Times* (Shenon, 1993). Despite these rising numbers, most international investment analysts still complain that U.S. businesses have barely begun to reap the potential of the Southeast Asian market. As for the Latin consumer market, it too should expand exponentially, at least doubling in size in every country. Brazil alone should provide a market of 11 million households, nearly triple today's level (Institute for the Future, 1993b).

The most obvious result of the phenomenal income growth over the past twenty years in Asia and, to lesser extent, Latin America is an explosive demand for consumer products. As incomes rise, the burgeoning megacities of these regions are becoming a chain of exploding firecrackers of demand. A 1993 survey of Asian business people in the ASEAN countries found that 50 percent had purchased a desktop computer in just the past year (Shenon, 1993). And the demand is not limited just to consumer products, like motorcycles, TVs, and PCs. To support these expanding urban pockets of con- sumerism, public infrastructure—roads, power plants, port facilities, universities, communications facilities—must ex- pand as well. One recent study cited by the *Economist* ("Mur- doch's Asian Bet," July 31, 1993, p. 13) projects that before the end of the century Asia (excluding Japan) will spend an as- tonishing $1 trillion on infrastructure. The demand for both energy and raw materials will be enormous—with a resulting strain on the natural environment.

Obviously, all of this expansion, combined with the slower-growing but vastly greater demand among the world's industrial economies, drives an ever-more competitive global marketplace in which the growing number of multinational firms, joint ventures, and alliances play the key role. Over the past decade, foreign direct investment through multinationals has grown at a rate exceeding 15 percent annually—almost two and a half times as fast as the growth in real output and almost three times as fast as the growth in trade of goods and services (*World Investment Report*, 1992). The average annual outflow of direct investment by multinationals is expected to double (in constant 1991 dollars) from the approximately $150 billion annually in the first half of the 1990s to $300 billion annually in the latter half (*World Investment Report*, 1992).

While the vast majority of this investment flows among the richest nations, the share coming from the big five indus- trial nations (the United States, United Kingdom, Japan, Germany, and France) declined from 80 percent in the 1970s to 66 percent in 1992, according to the 1992 U.N. World Investment Report (*World Investment Report*, 1992). Mean- while, the share of total foreign direct investment going to the new emerging markets is growing—especially in Asia, where investments are up 250 percent over the 1980s. Increasing flows are also showing up in China, unified Germany and Eastern Europe (particularly Hungary, Poland, and the Czech Republic), and the more developed former Soviet republics like Russia and Ukraine. The International Finance Corp., an arm of the World Bank, notes that the combined value of thirty-six of the principal emerging stock markets in the developing world multiplied elevenfold between 1982 and 1992, from just $67 billion to $774 billion (Sesit, 1993). This trend is expected to continue into the next century, by which time international equity investors will be routinely shifting dollars between stock exchanges in cities like Prague, St. Petersburg, Hanoi, Lima, Colombo, and Shanghai. Similarly, while almost four out of five of the Fortune Global 500 corporations are headquartered in the big five countries, the total number of countries hosting these multi- and transnationals has mushroomed to thirty-four, including Argentina, Brazil, India, Malaysia, Mexico, Thailand, Turkey, and Zambia (*World Investment Report*, 1992).

Predicting the location and force of tomorrow's consumer explosions is a relatively safe business, since the fuses are already burning. But figuring out how to participate in these markets successfully is a good deal riskier, for they are spread throughout a world of real and imagined barriers. Where they are already concentrated, in the United States and Europe, there is slow growth and fierce competition. Where they are growing fastest, they tend to be dispersed and hidden behind barriers of culture, language, tariffs, and exchange controls. Each of the major growth regions except for Japan is made up of several different countries with different languages, customs, cultures, markets, distribution systems, technology infrastructures, politics, government regulations, and controls, all of which affect the nature of the market and the work environment. How do you decide which markets to enter? What criteria will you use? What knowledge and skills will you need? Where are the maps and who are the pioneers of this new age of global discovery?

Business Implications. Tomorrow's global consumer market represents challenges on every front — technological, managerial, cultural, linguistic, and more. The implications are boundless, but among the most fundamental are these:

■ Cultural diversity in the global market must be recognized not simply as a fact of life, but as a positive benefit. Similarly, diversity in corporate life must be nurtured at every opportunity. This will require a wrenching shift of attitudes away from monocultural norms that value conformity and the rigid view that every problem has a "best" solution. And this shift will be especially difficult for the narrow cultural band of corporate chieftains governed by white, male, European-American values that have served so reliably and profitably for so many years.

■ Cultural competence must be recognized as a key management skill. American managers who have been highly successful in the national market may find that their tried and true management practices just don't work in the global arena. They will have to adjust to a world of extraordinary variety in consumer preferences and work practices by cultivating the ability to put themselves in others' shoes.

■ While not every corporation or every business team will have to function as a global enterprise, all may benefit from viewing themselves from a global perspective. The complex webs of interrelatedness that give even small and local businesses in North America a stake in the outcome of global trade negotiations in Geneva or immigration legislation in Washington are evidence of the global demands on every level of business activity.

■ Just as cultural knowledge and appreciation of diversity are the keystones of transcultural business activity, so is technological competence the key to leaping the global economy's boundaries of distance and time. Resources and training must be directed toward supporting global workers with the technology they need and the skills to use it, once those needs are clearly understood. There is considerable danger, though, in plunging headlong into this expensive undertaking without an objective evaluation of the real needs and the technology's functionality (which is often minimal).

▪ Workers, consumers, investors, and all the key figures in national economies must recognize the inevitability and opportunities of the global market and abandon the negative, protectionist thinking that has characterized recent debates about the extension of free trade. Globalization of jobs, products, investment, and markets is a fact of life; artificial barriers can only hinder the broad flow of the many benefits of globalization without halting the negative impacts, such as temporary job losses.

The Global Corporation: Networks of Lean Machines

The second major fault line is in the organization of work: the structure of the corporation. For two hundred years, ever-larger corporations have dominated business activity. Now, as the old technologies that served them and the old markets that they served change almost overnight, these unwieldy behemoths are experiencing some of the disadvantages known to dinosaurs: they cannot move fast enough or evolve fast enough to compete with smaller, sharp-toothed, quicker predators in the global jungle. To survive, many are virtually reinventing themselves through radical downsizing, reorganization, and the technology-enabled creation of worldwide spider webs of strategic partnerships and alliances. The resulting turbulence is upending all the old world's corporate relationships, work habits, and employer/employee bonds, leaving massive confusion, anxiety, and fear — and the promise of survival and greater competitiveness — in its wake.

Already technology and the centrifugal forces created by the global market's competition and expansion have flung the functions and missions of the traditional corporate structure far from the old centers of power and strategic decision making. Vertical hierarchies are being flattened. Middle management is disappearing. Even the very concept of the office as a warren of cubicles in a high rise is shrinking as managers find themselves working in an "anywhere/anytime" mode, connected to teammates and the company by electronic webs such as e-mail, teleconferencing, and local and wide-area networks.

The transformation of corporate structure has not, as some maintain, been driven solely by advancing technology. Market forces have played the greater role. But the technology has definitely made it all possible, in the same sense that mass production and low cost of automobiles led to suburbanization. Similarly, the technology of the interstate highway system in the 1950s helped transform a constellation of regional markets into a genuinely national market.

In fact, some academics, such as Stephen R. Barley of Cornell's School of Industrial and Labor Relations, have noted that corporate organization has adapted itself to the possibilities made manifest by "infrastructural technologies" (Kiechel, 1993). The electrical revolution and the development of the internal combustion engine and the telephone built the highway to the manufacturing economy and its hierarchical, professionally managed corporation. Now, Barley notes, "electromechanical infrastructure" is giving way to what some call the "computational infrastructure" based on computers. Computers are not only marvelous number crunchers; they have an almost unlimited capacity to take over many kinds of routine work from running assembly lines to tracking inventories and passing and filtering information along the far-flung corporate nodes — all tasks that have traditionally depended on human labor and management.

But it would be a mistake to conclude that computer technology's primary role in the new corporate structure has been merely that of replacing manual workers and the middle managers who orchestrated and coordinated it all. It has had at least one other major impact: it has the potential to radically augment the productivity of the higher-order information workers — the growing ranks of technical and idea people who are the greatest source of innovation in a service and information economy. Given that an estimated two-thirds of U.S. workers are in services, and that knowledge is itself becoming one of the global economy's most important "products" (a notion we explore below), the potential impact of the new technology on the corporate structure and workforce is far reaching. It undermines corporate hierarchy by taking over the work of that vast, fundamental layer of middle management that once served as the corporate glue. And, moreover, it augments the influence of innovative technical and knowledge workers, who function best in smaller, looser, decentralized and more flexible enterprises. Even though it is difficult to measure the productivity impacts of computer use, the overarching potential is to allow work to occur in ways that have never before been possible.

Given this rapidly expanding global market and the mounting pressures of competition from smaller, more innovative, and nimble global enterprises, it should come as no surprise that many of today's biggest transnationals and multinationals (which are two different things) are scrambling to break out of their molds. They are reinventing themselves through such strategies as downsizing, outsourcing, and networking through strategic alliances, joint ventures, and partnerships—all of which tend to alter the shape of the corporation by blurring the organizational boundaries and flattening the hierarchy into a horizontal division of labor based not on titles and authority so much as on specialized skills and knowledge. In effect, the corporation is being reduced to those core functions (see Figure 1.3) still needed to monitor and process the work of more specialized functions, such as accounting, advertising, legal services, training, and computer support, all of which operate in the still-evolving workspaces of the outsourced enterprise.

In these evolving networks of flattened, decentralized skills and information, the nodes that connect the largely autonomous fragments of independent contractors, outsourced firms, and allied enterprises become the prime structural and strategic asset. They are the building blocks of the networked global business—team leaders and members, often geographically dispersed, culturally diverse, and functionally mixed. With their communications networks, workflow software, and a growing array of electronic and human "groupware," they are the air traffic controllers of global enterprise,

Figure 1.3. Corporate Reduction to Core Functions.

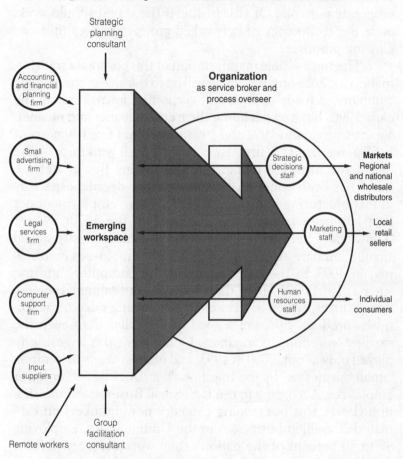

Source: Institute for the Future.

coordinating a vast array of distributed work and services—doing, in essence, alone what legions of middle managers once did. And the prime source of nourishment that keeps these teams functioning at high capacity is the *sine qua non* of the global corporation: information—instantly accessible, constantly updated, and reliably filtered to keep all teams fully informed of everything they need to know about the goals, processes, resources, and activities of all the other nodes in the corporate network. Or at least this is the way it should work, once the technology of networked groupware lives up to its glowing promises.

The most visible manifestation of this corporate transformation to those on the outside will be in the size of the average company. Already the wave of corporate downsizings in the early 1990s has pressed home the trend to leaner and meaner. Various surveys in 1992 and 1993 found that from 40 percent to 65 percent of U.S. firms were cutting their workforces—the bigger the firm, the higher the percentage. But in fact the trend has been going on for more than a decade, especially in manufacturing industries, where average employment per firm has been falling since it peaked in the 1970s. Newer "knowledge" industries have started small and mostly stayed small. Compare Apple's roughly 15,000 employees (and falling) in 1993 to the older giants of the computer industry, such as IBM, with more than 300,000 (and falling). Biotechnology firms, which are closer to the cutting edge of tomorrow's "product" line, are a good deal smaller than even the smallest computer companies. Genentech, the largest, employed only about 2,000 in 1993, and others qualify as genuine "small businesses" by the traditional yardstick of 500 or fewer employees. According to the U.S. Small Business Administration (1991), this burgeoning category now numbers an estimated 20 million businesses in the United States, employing 45 to 50 percent of the nation's total workforce. Small firms provide the vast majority of all the new jobs being created today—a fact that is not an unmixed blessing, since small businesses are inherently unstable and tend to pay lower wages and benefits.

Many large firms are in fact becoming collections of smaller establishments distributed across many locations around a small core. In the future it may even become difficult to determine where one company ends and another company or consulting firm begins, a fact that will have mixed implications for corporate culture, employee loyalty, and the feasibility of projecting a corporate vision. Although global statistics are not available on downsizing, there is growing evidence that the trend is occurring throughout the industrialized nations at varying paces as small and medium-sized business sectors expand and companies with a thousand or more workers contract. In the United States, a 1993 survey of 870 large companies conducted by the American Management Association (AMA) showed that 47 percent of them had laid off an average of 10.4 percent of their workforces over the previous year. It also revealed that for the first time in the survey's seven-year history, white-collar workers — management, technical, or professional positions — made up more than half of the layoffs (Gatewood, 1993).

One intervening factor outside the United States is the strength and role of labor unions, which are stronger in countries like France, Germany, Mexico, and Canada. Were it not for Britain's union strength, more than one-third of that country's mining employment would disappear overnight. Moreover, radical downsizing has yet to make a major impact on most Japanese firms due to the high cultural value placed on long-term employment as a reward for company loyalty. If and when it does strike, it is bound to have especially serious implications for social stability. Indeed, there may be reason for concern about social stability even in the OECD countries like France, Italy, and Britain, which have long lived with high levels of unemployment, if joblessness reaches 15 percent, and remains there, as some experts fear it might.

In any case, technological change and innovation will accelerate and continue to shape the already fragmented and distributed workforce, as well as the web of services that supports organizations. As information and communications become smaller, cheaper, more mobile, and more user-friendly, more small and medium-sized businesses will take increasingly sophisticated advantage of them, spreading work out across an even broader community to home offices and remote locations. While these trends contribute to flexibility and innovation, they also increase the complexity of managing work processes from both functional and social perspectives.

They are transforming not just the corporation but the society in which the corporation has become such a vital support.

Business Implications.   Corporate restructuring is at least as painful and risky as it is exciting and promising. Here are some of the likely impacts:

■ Downsizing (sometimes called "rightsizing") will continue to leave a negative legacy of possible long-term unemployment. A 1993 OECD study of employment trends in Europe (Cohen, 1993) noted that the record levels of joblessness in Europe's major industrial countries was less a function of a temporary economic slump or recession than a sign of fundamental shifts in the workplace and in the global economy. Noting that unemployment had become "endemic" and rising in Western Europe, it added that 45.8 percent of the unemployed had been out of work for more than a year. In the United States, the percentage of unemployed in 1993 reporting permanent job losses, as opposed to temporary layoffs or resignations, rose to more than 40 percent compared to less than 30 percent in the mid-1970s — and a rising percentage of these permanent losses was among white-collar workers (U.S. Bureau of Labor Statistics, 1993).

The easy response to these trends is to argue that corporations and the government need to provide better job retraining programs to blunt the social impact of high and persistent unemployment. But the reality is that rising rates of job turnover discourage companies from investing in skill training, perhaps because well-trained workers may be lured away by competitors before the training investment has paid off. This risk is all the higher in a downsizing environment, since workers in increasingly insecure positions naturally show less loyalty to employers, lower morale, and greater likelihood to grab a better job opportunity, A 1993 Conference Board survey of fifty-five large U.S. firms, with 10,000 or more employees, found that at nearly two-thirds of the companies job cutting had "lowered morale among employees who have survived" (Conference Board Survey, 1993).

The social impact of high and persistent unemployment traditionally has been viewed as an opportunity for business and a problem for governments, which must provide services. But eventually, government's problems become the problems of business, as well. Healthy markets and productive work-forces both depend on broad measures of social security at home and abroad.

The downsizing phenomenon, which is likely to con-tinue, must be evaluated objectively from all angles. For some companies, downsizing has become an end in itself rather than one of many steps in structural reforms designed to improve productivity, competitiveness, and profits. The evidence to date, however, does not suggest that cutting back middle management is an effective way to increase profits. The AMA's 1993 survey found that the most predictable result of the wave of corporate layoffs in the early 1990s was reduced employee morale (Gatewood, 1993).

■ While small may be beautiful in terms of efficiency and innovation, it is also risky—and the risks will be borne by the workers as well as the owners. The one-year failure rate of small businesses jumped from 36 per 10,000 in 1973 to 98 per 10,000 in 1989 (U.S. Small Business Administration, 1991). Small firms also typically offer minimal, if any, benefits such as health insurance and pension plans.

■ New corporate structures will require new corporate cultures to make sense of the new environment. But while the cultural changes will be easy enough to conceptualize on paper, they will require enormous effort to be effectively com-municated to the far-flung, largely autonomous teams operat-ing at the network nodes. Furthermore, the rapid growth of small and medium-sized firms entering the global market through strategic alliances and partnerships raises the ques-tion of whether any single corporate culture can actually en-compass this type of global enterprise. Perhaps a global enter-prise's vision—its shared view of broad goals—will have to substitute for the stronger and more complex glue of a corpo-rate culture. In any case, until new models of global corporate culture and vision are devised and implemented, workers will continue to operate with their old values and beliefs, inevitably creating cultural roadblocks to globalization.

■ New conceptual frameworks are needed for the creation and management of the diverse, distributed, and cross-functional teams that will be basic units of global business. The old models of individual initiative and hierarchical command will increasingly be seen to impede rather than advance corporate competitiveness.

■ To be competitive in the global marketplace, companies will have to develop new competencies in teamwork and leadership, the basic building units of global competitiveness.

Global Jobs: The Fragmented Workforce

The flip side of organizational restructuring is workforce fragmentation, a phenomenon that includes shorter rates of job tenure, a variety of new types of employment relationships, and increasing cultural diversity in the workforce. The days of lifelong employment in large, paternalistic corporations are over in many countries, especially the United States. Workers are spending less time with more employers under new employment arrangements (part-time, contractual, temporary, or other negotiated relationships). A recent OECD study (1993b) found that in 1991 nearly one out of three American workers had been with their employer for less than a year — and almost two-thirds for less than five years (compared to 10 percent and 37 percent, respectively, in Japan). In Germany and France, job turnover rates are closer to those of Japan, while the other major OECD economies are closer to the American rate.

The shift away from traditional work patterns in the United States has been under way for at least two decades (see Figure 1.4). The percentage of workers in the traditional full-time workforce shrank from 71 percent in 1970 to 66 percent in 1990. It is expected to wither even more dramatically to 57 percent by the year 2000 (U.S. Bureau of Labor Statistics, 1989, 1990, 1991, 1992). Using somewhat different measures, the National Planning Association reported that the United

Figure 1.4. Growth of Flexible Workforce.

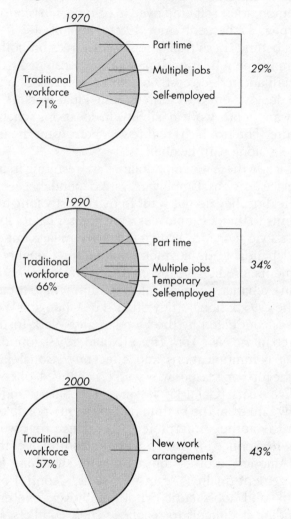

Source: Institute for the Future; U.S. Bureau of Labor Statistics, *Employment and Earnings,* 1991, 1992, tables 23 and 32; *Handbook of Labor Statistics,* 1989; labor force statistics derived from *Current Population Survey,* 1948–1987, table 21; *Monthly Labor Review,* 1990.

States' "contingent workforce"—consisting of roughly 45 million temporaries, self-employed, part-timers, or consultants—has grown 57 percent since 1980 (Henkoff, 1993). The demands behind these trends represent forces on both sides of the employment relationship: organizations need to trim full-time staff and reduce costly benefits, as well as gain flexibility in the deployment of resources; individual workers, for their part, want more work flexibility in location, schedule, and structure. The trouble is that few workers want the insecurity that goes along with flexibility.

Clearly these incompatibilities are resulting in inevitable workplace tensions. Employers want dependable, well-trained workers; but they do not want to make costly long-term commitments to them. Employees want greater flexibility to meet the life-style demands of two-income families; but they also want dependable employment, skill training, quality work environments, predictable incomes, and control over their own work in exchange for loyalty and commitment to their employers. The 1993 national study titled "The Changing Workforce" that was conducted by the Families and Work Institute and reported in the *New York Times* (Noble, 1993), found that lack of "open communications" and "effect on personal/family life" were the top two reasons why workers changed jobs within the past five years (Galinski, 1993, p. 17). Salary and benefits actually ranked in the bottom half of twenty possible reasons, which the authors interpreted as evidence that workers are willing to sacrifice income to get more control over their work lives. Among the other top reasons for switching jobs were "management quality," "gain new skills," "control over work content" and "job security." Both employers and employees are finding it difficult to reconcile such conflicts, but companies that attempt to downsize or reengineer without taking account of the new kinds of demands being made by workers may gain little more than "a view of the receding backs of their best people leaving for friendlier premises," warned one analyst in reviewing the survey (Noble, 1993, p. F-21).

The problem of opposing needs in this fragmenting work environment is especially acute in terms of worker training.

High rates of job turnover discourage corporations from investing in skill training, since newly trained workers are more able to skip jobs before their training investment has paid off. But companies that fail to offer job training are likely to have a less committed, less loyal, and less productive workforce. Different countries have approached this problem in very different ways. In Japan and Germany, which have low rates of job turnover, around 70 percent of young workers receive formal on-the-job training, which keeps them loyal, skilled—and, of course, on the payroll. In the United States, where high job turnover is the route to flexibility and increased profit, only 10 percent of young workers receive formal job training (OECD, 1993b).

The question all this raises is clear: Is it possible for employers to maintain the flexibility that comes with fragmentation of the labor force and at the same time maintain highly skilled, competitive workers? If the problem of worker training can be resolved, both workers and corporations in the United States and other high-job-turnover countries, like Britain, may benefit from a new kind of relationship evolving between employers and employees—one in which both interests engage in an increasingly open market for each others' services. Independent workers, especially those in the fast-growing ranks of skilled "technical" workers, will be strengthened in their negotiating power by the availability of information tools and the growing networks of business contacts that allow many workers to function outside the traditional organizational structure. These workers will be able to offer employers high-valued service, unique experience, and creative knowledge, rather than mere labor power and the ability to fill a niche in the chain of workflow tasks. They will be in high demand and wield growing clout in the employee/employer relationship.

Already, basic work conditions—salary, schedule, workplace—are being negotiated by workers themselves on a one-to-one basis with employers. The most sought-after workers are able to include new flexibility benefits, including job sharing, paid sabbaticals, child care, paternity leave, flexible hours, subsidized education, and constant retraining. In many cases, employers may be loath to standardize such benefits, since they enhance the very flexibility that makes it possible for workers to jump almost casually from one firm to another. But if employers can no longer offer continuous advancement up the corporate ladder (because the ladder has been knocked down) or even long-term job security, work flexibility must be treated as a virtue in order to attract the best workers. As some observers have noted, competition between firms over customers may one day be replaced by competition for the hearts, minds, and especially the skills of employees.

In the meantime, the forces of fragmentation continue to shape — or shatter — the job picture in the United States. Consider, for example, the number and increasing specialization of temporary help agencies, those who provide what might be called "just-in-time employment." These agencies have grown enormously over the past twenty years and have become key resources for highly skilled professional workers — now the fastest-growing segment of the temporary workforce. Temporary agencies for accountants, lawyers, and executives are an important new employment source for managers whose jobs have been eliminated through rightsizing as well as for young workers trying to learn new skills and office processes. *Executive Recruiter News* claims that as of 1993 there were at least 125,000 professionals working on temporary assignments (Henkoff, 1993, p. 47). And the National Association of Temporary Services reported in 1993 that the professionals' share of the $25 billion temp market doubled in one year to $1.3 billion (Henkoff, 1993, p. 47). A growing number of these professional "temps" earn well into six figures, although their earnings have to cover health care and the like.

Similarly, part-time workers (those working less than thirty-four hours per week) already number over 20 million and will surpass 25 million by the year 2000 (U.S. Bureau of Labor Statistics, *Employment and Earnings*, 1992). The surge in involuntary part-time work was a key driver of the growth of temporary workers during the 1980s, but both the voluntary and involuntary categories will grow throughout the 1990s, bringing the total share to approximately one-quarter of the workforce, according to the BLS's *Employment and Earnings* report for 1992.

Then there are multiple-job holders—a growing number of workers are holding down two or more jobs, either to make ends meet or to save up for an extraordinary expense such as starting a new business or paying for a child's education. The number of multiple-job holders is expected to increase by 7.2 percent a year through the 1990s, bringing the total number of multiple-job holders to 15.3 million workers by the year 2000 (U.S. Bureau of Labor Statistics, *Employment and Earnings*, 1992). And many second jobs go unreported, of course, so the number may be much higher.

Yet another sizable and growing segment of the fragmented workforce is made up of the self-employed, who now number almost 9 million. Their professional and business services form an important source of skills and talent for organizations of all sizes, as well as for other workers. In fact, many laid-off middle managers move beyond contracting to their former firm and start their own businesses. Their flexibility, affordability, quick turnaround, and personal attention to work are key criteria for strategic positioning in a complex and competitive economy. The limited time and resources available to the self-employed often motivate them to adapt innovative strategies and processes for managing and organizing work that may never have been considered in traditional organizations.

Ultimately, the core operating structure of organizations—the remaining full-time management staff—will face tremendous change as well. Maintaining high performance levels and demonstrating value to the company will be more important than ever to ward off the pink slip. But it will mean increasing levels of stress and tension on the job, more overtime hours, a rapid work pace, and the need to manage a set of new and difficult work relationships and contexts, including, especially, work across geographical and cultural boundaries. In the near future, too, the terms part-time, contract, temporary, and the like may become anachronisms as multiple forms of work arrangements become the norm. The old job definitions will begin to blur, and new terms may emerge that focus less on working conditions and more on the culture of work and the predominant activities performed by workers and their electronic tools.

Workforce fragmentation could also have profound impacts on the way corporations, professions, and corporate functions define themselves as unique cultural expressions. Legal professionals, engineers, scientists, psychologists, and the like have unique approaches to problem solving that differ from others in the organization. Strong corporate cultures have historically instilled abiding values and ways of doing things that cut across all the functions of an organization. But as corporate functions like advertising, marketing, and research fragment through outsourcing and more workers find themselves in multiple-employer relationships, corporate cultures are apt to decline in strength relative to professional and functional cultures. As organizations go global, new and unfamiliar strands of social cultures will be added to the already complex patterns created by domestic workforce fragmentation.

Finally, any discussion of workforce fragmentation must take account of the social fragmentation that is occurring through global migration. Indeed, the U.N. Population Fund warned in its 1993 State of the World report that global migration "could become the human crisis of our age" (U.N. Population Fund, 1993). Noting that "the growth of the global economy has emphasized rather than reduced inequality between nations," the report paints an alarming picture of tens of millions of people streaming across the economic gaps between nations and between cities and rural areas. It estimates that some 2 percent of the world's population, or about 100 million people, are now displaced from their own culture and national economy. More than half are regarded as economic refugees, most of whom find only marginally better economic circumstances — and increasingly bitter and repressive social conditions — abroad.

Whether they go from dirt farms to urban ghettoes or

from the underdeveloped to the developed world, economic migrants arrive with expectations that even healthy economies will find increasingly hard to meet as their numbers grow. In the recession-battered advanced economies of the early 1990s, these forces are already the source of divisive conflicts over social services, bottom-end jobs, and cultural assumptions. They may not have direct relevance today to the composition or organization of the global corporate workforce, but they have obvious relevance to the workforce of the future — and, right now, to the social stability and acceptance of cultural diversity on which healthy and prosperous global organizations depend. Their ultimate role in the global economy will depend largely on how governments in the developed countries respond to the phenomenon today: with xenophobic, protectionist, and probably unenforceable immigration restrictions or with generous aid and trade policies toward the developing world and the kind of educational and social service policies that turn immigrants into productive citizens. So long as gross economic inequalities persist, neither approach will eliminate the global movement of people from regions of poverty to islands of wealth. But development-oriented aid and trade policies promise at least to ameliorate the impact by narrowing the gaps, while doing so in a way that creates an even larger global consumer market.

Business Implications. In the patchwork webs of diversity and workforce fragmentation that characterize global businesses — each a virtual atlas of languages, cultures, histories, work styles, traditions, and employment relationships — how do workers identify with one another? For that matter, how do they identify with the employer in a manner that builds loyalty and maintains trust? Clearly there is an urgent need for proven strategies for developing commitment and shared vision in dispersed, fragmented, and diverse teams and organizations, as well as maintaining coherence and continuity in networked and virtual spaces and relationships. Given the extraordinary degree of diversity and fragmentation, these strategies will have to incorporate remarkable flexibility. Here are some of the ways these trends will affect the daily life of global managers and teams:

■ Cross-cultural, cross-functional, and multilingual knowledge and fluency will be among the most highly valued assets in the emerging managerial landscape, whether one works in a global, regional, or national organization.

■ The future networked, fragmented workforce will be reminiscent of the medieval craft guilds, where workers identify with their profession, their art or craft, their training and skill more than with their employer. We may even see function-based organizations—engineering associations, for instance—emerging to help fill the need for continuous training.

■ The growing sophistication of information workers will change the bargaining relationship between employers and employees, since for the first time in centuries workers will own the means of production (knowledge and information) and have broad access to the tools.

■ With ever more powerful computing and communication tools, growing numbers of workers will choose to create and sell services instead of their own labor. These workers, alone or in small firms, will constitute a vital web of resources upon which larger firms will become increasingly dependent if they are to compete effectively in the global environment.

Knowledge as a Global Product

Intangible products—ideas, processes, information—are taking a growing share of total trade in the information economy's global marketplace from the traditional, tangible goods of the manufacturing economy. But little attention has been given to either the magnitude of this trend or its implications.

Traditionally the transfer of new knowledge or technology across borders has been embodied in the goods and services sold for use in a foreign country. But increasingly, knowledge transfer is occurring in more direct forms: by transferring R&D facilities and people across borders as well as transferring the right to use a blueprint or process to a neighboring country so that local producers can turn out the products or services themselves. The question is whether such transfers represent a competitive advantage or disadvantage in an era of rapid globalization.

The payment of a license or royalty can be seen as the purchase price of an advanced technology or idea. Thus it is, in every respect, a product. While it currently represents only a small piece of total international trade (about 2 percent), it is growing 75 percent faster than world trade and 50 percent faster than overall world output for well more than a decade (*World Investment Report,* 1992). Manufacturers are finding that it is more efficient to transfer ideas and have foreign nationals produce the goods and services as close to the local markets as possible.

The United States easily dominates the market in idea transfers, accounting for more than one-third of all receipts. This market—including all royalty and license income and multinational profit returns—will grow to the equivalent of 20 to 25 percent of all U.S. export income by the year 2000.

Per dollar of trade, U.S. multinationals transfer between five and ten times more technology than either Japan or Germany (Institute for the Future, 1993). This is largely because the U.S. firms are playing more by free-market rules of globalization and operating full production facilities in most host countries. Meanwhile, the Japanese and German multinationals are more likely to be running only marketing or assembly operations, thus maintaining greater quality control and keeping key high-skilled and high-paying jobs at home. We believe that the U.S. approach is more in keeping with the full spirit of globalization in which information, not control, is the key commodity.

Business Implications. The content of globalwork will change as more information and knowledge, as opposed to goods, flow across borders. This trend has many implications for the work of managers and for the types of global teams needed:

- Entire business processes will need to be packaged and translated for multiple cultures. Initial implementation of transferred knowledge must be facilitated for some time with technical support.

- Putting complete manufacturing processes or R&D facilities in place of foreign countries will require high-level cross-cultural, multilingual, and cross-functional global teams.

- Exporting entire manufacturing processes—as is already occurring and may accelerate under a North American open trade agreement—will exact at least a short-term cost in U.S. jobs. Finding ways to reeducate and maintain a skilled group of workers for tomorrow's business teams will become an even greater challenge for both the private and public sector.

MANAGEMENT COMPETENCIES FOR THE TWENTY-FIRST CENTURY

If companies are to survive the inevitable eruptions and constant uncertainties of living on the four fault lines described here, they must face up to the need for a fundamental redesign of the ways in which they communicate, learn, and coordinate team activities within and across organizations. Globalization is not mere expansion. It is a different universe with an entirely new ecology that defies all the old assumptions. Those organizations that can adapt fast enough to the demands of the new environment will thrive; those that try to do things the old ways will suffer the fate of the dinosaurs.

How do we build the bridges of survival to the future? How do overgrown, tradition-bound, national companies learn to trim down, cut the ties to the past, and soar beyond the old boundaries of nations and cultures? The task depends on cultivating an entirely new mindset about work itself, the way work is organized, what it produces, and for whom. The foundations of that new mindset will consist of a new mix of essential competencies that we will explore in depth in the following chapters. The competencies are:

- The ability to understand and communicate across multiple cultures, an ability that begins with knowledge about our own culture

- Technological competence in a time of rapidly proliferating information and communication technologies, with a special appreciation of how they apply to teamwork in cross-cultural, decentralized settings

- The unique leadership skills associated with creating and sustaining business teams in a global setting

- And the elusive, ever-evolving art of "facilitating," or easing the sometimes painful and always complex processes by which organizations and teams accomplish work.

PART ONE

The New Competencies
of the Global Manager

TWO

A Multicultural Perspective: Transcending the Barriers of Behavior and Language

In the 1990s the art of managing cultural interfaces has become an everyday business challenge at every organizational level. In the twenty-first century, the ability to communicate and collaborate among racial, national, corporate, and functional "tribes" will provide an essential competitive edge.

The new global business landscape encompasses a myriad of cultures. Cultural diversity is more than a rainbow of racial colors or an ethnic babble of languages. In a multitude of less obvious but equally important ways, diversity permeates society, including the business environment, from its shallowest to its deepest roots. Professions like engineering, law, and accounting have special cultures, schools and religious groups have them, as well as corporations and organizations from Texaco to the Girl Scouts. There are cultures of gender, generations, social classes, geographic regions, even particular cities.

This is nothing new, of course. America has always had a multicultural and diverse workforce. But historically, businesses have viewed diversity as a chronic problem that had to be minimized and managed. The new challenge of globalization represents an opportunity to take a radically different approach: one that embraces diversity in ways that allow business to grow and profit from the many dramatically different cultural qualities that characterize most of our communities and organizations. Our diversity — as a world, as nations, regions, communities, as professions and businesses — can be turned to our advantage.

To effect such a change, we need to undergo a shift in the basic way we view diversity — that is, our mindset. While this shift away from the dominance of single cultures toward a more multicultural perspective has, in fact, been under way for several decades, the emerging sense of diversity as an asset is still more an intellectual than a visceral understanding. The mind opens new vistas, but old habits, myths, and fears — in short, old cultures — hold us back. The advantages of diversity over uniformity and the admonition to "invest in people" as our most valuable form of capital is proclaimed from bumper stickers and World Bank reports, yet our everyday practices — at home, at school, from corporate board rooms to city hall to Washington — remain mired in old ways of seeing, thinking, and doing.

How do we make the leap from conceptual understanding to instinctive behavior? Nobody has all the answers, least of all the managers of the thousands of business teams that are working in the midst of the enormous changes confronting them. While the business community, especially those sectors engaged in regionalization and globalization, is on the cutting edge of this cultural awakening, the day-to-day challenges remain confusing and much of the time painful. Businesses are pouring enormous investments in time and resources into acquiring new cultural skills, yet for many the rewards have been disappointing or illusory. Much of this pain comes from the sudden challenge to long-held values posed by exposure to new cultures. Inevitably, globalization entails learning as much about one's own culture as it does about others.

One thing that pioneering companies are discovering is that the cultural competencies they seek cannot be found in textbooks. Productive cross-cultural relationships require each individual to embark on a personal learning journey that initially can be even more frustrating than it is rewarding. Academic learning is useful, of course, but it is the direct knowledge accumulated in the day-to-day act of conducting business across cultures that is ultimately most meaningful. This is the kind of learning that allows people to understand not simply the surface signs of cultural differences — for example, that people of many Asian cultures tend to avoid eye contact with business associates — but, far more importantly, the invisible meanings beneath such differences: the fact that for such cultures avoiding eye contact is a sign of respect, which is exactly the opposite of the same behavior in American culture. Unfortunately, there are very few shortcuts, only guidelines and rules of thumb, to this long and arduous learning path.

Every successful journey begins with a map. Whether it is accurate or not, it should reflect the state of knowledge about the hazards and byways between the point of departure and the intended destination. Even Columbus had such a map, which embodied centuries of knowledge about navigation, when he set out for India. The fact that he never reached that country is inconsequential. Far more important, his basic knowledge — his map — gave him the confidence and competence to undertake a journey that would transform the world. This chapter constitutes a foundation for such a map: a simple but comprehensive overview of what is already understood about the role of culture in our lives and in our work. This is our point of departure.

THE COMPUTER AS
CULTURAL METAPHOR

Culture, according to the standard anthropological definition, is an integrated system of learned behavior patterns that is characteristic of the members of a society. Culture refers to the total way of life—the underlying patterns of thinking, feeling, and acting—of particular groups of people. It is learned, not inherited, and transmitted from generation to generation primarily through conditioned learning.

That's one way of looking at it. Here is another: culture is "a system for creating, sending, storing and processing information" (Hall and Hall, 1989, p. 179). If this definition sounds familiar, it's because, as Edward T. Hall and Mildred Reed Hall have shown, the computer is a particularly useful metaphor for understanding culture and its various layers, as well as how they all work together. The metaphor works at three levels: our bodies and physical cultures as hardware; our primary social, or national, cultures as basic operating systems; and work cultures, including professional and corporate cultures, as applications software (see Figure 2.1).

Bodies as Hardware

At the most basic level, the physical attributes we are born with—our gender, age, the color of our skin, the shape and characteristics of our bodies, including our brains—can be likened to computer hardware. These are all attributes that cannot be changed and, for the most part, are visible to others and thus are the most common sources for cultural prejudice and stereotyped behavior. They have a profound impact not only on how we are viewed and treated by others, but on how we behave toward others as well. And they provide an important foundation for our worldview and the kinds of activities we choose to pursue: intellectual or physical, athletic or artistic, for example. They are particularly relevant to the American business environment, where physical diversity is greater than anywhere else in the world and thus the clashes over

Figure 2.1. Computers as a Mirror of Culture.

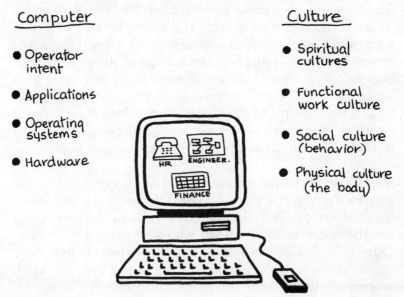

Computer

- Operator intent
- Applications
- Operating systems
- Hardware

Culture

- Spiritual cultures
- Functional work culture
- Social culture (behavior)
- Physical culture (the body)

cultural hardware are a persistent and debilitating problem. Let us examine just a few of the major characteristics.

Gender. Women and men in every society are acculturated differently as children to serve different social and work-related roles and values. In the workplace, this early cultural learning strongly influences what men and women can do and how they are treated. Certain management styles are considered to be feminine or masculine. Compromise and negotiation, for instance, are thought to be feminine characteristics in American culture but are highly valued by both men and women in Scandinavian countries.

In most countries, women are still not easily accepted in executive positions, particularly if their corporate behavior is seen as confrontational and aggressive. The "glass ceiling" seems to be characteristic of most cultures, although it is cracking at different rates and in various patterns, depending on each culture's level of economic and political evolution.

The various levels are themselves a source of intercultural friction when members of one culture criticize another for its lack of progress on gender and other "hardware" issues, such as race relations. With respect to gender, it is important to remember that assertiveness has a range of culturally correct behavior: all cultures have an inherent logic, and there is no single "best way" for all cultures at all times. What is clearly "sexual harassment" in the United States, for instance, could be acceptable behavior in another culture — just as it was labeled differently at another time in American culture.

Age.   The physical attribute of age has very different meanings in every social culture. The United States and other highly developed societies tend to view both the very young and the elderly as "dependents" who deserve legal protection. Other cultures view both age groups as positive resources to be utilized. American culture values the young over the aged, whereas in most Asian and many Latin cultures elders are revered — indeed, their age even takes precedence over skills and other work competencies. In many cultures, each age cohort, or generation, develops its own unique values, rituals, heroes, and behavior that become an important basis of self-identity, such as the Baby Boomers and the so-called X-Generation in the United States.

Skin Color.   The positive or negative values associated with skin color and race are obviously among the most deeply rooted cultural prejudices in the world — the source of centuries of conflict and untold suffering. Values assigned to skin color vary from culture to culture, depending on the majority race, which sets the cultural standard. Values can even be assigned to the various gradations of black or brown or pale. The values are extremely difficult to change — as witnessed by the U.S. experience over the last century, especially the last three decades.

Body Type.   What does a corporate CEO look like? Every culture has its own stereotype based on height, weight, and even the color of hair and eyes. Higher and lower values have been ascribed to different physiques beginning with the most ancient cultures. American women — and, increasingly, men — spend billions of dollars a year to shape and mold their bodies to achieve an ever-shifting ideal physique, one that another culture might find basically unattractive. Body types subtly smooth the path to certain positions in society and at work.

All of this physical diversity has serious implications in the business world, especially in multinational and global organizations. The legal supports for physical diversity found in the United States, such as the 1990 Americans with Disabilities Act, are rare in most of the world, where acceptance or rejection is often based on physical conformity. Physically challenged workers who function successfully in the American workplace, including the deaf, blind, and wheelchair-bound, are apt to find that the cultural barriers in the global economy are every bit as daunting as physical barriers. In some cultures, the physically different are even objects of fear.

Social Cultures as Operating Systems

If the physical state of our bodies is our cultural "hardware," the primary social culture, usually defined today by nationality, is our operating system. Constructed through conditioned learning, mainly via families, beginning virtually at birth, this is our DOS or Unix or System 7.

This most powerful level of culture represents the accumulated values and behavior that arise from society's most basic assumptions and beliefs. The primary social culture is mental programming that establishes patterns of thinking, feeling, and behaving at a deep, unconscious level. This culture becomes the powerful guide to making our life *work*. It provides the answers, automatically and by reflex, to life's most basic questions of survival: from what and how we eat to how we live in our environment, raise children, and approach the world of work.

This integrated system of values, beliefs, rituals, and rules is more or less permanent. It can change only over generations. And more than anything else it determines our basic level of compatibility to others. The various dimensions of this compatibility are the subject of lively debate among anthropologists, but many agree that the key variables include common language and common orientations to context, time, power and equality, and information flow. We will take a closer look at these dynamics later in the chapter.

Just as a DOS system has trouble communicating with a Unix machine, so does the member of one primary culture have trouble getting through to another. Relationships are possible — but mainly through applications (behavior) rather than through the underlying assumptions. Even then, misinterpretation of the behavior and practices of people from other cultures — glitches — is a common phenomenon. It is what underlies all the social problems of cultural diversity.

Operating systems, of course, have no real function beyond serving as a platform on which task-oriented functions, or applications, can be built. Likewise, the primary social culture serves as a platform for individuals or groups to act on the environment, or be acted upon, through the creation of conscious, choice-driven cultural overlays that may be thought of as roughly equivalent to applications software. This is especially so in advanced societies where social functions have outgrown the primary family or tribal unit and people look to larger social units — religions, schools, clubs, the workplace — for meaningful relationships. These cultural overlays can result in powerful individual proclivities throughout life. Some people attend high school reunions for fifty years or more. Where you go to college can have a great impact on how and where you work. Each person weaves a unique, distinguishing cultural pattern with his or her choice of social subcultures: Catholics are different from Methodists or Jews; Junior League members are different from NOW activists. In Canada even more than the United States, the major universities leave lasting and distinct cultural imprints on their graduates. And in Japan identities are strongly linked to one's work, a topic we will explore in the following section.

Work Cultures as Applications

Some of the most powerful cultures are the work cultures associated with corporations, various professions, and business functions. The mental software of the engineering culture, for instance, is different from that of marketing professionals or accountants. IBM has had its own button-down way of looking at the world, for example, which is quite different from Apple's more flexible approach, where individuals from all management levels are encouraged to pursue ideas and interests—no matter how divergent. Now, these two corporate cultures are intermingling.

People tend to gravitate toward certain corporate or professional cultures on the basis of their personal hardware and operating systems, looking for a mutually friendly fit. If they don't find it, their work lives may be characterized by discord, unhappiness, and low productivity—much like a word processor that is not wholly compatible with a system's hardware or operating system. If the choice is a good one, however, a synergism develops between the two levels of culture in which the values of each manifest themselves in similar patterns at every layer.

Corporate Culture.   During turbulent times, these higher-level work cultures provide essential ballast: they keep us from tilting off course. As André Laurent notes (Hampden-Turner, 1990b, p. 12), corporate culture "reflects assumptions about clients, employees, mission, products, activities, and assumptions that have worked well in the past and which get translated into norms of behavior, expectations about what is legitimate, desirable ways of thinking and acting. These are the locus of its capacity for evolution and change."

The development of an explicit corporate culture will need to include values about people and the equidistance of cultures. This is a necessary part of the attitudinal shift from a mechanistic view of organizational life to one that values the importance of people. Just the process of creating a corporate culture, or changing one, forces senior executives to think in terms of human beings with ideas, feelings, and patterns of behavior.

Because corporate culture can be deliberately shaped and is consciously learned, it can be changed when conditions demand new directions. This makes it a vital element in corporate survival strategies for periods like the present, when every day brings a new wave of change. The corporate culture should function like a ship's navigational system: taking readings from the changing environment, making corrections, steering the organization toward its goals. But like any navigational system, corporate cultures are also delicate and easily damaged. Radical organizational changes, such as sudden downsizing, can throw the culture out of kilter and harm the organization's ability to steer through the reefs and shoals of sudden change.

Professional and Functional Cultures.   Unlike corporate cultures, professional cultures are learned in highly structured and formal educational and training programs during formative years. Thus they are particularly strong. Moreover, they are often buttressed by strong organizational supports, such as professional associations, that continuously reinforce certain values and practices and lionize new heroes for members to emulate.

Professional cultures offer common ground globally, since their values and behaviors are often similar across the larger boundaries of nationalities and ethnic groups. A Nigerian electrical engineer, for instance, may have professional values that are strikingly similar to those of a Brazilian counterpart. The extraordinary strength of professional cultures means that they often have more meaning for people than a corporate culture. And why not? A professional culture is a lifelong choice—whereas a person can move in and out of a corporate culture on a daily basis, literally leaving it at the office. It can be left behind for good when one chooses to jump from one company to another.

Functional, as opposed to professional, cultures are the roles, practices, and habits associated with a particular work function, often defined by departments: finance, sales, marketing, personnel, R&D. Because these functions have traditionally been organized on a top-down basis, with little contact between them, they have been the foundation for the "stovepipe" corporate structure and a key impediment to enterprise-wide vision and action. The cultures that have developed within these "functional silos" (Dimancescu, 1992) are similar to professional cultures in that they develop their own languages and automatic patterns of behavior. The more successful and deeply ingrained they become, the more they become an obstacle to cross-functional teamwork—one of the richest sources of corporate innovation.

Cultural Synergism and Convergence. All these levels of culture operate on a synergistic basis, each influencing all others. For culture, of course, is more than a computer. It is a living, evolving entity.

In the dynamic relationships between the various levels of work cultures and the primary culture, it is no surprise that the underlying, unconscious, primary culture always predominates and is visible through the outer layers of the "applications" cultures. The social cultures we inherit literally permeate the work cultures we select and learn in later life. They also give cultural meaning to the physical hardware with which we are born. The significance of gender, age, skin color, and other physical attributes, in other words, is virtually nil without the meaning provided by the primary culture.

The predominance of the primary culture is evident from the way in which corporate cultures reflect the nationality of their members. For example, most Italian companies would be described by cultural researchers as "high context," meaning they put a high value on human relationships and harmony, as does the Italian social culture itself. Similarly, social cultures where status is highly valued and lines of authority are explicit, as in Mexico, tend to nurture corporations that value hierarchy and distance between corporate levels. To a greater or lesser extent, all work cultures are mirrors of the social cultures in which they operate.

This natural convergence between primary culture, work culture, and corporate culture represents one of the greatest challenges to national companies setting up foreign divisions or joint ventures—especially if they attempt to impose their corporate culture on workers from a different primary culture. Workers are capable of making such adjustments, of course, because corporate cultures are consciously learned behavior patterns as opposed to the conditioned learning of primary cultures. Corporate cultures can therefore be unlearned, though the difficulties may be great. (It would be interesting to know, for instance, what kind of cultural adjustments were necessary when the culture-intensive Disney Company set up its theme park operations in Japan and France with local managers.)

Similarly, the mirror quality of work cultures and primary cultures represents one of the greatest obstacles to genuinely global organizations, in which no single primary culture predominates. So far, globalization in all its aspects—economic, political, social—has yet to produce anything that could accurately be described as a global culture. This does not mean that it cannot happen, though. For already there are signs that something along these lines is slowly emerging, especially among global managers, building from basic values that are more and more widely shared throughout the world, values such as democracy, secularism, market-oriented economics, individual freedom, and fundamental human rights. As more national companies embrace globalization, and as more global workers and managers learn to build the necessary bridges across national and cultural boundaries, perhaps a fully developed global culture will indeed arise, originating in the peripatetic global business community and expanding gradually to influence all walks of life. But such a culture, when it does arise, will not negate the differences among the underlying social cultures. It will merely transcend these differences, including the various ways in which each culture pursues capitalism or its own interpretation of free trade.

Basically, cultures are capable of phenomenal flexibility and change. It all depends on whether they are learned in childhood or added later and internalized in adulthood. Understanding this can save a lot of frustration when events require cultural adjustments or when a "third way" has to be created to meet the demands of competing cultures.

Common Features and Compatibility

The interactions between the various cultural layers within each person are quite complex. Physical characteristics influence the primary social culture (and vice versa), which in turn influences the higher-level work cultures (and vice versa). But this complexity expands geometrically when we begin to look at the interactions between people of different primary and work cultures: Indonesian engineers working with Egyptian marketing specialists, for instance. This is where we get into deep cross-cultural problems — where we forget that one of the basic purposes of culture is as a vehicle of reliable communication, and where we easily misunderstand the meanings of behavior. To avoid such pitfalls, it is useful to keep in mind five common cultural characteristics.

First: *Cultures are inherently logical.* All cultures develop with integrity at their core. An absolute logic prevails over the system of values, beliefs, and norms that constitute a culture. A key challenge in the workplace is to learn to accept the logic of other cultures without judging them according to the very different logic of one's own culture. The discovery of this logic is essential to seeing the coherence between that culture's beliefs and its behavior. This is the key to accepting rather than rejecting behavior that might otherwise appear illogical and result in unproductive emotional responses.

Second: *Culture is communication.* Communication is more than the words in which a message is packaged. Verbal communication, for instance, seldom counts for more than 20 percent of a communication. The nonverbal 80 percent — greeting styles, gestures, posture, and so on — has certain culturally based meanings to the participants. When these meanings are not shared across a common culture, misunderstanding is inevitable. Low-context American culture places so much emphasis on words and their meanings—to the exclusion of the surrounding context—that Americans are often perplexed at the seemingly inappropriate responses that result from a carefully crafted verbal or written message. Without some system of shared meaning, communication is not possible.

Third: *Culture is the basis of self-identity and community.* Culture is the answer to the universal human demand for self-identity—that is, how we communicate to the world who we are and what we believe. In primitive societies, the culture of the family or tribe provides the necessary trappings for identity. In modern societies, each person must continuously build his or her own identity through a choice of cultural overlays and refinements added to the primary culture. The kind of work we seek, the kind of company with which we associate— these are major expressions of our self-identity. They help to keep us oriented to our environment so we can function well and maintain a sense of continuity.

Fourth: *Culture is visible through practices and behavior.* Practices—the things that people do repeatedly to accomplish certain recurring tasks of daily life and work—are the most visible parts of the culture to outsiders. But they are only the tip of the iceberg. The meaning behind the outward symbols, behavior, and practices is incomprehensible unless we understand the culture's inherent logic. Even then, culture can be deeply appreciated only by its own members.

Fifth: *Cultures can adapt to outside forces.* Cultures can adapt when major outside forces demand changes in belief and behavior. Corporate cultures can adapt fairly quickly, professional cultures less quickly, and primary social cultures not quickly at all. Likewise, it is easier to eliminate a corporate culture than a professional or primary culture. The recent reversion to old cultural values and practices in Eastern Europe, for instance, following years of imposed communist culture, is a dramatic example of how resilient these primary social cultures can be. By comparison, corporate cultures can adapt to changing market demands with relative ease—as witnessed in numerous corporations in recent years. If Russia could adapt to democracy and a market-based economy as quickly and efficiently as British Airways, for instance, adapted to the globalization of the transportation industry, the new world order might look a lot more orderly.

FIVE CULTURAL LENSES

The preceding overview of the layers of culture in a society gives some suggestion of the complexity of cultural diversity. When we add distance to the equation, however, and then multiply all the layers by intermixing various primary cultures, the complexity of the problem begins to seem mind-boggling—all the more so when we focus on the specific challenges of the workplace or "cybernetic workspace."

And yet these challenges are the everyday reality of today's distributed and cross-cultural business teams. As we were writing this book, for instance, one colleague was leading a global team with members in Costa Rica, Kenya, Britain, and two locations in the United States. Simultaneously she was leading a separate regional team with members in Canada (whom she had never met face to face), Mexico, and San Francisco. This regional team was cross-functional, as well, with members representing such diverse disciplines as computer science, law, sociology, organizational development, graphic design, and journalism. Both teams had competing priorities, sophisticated work goals with short deadlines, and a variety of technological supports (which worked only some of the time). A typical day involved using both English and Spanish, switching contexts at a moment's notice, spanning eleven-hour time differences, and managing a small mountain of varied data and analysis.

There is almost no way to make sense out of this much diversity and distance at the micro level. In the business environment, especially, we need a firm cultural understanding to address at least the key macro-level questions: What are the cultural influences in this situation? How can they be understood so that a good, people-oriented environment is maintained and productivity is enhanced? We need a way of peering through the fog of cultural diversity—a way to focus on the common features, the differences, and the interrelations among cultures at all social and work levels: a multifaceted lens.

There is, in fact, a broad array of cultural variables that might serve as facets in such a lens. Here we will rely on what we have found to be the five most useful variables:

- *Language:* The agreed upon structure, vocabulary, and meanings of written or oral communication, such as Spanish or English. Also, the specialized dialects or jargons adopted by subcultures (such as professions).

- *Context:* The elements that surround and give meaning to a communication event. In a scale of high to low, low-context communications hold information in the single message or event-objective, and high-context communications are more subjective and distribute the information in the person. The meaning of the event is deeply colored by elements including relationships, history, and status.

- *Time:* Cultural attitudes toward time are generally *monochronic* (one event at a time) or *polychronic* (many events at once). Polychronic time is a state of being, monochronic time is a resource to be measured and managed. Concepts of time differ in interrelationships between past, present, and future.

- *Equality/Power:* The distance and types of relationships between people and groups as regards the degree of equality, status, and authority.

- *Information Flow:* How messages flow between people and levels in organizations, and how action chains move toward communication or task completion. The general flow patterns can be sequenced or looped.

Each variable is holographic—meaning that each exists in a dynamic relationship to all others, which results in cultural

**Figure 2.2. The Five Cultural Variables in
Holographic Relationship.**

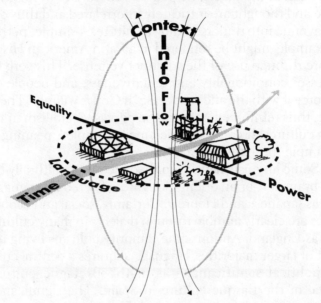

patterns (see Figure 2.2). Concepts of time, for instance, are dynamically related to concepts of equality, information flow, context, and language. Aspects of each variable are reflected in all the others.

Our treatment of these variables is generally in keeping with standard anthropological definitions, especially the extensive work of Edward T. Hall and Mildred Reed Hall (Hall and Hall, 1989). Each of these dimensions is a deep subject unto itself, and anyone with the appetite to delve more deeply into these and other fascinating dimensions of culture will profit from doing so. (The recent work of Fons Trompenaars and Geert Hofstede [Trompenaars, 1993; Hofstede, 1984, 1991] is particularly recommended.)

Language

Language is the deepest and richest expression of a primary social culture. It reflects and interprets the culture, providing vital insights into how it operates. Language is not simply an expression of thought; it helps give structure to thought. Language and thought are intricately interrelated and thus offer a vital avenue into understanding a culture. A simple "perhaps," for example, might be rendered in a Latin American Hispanic culture through use of the subjunctive tense. This verb tense expresses conditionality and tentativeness, and people often reinforce it with the add-on phrase "if God is willing." The verb tense, thus reinforced, reflects the pervasive fatalism in many Latin cultures. It carries a much more complex meaning than the simple "perhaps" in English.

Some linguists have even theorized that culturally based right-brain/left-brain orientations are reflected in languages — such as Japanese and Hebrew. Certainly, social and economic classes are clearly audible through dialects in many cultures — such as England. And in some minority cultures living in the midst of larger majorities, language acquires a central cultural and political significance — as in the Bretagne culture in France or the Basque culture in Spain. The significance of language for such cultures springs from the popular recognition that the traditional language serves as the central repository of cultural knowledge. Its loss through suppression or negligence, therefore, would represent the loss of the very heart and soul of the culture. Small wonder, then, that so many people have been willing to fight wars for the preservation of their language.

Jargon.   The increasing use of special languages and jargon by professional and functional cultures — a trend that has paralleled the advances of the technical and scientific revolutions over the past forty years — has become a major barrier to effective communication and productive work, especially in cross-cultural teams. While many technical specialties require the use of special vocabularies, these "proto-languages" inevitably result in the exclusion of some team workers. As a senior manager of a global consumer products company noted: "It's not simply that jargon should be avoided, because sometimes it really does facilitate communication. But the conceptual structures and assumptions behind the jargon need to be addressed explicitly or cross-functional work will never succeed."

Business Implications.   Facility in several languages clearly enables a greater range of meaningful relationships and confers a distinct business advantage. Without more than passing familiarity with the language of a culture, it is virtually impossible to scan the environment for business cues, negotiate, or evaluate performance. And because people are their most creative in their native language, forcing workers to use a second language for business can deprive the company of their best performance.

This problem, moreover, may grow in importance as the increasing number of Americans who speak a primary language other than English gain greater influence in business management. Already, the American insistence on speaking English has created bitterness and serious communication problems at the less skilled levels of the workforce. A less serious but equally pervasive set of problems involves the heavily accented English spoken by many immigrants. Some accents trigger negative stereotypes; others, such as French or British, are considered sophisticated and attractive. In some cases, accents are thick enough to represent genuine communication problems, especially over the telephone. In response, many companies have instituted accent improvement training.

Overcoming language problems requires a substantial investment. Acquiring language facility takes, at an absolute minimum, a year of intensive study, and fluency is virtually impossible without living in the culture. Because it's almost impossible to learn every language that might be useful, it's important to know how to manage language needs in different situations. Companies should have explicit language policies for all cross-cultural business environments. And they should invest in language competencies, including English-as-a-second-language (ESL) training, wherever needed and reward employees who achieve it.

Strategies for overcoming the barriers of professional jargon should focus on "plain-speaking" alternatives to unnecessarily obtuse terms and offer cross-functional training in the more common usages that persist. To stabilize the proliferation and shifting meaning of jargon, some companies have gone so far as to develop on-line dictionaries.

Context

Context is probably the most important cultural dimension — and the most difficult to define. It refers to the entire array of stimuli surrounding every communication event — the context — and how much of that stimuli is meaningful (Hall and Hall, 1989, p. 6).

Everyone has automatic filters, learned during childhood, that select and color what they perceive in the daily course of living and interacting with others. Cultures vary dramatically as to how much of the total environment, or context, is meaningful in communication. High-context cultures assign meaning to many of the stimuli surrounding an explicit message. Low-context cultures exclude many of those stimuli and focus more intensely on the objective communication event, whether it be a word, a sentence, or a physical gesture. Thus in high-context cultures, verbal messages have little meaning without the surrounding context, which includes the overall relationship between all the people engaged in communication. In low-context cultures, the message itself means everything.

Since context perception is a cultural pattern, most cultures can be placed on a high/low context scale (see Figure 2.3). China, Chile, and Iraq, for instance, are high-context societies in which people tend to rely on their history, their status, their relationships, and a plethora of other information, including religion, to assign meaning to an event. The totality of all this information, implicit and explicit, guides their response to the event. This pattern is in sharp contrast to Norway or Austria, for instance, where people depend for meaning on a relatively narrow range of objective information in specific verbal or physical form.

Figure 2.3. High/Low Context by Culture.

Source: Copeland and Griggs (1985, p. 107).

High-context cultures are characterized by extensive information networks among family, friends, associates, and even clients. Their relationships are close and personal. They keep well informed about the people who are important in their lives. This extensive background knowledge is automatically brought to bear in giving meaning to events and communications. Nothing that happens to them can be described as an isolated event; everything is connected to meaningful context.

People in low-context cultures, on the other hand, tend to compartmentalize their lives and relationships. They permit little "interference" of "extraneous" information. Thus, in order to give detailed meaning to an event, they require detailed information in a communication. The "context" must be explicit in the message. One might expect, therefore, that low-context communications are perforce wordier, or longer, than high-context messages, since they have to carry more information. In fact, the opposite is sometimes true: low-context cultures use language with great precision and economy. Every word is meaningful. In high-context cultures, language is promiscuous: since words have relatively less value, they are spent in great sums.

High- and low-context cultures have radically different views of reality. And the further apart they are on the context scale, the more difficult it is to communicate between them. This applies not only to different primary cultures, but also between different professional and functional cultures within a single primary culture. Indeed, context differences between work functions can lead to holy wars.

Consider, for example, the context orientations of marketing people compared to engineers (see Figure 2.4). The marketing culture is driven by rapport-building practices that attach high values to relationships. The best marketing people are good at understanding, accepting, and blending with the views of their customers. They are always selling—either themselves or their products or their clients. Engineers, on the other hand, tend to be driven by analytical thinking. They value precision and skepticism. To the engineer, the marketing people look fuzzy and even unprincipled: "They'll do anything to get a sale—including promising what we can't deliver." But from the marketing perspective, engineers often seem insensitive and rigidly boorish.

Space as Context. In relations between high- and low-context people, spatial cues, which are a type of information, are almost invariably misinterpreted, often with harmful results. Office layouts in China, for instance, do not conform to American ideas about organizational hierarchy and structure. In the United States, corner window offices often signify high status; in Japan, they can mean "close to retirement."

Automatic responses to spatial context also govern the

Figure 2.4. High/Low Context by Profession.

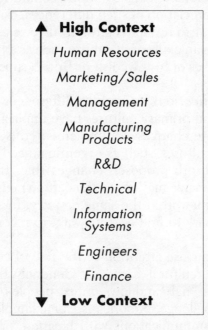

appropriate amount of space between people in conversation, which varies from culture to culture. Moving away from an Arab whom you think is too close, for instance, can be taken as an insult. In Saudi Arabia, men often engage in close physical contact—the complete absence of space—which would be distinctly uncomfortable for most American men. As a rule of thumb, Northern cultures tend to value distance in business relationships while Southern cultures value intimacy. The amount of stress that can result when these norms are violated should never be underestimated.

Emotions as Context. Just as spatial distance versus intimacy is related to context, so too are all expressions of emotion. Scandinavians are often quite neutral in terms of showing emotion, whereas Americans are comparatively expressive, which is one source of the intercultural misunderstanding. Latin cultures tend to be very expressive. The British are known for masking emotions behind humor. Again, without an appreciation of such differences, clashes and misunderstandings can result in culturally diverse teams when an employee from an expressive culture such as a Hispanic over-reacts in the eyes of his Swedish or British supervisor.

Business Implications. Context differences among both professional and primary cultures have implications for how major corporate changes are implemented (see Table 2.1). High-context cultures, such as Argentina, need more time to discuss and absorb proposed changes than their northern neighbors. The same may be true for certain members of cross-functional teams within the same country. In some cases, it may be necessary to find a "third way" to reconcile extreme differences.

The same close attention to the role of context should apply to all intercultural teamwork. Generally, the greater the spread between high- and low-context people on a team, the greater the challenge. Americans, for example, are always feeling that communications with Japanese or Costa Rican colleagues are ambiguous at best. They constantly have to "read between the lines"—difficult enough in their own culture and certainly not expected in important business relations. Americans can never get enough information. Part of the problem can be traced to the fact that both Japanese and Spanish are inherently vague languages. Greater fluency in nonverbal behavior is needed to function well with high-context cultures.

The role of context in business affairs naturally spills over into personal relations when high- and low-context cultures mix. Low-context cultures such as the Swiss tend to compartmentalize their business and personal lives, keeping them separate, while the French love the art of relationships and enjoy playing it out in the form of the elegant business lunch. Filipinos working in domestic American companies may perform better if they have a personal relationship with their colleagues. The same applies to cross-functional or professional relations: human resource professionals are more likely

Table 2.1. Common Context Differences in Business.

High Context	Low Context
■ Executive offices shared and open to all	■ Executive offices separated and access controlled
■ Do not expect or want detailed information and feel irritated when pressed for it	■ Heavy reliance on detailed background information in written or verbal form
■ Information shared with everyone	■ Information highly centralized and distribution controlled by a few people
■ Relationships more important than objective data	■ Objective (information based) rather than subjective (relationship based)
■ Overlap between business and social relationships	■ Business and social relationships compartmentalized
■ Authority and status more important than technical skills	■ Competence given equal/more weight than position and status
■ Invitations to functions based on person's status rather than competence	■ Business meeting invitation based on competence
■ Meetings often announced on short notice, key people always accept	■ Meetings with fixed agendas and plenty of advance notice
■ Each new factor and item cautiously evaluated to be sure of implications	■ Reluctance to act without a great deal of current information
■ Comfortable in a sea of information	■ Overload if information flows in a fast, disorganized manner

Source: Hall and Hall (1989); Samovar and Porter (1991).

to organize social events with their colleagues than are the low-context accountants down the hall.

One of the most hazardous management functions in a mixed-context environment is that of personnel evaluation. High-context cultures take all feedback as personal: there is no such thing as an objective evaluation. Openly discussing poor performance with a Thai or Chinese worker, for example, is considered very aggressive. Similarly, individual rewards for performance are not particularly motivating in cultures that put a high value on working for the good of the group. A range of reward systems may be necessary in many cross-cultural situations.

When cross-functional and multicultural teams are formed, the choice of communications technology has major implications. Clearly, some linear communication tools, such as e-mail and fax, operate at a low-context level—which is appropriate for direct data transfer and simple point-to-point communications but inadequate for the elaborate emotional requirements of high-context cultures. Video and audio conferencing come closer to meeting these needs, though nothing really substitutes for face-to-face encounters.

Time

All cultures have unique concepts of time and ways of managing it. Americans tend to worship time and manage it as though it were a tangible and scarce resource: "Time is money." Few cultures—perhaps the Germans and Swiss—can compete with the American obsession with time. In most countries, time is more flexible. Being late to an appointment, or taking a long time to get down to business, is the accepted norm in most Mediterranean and Arab countries. Cultural time differences can be categorized according to whether they are monochronic (sequential) or polychronic (synchronic) and according to the culture's orientation to past, present, and future.

Monochronic/Polychronic Time. Time can be thought of as a straight line or as a circle: the linear, sequential march of days and years, or the rotation of the seasons. Our cultural orientation to time has a profound effect on our daily lives and business functions. As Edward and Mildred Hall have noted, "It is impossible to know how many millions of dollars have been lost in international business because monochronic and polychronic people do not understand each other or even realize that two such different time systems exist" (Hall and Hall, 1989, p. 16).

Monochronic time is one-track linear: people do one thing at a time. Polychronic time is multitrack circular: it allows many things to happen simultaneously, with no particular end in sight. Monochronic time is tightly compartmentalized: schedules are almost sacred. Polychronic time is open-ended: completing the task or communication is more important than adhering to a schedule.

People from polychronic and monochronic cultures have the same difficulties adjusting to one another as people from high-context and low-context cultures. In fact, polychronic time is characteristic of high-context people and monochronic time is characteristic of low-context people. Similarly, the first approach tends to characterize Southern cultures, while the second rules in the North (with some notable exceptions). Monochronic people tend to sequence communications as well as tasks. They would not be inclined, for instance, to interrupt a phone conversation in order to greet a third person. Polychronic people can carry on multiple conversations simultaneously — indeed, they would consider it rude not to do so.

Past, Present, and Future Orientations.   Different cultures function according to different orientations toward the past, present, and future. In general, cultures are either future-oriented or past-oriented. That is, activities in the present are either designed to influence future events or likely to be influenced by past events. In the United States, the present is heavily influenced by the short-term future. Asian cultures tend to be oriented toward a more distant future. Mexicans and many Latin cultures, on the other hand, are more heavily influenced by the past. Part of the difference may be related to cultural concepts of control over the environment, which may in turn be related to religious tradition. Mexico, for instance, is usually viewed as a fatalistic culture where the past is in

Table 2.2. Common Time Differences in Business.

Monochronic People	Polychronic People
▪ Do one thing at a time	▪ Do many things at once
▪ Concentrate on the job	▪ Highly distractible and subject to interruptions
▪ Take time commitments seriously (deadlines, schedules)	▪ Consider time commitments an objective to be achieved only if possible
▪ Low-context and need information	▪ High-context and already have information
▪ Committed to the job	▪ Committed to people
▪ Adhere religiously to plans	▪ Change plans often and easily
▪ Concerned about not disturbing others; follow rules of privacy and consideration	▪ More concerned with relations (family, friends, close business associates) than with privacy
▪ Show great respect for private property, seldom borrow or lend	▪ Borrow and lend things often and easily
▪ Emphasize promptness	▪ Base promptness on the relationship
▪ Accustomed to short-term relationships	▪ Strong tendency to build lifetime relationships

Source: Hall and Hall (1989).

control of the present and future. Americans, by contrast, have a greater sense of control over present and future events.

Business Implications. Like context, time is a variable across all levels of culture—social, professional, and functional. And its implications in the business environment are almost endless: management of appointments, agendas, schedules, decision making, lead times, and much more (see Table 2.2).

Some of the most important time differences have to do with personal and business relationships. Polychronic people tend to be more group-oriented in keeping with their high-context orientation. They see relationships as deep and long-term, spanning past, present, and future. They seek out business relationships that offer this orientation — even over other factors including competitiveness. Monochronic cultures often value relationships according to more practical, future-oriented criteria — and even discard relationships that don't seem useful to future business goals. Likewise, polychronic employees tend to value long-term employment relationships, as in Mexico. Promotions are based on somewhat subjective criteria linked to one's network of relationships. In contrast, Canadians and Americans link promotion to achievements in the near past and likely success in the near future.

Time orientations have great relevance to cross-functional teaming, where it can become a major source of frustration. Functional cultures, no less than primary cultures, tend to be more or less polychronic or monochronic and oriented to past, present, or future. R&D people typically have a long-term perspective, which is reinforced by the tendency to measure their productivity by the frequency of "big ideas." Accounting, on the other hand, must have a short-term, incremental point of view and a present-tense orientation or face chaos. People with polychronic-oriented functions, as in marketing or advertising, are better able to blend into cross-functional teams because of their ability to handle concurrency and simultaneity. Monochronic, present-oriented individuals, such as accounting and information systems specialists, find this challenge much more daunting.

We may find that in turbulent business times such as the 1990s, polychronic-time planning could have unforeseen advantages: after all, relationships tend to outlive even the most objective data. Furthermore, the polychronic workers function with far greater comfort and assurance in that sea of information which threatens to swamp monochronic cultures.

Power Equality

The distribution of power and the importance of equality differ widely from culture to culture and even among subcultures. The different degrees of power and equality assigned to people within a particular group usually relate to social class, age, wealth, education, race, and family. Cultures that ascribe power and equality on the basis of predetermined qualities such as family status or social class have more rigid power structures and more inviolable distance between social groups than cultures that award power on the basis of achievement.

Naturally, the distribution of power and equality in work cultures mirrors that of the social culture itself. Professions and functions can be ranked by power and equality according to how the host culture values the respective services. In most cultures, as might be expected, skilled professionals have more power than unskilled workers. Within the realm of skilled workers, however, differences commonly arise over how various cultures ascribe power to, say, business executives and managers, educators, athletes, intellectuals and writers, lawyers, religious leaders, and physicians.

Asian and Latin countries typically have more culturally ascribed power and less equality among groups than in the United States and Northern Europe—and the inequalities, including uneven application of rules, are more accepted in these cultures. The revolutionary idea that all humans are created equal has not yet penetrated deeply into very many cultures, social or corporate.

Business Implications.   Probably no cultural variable will have more immediate impact in global business than power. The implications for corporate power structures are obvious: How much can hierarchies be flattened in cultures that are accustomed to ascribed power and a high tolerance of inequality? Can decentralization proceed without creating havoc among those accustomed to enjoying power and creating uncertainty among the traditionally less powerful?

The trend toward "total quality" will also upset the delicate power balances among functional cultures. The elevated status long enjoyed by financial professionals, for instance, is already giving ground to workers closer to the customer level—sales, human relations, and marketing, for instance—as quality-driven competition becomes more focused on customer relations. As companies adopt quality programs and continuous improvement philosophies, the power differential between various business functions will inevitably diminish. Understanding this fact—and making an effort to equalize relationships before conflicts erupt—can avoid unnecessary tensions and enhance productivity.

Moreover, the trend toward greater market responsiveness, which requires quick and open communications, is bound to force changes on social and corporate cultures that favor a rigid hierarchy and tolerate considerable inequality between functions and corporate levels. The social cultures of Thailand and Korea, for instance, have given rise to highly centralized corporations with rigid lines of authority. In such corporate cultures, workers are used to taking direction from leaders whose authority is based more on status than superior competence—indeed, they may even find it difficult to work without clear direction from such leaders. Self-managed teams in these cultures will obviously have to be very different from their U.S. counterparts.

Similarly, hierarchic companies undergoing systematic leveling will experience painful contradictions at the level of functional cultures. At the very top levels of corporate hierarchies there is often a turf mentality. At lower levels, the work is often raining down so hard it encourages a spirit of covering for one another. The result, on teams with people from different functional levels, can be confusion. Senior managers may say "treat me like everybody else," but in fact they are not like everybody else. Telling people to ignore hierarchies won't work if the patterns and habits are built into the corporate culture.

Even in the United States, work cultures that have developed around hierarchy will not disappear overnight. Employees at middle and lower levels tend to be skeptical, at best, when told they are getting more responsibility and power. Many have been told that too many times in the past, only to have the promise evaporate. Most of the old hierarchic practices will thus remain in place long after top management issues the edict to decentralize.

The power/equality variable is often visible in office layouts—just as the context variable is. The French executive likes an office in the middle of everything to maintain a central position of control in the information network (Hall and Hall, 1989). Japanese managers prefer to work at desks in rooms full of subordinates. German executives communicate their power and status through the seclusion and privacy of their large and plush offices.

Information Flow

"There is no point in getting straight to the point. Getting straight to the point is a uniquely Western characteristic. In the West we try to get a deal; others try to know us. We like facts, while others like suggestions. We specify, while others imply" (Copeland and Griggs, 1985, p. 103). Cultures such as the United States and Germany prefer to travel the shortest path between two points. This is not true for many other cultures, where looping and making important connections with others somewhat removed from the process at hand is valued.

Information flow consists of both the path and the speed of communications. Clearly, it is closely related to context, time, and power orientations. And thus it can be one of the greatest stumbling blocks in cross-cultural business.

How fast does a message travel from one part of the organization to another? How must information be linked and sequenced—or looped—to produce the intended results? What are the most effective means of packaging information to produce the right responses? Why do some cultures prefer words to graphics? Why do some prefer written communications to oral directives? Why does informality in a business presentation cause the French to stop listening? These are questions of information flow (Hall and Hall, 1989).

The ability to master these problems will have a major impact on the success of cross-cultural business teams. One useful technique is to have a knowledgeable source map the culture's information-flow system in a general way to show

how action chains and human relationships function in various business processes. These flow patterns tend to follow the same general contours as context, time, and power relations. High-context and low-context cultures—and those that are monochronic and polychronic—have different flow patterns. Information flows freely through interpersonal contacts in high-context cultures, such as Argentina, where people more naturally share as much information as they can. People swim comfortably in the sea of information and seldom drown in it, as Americans do. Because they are in constant contact, they are continually storing and linking information. By contrast, low-context cultures control information and keep it departmentalized—accessible only to carefully screened people within functional silos. The rate of information flow is thus much slower in low-context, monochronic systems.

Equality and power relationships also shape information flow. In a hierarchic culture such as Mexico, for instance, a lower-status worker would normally be "out of order" if he were to question a superior or appear to pass information up the hierarchy. Information typically descends from the top to the grassroots, not the other way around.

Business Implications.   There are cultural rules that govern the flow of information, just as they govern the structure of action chains—established sequences of events designed to accomplish a goal. Although the differences between these rule systems are most significant in a global context, they can also create problems in national teams representing diverse professions and corporate cultures. In multinational corporations based in a host country, the dominant social culture will govern action chains—and workers from other cultural backgrounds will have to adapt. Since business is replete with action chains in everything from hiring policies to workflow, it is best to get a general sense of how things flow and the general rules that govern the sharing of information and communications. This will keep people oriented when problems erupt in specific situations.

From the American perspective, action chains appear

much more efficient in low-context, monochronic cultures. They are designed to meet goals in the shortest, most direct route possible — and deviations are discouraged. Action chains are more easily broken by high-context people because so much of the information they value is based on human relationships. As well, they are able to create alternate paths more quickly and feel more comfortable in changing course midstream. Italian managers, for instance, are apt to make such a change whenever they sense that a process is not working smoothly. The same change might be anathema to a Swiss manager. Neither will be right or wrong every time, but both ways work some of the time.

Despite American preferences, high-context cultures, with their tolerance for change and their ability to handle great waves of information, may well prove more flexible and adaptable to turbulent times. On the other hand, the flattening of hierarchies in many low-context cultures could result in a shift to a more relationship-based flow structure, which would improve their ability to handle change. When the corporate culture truly values cross-functional work, major shifts in information flow are almost inevitable. For example, sequential task processing — the usual work mode for functions — must give way to simultaneous multiprocessing on cross-functional teams. In the global business environment, slowdowns or even breakdowns in business processes often result from clashes over appropriate action chains. Negotiation processes, for example, differ radically from culture to culture. Often managers should look for "third ways" rather than try to impose one or another cultural system — perhaps by asking team members to help design a good team-based action chain of their own.

Here are some useful rules of thumb for dealing with the challenges of information flow:

- High-context cultures may resist heavy reliance on computerized, "objective" information systems if they are thought to interrupt vital interpersonal relationships.
- Low-context cultures are more vulnerable to broken action chains because they are so dependent on tightly scheduled activities.

- The "old boy network" is the strongest channel for information flow at the top in high-context cultures.

- High-context action chains rely heavily on personal relationships.

- Learn to slow down and sneak up on information in high-context cultures. You have to become part of the informal, interpersonal information-flow system.

ACCEPTING THE CHALLENGE OF CULTURAL LITERACY

Cultural literacy is not simply desirable—it is a global business prerequisite. While the learning process is endless, simple frameworks can help you develop a sense of competence. Understanding the various levels of diversity—physical, social, professional, functional, even spiritual (a level we have not explored here)—provides a good beginning. Learning to view each of these levels through the lens of language, context, time, power/equality, and information flow adds invaluable insights.

Still, even after years of direct exposure to cultural diversity in the workplace, the problems can seem bewildering. They are best approached simply, directly, and in familiar terms. The following guidelines should prove useful:

- Accept diversity—this is the first step toward managing it. Most of us resist the challenges of diversity deep in our hearts, however politically correct multiculturalism has become. Embracing diversity represents a profound cultural change for everybody—those at the top and the bottom. People need to take time and give themselves plenty of room for learning.

- Start out learning some basic knowledge and explore in depth later. The five variables of language, context, time, power/equality, and information flow are tried and true cultural concepts that have deep and rich meanings but can also be understood intuitively by most people. They can be used as a conceptual framework for academic learning about cultures and, later, as reference points for direct experience.

■ Use simple concepts like the five cultural dimensions for mapping the differences and common features of cultures. Sorting out complexity in a few inclusive categories — such as physical diversity, social cultures, and work cultures — helps break problems into manageable chunks.

■ Think about your own corporate and functional culture in terms of values, rituals, heroes, and behavior and how they do or do not support corporate missions. And remember, without conscious effort our own cultures are invisible to us. The best way to see them is in comparison to other cultures.

■ Provide first-rate training for leaders of diverse and distributed teams. Leading multicultural teams is not a task for everybody. It requires special skills and attitudes.

■ Accept personal responsibility for your own intercultural learning.

Each of these approaches can be greatly enhanced through the use of a conceptual model of the intercultural learning process. Although models are no substitute for experience, they do support learning by providing an orienting context and a guide to interpretation. The seven-stage Intercultural Learning Model (see Figure 2.5) depicts the major phases that we tend to encounter in moving from a position of rigidity and resistance to other cultures to an attitude of openness and appreciation of diversity:

Engaging Stages

1. *Anticipate similarity.* We enter cross-cultural experiences with a subconscious expectation that others will be similar to us. Deep within we believe that everyone thinks and feels the same way we do.

2. *Encounter shocks.* A cultural shock occurs when others do not behave as we expected. An intense emotional reaction occurs and no sense can be made immediately of the differences.

3. *Consider possibilities.* A struggle exists between the desire to understand the new behavior and our intense, uncomfortable emotional reaction. Interpretations are based on our own cultural knowledge.

4. *Open to the culture.* Awareness that feelings are a personal reaction to other cultures allows the feelings to subside and opens the way to experiencing the true cultural situation despite continual discomfort.

Learning Stages

5. *Pursue learning.* Now there is an opportunity to see and assimilate the logical reasons behind behavior from the new cultural context and to make accurate interpretations.

6. *Transcend boundaries.* Knowing another culture is also an inward journey to learning about one's own culture. Crossing the boundaries allows ourselves and others to experience one another fully.

7. *Appreciate diversity.* We approach each new opportunity with enthusiasm and feel an easy pull toward engagement. Cultural differences are more readily apparent.

The model traces the predictable pains and the resolutions associated with each of the seven stages that people experience when deeply engaged with another culture. It illustrates both the inner and social process of cultural learning. Used with a team, it can serve as a common framework to support mutual understanding regarding the frustrations—and the surprises—inherent in cultural encounters. The unresolved and resolved issues associated with each of the seven stages are continuous and always present. And each stage builds on prior ones in an inclusive way.

Figure 2.5. Intercultural Learning Model.

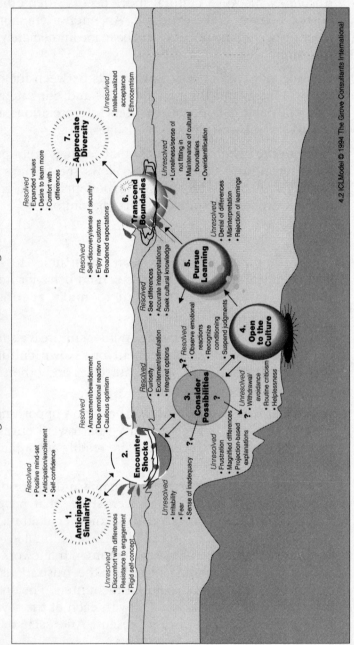

Resolved
• Positive mind-set
• Anticipation/excitement
• Self-confidence

1.
Anticipate
Similarity

Unresolved
• Discomfort with differences
• Resistance to engagement
• Rigid self-concept

Resolved
• Amazement/bewilderment
• Deep emotional reaction
• Cautious optimism

2.
Encounter
Shocks

Unresolved
• Irritability
• Fear
• Sense of inadequacy

Resolved
• Curiosity
• Excitement/stimulation
• Interpret options

3.
Consider
Possibilities
?

Unresolved ?
• Frustration
• Magnified differences
• Projection-based
  explanations

? *Resolved*
• Observe emotional
  reactions
• Recognize
  conditioning
• Suspend judgments

4.
Open to the
Culture

? *Unresolved*
• Withdrawal/
  avoidance
• Routine criticism
• Helplessness

Resolved
• See differences
• Accurate interpretations
• Seek cultural knowledge

5.
Pursue
Learning

Unresolved
• Denial of differences
• Misinterpretation
• Rejection of learnings

Resolved
• Self-discovery/sense of security
• Enjoy new customs
• Broadened expectations

6.
Transcend
Boundaries

Unresolved
• Loneliness/sense of
  not fitting in
• Maintenance of cultural
  boundaries
• Overidentification

Resolved
• Expanded values
• Desire to learn more
• Comfort with
  differences

7.
Appreciate
Diversity

Unresolved
• Intellectualized
  acceptance
• Ethnocentrism

We suggest using the model to map the course of your own cultural learning. But whether you use the model or not, a major investment in learning is vital for all those who hope to survive and prosper in the sea of cultures that is the global economy.

THREE

Technical Competence:
Managing Team Connections
with Groupware

Can information technology overcome the problems of working together for a fragmented, global workforce? Is technology up to the challenges of distance and diversity? The answer is a very qualified yes. Yes; but the available technologies are still extremely limited. Yes; but the existing global information infrastructure is erratic at best. Yes; but global managers must be trained in the special skills of computer-aided collaboration.

And yet, despite all the "buts," information technology is not just an option for global business, it is a requirement. Global organizations cannot function without information technology. But the technology itself is not the answer to the myriad problems of working across geographical and cultural boundaries. The ultimate answers to these problems remain in the realm of human and organizational relations. The technology merely enables us to begin to confront them. In fact, using technology to connect people across distance and diversity is often more frustrating than futuristic, for at this point it does little more than hint at what is possible without making it so.

Even when the technology matures, it will take organizational sophistication and human sensitivity to bring it to life as a living central nervous system for globalwork. This chapter tells what tools are likely to be most useful and what competencies should be developed. To lead with our conclusion, the best overall rule of thumb is this: Less is more. Do the simple things well.

A true story illustrates the point. While we were writing this book, Robert Johansen was invited to speak in Australia. In the interest of finishing the book, he turned down the trip and suggested a video teleconference presentation. "Great idea," said the conference chair, a world-class professor in a technical field. A date was agreed upon and Robert (an experienced global teleconferencer) requested that the presentation be scheduled before noon Australia time so that it would be at a reasonable hour of the night in California. He also requested that his connection point be a video teleconferencing facility in San Mateo, California, where he lives. Agreed. A time and date were set.

Months passed. As the date approached, an urgent fax arrived to confirm details. It asked for a response via Internet, which Robert provided the same day. Unfortunately, Robert's Internet message was never received in Australia and he was never notified by the network that the message was not delivered. The message was lost in the ether.

Another urgent fax. This time the conference organizer requested a response via voice mail. Robert called immediately, prepared to leave a detailed message about what he needed. The voice mail at the conference organizer's university, however, was programmed to accept only brief voice messages, so he was cut off after barely giving his name. Robert tried the fax again. The conference organizer, needing more details, phoned back several times before reaching Robert on a Saturday morning and informed him that his speech had been scheduled to close the conference — and thus it had to be late afternoon Australia time, which is the wee hours of the morning in California. Too late to change the program now, he said.

It was also too late, as it turned out, to book the San Mateo video room, which had not been reserved. More urgent faxes flew back and forth. Would Robert mind doing the teleconference from downtown Oakland at 2:00 A.M.? An alternative site in nearby Sunnyvale was eventually found. Finally, three days before the actual speech, Robert mentioned casually in a (brief) voice mail message that he would talk to the conference organizer before his presentation in the wee hours of Friday morning. This brought another urgent fax informing him that the schedule had actually been shifted long ago and the speech was now to be on Tuesday morning — when Robert was scheduled to be on vacation. Nonetheless, since he would be in town anyway, he agreed to the new schedule and re-booked the video room. "We should have a virtual Australian beer together and reflect on all that we've learned from this," quipped the last fax from Australia.

The teleconference itself came off without a hitch, but it left a lot of people wondering if it wouldn't have been easier for Robert to have flown to Australia after all. This was a relatively simple video teleconference, by experienced global workers with plenty of time for planning. But not enough planning was done and all the fax, phone, voice mail, and e-mail resources of a major university could not make much of anything work smoothly. The failure was not in the technology. The glitch was the human factor, which in this case included bright, sophisticated, technologically competent people.

It is silly that such mistakes still occur, but they happen every day. And they will continue to happen, frustrating the richest promises of the globalwork environment until the social and organizational skills of global workers catch up with the trailblazing gains of information technology.

The challenge goes well beyond the human skills of organizing a conference. It ultimately involves the fundamental skills of organizing communities, governments, business enterprises, and global relations with a delicate mix of responsibility and freedom as well as incentives for individual initiative and group interaction and loyalty. But in composing that mix, we must be careful to resist the temptation to let regulation, planning, and technology get in front of the human engine. As Nobel Prize economist Gary Becker noted in a speech to the Citibank–Hongkong University of Science and Technology Business Forum: "The focus on human capital places individuals' behavior and their responses rather than machines at the center stage of the process of economic developent and prosperity" ("East Asian Miracle," 1993). In other words, technology is here to serve us, not lead us. Once we learn to master the tools we already have, then, and only then, can we contemplate the rich possibilities of globally dispersed, culturally diverse business teams operating to their full creative and productive potential in tomorrow's virtual offices of cyberspace.

GLOBAL GROUPWARE: TOOLS FOR TEAMWORK

With this cautionary thought in mind, we move into the subject of information technology for dispersed and diverse business groups—"groupware" is the buzzword of the day— with a proper emphasis on the human side: the group is always more important than the ware. In fact, some of the most valuable groupware being used today is not even electronic. It consists of the skills and well-honed strategies of "meeting facilitators" who often use nothing fancier than colored markers, wall boards, group graphics, psychological techniques, and gentle persuasion, admonition, and insight to help two or more people function productively as a group.

The term "groupware" was coined in the early 1980s, but

the reality of electronic groupware has only come about in the 1990s. What is it? Peter and Trudy Johnson-Lenz once defined it as "intentional GROUP processes and procedures to achieve specific purposes + softWARE tools designed to support and facilitate the group's work" (Johnson-Lenz and Johnson-Lenz, 1982, p. 47). More recently, they have offered a more open-ended definition: "computer-mediated culture" (Coleman and Kaufmann, 1992), which hints at the pervasive impact expected of groupware in the near future. We define it simply as electronic technology and group processes to support teams and organizations as they work together.

While the term can be useful as a conversation starter, it runs the danger of suggesting more originality than is actually the case. Indeed, groupware is the incarnation of computing pioneer Doug Engelbart's visionary Augmented Knowledge Workshop at the Stanford Research Institute twenty-five years ago. This workshop demonstrated technical capabilities for facilitating group collaboration that the marketplace is still pursuing today. While we see some value in groupware as an umbrella concept, we recommend that this term be used with caution. In time, as computation and communication merge into truly comprehensive systems, it may even be accurate to describe all software as "groupware." It is what our computers and telephones are becoming.

Groupware is one of the few emerging technologies that is clearly being driven by users' needs: the literally millions of business teams working in the chaotic business environment of the global marketplace. Clearly, the social and business trends discussed in Chapter One are the prime drivers. In today's flattened, downsized, networked organization—in which cycle times have been reduced, responsibilities have been pushed downward, and all effort is directed toward working closer to the customer level—important information that was once the property of an elite few must be accessible to a greater number of lower-level staff. These people must be capable of making more and more independent decisions. And to do so they need not only information and autonomy but also a comprehensive vision of the organization's direction and goals. And they must have constant access to all the resources they need, and to one another, without the mediation or coordination of the disappearing middle managers. Additionally, the far-flung business teams that are the basic units of measure for global, networked organizations must be capable of sharing, analyzing, and utilizing information across vast distances and time zones.

Along with these business drivers, several key technical trends have pushed (and been pushed by) the networking of corporate structure. These trends include, especially, the phenomenal growth of networking through local-area networks (LANs), their broad-based cousins the wide-area networks (WANs), and electronic mail—all of which taken together constitute, in effect, the infrastructural backbone of groupware.

Clearly, the globalization and fragmentation of business—combined with the network and communications orientation of recent software developments—have resulted in a dramatic shift in the basic paradigm of computing: a shift that basically parallels the transformation from hierarchical to networked or from local to global organizations. We are moving from a human-to-machine problem-solving orientation to a human-to-human/group-to-group orientation in which groupware performs, in part, the functions of the missing middle managers.

Mapping the Groupware Territory

Unfortunately, we are far from having any single groupware system or toolkit that replicates a range of functions of the middle manager. Today's groupware products animate several discrete group functions, from basic e-mail to complex meeting-support systems, group writing, audio and video conferencing, screen sharing, group scheduling, filing/retrieving, filtering, workflow, and more. Most of these applications are transported over the standards-based e-mail backbone, but a key hurdle remains: cross-platform interoperability. Before truly comprehensive groupware is possible, developers must meet the challenge of allowing systems based on current and future platforms — DOS/Windows, OS-2, System 7, IPX, and various flavors of UNIX, among others — to share workgroups. Interoperability is a major challenge, with little hope for break-through solutions. Even scalability (moving from teams to teams of teams) is difficult.

As Richard Dalton of the Institute for the Future has noted (Dalton, 1992), today's groupware tools are probably fusing toward three supercategories:

1.   Group communications
   - Teleconferencing
   - Screen sharing
   - Group scheduling
   - Meeting support
   - Group writing

2.   Group memory
   - Existing data bases
   - Group filing
   - Filtering & refining

3.   Group process support
   - Managing groups
   - Workflow

Many of the functions now sold as separate applications will be absorbed into operating systems or even hardware. Even-tually, toward the end of the decade, we may have something close to a genuine "group information system" — an aggrega-tion that combines the core groupware functionalities: com-munications, collaboration, and coordination. In the mean-time, it is still easier to conceptualize current groupware options as falling within the cells of a groupware matrix based on the various possible configurations of time and place (see Figure 3.1).

Same-Time/Same-Place.   This mode is the most comfort-able for most people. It is the familiar face-to-face meeting, which so many groupware applications attempt to emulate in

Figure 3.1. The 4-Square Map of Groupware Options.

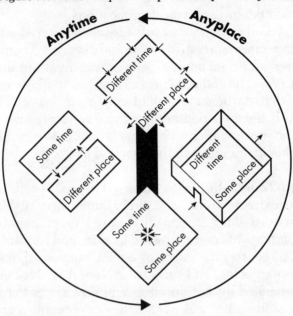

Source: Institute for the Future.

one way or another. Of course, the kind of face-to-face meeting that most people are familiar with is the kind with no technology (unless a blackboard counts as technology). But in fact, a great deal of productive effort has already gone into developing technical enhancements for face-to-face encounters—ranging from low-cost copyboards and overhead projectors to expensive, integrated software packages shared through each participant's computer workstation. These products focus on facilitating such group activities as brainstorming, idea organizing, rating/ranking/voting, group memory, and work process support. Activities such as group writing and modeling are also used with increasing success.

The groups that benefit most from such technology are those that depend on recurring processes and procedures. The software can guide them through the process and document it—even to the extent of providing a complete electronic record of the meeting for later reference. Strategic planning, total quality, and systems analysis/planning (such as joint application design) are typical applications.

PC-based conferencing software allows everyone to carry on a conversation spread over time and distance. Anonymity is sometimes a distinct advantage in group situations involving difficult cross-cultural communications, as it allows issues to surface that participants might otherwise be reluctant to voice. Also, the text orientation of these systems allows participants who speak a different primary language to carefully read what is being discussed in their second language.

Different-Times/Different-Places.   This cell, which is at the opposite extreme from same-time/same-place, depends on asynchronous links among distributed team members, in which participants communicate in store-and-forward mode. This is, of course, the realm of e-mail, voice mail, fax, computer conferencing, and various LANs and WANs that allow teams separated by vast distances and time zones to function virtually around the clock even if they never come together in the same place at the same time.

E-mail and its group equivalent, computer conferencing, are often compared unfavorably to synchronous communication modes because they lack the capability for the sequential processes that face-to-face groups engage in when solving problems. This alleged weakness of asynchronicity may, however, be a strength — especially in very diverse groups made up of people who approach complex problems from radically different perspectives. Whereas the sequential, real-time problem-solving processes of face-to-face meetings often inhibit intellectual and creative diversity, asynchronous discussions, by their very nature, encourage people to approach problems from their own perspectives and at their own convenience, regardless of what others in the group may be doing. The result can often be a degree of innovative collaboration that is rare in synchronous discussions.

Another advantage to asynchronous group conferencing via e-mail lies in its text-based, evanescent nature. Researchers exploring the social and cultural effects of computer con-

ferencing have found that participants tend to be less influenced by the status of other participants (and thus more
democratic). They also are more relaxed, vivid, and innovative
in their use of language than face-to-face groups, less constrained by culturally based conventions and norms, and more
apt to take risks. The downside, of course, is that the "disinhibi-
tion" aspect of computer conferencing can also result in nasty
name-calling, brusque and impersonal communications, and
an almost total loss of the social and cultural contexts that
structure face-to-face communications.

For these reasons, e-mail conferencing may be less appropriate for cross-cultural teams than in more homogeneous
settings. Many Asian cultures, for instance, regard off-the-cuff
responses insulting and deem intellectual banter as rude.
Blunt, untempered criticism, which is common on e-mail
systems, is particularly offensive for many cultures. Too, irony
and sarcasm are easily misread even in homogeneous
groups—which is why IBM's in-house computer conference
officially discourages their use, along with all discussion of
religion or politics. Robert Kraut, former director of interpersonal communications research at Bellcore (now at Carnegie-
Mellon), has concluded that while e-mail communications are
useful for sharing hard data among group members, their
insensitivity to cultural norms and their inability to convey
situational context and subtleties make them inadequate "to
support the planning and social relationships characteristic of
intellectual teamwork" (Scott, 1993, p. 1). On the other hand,
our study of global teams suggests that some teams can learn
to use text media in very flexible ways—provided they have
done orientation and trust building in the face-to-face mode.
It's too early to make final judgments regarding which medium
is good for what.

Another weakness of all globally distributed communications is the extensive differences that exist from country to
country in hardware, software, and telecommunications regulations, tariffs, and infrastructure. Most of Europe, for instance, is within a year or two of catching up to the United
States in terms of its networking infrastructure (some of

Europe is already ahead), but the European business culture's more traditional, top-down approach to network connectivity has inhibited the movement to distributed desktop computing. Many European firms still favor highly centralized mini-computer and mainframe-based systems, and they have been slow to cede their control to networks.

While most of the developed economies of Asia have embraced networking, Japan remains a curious holdout, partly because of the language problems of kanji computing. Thus LAN connectivity among PCs in Japanese firms is believed to be roughly one-third the level achieved in the United States (Powers, 1993). Elsewhere the situation is about as one would expect: the United States, Western Europe, South Korea, Hong Kong, Singapore, Australia, and New Zealand are all highly networked; Africa and South America are barely on the charts; the rest of the world is somewhere in between but struggling hard to catch up. Meanwhile, the first major conference on groupware in Japan was held in December 1993 and January 1994. Groupware in Japan, finally, is growing.

Same-Time/Different-Place.   The systems in this configuration have developed from one of the most successful and prosperous grandfathers of groupware: conference calling. For most people, a group meeting by telephone is not perceived as groupware, but it is nevertheless today's most common means for electronically linking distributed groups. In fact, audio conferencing is already a billion-dollar market in North America and growing at a rate of 20 to 30 percent a year, even without a marketing push.

As simple as it sounds, conference calling and all its variants can be fairly tricky — particularly in cross-cultural groups in which some participants are always forced to use a second language and the component of body language is mostly lost. Connections are inconsistent, as well, and it is often difficult to know who is speaking. Moreover, conference calls can be hard to control, especially if the leader is not experienced in the medium. Successful use depends on developing protocols and group processes well in advance.

Nonetheless, audio teleconferencing is a low-cost, highly efficient, real-time group tool with a large installed base of audio rooms and speakerphones, at least in the United States. Also, audio rooms and desktop systems can be equipped to allow exchange of real-time graphics or images while people are talking. These audiographic systems are especially potent for real-time, dispersed, design-oriented work, where graphics is important and there is need to talk frequently.

The top end of teleconferencing is video conferencing, which has evolved gradually from its commercial introduction in the late 1970s when a fully equipped room cost roughly $1 million. The technology has now reached a critical mass: more than 10,000 two-way video rooms worldwide, many of which can now be interconnected. Inexpensive rollabout units account for most of the sales, and transmission costs are falling. Modular systems with built-in microphones, monitors, and computer support have become the norm. There is no reason why the price of video coder/decoders should not fall further, so that video could become a basic feature on desktop computers by the late 1990s. (A less expensive version of video conferencing is screen sharing: a still image/audio or video/audio hybrid in which participants see the same image on their workstation screens while having a parallel audio connection.)

The key question behind video conferencing is user demand: Will users perceive a compelling need for video at the desktop? Are visible talking heads important to synchronous, collaborative work at a distance? Possibly not. In fact, it may be that in attempting to replicate all the information and social interaction of face-to-face meetings in same-time/different-place "media spaces," video conferencing is being asked to do the impossible — and then being faulted for failing. Instead, we should be looking to audio/video to improve collaboration over distance in more specialized and narrowly defined ways. Consider, for example, the idea of video as data, where team members can access the same video information (such as focus group videotapes, TV commercials, or videos of manufacturing lines in operation) from remote sites. Video mail also offers intriguing possibilities for different-place/different-time collaboration. We are, in fact, just at the threshold of discovering video's powerful capabilities — so long as we don't expect it to do what it cannot, which is substitute fully for face-to-face meetings.

Same-Place/Different-Time.   This is the least familiar of the four exchange modes in the time/place map, but there are many possibilities for such collaboration:

- A bedside hospital terminal where a team of doctors and nurses cares for a patient in a single room or bed, caregivers coming and going at all hours and needing detailed group memory and work process support

- A financial trade room where traders come and go around the clock as markets around the world open and close

- A factory floor where three different shifts of workers come and go, all needing to collaborate and exchange information between shifts, just as in the hospital room

- A computer-facilitated meeting room assigned to a team for the life of a project and dedicated to the support of the team at all times

While fewer people may be working in traditional office buildings, many of the buildings that are left will be used by different people and at different times. Office buildings could become flexible work hubs supporting a constant stream of people that continues round the clock. Through creative use of groupware, the same places can be used at different times by a wide range of people — some of whom are communicating with each other asynchronously.

Anytime/Anyplace.   This cell does not exist in the time/place map, but ideally it is at the juncture of same-time/same-place and different-time/different-place. A comprehensive, integrated groupware system should eventually provide the familiarity and something close to the contextual richness of face-to-face meetings with the flexibility and convenience of dispersed, asynchronous communications. Moreover, groups should be able to use the same system interface to move easily among any of the cells in the matrix. Stan Davis, in his ground-breaking books *Future Perfect* and *Vision 2020*, argues convincingly that such anytime/anyplace work will be required by the changing nature of the global economy (Davis, 1987; Davis and Davidson, 1991).

Beyond Place and Time: The Anyplace/Anytime Office

The key to the anytime/anyplace workspace is mobility, which consists of portability plus connectivity wherever one happens to be: in a car, on a boat or a plane, on a remote mountaintop, or at home. It is no secret that mobility is blossoming, as there are increasingly attractive quality and price tradeoffs in the move from fixed to flexible.

Many modes of mobility are coming together. Laptops will continue to get lighter, more powerful, and cheaper. Software is now mature and stable enough to support a wide range of applications. Subnotebook and hand-held computers will soon be as powerful as desktop units, and the cost premium associated with portability will continue to decline. Many of the portable devices (but not all) will be able to recognize speech and handwriting, use smart cards for applications, include a cellular phone, and, most important, communicate over a two-way switched wireless voice and data communication network. Such a network, currently in its formative stages, is popularly referred to as the personal communication network (PCN). These PCNs will also be able to support other wireless-oriented communication devices, such as two-way pagers, smart telephones, and worldwide locational devices.

As such information appliances become common, global workers will be able to carry or wear special-purpose devices designed specifically to support their work and help them share it with others. Just as personal computers jarred people's thinking about what a computer was and who could use one, so information appliances are destined to shake our understanding of groupware in often-unpredictable ways. The technology for such multimedia ubiquity is already present and rapidly evolving: pen and voice input, ministorage devices, low-power microprocessors, and communication networks like the PCN. In effect, this means that mobile executives will be able to carry their desktop computer in their pocket wherever they go, able to do whatever they do in the office from any place, any time.

As these appliances incorporate communication features, they will likely become important groupware integration tools. Imagine a pen-based "dynabook" (Alan Kay's original term), with a built-in cellular phone/modem that can send and receive Group III fax formats. It would be an ideal platform for sending and receiving faxes, files, and messages while traveling. Its users could dispense with paper entirely. Or if they need a hard copy, the nearest plain-paper fax machine (ubiquitous by 1995) becomes their on-the-road printer.

Sales organizations could make even more effective use of such a device, using it to stay in touch with their office ordering and warehousing systems, as well as keeping up with messages and sales leads. The absence of a keyboard makes the device less obtrusive in front of clients, so a salesperson could use it on sales calls, checking pricing and availability on the spot. (Such an appliance assumes the use of software agents unobtrusively executing such tasks as checking stock and correcting orders.)

The message for users is this: prepare to go to work in the anytime/anyplace office with (indeed probably wearing) a wide range of portable, task-specific computer devices capable of performing such on-the-road jobs as calendaring and note taking, document reading, or voice and text communications. Even the long-held dream of information at your fingertips could become a reality, at least in certain domains.

The key to the full realization of anytime/anyplace will be to provide the infrastructure that allows easy movement to whatever communication channels are necessary to follow users wherever they go. Providing an "intelligent environment" like this will be difficult enough in single office buildings or cities. On the global scale, it will be one of the defining challenges of our time.

A Groupware Manager's Reality Check

Before we get too far ahead of ourselves, we will do well to come back to earth and confront some of the more modest, and often frustrating, realities of groupware today. As we have already noted, the information technology infrastructure for global teams is getting better, but in erratic and inconsistent ways that still leave distributed work a difficult and sometimes painful experience. Obviously, the technologies that support globalwork are the same tools we depend on in any environment. In the following survey we limit our observations to ways in which these tools represent problems or solutions that are special to the global environment.

Basic Lesson 1: Beware of Culturally Biased Technology. Today's groupware may help us leap over great distances and time zones, but it is largely incapable of crossing cultural boundaries. In fact, it is often a hindrance. As researchers in a trinational study of culture and group support systems have found: "Information systems (IS) theories and research, like those of management and social psychology, are heavily influenced by North American cultural values. Considerable IS research has been conducted by North Americans based on observations in North American organizations or using North American subjects. However, theories grounded on North American cultural values may not necessarily apply in other cultures" (Tan and others, 1993, p. 132).

Groupware will work only if it fits the users' culture — which is why it (mostly) works for North Americans, since it reflects our own values of rationality, verifiability, measures of efficiency and productivity, a preference for problem solving over acceptance of what is, and the view that we have the right to manipulate natural forces and human institutions as objects. Cultures with less direct approaches to problem solving do not necessarily find these values understandable or the processes user friendly.

Microsoft learned this lesson when it introduced Windows 3 in the Japanese market, where it sold only 440,000 copies over two years. Before launching Windows 3.1, the company did something unique. It totally redesigned the program along Japanese lines after studying the work habits of 6,000 Japanese computer users. The result: Windows 3.1 sold 200,000 copies in the first two weeks, and Microsoft managers in Tokyo predicted that sales would top 1 million within a year. The company followed up that success by repeating the process of cultural redesign for China and South Korea (Read, 1993).

Global team managers must consider similar issues when choosing information technology for their own teams. For example: Will a person from a visually oriented culture be more comfortable with video teleconferencing than with audio? Is this increased comfort worth the difference in cost? Is there some special meaning assigned by each culture to a particular channel of communications—such as text? Are there some topics that people are comfortable talking about but not writing about (or vice versa)?

One of the most obvious questions for global teams is how to overcome the multiple language gaps so that no member is working at a disadvantage in relation to others. Automatic foreign language translation, for instance, has been dangled before eager global teams who would love to have access to such a device. But are the current products worth the bother? In fact, practical systems are starting to become available, but there is still more hope (and hype) than reality. Nonetheless, the Los Angeles Times-Washington Post News Service recently contracted with a small software vendor to provide real-time translations of news stories for Spanish-language media using an inexpensive device that its manufacturer claims can produce draft-quality translations of text with up to 90 percent accuracy (Southerland, 1993). Such tools may soon prove useful for text-based communications, but what about face-to-face or audio communications? In both the short and the long run, systems for foreign language teaching and relearning may be more promising. A mix of machine and human translation will be most attractive for the foreseeable future.

In any case, such questions must be addressed as early in the process of technology choice as possible, since it is often difficult—or at least expensive—to switch media once initial choices are made. Generally speaking, it is easier to support cross-cultural information sharing than it is to assist cross-cultural teams in thinking and making decisions together. And the use of group facilitation with graphic tools is proving to be very useful for both same-time/same-place and different-time/different-place teams.

Basic Lesson 2: Don't Forget to Phone. For globalwork, the simplest technologies are most important—at least in the short run. Save the exotic technologies for more controlled situations. Focus on the telephone (and its voice mail and fax extensions) as the cornerstone for globalwork.

Unfortunately, getting good telephone service around the globe is not a trivial matter and it is not cheap. One American company we interviewed recently put in a high-quality satellite link to one of its regional offices in South America. The result was an overnight change from crackling telephone connections that were always in danger of breaking off to very high-quality voice communications. Telephone use to the region had been increasing at a rate of less than 10 percent a year before the new satellite system was installed. After the installation, it increased at more than ten times that rate. The increased traffic was only part of the difference. The qualitative sense of closeness may be even more important. A high-quality telephone signal conveys a psychological close-ness that is difficult to measure but obvious when experienced. And telephone communications tend to be among the least sensitive to cultural differences.

Satellite, cellular, and other wireless technologies are creating an opportunity for developing areas—where global team players have been on an unequal communications foot-ing—to leapfrog the evolutionary path followed by the more advanced nations. The results can be staggering. In Eastern

Europe, for example, salespeople used to assume they would be completely out of touch when they went into the field for a month. Now, in some regions, these same people have gone overnight from having almost no communications to wearing flip phones on their belts. In China, ostentatiously displayed cellular phones are a sign of prestige that no self-respecting entrepreneur would be without.

A major constraint of the telephone, of course, is its requirement for a same-time connection, even when the person you want to talk to happens to be on the other side of the planet and sound asleep. That's when it's time to go for voice mail, which is something of a hybrid of e-mail and the telephone. It is store-and-forward telephony that allows people to work across time zones. One strength of voice mail is that it builds directly on the telephone, which people already know how to use. A weakness lies in the fact that the messages are not in a form that is easily turned into text for storage in corporate or group data bases. For this reason, voice mail can be somewhat competitive with e-mail within a company. Bridges will probably be built between these two media, but for the moment they remain separate worlds.

When voice mail won't do, put the phone to work with a fax. Facsimile bores the technologists, but it still thrills many users. It works. Fax machines are ubiquitous globally and, where the telephone infrastructure is adequate, they usually work. Fax is a simple medium that most people know how to use. And because of its interoperability it can be installed rapidly in most parts of the world without special infrastructure. There is a downside, of course. Fax is not yet commonly linked to personal computers, though the technology to do so is cheap and widely available. In the short run, fax will remain a basic building block for global organizations.

Basic Lesson 3: Create a Network as Soon as Possible. Electronic mail is the backbone for globalwork, representing an infrastructure on which more sophisticated systems can be built. For global companies spanning many time zones, e-mail has the distinct advantage of allowing people to communicate

Figure 3.2. Electronic Connectivity of Workforce.

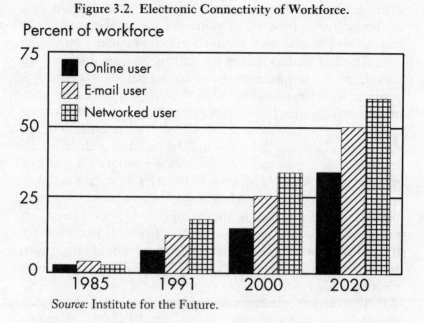

Percent of workforce

Legend:
- Online user
- E-mail user
- Networked user

Source: Institute for the Future.

around the clock. Text messages (sometimes with data, graphics, images, or even embedded programs for responses, filtering, and group distribution) can be exchanged at any time. An e-mail address is independent of location, so with the right hardware and software you can check your mail from anywhere. The world's largest computer netowrk, the Internet, now has connections to more than a hundred countries, and subscriptions are growing at a rate of about 15 percent a month. Commercial e-mail networks are experiencing similar growth and with ever-improving global access. As Figure 3.2 illustrates, the electronic connectivity of the workforce is growing rapidly.

E-mail and its group version, computer conferencing, have important potential for continuing relationships begun on overseas visits. These store-and-forward text media allow informal exchanges and organizational learning to continue between visits. Management should encourage such exchanges, even if they are not directly related to company business. Just as trips overseas involve informal learning that has indirect business value, so do informal e-mail exchanges.

Another potent reason for getting an e-mail system up and running is the number of workflow-related programs that piggyback on the e-mail network. Among the most common, and increasingly useful, are group scheduling, project management, and resource management tools — all essential aids for group coordination. Resource management programs, for instance, allow group members to access central data bases of meetings, conferences, electronic libraries, or even employee in/out boards. Scheduling has always been a tough coordination challenge for groups, especially for dispersed teams. A number of group scheduling products now available go far toward automating the cumbersome process of finding a convenient time for a group to get together, either in person or electronically.

But certain behavioral and cultural issues still complicate the challenge. Some people, for instance, treat their calendars very privately, and group calendaring requires that participants keep them on line and up to date (though some systems now make it possible to hide the identity or purpose of a scheduled appointment). Another problem is that monochronic and polychronic cultures can have such radically different concepts of time. Most of the American-developed scheduling programs are biased toward America's own monochronic view of time as a valuable resource.

Of course, e-mail itself has cultural biases, as mentioned earlier, as well as some liability issues. Many senior executives are concerned that employees will use e-mail systems for personal communications. Their apprehension is curious. There is no concern about personal conversations around the coffee pot or the water cooler or in the company cafeteria. Ideally, e-mail *should* function as a "virtual coffee pot." Such social uses of e-mail can promote a team spirit and corporate culture and improve overall communications.

Basic Lesson 4: Do You Really Want to Be a Video Star?
Full-motion video conferencing is becoming practical — cer-

tainly in video conference rooms in North America, Europe, and Japan — and it will soon become practical at the desk, as well. But the global infrastructure for two-way video is still erratic. Connections can usually be made between major international cities, but reliability is still a problem. And in a global setting there is always the hurdle of time zones. Business hours for one site can be the middle of the night for another. Too, there are numerous potential problems in cross-cultural video communications. The best advice may be to hold off on video conferencing until there is more compelling evidence of its usefulness.

Basic Lesson 5: Cultivate Nomadic Technology Brokers. The purchasing and installation of computer or telecommunications equipment in different countries, as well as the transportation of such equipment across borders, is often a problem. Every successful company we have encountered had at least one person on staff who had become adept at getting the right piece of technology to the right person in the right place at the right time. These people are young global nomads with a technical bent, but they have also developed the ability to work with, through, and around customs officials and other legal barriers. Many of the remaining Cold War era laws restricting the flow of computer and telecommunications equipment are outdated and rarely enforced, but they still create problems. The informal technology brokers run by this simple rule: It is often easier to apologize than to ask permission. The game for them is to find ways to install technology without running into local or international restrictions. In these days, it is a game of bypass, flexibility, and balance where there are no rigid rules — except those that you try to avoid. This is a strange game for many companies and many people. The cultural norms vary wildly. What is accepted business practice in one culture may be illegal in another.

Basic Lesson 6: Think Security. Today's analog wireless communications are an invitation to eavesdropping. The legal system that has strict wiretap laws for hard-wired communications is still playing catch-up when it comes to the privacy and security issues of wireless systems. This situation is unlikely to change in the near term.

Even apart from wireless tapping, there are other real-world experiences to consider. In late 1990, for example, David Farquhar, a wing commander of the Royal Air Force of Great Britain, left his car parked in downtown London for five minutes to pop in and take a quick look at the new Jaguars. While he was inspecting the cars in the showroom, a thief was inspecting the laptop computer in his car, which just happened to contain plans for the coming U.S. air strike against Iraq. The thief worked quickly and the laptop was gone when the wing commander returned to his car. Farquhar was court-martialed, demoted, and fined even though the laptop was returned a week later with the Desert Storm data intact. At last report, Farquhar had not looked at a Jaguar since.

How many similar stories from global corporations have happened but were too embarrassing to report? As information technologies become more portable and less dependent on wired infrastructure, a host of new security and organizational issues will appear. These issues are just now coming to the surface—and appropriate responses are not at all clear.

Basic Lesson 7: Support, Support, Support. Groupware technology is still in the early, largely experimental, stages of deployment, and the opportunities for confusion, frustration, and misuse are vast. Think back to the horror stories of the early days of initial LAN installations in single departments or divisions, and you have just a glimmer of the adjustment problems that an initial implementation of globally dispersed, cross-functional, and cross-cultural groupware applications can involve. The installation, training and support requirements are virtually endless. To ignore them or shortchange them is to doom an expensive system—not to mention the group itself—to failure from day one.

Groupware support on the global scale means much more than instructing users on new applications. It means continually supporting users on the evolution of applications that are designed to grow in functional complexity and eventually integrate with other applications as cross-platform problems are resolved. It also means supporting users in making the transition from the human-to-machine model of computer tools to the human-to-human model that groupware is supposed to facilitate.

One of the unique aspects of groupware support arises from the ways in which the technology helps teams not only to do the work but to redefine it. Thus support also means helping users understand these new work processes and accept them. This is a task that may require support workers who combine the skills and knowledge of motivational psychologists, organizational systems analysts, technology information systems and veterans. For the corporate executive implementing global groupware, it requires a top-priority, long-term, enterprise-wide commitment to continuous learning in the realms of culture, work process, and technology.

Final Basic Lesson: Accentuate the "Group" in Groupware. This is a short lesson but maybe the most important of all: The "soft" problems are the hardest. Group dynamics are even more poorly understood than group technology, and they are infinitely more urgent. Many of the human, cultural, and organizational challenges of global teams are still more amenable to sensitive human interventions than to technical solutions.

The Next Stage: From Workflow to Continuity

As we move into the middle and late 1990s, many of the shortcomings of the current crop of groupware applications will be resolved—including, one hopes, the question of common standards and cross-platform interoperability and integration. At that point, what dispersed organizations are going to need more than anything else is continuity—that delicate balance of key variables and work processes that leads to high performance teamwork. In the race to meet this demand, workflow products are already at the starting line. But it will be a long and hard run, under intense competitive pressures, before anyone is even in sight of the finish line.

Workflow is, quite simply, the complex process of "who has to do what with whom by when." Workflow products are tools that help automate, rationalize, and navigate that flow of work. In 1993 there were at least forty workflow products on the market, and the list is growing. The problem is that no-body—and no software tool—can really *do* workflow yet, except in very limited domains where there are predictable, recurring activities. Mature, enterprise-wide workflow systems are still a pipe dream, just as large-scale office automation was a pipe dream a decade ago.

Certainly the vision for workflow is lofty: nothing less than to lubricate the flow of information and work through an organization and to glue together all the key elements. But today's vendors and users alike have not gone for the lofty heights. Rather, they have focused on the mundane, pick-and-run strategies—on work processes that can, in some sense of the word, be automated (for example, shepherding an invoice through a series of signoff procedures).

Nonetheless, the pressures for more comprehensive workflow systems are building rapidly. Large organizations are realizing that they have a middle-management vacuum after all the downsizing and reorganization of the past few years. And it is now becoming clear what all those middle managers used to do: they were the organization's memory. At their best, middle managers knew how to get things done. They were the essence and the means of coordination. They were the energy and activity of workflow. The hope is that information systems in general, and workflow tools in particular, will supplement the organizational memory, the coordination, and the process support needed in the zone of the missing middle.

For now, the notion of comprehensive workflow systems must be regarded as nothing more than a fond dream. It is best to focus attention on today's realities and the actual market trends that show some promise. Among them:

- Middleware is maturing. Lotus Notes, to date the most successful product that calls itself groupware, is more accurately described as "middleware"—not an application itself but an environment within which applications can be developed. Users or third-party providers need to develop workflow applications within the environment. Other middleware developments include Microsoft's Windows for Workgroups and Apple and IBM's Taligent venture, which is building up to middleware from the operating systems level and may provide some big answers.

■ Organizational memory is becoming practical. Remember the days of data bases, of information storage and retrieval, of keyboard searches? With any luck, we'll be able to forget them soon. The new tools for organizational memory are advancing in leaps toward what John Clippinger calls the "information refinery." Information—like oil—is not a finished product but something that can be refined and produced in new ways that are useful to different people at different stages in the work process. New general-purpose systems to support organizational memory will be on the market soon.

■ Workflow systems are limited to "factory-like" work processes. For the foreseeable future, wide-scale workflow does not seem practical for all work environments. Realistically, then, workflow systems will play a useful role in the important but boring world of repetitive, regularly scheduled work processes, especially relating to managing documents and images. Workflow in the irregular, interrupt-driven world of knowledge will remain elusive. And systems that attempt to compensate for American cultural biases toward work processes—our low-context, monochronic, sequential, democratic, and direct action-chain orientations to work—are not even on the drawing board.

BUILDING A FOUNDATION

What does all this mean? It means that users, as usual, are caught in the middle. The great uncertainties surrounding collaborative environments mean hard choices must be made.

What platform to choose? What environment to build from? What tools to invest in?

Workflow will not really work unless people can fiddle with it without negatively impacting others. You can't "install" workflow and forget it. Workflow is nothing if it is not flexible and capable of growing—or even dying when appropriate. The worst possible nightmare is implementing a new work-flow system and then being unable to change or adapt it when the work changes.

To make networked organizations viable, there must be network-based computing. We can think of this situation as if we were building a corporate house for the late 1990s. Vendors have a few building blocks, a range of tools, some interesting architectural plans, and a willingness to experiment. But they have no idea how to build a house, and many don't even know what a house looks like.

The vendors are experimenting on corporate users, by necessity, because nobody really knows yet how to grow work-flow systems. And the users have no choice but to participate in this real-life experiment.

How can the poor subjects of this experiment protect themselves and reap some benefits from all this? Here are three suggestions for action that will build a foundation for future growth:

- Do *something* with a product like Lotus Notes. Notes requires organizational effort to develop applications. But this effort will pay off, even if the product fades, by nudging companies in the right direction.

- Develop a strategic plan for moving toward workflow. What will it take to balance your vital work processes, key players, and other important business variables? After the plan is done, build in activities that can move you toward the plan.

- Take the long view. Continuity will not come easily, but it is a mandatory pursuit. Continuity will be a concept for the millennium, taking most of the rest of this decade to become practical on a large scale.

To go back to our original question: Can information technology help overcome the problems of distance and diversity? It must. There is no other way to make dispersed organizations work in the 1990s and beyond. But information technology can only enable the changes that must take place — and only some of the changes, at that. It will be up to the people and organizations themselves to figure out how to use the technology to bridge vast distances, time zones, and, especially, cultures. For now, assessing the technological options is important and learning from the pioneering organizations is critical. Only those who are working in the field have a firsthand sense of what is needed, what is possible, and what might be.

As the vision takes shape, it will become obvious that groupware is not just a new class of products. Groupware signals a shift in perspective: the end user is now a collaborative work group rather than a single user or an aggregation of single users. Groupware is a temporary term, a banner, signaling the transition from the personal computer to the interpersonal computer and eventually the collaborative computer. Groupware is what all of us will expect our computers and telephones to do for us within the next five to ten years. In each of the following chapters, the role of groupware in meeting the myriad challenges of globalwork is addressed — both as it exists now and as it might be used in the future.

FOUR

Process Facilitation: Mastering the New Leadership Skills

Today's global teams straddle the gap between the expansive visions and the day-to-day realities of global business. They are being asked to chart new pathways across international borders, pioneer through the fog of cultural diversity, and meander through the maze of organizational restructuring. They are seeking the elusive vision of anyplace/anytime success—typically without a road map, assistance, or role models.

As we noted in Chapter One, traditional corporate hierarchies have flattened to meet the challenges of global competition. This restructuring has shifted focus away from the middle manager as the hub of all communications, organizational memory, and workflow coordination to a new view of the manager as leader/facilitator of teams and technology. Senior managers and key professionals find themselves as leaders or members of teams that span multiple cultures as well as vast distances and time zones. When all these factors come together, even with the aid of technology, the result is something much more complex than the mere sum of the challenges. It is a bewildering sea of difficulties, improbabilities, and seeming impossibilities.

In companies that are reinventing themselves to compete in this global whirlpool, the surviving managers are finding that traditional management practices and the old rules of team dynamics are largely obsolete. In the scramble to stay competitive, they are proceeding by the seat of their pants, making up the new rules as they go along. Is it any wonder that the people involved—the team leaders, the members, and the nomadic global managers who oversee and participate in multiple teams—are convinced there are still more challenges than solutions, more blind corners and forked roads than straightaways?

TEAM LEADERS:
MANAGING THE GLOBAL VISION

Developing the capacity to create and sustain global teams is the business challenge of the twenty-first century, and the challenge rests largely on the shoulders of those who are designated as team leaders. Where are they to come from? How are they to be selected? How do we train them? What special skills do they need? These are among the key questions at the front end of the transformation to the global workplace.

Because the challenges of distance and diversity are first and foremost human challenges (and only secondarily technological), insights into the nature of global team leadership are among the most critical to understand. Human beings and their cultures are incredibly complex organisms with extraordinary learning abilities and elasticity—but also remarkable rigidities and devotion to the status quo. Helping them to manage a sea change as fundamental as the mindshift required to deal with distance and diversity is a task for a new and very special kind of leadership—one that can combine the sometimes contradictory messages of facts and entrepreneurial imagination to deal with the ambiguities of day-to-day global management. "What," managers ask, "is the right way when there is no longer one right way but many . . . and when most of them include difficult choices regarding which medium to use when?"

This may be the first rule of team management: There is no one best way. The path you select must accommodate the cultural conditions, geographical distribution technological possibilities, and operational mission unique to the team, and every team is dynamic and evolving in its own ways. Thus global team managers, like pilots, must be able to take constant bearings by using the five fundamental dimensions of culture—language, context, time, power/equality, and information flow—throughout every global flight path (see Figure 4.1). Reorientation is required for different locations in the global landscape. Navigating through the different cultural weather patterns requires new skills and the ability to correct quickly pre-prepared flight plans that are not working.

Besides cultural competence, team leaders must also develop process facilitation skills: the capacity to coordinate and collaborate across time, distance, and cultures with a minimum of formality and centralization. With the help of technology—and the skills to facilitate its use—they must manage teams whose members speak different languages, have different beliefs about authority, time, and decision making, have access to different technological capabilities and supports, and bear a variety of direct and indirect relationships to the company and the mission. And they must do so even though members often have little time to work face-to-face and in some cases never even meet one another.

Finding Tomorrow's Leaders

In selecting future managers, says Dr. Wisse Dekker, chairman of the Board of Management at Philips, "we must look

Figure 4.1. Navigating the Global Workspace.

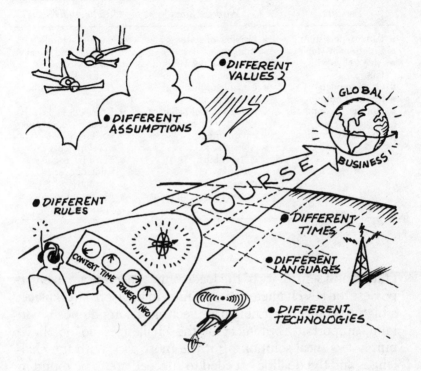

not only for professional skill and business acumen as our criteria, but also for the capacity to be able and willing to listen to others, openness, accessibility, and communication skills. Last, but not least, we must look for an understanding and knowledge of social developments. Managers no longer make the grade who treat society as something that bothers one, to be given a wide berth" (Bartlett and Ghoshal, 1989, p. 186).

As Dekker notes, leadership and management in the global marketplace require special skills, as well as unique personal characteristics, and for the most part these qualities develop only through years of direct experience in cross-cultural work. Those who bring a breadth of cultural back-

Table 4.1. Characteristics of Successful Global Team Leaders.

Personal	*Work-Related*	*Intellectual/Social*
■ Patient/persistent ■ Emotionally stable ■ Able to live with failure ■ Open-minded ■ Sense of humor ■ Humble (as opposed to modest) ■ Strong imagination	■ Capable of systems thinking ■ Can make decisions in ambiguous situations ■ Capable of pushing cultural limits ■ Able to model behavior valued in each cultural environment ■ Able to read cross-cultural business cues ■ Able to adapt management style ■ Technically competent	■ Curious—intellectually and socially ■ Able to form personal relationships and build rapport ■ Knowledgeable about historical and current social developments ■ Sensitive to the value of every person ■ Motivated to work cross-culturally

ground and sensitivity to the leadership challenge are likely to possess the key characteristic required in the global workplace: a high tolerance for ambiguity. Technical competence is certainly important, but most of the challenges do not have purely technical solutions. For the most part, both the challenges and the qualities needed to succeed are to be found in the human personality.

The key characteristics noted in Table 4.1 are all aspects of the overriding need in global team management for flexibility—the ability to be "hard like water" (Copeland and Griggs, 1985, p. 210)—and for a deep appreciation of the fact that there is more than one good way of doing things. In addition, it is often said that a sense of humor is one of the most important leadership qualities, along with the ability to fail. This is particularly true for global teams, where culture shock, embarrassment, frustration, and failure are among the givens of managerial experience.

Two work-related characteristics—the ability to adapt one's management style without sacrificing authenticity and the ability to mediate cultural differences—are critical competencies in the global realm. Managers who are able to open themselves to other cultures will soon realize the value of management practices that might otherwise seem totally alien. Team leaders are the interface between management and employees and between team members from different cultures. They need to interpret and communicate in all directions in culturally appropriate ways.

Management expectations of employee behavior are often culturally biased and reflect the norms of traditional, hierarchical office relationships rather than the new group dynamics of electronic networks. For example, American managers, with a bias toward individual initiative, are likely to instruct a team to complete a particularly urgent task by approaching it through individual work assignments. This strategy could be counterproductive if the team includes members of cultures, such as the Japanese, in which work is performed more efficiently in pairs or small groups. Moreover, different cultural groups require different styles of leadership: how assertive, aggressive, or direct one can be is governed by cultural norms. North Americans like egalitarian relationships with their superiors, while many Asian cultures, such as those of Thailand and Korea, expect bosses to lead a group without much feedback. And different cultures may be more or less inclined to provide feedback via electronic media. (In fact, the degree and form of feedback could vary from medium to medium.)

In addition to skills, a team leader's style must fit whichever culture or mix of cultures the team embodies, which often makes facilitating team interactions a tricky business. Brainstorming can be very threatening to hierarchical cultures like the Chinese, for instance, who find the process too egalitarian. The very word for brainstorming in Chinese—*zhu geliang*—comes from the name of a general and implies a strategy to defeat others. The complexities of these situations call for careful selection of team leaders, matching the unique demands of the environment with the characteristics most likely to succeed.

Another key characteristic vital to cross-cultural work is the ability to form personal relationships and build rapport. As noted in Chapter Two, in many high-context cultures people work most productively when they have a close relationship with the leader and other team members. In the United States and other low-context cultures, however, personal relations play a less significant leadership role than professional competence. In either case, the significance of personal relationships is further complicated when they must be established and maintained via electronic media.

One of the most common mistakes in selecting a leader is the assumption of transferability: assigning a manager who has been successful in a local or regional business unit to a diverse and distributed environment on the assumption that his or her skills are equally applicable. "We used to select and promote our most successful local managers to global positions and just assumed they would succeed at the job, and then we gave them little support. Even though they worked hard they would make mistakes and get labeled a failure. It was a real setup where we both lost," said a vice president of human resources at an American high-tech company with extensive operations in Asia.

In such cases, expectations are always high; and when failure comes, as it often does, both sides are bewildered. Local success does not ensure global success. Even managers with extensive American cross-cultural experience are often unprepared to cope with the scale and intensity of the differences they encounter in a foreign country—differences that they cannot escape by going home to their own culture after each workday.

Finally, leaders must be at ease with risk and uncertainty, able to act on instincts honed by experience. Leaders who lack in-depth exposure to other cultures are prone to try to please everyone all the time, and in so doing they often fail to act promptly or at all, thus pleasing no one. Experienced global workers acquire a sixth sense about when to trust themselves in ambiguous situations.

Companies that have deliberately developed specific criteria and processes to select cross-cultural and distant team managers have naturally had the best success. The process of

explicitly stating the selection criteria creates a shared understanding of what will work best for one's company, because
each company is unique in its special needs and its culture.
This process begins with collecting information about successful and less-than-successful team leadership cases in the
organization and throughout the industry. The result should
be a list of desirable characteristics that can be further refined
and customized into a meaningful set of criteria.

Matsushita, for example, has a selection process they call
"SMILE" — for Specialty (the needed skill, capability, or knowledge), Management ability (with the emphasis on motivational
ability), International (meaning the willingness to learn about
cultures and the ability to adapt), Language (the ability to
speak the languages of most team members), and Endeavor
(vitality and perseverance in the face of difficulty) (Bartlett and
Ghoshal, 1989). Certainly the time spent in addressing the
unique needs of global managers begins to build a shared
understanding of what characteristics a company values most.
This understanding, especially among top managers, is almost
as important as finding team leaders with the right personal
characteristics. If screening for a dozen or more key leadership
characteristics seems too cumbersome, it is possible to begin
the process by focusing on the two major filters: cultural
experience and technical competence.

Because cultures reveal themselves in small bits and
pieces as the shared journey unfolds, there are no shortcuts to
cultural experience. Thus it would be sensible to expand the
traditional criteria for management positions to include life
and work experiences such as the Peace Corps, foreign exchange student programs, or even inner-city work among
ethnic minorities. Often these experiences confer more cultural understanding and prepare a person more effectively for
working across cultures than any amount of academic preparation. Such people have usually encountered, if not mastered,
the intercultural learning process and tend to see themselves
as global citizens comfortable in many cultural situations.

Norma M. McCaig, founder of Global Nomads International, which brings together people who have spent their

childhood years living outside their country of passport due to their parents' occupations, notes: "We aren't really rootless. We're just rooted differently—horizontally, not vertically. Our root system is defined more by people, less by place" (McCaig, 1992, p. 2). One could hardly ask for a better description of the global corporate culture. The attitude is prophetic of the kind of root systems that many global managers and their corporations will have to develop as nationality becomes less central to concepts of identity. Companies must begin to acknowledge the value of these experiences for leaders in today's global society.

Another aspect of cultural competence, of course, is linguistic ability. Team leaders should be willing to learn the language of the local culture if at all possible. Language competency is vital if they are to enter the culture and work fluently in it. Certainly they can get by for short engagements without real fluency, but "getting by" won't keep them competitive in the long run.

Supporting Global Workers

The need for technological competence among leaders in global, networked organizations is fairly obvious, but the needed depth of that competence may not be so clear. Competence with existing groupware and familiarity with all forms of communications technology is no longer an option but a requirement. Tomorrow's global managers will have to make choices about which technologies to use in different situations, often on a daily basis. As the last chapter noted, groupware technology is still in its infancy, and global managers will be continually bombarded with new products, many of which will have limited use in global work. Assessing their usefulness and determining their cost effectiveness are critically important managerial functions.

The challenge of technical support means the ability to plan communications, collaboration, and coordination not only for the far-flung mobile workers around the globe but for those back in the traditional everyday/same-place office setting as well. In fact, effective support requires new ways of viewing the types of workers in a global enterprise and categorizing their various technical needs. For a large share of the 49 million American workers classified by the Bureau of Labor Statistics as "office workers" are in fact involved in varying degrees of mobile work. Some 23 million of these workers fill the back offices, central business offices, headquarters, and other traditional office spaces. They include administrative and clerical support workers as well as supervisors, technicians, and professional specialists.

The new roles for these organizational staff workers will have to evolve quickly and efficiently when other parts of the organization move toward greater mobility, for they constitute the mobile field workers' key supports. They will be expected to produce and distribute new and more complex data bases for field workers, including information created by events in the field. They will monitor the client activities of field workers as well as coordinate, track, and manage the workers themselves. And they must be able to do all this despite a shrinking base of on-site managers. Furthermore, these back office support staffs are being liberated from their own desks and are gaining a broad degree of mobility themselves, which creates its own support requirements. In fact, it is fair to say that all 49 million "office workers" will feel the impact of mobility on their work, if not experience it directly.

It is useful, from a leadership standpoint, to consider the support needs of the global, distributed organization from a perspective that includes not only the "nomadic professional," who is constantly on the road and the airways, but these increasingly mobile home-office support staffs. Andrea Saveri and Paul Saffo of the Institute for the Future have developed a somewhat unorthodox framework for categorizing workers in global organizations in a way that focuses on the content of their work and their unique support requirement (Institute for the Future, 1993b, pp. 30–32). Among the traditional office-bound workers, they cite four basic categories:

- "Corporate Rangers" include professional and technical specialists and certain administrative positions that require a great deal of mobility within a limited domain: short and infrequent visits to branch offices, frequent trips to nearby corporate labs and R&D sites, and constant roaming of the buildings and hallways of the corporate campus. They require support tools to locate and exchange information and work with many colleagues within this expanding inner circle of the broader corporate universe: LAN connections, voice mail and e-mail, electronic corporate archives, and such nontechnical supports as receptionists, office nurses, libraries, and on-site electronic systems technicians and training.

■ "Scouts and Traders" include more mobile workers—such as regional salespeople and managers who explore remote territories and markets in the global landscape. Their roamings may be fewer in number but much greater in distance, and their territories are far less familiar. They require specialized skills in orientation, navigation, and cross-cultural communications, and the distances involved demand a more sophisticated and mobile electronic toolkit to plan and execute their work. While these workers may rarely see one another, they have to stay in touch regularly—both with each other and with the central office—via electronic conferencing.

■ "Corporate Astronauts" are the most publicized but least common of the global workers. These are the executives who appear in business meetings around the world—today in London, tomorrow at New York headquarters, a few days hence at a manufacturing site in Thailand. Their global appearances in any given city may not be frequent, but they involve the outer limits of the corporate universe. Unlike their outer-space cousins, who can count on a stable mission control, the astronauts have to carry their everywhere/everyplace office in their briefcase: laptops, phone converters, extra cables and adapters, batteries, and all the essential devices that keep them connected and informed in a foreign environment.

■ "Air Traffic Controllers" may never leave their desk, but the workspace they coordinate and control is vast. They depend on a complex, information-rich set of communication tools that literally spans the globe. Project and operations managers, financial controllers, administrative assistants, and sales account managers are some of the positions that could soon be elevated into this new role—the ground controls of cyberspace.

Business Implications.   What are the implications of all this for the support role of corporate leadership? Above all, the work responsibilities and needs of all types of global workers— whatever their degree of mobility—are changing radically, challenging current management techniques and transforming not only the physical but even the functional boundaries of the organization. A good illustration of the changing roles and supports is provided by the experience of Frito-Lay Corp. when, in the mid-1980s, it responded to flattened sales and saturated markets by reconfiguring its information infrastructure and adopting new technological supports for its field workers that were designed to provide greater flexibility and more timely information (Applegate, Feld, and Jordan, 1993).

Charlie Feld, the company's vice president of information systems, distributed hand-held computers to Frito-Lay's 10,000-member sales force. With these devices the salespeople logged detailed information on every transaction involving a hundred product lines in 400,000 stores. Regional sales managers were able to tap into the system to obtain up-to-the-minute data to plan promotions and sales and introduce new products. In addition, the data provided headquarters with constantly updated status reports, by product and region, that allowed managers to respond to the rapidly changing market demands on a regional rather than national basis.

But the technical innovation at Frito-Lay probably would not have worked had the company not undertaken a parallel organizational restructuring to accommodate the technology. During an eighteen-month period, the company was restructured twice. It was divided into area business teams responsible for profitability, promotions, and product mix decisions within a defined geographical market. The cross-functional teams included representatives from marketing, sales, manufacturing, logistics, planning and control, and human resources—all linked together through the new information infrastructure.

Frito-Lay estimated that the new technology saved more than 40,000 worker-hours per week while maintaining a more accurate inventory and ensuring the freshness of its product line. Moreover, the team-based reorganization, supported by the technology, led to a change from annual, corporate-wide planning to thrice-annual planning by the area teams, which now use one-week-old data instead of the six-week-old data under the old system. By 1992, the company's profitability had returned to more than 20 percent, up from just 2 percent in 1985, and its market share was growing again.

Frito-Lay's experience was not global in nature, but it could have been. The technological support tools would be much the same, as would the organizational supports. The keys to making it work—either within national boundaries or in the global environment—are not so different (excepting the cultural component). The main requirement is a kind of leadership that is capable of viewing its mobile and nonmobile workforce in terms of its evolving roles, responsibilities, and needs and then giving the workers the organizational support they need to meet their new responsibilities.

In contrast to the Frito-Lay experience, which focused on supports for fieldworkers, top managers in global organizations increasingly will need ways to visualize and monitor the whole picture of their operations. The Pit, as the people who work there have dubbed it, is buried in the high-rise and high-tech Volpe National Transportation Systems Center at Kendall Square in Cambridge, Massachusetts—in the shadow of MIT. The Pit is a room designed to shift your perspective on the data you are viewing, to provide a top-down or global view. Rather than offering the typical small window on the world that most users get as they sit at their workstations, The Pit provides a giant window that can deliver a sense of the whole—not just an analysis of the parts. For example, the Enhanced Traffic Management System (ETMS) is a software program designed for use in The Pit to give a top-down view of the 30,000 plus commercial and military flights that happen every day in the life of the United States. During peak travel times, as many as 4,000 aircraft may be airborne simultaneously. Obviously, there are safety issues—especially for the 1.5 million people who fly every day—but there are also cost issues, since the cost of operating large aircraft can be as much as $12,000 per hour and delays are deadly for the financially strapped airlines.

The Air Traffic Control System in the United States has evolved since the early 1950s, moving from the individual controller peering into the sky from the control tower to the controller peering into a screen, following each aircraft off of one controller's screen onto another's. This was a system designed for the individual controller and aggregations of individual controllers, with impressive jumps in technical capability to track individual flights and route them safely around each other. The tools available to individual controllers improved steadily, but each controller still had only a narrow view of individual aircraft—not a wide view of overall traffic patterns.

The ETMS as displayed in The Pit offers a view from the top, with an attendant visual and temporal shock. Rather than focusing on individual aircraft and individual controllers (a bottom-up view), ETMS focuses on air traffic flow control and congestion management (a top-down view). Each aircraft in the United States carries a small transponder that signals the ETMS about its position and progress, as well as providing basic information about itself (flight number, destination, and so on). The ETMS assembles the whole picture, a snapshot of air traffic status in the United States at any point in time. And, of course, the snapshots can be animated to show changes in flow across the country. Past or anticipated future and animated patterns of congestion can be produced or the picture can be spiced by a continuous flow of information about thunderstorms and lightning.

The ETMS display in The Pit is awesome. People in The Pit see a view of air traffic that no individual controller, or anyone else, has ever seen before. The visionaries who created The Pit and the ETMS were driven by a need to "see it all at once." These innovations provide a dramatic example of what can happen when you use information technology to shift people to a wider view. The use of large displays such as that described in the case study of The Pit could become a top management groupware tool of the twenty-first century. Executive boardrooms could be equipped with wall-size projection screens where strategic planning, monitoring of business operations, and video conference briefings are held, all linked with a relational data base system where information — numbers, graphics, still photos, and video segments — can be brought up with the click of a mouse.

Top managers need to see the pattern of their operations and their interconnectedness, not just the individual processes. They need to move in and out of a global operation, having access to key strategic information — both historical and present — when they need it. At the same time, they also need to be able to get underneath the surface to understand all the layers — to "drill down" to successively local views, giving the many global players their own view of the information in comparison to others'. Imagine a large screen divided into quadrants where a consumer goods company could look at displays of products in four different countries in the four different quadrants layered with statistics, video briefings, sales projections, and so on.

Such global and layered views also have application to other types of operations, such as complex manufacturing operations. Their use of multimedia and layered information provide for multiple views of different parts of the process and offer a rich opportunity for cross-functional teams to make improvements. Although these customized systems are still very expensive, their cost could be well worth the investment, depending on the importance of the operations they illuminate.

Not only is the macro view of global operations needed; often, access to the micro view is needed as well. Other technology in The Pit (and linked to the technology systems mentioned above) was designed to monitor a global transportation tracking system, where shipments of all types are tracked worldwide. The system allows close tracking of both the ship or truck and the shipments. Because shipments are sometimes lost, each transportation unit (ship, truck, container, or whatever) has a smart card buried in it that can track whether the shipments are still in the container on the transport. E-mail messages can be sent to truck drivers, navigators of ships, and airplane pilots if communication is needed or if the system notes problems with the cargo. With a click of the mouse, all of Europe can be displayed and the various shipments seen at a glance. Each one can be zeroed in on and that day's data gathered in seconds. The tracking system automatically stores the information in memory so that it can be retrieved at any time. The technology provides a top-down view of the transportation system in operation that no one has had before.

Such an overview gives the truly global manager information and a perspective that support better decisions faster as well as an electronic organizational memory to fuel learning for improving future operations.

Both the Frito-Lay and The Pit case studies provide a glimpse of work with global organizations and mobile workers as it is likely to evolve in the near future. These new workspace arrangements will offer many new management challenges. Leaders who have taken on such challenges are still refining the competencies they need and defining the strategies that work. Among the rules of thumb some have suggested:

- *Develop a broad conceptual understanding of the workforce.* To be effective in planning work and integrating work processes, managers need to develop a larger picture of the organization and its functions, including new understandings of the physical and electronic work environments.

- *Find out the specific roles and technology needs of workers.* Approach the assessment on the basis of workers' patterns of mobility and their use of information resources. Which work groups, departments, and teams are mobile in a local setting and which travel outside the boundaries of the office facilities? Which groups require new supports, and which groups support other groups?

■ *Identify business processes that span geographical locations.* Some functions or processes may span different areas and involve individuals and teams that are both mobile and nonmobile. How are workflow and communication patterns within different processes affected by distance and diversity?

■ *Create a nomadic drumbeat.* When project work is spread across locations, especially globally, it can lose momentum. Switching time zones, difficulties getting in touch with remote or traveling workers, lack of regular meetings, and unclear direction all present obstacles. Leaders must discover the methods and technologies that will keep the drumbeat going on projects conducted by a dispersed workforce. Mobile workers, especially, will benefit by being able to plan and organize their work and travel around a structured pattern of communication. Drumbeat communications via telephone, e-mail, and audio and video teleconferencing also improve integration between mobile and nonmobile workers.

Corporate Commitment to Leadership Learning

The kind of global support strategies suggested here do not materialize out of good intentions. Every one of them is a skill that has to be learned. And while there is no school to equal the "institute of hard knocks," the need for formal classroom training for global managers and leaders is greater than ever. The resources that corporations commit to such learning, and the care they take in cultivating and refining it, is a sure sign of an organization's overall appreciation for the challenges and opportunities of globalization.

Traditionally, American management training has been weighted heavily toward formal, university-based MBA degree programs, while nondegree "executive education" programs were treated as prestigious perks and excuses for three days on the golf links. That has been changing radically in recent years as U.S. corporations have expanded global operations and discovered the need for more formal training for top managers in multinational and multicultural business practices. Increasingly, the best executive training programs are focusing on leadership in global settings, international competitiveness, customer satisfaction, global team processes, and product quality.

American universities have adapted their own business school programs to the new demands by offering more nondegree, customized executive training programs, either in-house or university-based, designed for specific companies. Many of them are offered in conjunction with overseas universities or management institutes. An estimated three-quarters of the roughly $3 billion spent by U.S. corporations on executive training now goes for such customized programs, according to a 1993 survey by the *Wall Street Journal* and *Brickers International Directory*, a leading guide to executive education. The average training session lasts two and a half weeks and costs just under $5,000 in 1994 (Fuchsberg, 1993).

While most U.S. nondegree training programs still focus on fairly broad general management issues, programs on global concerns are increasing in availability, sophistication, and popularity (and are attracting numerous foreign business leaders). As Alan F. White, director of executive education programs at MIT, told the *Wall Street Journal:* "Every corporation now realizes it has to compete internationally, and what's happening is that our [executive enrollment] is beginning to resemble the distribution of the world's GNP" (Naik, 1993, p. R-10).

Examples of the movement toward globalization of training among top-flight U.S. business schools abound (Naik, 1993). The University of Michigan, for instance, recently instituted a five-week "global leadership" program that takes participants to China for two weeks, where they are required to develop a business plan in a totally alien environment. In 1992, Stanford University started a joint program with Mexico's Monterrey Institute of Technology and Higher Education to address business issues specific to the proposed North American Free Trade Agreement. INSEAD (the French acronym for the European Institute of Business Administration) has begun a weeklong program for Western managers seeking planning to expand into Eastern Europe and Russia. And the University of Chicago has started an executive MBA program in Barcelona.

Admittedly, foreign training is far more expensive than in-house or even university-based programs, and so far no one has figured a way to quantify the costs versus benefits of such training. After all, no one can prove that a manager's success in implementing a major cost-saving process among foreign subsidiaries, for example, was the direct result of his formal training ("his" because the glass ceiling of sexism is a notoriously prevalent feature of most executive training programs). But, as Christopher Bartlett, chairman of Harvard University's International Senior Management Program, says: "The ethnocentric American view of doing business has to be broken down" (Naik, 1993, p. R-12). That process cannot succeed so long as all leadership training occurs in an American context. If American firms are to develop genuinely global business leaders who know how to support a global workforce, they must be willing to expose these future leaders to the cultures, business environments, political and legal systems, and everyday realities of the global markets in which they plan to do business. If you want to fly around the world, you have to leave the airport.

Finally, effective leadership development depends on the corporation's own long-term commitment. Companies need to spell out the value and nature of the management competencies that fit their needs and then create the expectation that all team managers will develop them. One three-day workshop, no matter how expensive or informative, won't be sufficient. Indeed, any formal training program is but a small part of the total process of global leadership training and development. Even mastering the four core competencies discussed earlier only provides a framework for continuous training both formal and informal. And much of the deepest, most useful learning will come from "just-in-time," hands-on experience.

Most of the companies we have studied were still grappling with the best approach to the team leadership selection and development process long after they had acknowledged that there was an urgent need to develop one. Companies must look at this task as an investment that will pay off over time. With the proper commitment and cultivation now, these companies will have a large and sophisticated cadre of global managers capable of the diversity and distance skills that constitute at least half of what goes into successful team leadership. Those that fail to make the investment will find themselves far behind the competitive curve.

PROCESS FACILITATION: A NEW APPROACH TO GLOBAL TEAMS

The many facets of the leadership challenge—cultural competence, technical knowledge, workforce support, and all the rest—come together in the ability to facilitate team-based processes: coordinating and collaborating across geographical and cultural boundaries via technology and with a minimum of centralization and a maximum degree of autonomy. Facilitation is the art of helping people navigate the processes that lead to agreed-upon objectives in a way that encourages universal participation and productivity. Indeed, process facilitation has come to represent a leadership skill that is just as vital in the global theater as cultural and technical skills. It is virtually inseparable from the broader art of creating and sustaining teams.

Why "process facilitation"? Some prefer the more straightforward "coordination" to describe exactly what the new team leader actually does. A coordinator, though, is someone who stands on the sidelines and helps others work as a team. Others prefer "mentor," but both of these terms suggest the old command and control, hierarchical type of leadership that is inimical to helping distributed and diverse teams work together productively in today's networked organizations. A process facilitator, on the other hand, is an active player in the same processes through which he or she is guiding a team — whether it be forging shared understandings in a multicultural context, mastering remote communications, devising systems of consensus decision making, or creating and maintaining a sense of team identity. And in our experience, the best process facilitators are like good coaches because they themselves are avid learners.

Because cultural issues are too complex for anyone to grasp completely, the most fundamental leadership principle required for successful process facilitation is self-acceptance and authenticity — the ability to feel at ease in one's own role and to project to team members a sense of one's own integrity. No one expects the team leader to know all the ins and outs of every culture or to speak every language, but they should be expected to know their own place in the organizational culture and to be guided by a set of consistent principles. This kind of centered self-confidence allows members to address the inevitable disagreements that arise, even over basic principles. Such conflicts are less important than consistency and a self-assured willingness to facilitate "third way" solutions as an alternative to "my way" and "your way." Without this kind of centeredness, leaders easily fall prey to the "do as the Romans do" approach in every cross-cultural situation. Going native — always adapting to local ways — is neither productive nor appreciated. Most people recognize that global teams need to make constant compromises, and they expect the leader to create a safe working environment where all relevant input can be gathered to produce a best solution.

As a core competency, process facilitation is needed for all levels of business relationships: in personal relations meetings, long-term teamwork, and organization-wide efforts. The techniques vary at each level, but general principles apply. Facilitation almost always involves clarifying purposes and missions. It invariably addresses the issue of trust. All facilitation aims at clarifying communications — the who, what, how, why, and when questions, as well as the unspoken interpersonal issues that stand in the way of a successful process. And it struggles constantly with issues of commitment, decision making, and implementation.

All facilitation requires leading at times and supporting at times. And there is the continuous challenge of recognizing the point at which group momentum has taken hold to move the process forward on its own — no easy task when working at a distance or across cultures. Few of today's team leaders and managers have had much formal training in process management and facilitation, since it is not a discipline recognized by many business schools. But slowly and surely a body of discipline is emerging, along with a few pioneering masters.

Facilitating Across Diversity and Distance

Consider some of the process facilitation challenges confronting today's global team leaders. In the realm of cultural diversity, for instance:

- Facilitating headquarter/subsidiary interactions can be like tiptoeing through a mine field under the best of circumstances. But how does a newly assigned American joint-venture manager open up communications with a proud management team from a former French company in Indonesia that has been bought by a Japanese partner? To complicate matters, how does one do it through electronic media?

- Conflict resolution styles vary widely from culture to culture. How does an American manager accustomed to the direct, confrontational style of New York resolve a problem with a senior-level team member in Bangkok who expects all conflicts to be settled behind the scenes in a manner that never directly impugns one's personal judgment?

- Strategic planning depends on different action chains in low-context and high-context cultures. How does one balance expectations between Chinese colleagues who want to start the process with building relationships and German colleagues who want to move quickly and directly toward logical objectives based on hard data?

■ Social cultures always penetrate work cultures. How does one set global time standards between Brazil, for instance, and the United States when "do it now" means immediately in Chicago and sometime soon in São Paolo? The potential misunderstandings are myriad—particularly when electronic media are involved.

■ Part of the facilitation challenge is knowing which behavior signals success: reading the cultural cues. During a facilitated team meeting North American members might participate through direct and plentiful verbal input. For Asian members, participation might involve little actual discussion; the real action might be happening out in the corridor or back at the hotel. What is the electronic equivalent of the "after-hours" meeting for such people? If there is no equivalent, what will this mean to cross-cultural team communication? After a recent face-to-face meeting in Seoul, American participants were surprised when their Korean counterparts turned down a deal for electrical parts that the Americans thought had been settled in the meeting. They had mistaken a polite technical discussion for a commitment.

■ Reward systems, too, are functions of cultural variables. High-context cultures are compensated through personal relationships, not just pay. Even though a Nigerian manager might be promoted and given merit pay increases by his Swiss supervisor, he is apt to feel diminished motivation and disappointment if the supervisor fails to lavish personal attention on him, either electronically or in person. Universal reward systems are an urgent need, yet there are no good models. Team leaders must innovate and customize rewards to meet the range of cultural needs.

Distance, like diversity, poses unique facilitation challenges and demands skills that are radically different from those that work with same-time/same-place teams:

■ How does one facilitate a complex implementation plan at a distance? A regional bank manager in Canada was amazed at how much personal time he spent on the phone and on the road providing support to supervisors when new loan processing procedures were put in place. He soon learned to provide more detailed documentation and group training as a substitute for all the one-on-one support.

■ Distance demands more sophisticated communications in a more structured and therefore nonspontaneous mode. Distributed teams do not have many face-to-face communication opportunities — no "water cooler" occasions to exchange information and build relationships. This lack of direct contact can be persistently uncomfortable because it feels so "out of control." Everything seems to take more effort. Maintaining good communications and workflow at a distance depends as much on the art of facilitation as on technology.

■ Distributed team members stay oriented to each other and their tasks through high-level shared visions, goals, and roles rather than through detailed implementation plans. This level of understanding is a critical substitute for the informal, face-to-face meetings that play such an important role in keeping on-site teams in tune with one another. But how do people develop such sharing across vast distances? Some teams use simple graphic reminders of team visions and goals that appear on their computers every time they log onto a shared filing system.

Learning to cope with such challenges may be easier if one confronts them first in the comfort of one's own culture — with plenty of unambiguous feedback and coaching — before moving out into more diverse and distant situations.

Facilitating Electronic Meetings

Technological and facilitation competencies converge in the global team meeting, one of the most common challenges of the global workspace. Most global meetings are not held face to face but in an electronic space that requires special knowledge and skills. How do you have a productive audio or video conference — or use an electronic bulletin board or a shared data base to research and develop new ideas? When is it best to use a certain technology to support a meeting? What are the best uses for each type of technology and the common problems associated with it?

Electronic meetings, like all meetings, go better when extensive preparation has been focused on the purpose of the gathering. One does not plan meetings casually when some team members are more than seven time zones away. Moreover, all meetings are expected to meet common but fairly sophisticated expectations — including the sharing of information, forming relationships, and helping people attain a common understanding of the project. These already difficult problems are exacerbated in electronic workspaces. People continue to bring very different expectations to meetings, including those in cyberspace. It is hard to serve the whole group if the technology is deeply biased in favor of a single set of cultural values. Some cultures see the most important function of meetings as building or reaffirming personal relationships, not getting productive work done. And because it is much harder to improvise and change the agenda of a dispersed meeting in any significant way, it is common to limit the scope of these meetings and skip the social amenities, even though they may be critical to some members' involvement.

Despite the challenges, there are some useful rules of thumb for facilitating electronic meetings:

Before the Meeting

- *Plan extensively and early.* Early and extensive preparations for electronic meetings are essential. Distributed teams that have participated in many regularly scheduled meetings may require less formality than less experienced teams, but it's hard to overplan and oversupport distributed meetings. The planning should consider how much can be accomplished in a given time and how the timing of the meeting fits in with the team's workflow.

- *Send OARRs and participant map in advance.* The leader should distribute to all team members a list of participants, along with their title, role, and location, as well as prepare the meeting's intended outcomes, agenda, roles, and rules (OARRs), which are also sent to members to ensure agreement on the purpose and the process. This is itself a facilitating practice since it gets everyone involved in the meeting before it even begins.

- *Identify decision points on agenda.* The agenda should be time-blocked with decision points clearly identified so that people will be prepared for both the allotted time per activity as well as when and how they will be asked to make decisions. (Some scheduling leeway may need to be provided for polychronic participants.) Also, someone must be assigned to document the meeting.

During the Meeting

- *Begin with introductions.* Beginnings set the stage and tone for the entire meeting. Even though participants should have prepared documents, the leader should firmly establish his or her control as meeting manager, review the OARRs, and have all the members introduce themselves. It is easy to become disoriented and lose track of who is "talking" in electronic meetings, even when they are videotaped. Right away, be sure to allow each site to describe what they are seeing and hearing through the electronic medium through their site. Often, differences in system configurations can make a difference in group interactions.

- *Summarize key points after each agenda block.* At the end of each agenda block, key points should be summarized and questions dealt with before moving on to the next agenda item. Interaction should be encouraged and ample time allowed for pauses and thinking — especially during audio-only meetings. A good rule of thumb is to pause at least fifteen seconds after asking if anyone has anything else to contribute before moving on to the next item.

- *Establish "turn-taking" rules.* Turn-taking rules are essential and must be followed.

- *Identify sender and receiver with each message.* When people ask questions, they should state the name of the person they are addressing. People should always identify themselves before making a comment.

- *Leave plenty of time for summarizing.* At the end of the meeting, all decisions, issues, and action items should be summarized, and time should be left for a five- to ten-minute evaluation of the meeting.

After the Meeting

- *Make documentation available, fast, and interesting.* Meeting minutes, decisions, and action items should be sent out to all members within twenty-four hours. The follow-up document should be available in one electronic file to which everyone has equal access. If electronic distribution is not possible, fax or hard-copy distribution by overnight express is an acceptable alternative.

A Process Facilitation Framework

Having a mental framework for conceptualizing process facilitation in a context of ambiguity and persistent discomfort is a key to maintaining a degree of objectivity and orientation. Such mental guides, or maps to the territory, allow leaders to be flexible but firm and keep business processes moving forward despite the barriers of distance and diversity.

One successful model that has been refined for various multicultural business as well as community settings is the seven-step "arc" model for process illustrated in Figure 4.2. Based on the process theory articulated by cosmologist and inventor Arthur M. Young, it has been adapted to organizational work over a 25-year period by David Sibbet and used extensively in cultural and distance work (see Sibbet, 1993).

Figure 4.2. Seven-step Arc Model for Process.

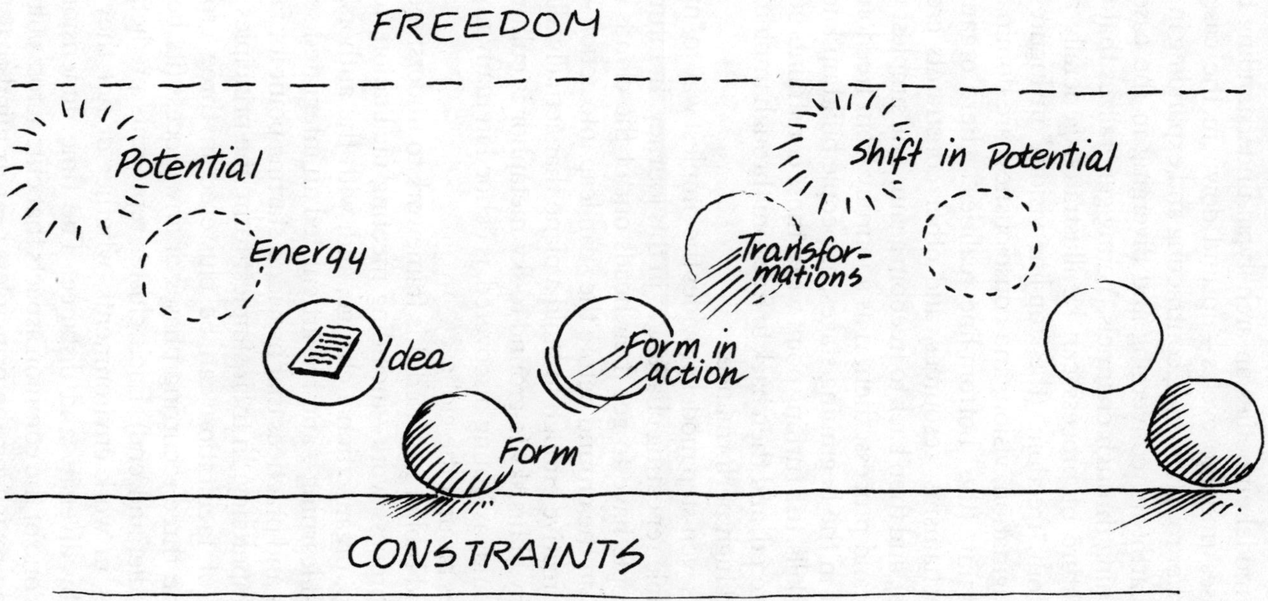

FREEDOM

CONSTRAINTS

Potential

Energy

Idea

Form

Form in action

Transfor-mations

Shift in Potential

The model embodies an archetypal understanding that all processes undergo cycles—up and down in the case of journeys over rough terrain, contracting and expanding in the case of heartbeats, converging and diverging in the case of rivers running through channels. Young generalizes that this pulsing nature of process can be illustrated generally as a journey from "freedom" (the "top-line visions" in Figure 4.2 where imagination, vision, and consciousness are dominant), to "constraint" (the "bottom-line realities" where organizational mechanisms, resources, and other constraints create true limits), and then back to freedom again. The simplest way to understand process, then, is as a journey from freedom to constraint in the beginning stages, as people build up knowledge and skills, to a turning point when these constraints begin to be mastered, and then back to freedom through implementation and high performance.

The seven-step model provides the simplest way to "map" the principle repeating challenges in this journey. In intuitive terms, people have to get their heads out of the clouds and their feet on the ground before they can leap into action—let alone be creative enough to build a plane that actually allows them to fly. This sky-to-ground-to-sky metaphor is culturally universal and, as Young discovered, is echoed in many myths and stories around the globe.

David Sibbet has used this framework to understand all kinds of process work—including meeting facilitation, team leadership, organizational change, and, with the authors, intercultural learning—and has articulated an integrated set of principles and practices that provide a starting point for facilitation competency. In their simplest form, the principles and practices of facilitation can be clustered in three groups around the three recurring phases of any process (its beginning, middle, and end). Each cluster represents predictable challenges in work environments, whether or not they are affected by diversity and distance. The time dimension of process is one of the common aspects that cuts across culture.

When reviewing the principles, bear in mind that they reflect a paradox. While process challenges are very similar as a result of the inherently cyclical nature of dynamic systems, people's practices and responses to these challenges are not necessarily similar. They reflect as much diversity as the world's cultures themselves. Our suggestions, therefore, should be read as just that: a stimulus to gain insight into one's own repertoire. The principles advanced here are those that seem to have the widest reach.

Cluster 1: Getting Involvement and Setting the Pace.   Initially and indeed throughout the life of a team, a critical challenge is creating a safe, inclusive space where everyone can participate and all styles and cultures are honored. The following principles help team leaders get things started well.

■ *Imagine various potentials for every situation.* Since there are so many unknowns in most diverse and distant workspaces, the leader is constantly called upon to improvise on the spot. The best cross-cultural managers learn to play a mental game of imagining various work assignments from different cultural perspectives. Applying the Intercultural Learning Model (Figure 2.5), one should try to cycle through stages four, five, and six — open to the culture, pursue learning, and transcend boundaries — while imagining a task or process such as a new marketing strategy for global product from an Arab or Indian member of a work group. In the course of actually facilitating communication about the task, the exercise makes it easier to accommodate a variety of viewpoints rather than feeling disoriented by all the competing paradigms.

■ *Create a safe environment.* Competence in process facilitation requires knowing how to establish a level playing field where everyone involved can participate. This means helping your group establish baseline operating assumptions or ground rules, agreed-upon outcomes, the role of individuals or subgroups, and a sequence of activities that maintains overall cultural perspectives. (We cover this concept of "third ways" at the beginning of Part Two.) The considerable time spent on such groundwork reaps big rewards in the long-term flexibility and viability of the work environment that results. A clear structure leads to full participation.

■ *Assume a "we" frame of mind.* Trying to create a team culture is difficult under any circumstances and extremely so across cultures and distance. There is a natural tendency to avoid all the barriers. This is particularly true for low-context cultures with a high value on individuality. Their orientation is to the task and getting the job done. Thus the leader must keep the group perspective—the sense of "we"—to the fore-ground in every interchange. Remember that the power of group intelligence is greater than that of any individual. High performance and innovation are more likely to arise from "we" than "me."

■ *Set a pace you can maintain.* Consistency creates trust, which is essential for leadership. In cross-cultural situations, managers often vary their pace of action erratically as they worry about language problems, cultural conflicts, and other barriers. Ultimately the erratic pace creates confusion and stalls the entire process.

■ *Deal with conflicts through "third ways."* Dealing with the inherent conflict in cross-cultural situations is the ultimate challenge of global team management. The intensity of the inevitable conflicts can be reduced by acknowledging at the beginning of every relationship that cultural conflicts are bound to arise—but adding that one is eager to seek creative solutions, such as "third way" blends and innovations. Unfortunately, there are no golden rules for handling all situations. Many techniques that work in the open, confrontational American culture will not work elsewhere. In most of Asia, for instance, direct communication about controversy is itself a source of conflict. Leaders will have to discover the specific ways that individual cultures handle conflict.

Cluster 2: Making Decisions and Managing the Flow. Global team leaders have to make a lot of decisions on their own as well as facilitate consensus decision making. They must actively manage the flow of the process at the top level, keeping team identity alive. This middle set of principles looks at the point at which process hits those constraints that must eventually be mastered to achieve performance.

- *Use vision to pull through constraints.* When you're in the middle of a process and the constraints are greatest, you'll need to make decisions about how to proceed and lots of compromise and cultural methodology are called for. It's the most difficult phase of any process — and, moreover, the phase in which competing cultural action chains and rules for decision making are most apt to come to the surface. At such times, appeal to the fact that at least all business cultures understand the importance of reaching an outcome. People may differ about how to get there, but the promise of a shared outcome represents common ground that the leader can use to facilitate progress. And frequent checking back to past shared outcomes can help you regain direction when the group is getting lost in the interweave of different cultural action chains.

- *Know when to lead and when to follow.* Team leaders need to know enough about the ever-shifting cultural dynamics of their group so they can determine an appropriate level of leadership intervention: from stepping back and letting the group's wisdom pull the process forward to restating choices or jumping in with suggestions that jolt the group into awareness. Supporting group process at an optimal level involves consciously defining and setting aside one's own desires in order to reach the group's goals. This ability to subordinate one's personal preferences to those of the group runs counter to traditional Western values. In general, lead people to address visions and constraints and then support them as they work to master the constraints in action.

- *Balance cooperation and competition.* Conflicting values about competition and cooperation characterize most global business relationships. In either one-to-one relationships or team endeavors, it is best to explore feelings about this important source of conflict from the beginning. All cultures both compete and cooperate, but they do so in unique ways. Go for *"wa"* (harmony), as the Japanese say.

■ *Agree on decision-making limits.* Always deferring to shared decision making is a dangerous pitfall in cross-cultural work. Many cultures expect the leader to make decisions. It is thus essential to be explicit about which decisions fall within the leader's ambit and which ones require group consensus. The leader must be able to foresee decision-making conflicts and resolve them before they arise. Again, exploring cultural differences at the beginning of a team's work is itself a good way to build cohesion and a positive group dynamic.

■ *Use helicopter thinking.* "Helicoptering" means zooming up to where you can see the entire landscape — something that in many situations only the leader can do because only the leader is familiar with all the sites. You must make sure that the whole is working, not just some of the parts. Helicoptering also means being able to zoom down and focus narrowly on one geographical area or one cultural perspective in order to examine a troubled process or get deeper into one perspective to resolve a problem. It also means flying backward or forward to the past or future, depending on what perspective is needed. Many cultures are more past- or future-oriented, and it is frequently necessary to examine the work situation through their eyes and interpret it for the whole group.

Cluster 3: Tracking Progress and Supporting Performance. Once constraints are mastered, the global leader's attention turns to keeping the milestones visible, supporting creative performance at each worksite, and facilitating team and organizational learning.

■ *Set milestones.* Team leaders should ask the group for "benchmarks" that everyone can agree to. In a distributed work environment, managing by milestones avoids many of the pitfalls of trying to micromanage each individual site.

There may be difficult choices regarding the action plans between milestones. It all depends on the cultural variations over information flow and context, as well as the local business environment. High-context cultures often have more time-consuming loops through important people as a critical part of their preferred action chain to complete a business process successfully. These local variations, at times mysterious to others, make it especially crucial to set observable milestones for any important process.

■ *Keep in touch.* Under the pressure of work it is easy to lose touch with far-flung participants and fail to assess progress regularly through formal reporting. Regular, periodic communications with all players must be maintained despite other pressures.

■ *Concentrate on what works.* In a dispersed environment frequent negativity, unbalanced by positive gestures, can assume larger-than-life proportions and undermine group or individual performance. Some cultures — the United States is one — delight in digging into what is wrong, but they are in the minority. American managers in cross-cultural team situations must deliberately suppress their inclination to always confront and analyze problems without balancing their criticism with positive attention to what is working.

■ *Create links and memories.* Supporting the group memory process in explicit, documentary form is a key to successful group dynamics. Individual group members often recall group actions and encounters through their own cultural frames, which may distort the reality of the group. Visual memory links, however serve as shared models that continue to guide work. Special attention should be paid to major transitions in a process, since it is often important to refer back to past action chains in order to see around the next corner. This is impossible without some form of reliable group memory.

Making the Process Visible.   The systematic use of graphics, in addition to text and spoken language, helps communicate

Figure 4.3. Benefits of Graphic Frameworks for Teams.

❏ Publicly recording each others' ideas on graphic frameworks during team meetings acknowledges contributions and builds trust.

❏ Graphic frameworks offer a bridge between different spoken languages.

❏ Open and incomplete frameworks stimulate thinking and draw people into discussion.

❏ They offer a common visual language for visioning as well as day-to-day team tasks.

❏ When designed and used consistently, they provide a way to document work to measure team activity and results.

❏ Context maps promote systems thinking and a process approach to teamwork rather than a mechanical one.

❏ Graphic frameworks help capture information from action research projects that can become organizational development tools.

❏ In a small space, graphic tools hold much information in context.

❏ They provide a memorable way to capture individual, team and organizational memory for storage and dissemination.

❏ As pen and paper technology, graphic frameworks are an inexpensive way to map and study the team learning process for later translation into electronic support.

ideas, processes, and results across all cultures in an explicit, accessible visual language (see Figure 4.3). The roots of graphic language go back to the earliest forms of human communication: to the practice of drawing on walls and in the dirt. It taps into the common visual culture, a "third way" in which all can share—assuming, of course, that the group agrees on the meaning of the symbols.

Visual images used for communication have evolved into basic business tools in the United States. They can fill a critical need in globalwork by supporting the development of "third ways" to understanding and trust. Although no technology or methodology is completely free of cultural bias, graphic language is about as close as we can come to a neutral forum for sharing ideas and decisions. In group meetings, carefully selected and sequenced graphic frameworks can tap the group intelligence and help steer the group toward strategies and practices that apply across cultures. Even outside the setting of meetings, graphic frameworks help structure written communications, such as fax transmissions, so long as the frameworks and symbols have been widely agreed to. Graphic process maps (project diagrams) keep people focused on the same big picture.

In multicultural groups, graphic tools are especially useful for three key activities: creating and communicating a vision; creating and sustaining teams; and managing project workflow. In each of these processes, the basic rule of communications should be: When words fail—and they always do—turn to universal symbols through agreed-upon graphic languages.

Although the global leadership puzzle resists casual solutions, it can be solved—in many different ways—by managers willing to practice intercultural learning and to take risks. One must be willing to experiment, on the basis of informed instinct, with all the pieces of the global teamwork puzzle—culture distance, time, technology—to discover how they fit together in a variety of ways. The first and greatest challenge is the personal challenge. Leaders accustomed to working in the "same-time/same-place" mode, in the comfort of their own cultural environment and with traditional command-and-control practice, will find for the first time that success in the global arena is always slightly out of their reach.

FIVE

Team Leadership: Managing the New Global Business Unit

The cultural, technological, and leadership competencies discussed in the previous chapters provide the basic building blocks for managing teams across the formidable barriers of the global workspace. But without the final ingredient, teamwork itself, no amount of leadership, technology, or cultural sensitivity can begin to deliver the promises manifest in this bewildering new environment. Teams are the basic business unit of the global economy. Their level of performance is the key to the competitiveness and productivity of the new, network-style global organization. Teamwork—the skills and knowledge that go into making teams work productively—is the final ingredient that makes all the other parts add up to something greater than the sum of their parts. The challenge of bringing all these competencies together is the business challenge of the twenty-first century, which in fact has already dawned.

Teamwork, of course, is hardly a new invention. Even in the local, monocultural arena, teamwork has become a buzz-word in the "total quality" lexicon. Teams (as distinguished from other work groups that can reach goals without close coordination) present a commonsense option to the clunky bureaucratic structure of the traditional corporate hierarchy. As a work unit they have proved responsive and resourceful in responding to the time-driven, task-oriented, cross-functional challenges that have always been the bane of complex, top-down organizational structures.

But if teamwork has proved to be of essential benefit to the successful reengineering or reinventing of local and national businesses, it is a *sine qua non* of productive global business. The powerful, creative dynamics of teamwork are the electricity that lights up the global economy. This is not the place to discuss the fundamentals of team dynamics, a subject that has received plenty of attention in recent years (Scholtes and others, 1988; Reddy and Jamison, 1988; Katzenbach and Smith, 1993; Weisbord, 1989; Hirschhorn, 1991). Rather, we will examine how global or transnational teams actually function by looking at some of the key challenges they face and the strategies they have devised for meeting them. We will also explore the basic growth process through which global teams evolve.

First, though, we should be clear about what we are talking about and what we are not. There are all kinds of teams, just as there are all kinds of organizations, groups, or even families (the prototypical team). Obviously, not every team needs to be transnational, cross-cultural, or cross-functional, even in global enterprises. Many tasks are strictly local in scope and are best dealt with by the least complex group configuration. Some groups whose work is not highly interdependent do not even need to function as teams. Knowing when and where to make the considerable investment in the time and resources required by complex global teams is a key strategic decision.

The challenge for top management is to some extent a challenge of vision: an ability to look across an entire global enterprise and construct a configuration of teams that supports organization-wide cross-cultural and cross-functional learning and innovation without interfering with local activities. This requires a systematic distribution of assets, resources, knowledge, skills, tasks, and responsibilities, all organized within the team context. Christopher Bartlett, in his influential work on the transnational corporation, highlighted this essential process: "Perhaps the most important requirement for facilitating transnational innovations is that the organizational configuration be based on a principle of reciprocal dependence among units. Such an interdependence of resources and responsibilities breaks down the hierarchy between local and global interests by making the sharing of resources, ideas and opportunities a self-enforcing norm" (Bartlett and Ghoshal, 1989, pp. 128–129).

Of course, simply telling people of different cultures or professions to work together as a team is not going to ensure innovation and productivity. Making disparate parts function as a team is where leadership and cultural and technological skills come into play. Also, global managers and team leaders need a clear understanding of the strengths and weaknesses of each business unit throughout the global network and how they function together. This means, in part, understanding how teams are best deployed for various strategic or tactical purposes and what kinds of technological support they need.

In discussions of the function and organization of global teams, the focus is too often on the challenges and difficulties while overlooking the obvious opportunities inherent in distance and time differences. These factors should not always be looked upon as "barriers" to be overcome, for they often function as "freeways" through old boundaries. Widely dispersed team members, for example, are able to conduct business on a 24-hour-a-day basis six or even seven days a week, depending on the team's geographical span. And the rich cultural diversity of global teams means that multiple perspectives and insights are brought to bear in the search for innovations.

THE OBJECT IS
HUMAN CONNECTIVITY

While technology is the key enabler of all types of global teams, it remains just that. It cannot substitute for the human interactions that constitute the real substance of global teamwork. Links between human beings, not between machines, is the real challenge of globalization.

In the following pages, we will examine some of the ways in which technology enables teams to maintain those human links over the primary barriers in a global environment— specifically, the constraints of time, the difficulties of maintaining the team's identity, the need for shared models, the absence of context, the challenges of decision making, and requirements for information sharing.

Transcending Time

"I've got a lot of people averaging four hours of sleep a night because of the need to be available around the clock," complained an information technology manager in a U.S.-based global consumer products company. "Any scheduled meeting of a truly global team means the middle of the night for somebody."

Communication across multiple time zones is always trickier than it seems. Even in transcontinental communications, the windows of opportunity during normal work hours are narrow, what with New Yorkers sitting down to lunch just as San Franciscans are arriving at the office. When the communications span global distances, it usually means someone is working from home in the middle of the night. E-mail, fax, and most importantly voice mail have sidestepped the hated "phone tag" syndrome, but not all communications can be done electronically and asynchronously. A certain amount of any team's work requires instant feedback, but the traditional method of instant feedback for the traditional same-place/same-time team — face-to-face meetings — is not an option in globalwork.

For many managers, this means travel — and lots of it. In fact, many managers travel too much to be productive, and many travel at the wrong times in the life of a project. In our interviews, we spoke with many managers who are in a travel frenzy, addicted to global travel but gasping for business results.

How does one decide when to travel? The decision whether or not to get on a plane depends on the situation, of course, but global travel should not be undertaken without considering all the relevant variables. Before traveling, there are some good questions worth asking:

- Are there trust issues that must be worked out? If a team is in the early phases of formation and the members represent a mix of high- and low-context cultures, it may be worth the expense and time of long-distance travel to resolve the tough issues of trust and team orientation.

- Can this task be supported with technology in lieu of travel (for at least some of the team members)? At various stages of a team project, electronic communications may even be preferable to face-to-face meetings. In other phases requiring more direct contact, video conferencing and screen sharing may serve as acceptable substitutes. It may also work to send the best generalist to a remote site but use teleconferencing to communicate with others who don't make the trip.

- Are there tough major decisions to be made that require fast iterations?

- How important is the task? Is it so urgent that it's worth the cost of travel and the even greater cost of wear and tear on the traveler? Are there opportunity costs involved?

- Does the problem involve highly sensitive cultural differences that may not be resolved electronically? Sometimes an overreliance on information technology has created the problem in the first place.

- Can travel kill several birds with one round-trip ticket? Sometimes a secondary mission can give traveling the edge over telecommunicating.

Managers often get sucked into a travel whirlwind in which they are constantly on the road but rarely in balance with the overall work of the organization. Everyone has a travel threshold. Overstepping it can result in serious errors. Even when business mistakes don't result from excessive travel, the strictly emotional costs can be high for the itinerant global worker. "My managers who travel a lot are lonely and suffer from low morale," reported a global director of training and education of a well-established consumer goods company. "It surprises me. I thought they would be up to this—I picked them myself. I find I spend a lot of time doing counseling and support on the phone—it's my biggest problem and I don't know how to solve it."

Cultures vary greatly as to how they treat visiting business team members, but even when the global worker finds himself well supported after hours by colleagues and their families it is still a grind. You can never really go "home" to dinner. There is a deep fatigue, often poorly understood by those new to global work, that comes from working in a cross-cultural environment, and it cannot be remedied by a good night's sleep. Every global worker needs to calibrate his or her own tolerance level, because effectiveness diminishes rapidly when that level is passed. In our researches among global teams, complaints about loneliness and cross-cultural fatigue have been among the most frequent and impressive.

Keeping up morale and a sense of community for those on the road more than a third of their time will no doubt remain a major challenge. Like space travelers, teams must create their "atmospheres" while on the road, and allow both compression and decompression time at either end. Team leaders must take responsibility for their own well-being as well as for others who have heavy travel schedules. The worst response is to simply deny the problem exists and expect people to tough it out on their own.

The need for easy and frequent accessibility to partners on a global team is another time constraint of almost equally daunting proportions. Global team leaders should therefore promise (and provide) at least as much access for their dispersed team members as they would offer to colleagues located in the same building. For example, team leaders can promise a response to any voice-mail message within four hours if it is received during the business day (or within eight hours if received at off-hours). Difficulties arise when an issue is "hot" and a problem cannot be resolved without immediate contact. For these occasions, dispersed teams must establish access protocols that fit with the task and style of the team early on. And it is critical to establish a discipline of response and stick to it. Because of different cultural concepts of time, some definition of a "reasonable" response time must be decided and explicitly communicated to all team members. It might be within so many hours or even so many days, or an assistant might be delegated to cover for times when the leader is out of touch. Global teams also need a common agreement as to what is "urgent" enough to get somebody up in the middle of the night. As a senior financial officer of a global construction company said, "I'd rather get a phone call at 2 A.M. and fix the problem by morning than lose a whole day."

The demand for accessibility requires that global teams map out their use of preferred technologies to support their different needs according to the times and places they will be working, as well as each site's technology resources. Video conferencing, for instance, is not an option in certain underdeveloped countries. Figure 3.1, the 4-Square Map of Groupware Options, is a good starting point for guiding these decisions.

Many senior managers now carry pagers and accept home telephone calls to provide greater access. In some cultures, voice mail may be preferable to e-mail because it allows an emotional component to flow with the message. A more satisfying range of options for balancing access, emotion, and privacy should be available in the near future—such as personal information appliances that can receive your wireless messages in various forms and store them until you are ready to review them.

Also, the future may bring greater personal confidence and comfort with e-mail and other text-only media. People are learning (or relearning) the ability to communicate emotions through writing (a skill we may not realize we've lost until we sit down and try to write a love letter). Already, electronic bulletin boards are providing an early taste of how electronic friendships might develop and be sustained without face-to-face encounters. In the meantime, one useful strategy is to encourage team members to choose survival "buddies"—fellow members with whom they create a particular bond and make an explicit agreement to call on in difficult times.

Maintaining Team Identity

"Out of sight, out of mind," said the CEO of a global accounting firm. "That phrase describes our most common problem."

How does one develop and maintain a sense of team identity—so vital to winning employee commitment—when colleagues rarely if ever gather in face-to-face encounters? Is it even possible? Possible, yes. Difficult, absolutely—especially for distributed teams that work together for only a short time or for people who work on several distributed teams. Teams need to develop shared understandings of the overall purpose of their work. Many cultures, particularly high-context cultures, find that sustaining productive team relationships in a predominantly electronic environment is extremely uncomfortable unless solid personal relationships have been formed early on.

Even when strong team identities have been built on solid relationships, these can easily fade in distributed teams under the pressure of local work and the demands of colleagues who are physically present. Everyone has lots of competition for their attention. Low-context Americans, who do not place a high work value on personal relationships, tend to respond to the "squeaky wheel" and answer short-term demands before they address the priorities of distant colleagues they do not know well.

People working in more than one distributed team face special difficulties. Although each team has its own leader, every member actually answers to a variety of managers in local offices and on other teams. This leads to frequent conflict unless there are strong communications, shared priorities, and operating rules between managers—tough to achieve in a global company where the managers may be as distant from one another as they are from their team members.

Getting necessary resources for distributed teams, such as funds for travel, expert consultants, or computer runs, is always a challenge, given the competition from on-site teams that have better access to top management. Without a serious commitment at corporate headquarters to the value of distributed and diverse teams—a willingness to "walk the talk"—resource competition will remain a serious problem. Part of walking the talks includes management's obligation to create corporate-wide values such as "all cultures are equal in this company" and "cooperation not competition." It is astonishing how many global enterprises find themselves competing against themselves because of the failure to make sure all teams are working in common directions with clear understandings of their place in the overall enterprise. The dissemination of a global corporate culture can provide some glue if it is explicit enough to be tangible, yet flexible enough to stretch and hold across distance and cultures. Top management needs to review existing values, principles, and goals and prepare them in simple documents and relevant languages. Committing to values and strategies that include all cultures participating in the organization is critical. A shared corporate vision and shared values that cross company and team levels can provide an invaluable link between the work of teams and goals of the corporation. It pulls the distributed team forward and puts it in a learning mode.

One simple, low-tech strategy for addressing team identification is to distribute to all members a well-produced wall map of team locales embellished with pertinent and even personal information about each member. Some of our study teams actually created collages that included pictures of each other's offices. Other teams have been known to place photographs of team members on their desks so they have a constant visual image of the people they're working with. Team leaders should give serious attention in the early stages of team development to creating a team metaphor that can begin to take on a life of its own. This metaphor can even be printed on t-shirts. Some teams have designated a volunteer as team historian to maintain and distribute team stories on e-mail. All of these techniques promote team bonding, which is essential for group identity over distance.

If teams are to be more than isolated individuals working on common goals, leaders have to provide the bonding and serve as guide to the territory. They must set a drumbeat of communications that the team can count on and come to expect. Nothing can be left to chance. For the clues that same-time/same-place, monocultural teams fall back on when in doubt simply do not exist for global teams. Leaders must regularly translate team goals and messages to all participating cultures — and do so in a way that is certain to elicit the right responses. If feasible, it helps, too, if the team leader visits each site early in the life of the team to build bonds and develop the work context for each member.

But it takes more than this. Distant teams often fall into the trap of having relationships built only between the leader and individual members. It is equally important for members to establish good working relations with one another. Without these relationships, distributed subteams may find they have no rapport without the trusted leader.

So far, groupware technology has not really focused on identity needs. As desktop video becomes widely available over the next few years, it may offer some valuable help. Telephones will become smarter, too, and be able to give personal information about a caller and the appropriate degree of access. For now, simple electronic systems can provide reminders of team identity, such as graphic summaries of goals or work plans whenever a team member accesses a shared system. Most global teams will do well to work on creative uses of simple core technologies rather than wait for universal access to advanced systems.

Creating Common Ground in Cyberspace

Every culture views the world and the roles of individuals and groups through its own unique lenses of language, traditions, myths, and patterns of behavior. It follows, then, that differences of experience and meaning can be very profound from one culture to another. For members of multicultural, distributed teams, these contradictions in fundamental vision are exacerbated by the need to rely for communications on nonnative languages, which by definition lack the rich metaphors that normally embody a culture's shared visions and interpretations. Thus, electronic communications among multicultural team members often seem dry, too objective, even nonhuman. To give these teams vitality and creative energy requires providing them with a system of shared meaning—a virtual island of common ground out in cyberspace.

Sharing a common understanding of team goals and actions is difficult enough even in monocultural situations. In the global workplace, one cannot even assume that all team members have a common understanding of what a team is. Some cultures have little experience of teamwork; some languages even lack a word for team. What does teamwork mean to the Saudi, the Pakistani, the Hungarian, and the Venezuelan members? Probably four rather different things. Expectations of authority, peer relations, group planning and workflow, information sharing, styles of communication—all operate on different assumptions, making the creation of "third way" solutions the only realistic way forward.

Figure 5.1. Graphic Framework: Vision Chart.

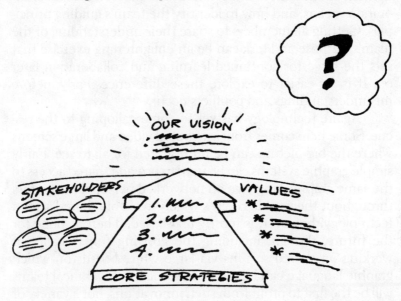

Even the creation of these "third ways" depends on a common language, which is why informational graphics — the use of visual imagery for communication — has become such a basic business tool in the United States, where more and more companies depend on it to create mental models for cross-cultural work. Large graphic frameworks, such as those that display the corporate vision and strategy, as well as less grandiose team action plans, help people bridge the gaps of meaning and focus on common tasks (see Figure 5.1). These visible frameworks offer a neutral place to share and develop ideas and make decisions without the interference of language.

In addition to graphic frameworks that are open and collaboratively created, there is also a crucial need for adaptable, robust models of repetitive processes, such as the Intercultural Learning Model (Figure 2.5), the 4-Square Map of Groupware Options (Figure 3.1), and the Team Performance Model. The Intercultural Learning Model, particularly, offers a framework for discussions in the early phases of team development about each member's values about work, what collaboration means, and how to identify the team's guiding principles. Getting all members to share their understanding of the team's purpose and task can be an enlightening exercise that sets the stage for continued learning and collaboration later on. It is far easier to explore these differences early, before misunderstandings and conflicts occur.

Again, technology has yet to come galloping to the rescue. Some help comes from integrated video and large screens where the big picture can be represented for all to see. Fairly simple graphic systems can be used to provide shared access to the same graphic language on networked personal computers throughout the world. Today's widely available shared-screen technology, however, is mostly text-based. There is hope for the future, though, including the growing functionality of working on shared screens via large white boards on which graphic language can be created. Specialized technical teams will be the first to profit from such innovations, but a variety of global teams will eventually have access to improved shared graphics. When these shared-model groupware technologies mature and come into mainstream use, the true promise of innovation through multicultural perspectives will be more fully realized.

Working Without Context

"Electronic messaging tends to strip off everything but the message and leave the rest to inference," said a Japanese-American global team member. "It intensifies all the differences in work style and values among team members."

Compared to the rich contextual information available in same-time/same-place team interactions, the main modes of distant team communications are meager indeed. The most common communications tools — voice mail, fax, and e-mail — are primarily linear, which is appropriate for certain types of information sharing, such as logical stream-progress reports, data, logistical information, and the like. But linear modes cannot communicate the "collages" of information that one encounters by walking into another person's office and sitting down in a face-to-face meeting. Just how much contextual information do people need? How do you provide it across time, distance, and culture?

Few global enterprises have grappled with the context challenge with much success. It is a measure of enlightenment when companies even recognize that the problem is a serious one, for it is natural to take context for granted. After all, most of us are unaware of the amount of relevant information we casually obtain from our work environment. For the manager sitting at the headquarters of a global company, that environment is a deep pool of cues, nuances, gossip, and other unspoken, unwritten sources of vital information. But team members laboring away in remote corners of the world— connected only electronically to fellow members and dependent mostly on short, telegraphic-style communications—are acutely aware of the lack of such information. And if they are culturally isolated, as well, they are apt to misinterpret even the scraps of information that come their way.

"Contextual information about the other pressures and projects pulling at team members is generally missing," notes a health care division manager of a global company. "Developing sensitivity to each other's time and responsibility commitments, in addition to the team's work, is an ongoing problem for us. The constraints tend to focus communications on the work at hand. As a result, it's difficult to interpret delays, unreturned calls, hesitancies." Mole hills become mountains, oversights look like insults. "When miscommunications result from not having enough of the right information, or reading it incorrectly, it's difficult to handle, especially if multiple parties are involved," said the president of a global consulting business. "Long-distance team members have to learn to question their own interpretations and put quick reactions on hold."

How can distributed teams replicate the "water-cooler" information channels that operate for same-time/same-place teams? They can't. But given recognition of the problem, and discipline and determination in coping with it, they can avoid the more obvious pitfalls. Building trust in the early stages of team development is perhaps the most effective measure. Team members who know and trust one another are less likely than relative strangers to attach negative interpretations to incomplete communications. "When things go wrong, which they always do, and there's no immediate explanation, it creates an open space that's often filled up with half-truths or outright falsehoods," said a regional manager of a large national bank. "Without feedback from trusted colleagues, it's easy to imagine the wrong explanation and hold onto it for a long time." Such problems are especially common on teams with both same-place and different-place members: poor results get blamed on those who are not around to defend themselves. Once this behavior begins, it can quickly undermine a team's ability to develop lasting trust and work productively.

Another common type of miscommunication is created by cultural differences. Global managers often have trouble getting accurate information from distant sites, especially the bad news. "Our business units, especially those in Asia, never want to tell us when things are going wrong. It's a cultural thing," complained the director of human resources of a large technology company. Different cultures have different protocols and action chains for reporting to managers, especially foreign managers who make periodic visits. The team leader needs to be keenly aware of the information flow patterns of all team members in order to evaluate their input properly.

Even in the low-context American culture, trust must develop from a basis of interpersonal knowledge. Distributed teams do not usually have time to get to know each other well. And despite the occasional face-to-face meetings, the focus is usually task-oriented, with little time for building relationships. Deliberately programming "bonding" time into all face-to-face meetings is crucial. It is easier to handle task-oriented teamwork at a distance, even in a slightly disoriented state, than to build trust at a distance.

Generally speaking, authoritarian supervision styles do not contribute to building trust over distances. A more effective approach is instituting drumbeat communications consis-

tently across all locations. This policy provides frequent opportunities to clear up troubling or ambiguous communications
and maintains a sense of continuity and accountability. As the
American-based leader of a global team with participants in
Europe, Latin America, and Asia told us: "In the end, we're all
like high-wire walkers. The other people on the team are our
safety nets. Trust is required. This is especially true when
you're working on a risky task."

Given the inevitability of misunderstandings in a work
environment without much context, managers should give
serious attention to the presentation and delivery mode of
every message. There are a variety of technology aids, each
with its own strengths and weaknesses. Often leaders use the
method they are most familiar with rather than seeking the
best choice for the team members. To meet the demands of
diversity in distributed teams, communications should follow
explicit protocols: commonly understood definitions for business processes, jargon, and cultural symbols, all of which can at
least minimize the hazards of ambiguity. It is important, too,
that different cultural preferences for formal versus informal
communications be taken into account. The Chinese, for
example, have highly formal business communication protocols; Americans and many others are more at ease with
informality.

The same attention applies to the choice of communication media. Information that is best conveyed with emotional
context, for instance, is better sent via voice mail than by
e-mail, which strips out virtually all context. Hard data, on
the other hand, are best transmitted in written form, such as
e-mail. Close attention to writing skills is vital on teams that
communicate primarily through compressed modes such as
e-mail and fax. Serious misunderstandings can result from
even minor slips in grammar or vocabulary. Often, for instance, a written suggestion can sound to the reader like a
command. Detail and explicit intent are vital, too, especially
when some team members are working in a second language.

To increase the flow of informal communications, leaders can introduce policies to encourage personal communica-

tion via e-mail. Some teams hold informal audio conferences periodically, in which any concern can be aired. Leaders should act as models for this behavior and encourage members to participate.

Decision Making at a Distance

"It's hard to delegate decision making to a distant team or business unit dominated by foreign cultures," noted a vice president of a global consumer goods company. "It takes extraordinary cultural learning and acceptance by top management."

All the research on numerous global teams indicates that decentralization of authority is a key to improving decision-making processes. Without adequate authority at the team level, low productivity and workflow stoppages are the norm. Delegation of decision making involves building trust between central management and those working at a distance. This means, for the most part, helping management get over its ingrained command-and-control habits so it can feel at ease with the decentralization it claims to espouse. Team leaders can help this process by keeping top management well informed of progress. The process can be greatly aided too by clearly written agreements regarding responsibilities and the scope of authority.

Reliable and easily accessible information tools are an essential precursor of decentralization, since good decisions rely on good data. Imagine how frustrating and unproductive it is for sales and marketing people, for instance, to be expected to make quick decisions when technology fails to keep them constantly updated on centrally generated pricing and product changes. The pace of change in today's business environment makes information quickly obsolete, and distant decision makers often lack access to alternative sources.

Well-functioning, inclusive, decentralized decision-making strategies are rare indeed on distributed teams. Commonly, decisions are simply left to the leader in the absence of any well-planned process. The difficulty of building and communicating team consensus across distance is one major aspect of this challenge. It is hard to know when to push for closure on an issue, for instance, if communications are highly formal and linear. There are none of the nonverbal, informal communication cues—such as smiles and heads nodding—that signal understanding. Supporting group decision making can be challenging even when audio or video conferencing is available, since these modes do not lend themselves to the kind of spontaneous discussion that builds momentum for consensus.

Distributed teams often overestimate the amount of togetherness they need. Teams work best when they take the time early on to determine exactly when and how to divide work in the most efficient way. They often see that the whole team is only needed in face-to-face meetings at specific times, that subteams can accomplish a great deal, and that individuals can learn to work alone and still feel part of a team effort. Taking a macro view of the team's interdependence needs on all the various tasks at the beginning helps people see how they can work together effectively and comfortably. This view should include explicit understandings about when collaborative decision making needs to take place and when people can make decisions independently.

Most global teams cannot be run on consensus decision making alone. It is important, therefore, to decide exactly when the extra effort to get full team consensus has the biggest payoff. Efficient decentralized decision making will provide a distinct competitive edge.

Information Sharing

Sharing information across great distances can be a mind-boggling, time-consuming task, even with the most sophisticated technology. And the issues are not all technical. For instance, who should have access to what information and by what means? Should all team members have open access to all team information systems? What is the proper balance between too little information and too much? How does one determine the amount of context that is needed to make information meaningful?

Information overload, for instance, is a common problem that looks mostly in vain to technology for solutions. It is epidemic in the United States and will inevitably spread to the rest of the world. Information managers will have to prioritize and sort the mountains of incoming data until better filtering technology catches up. Until then, teams must address the problem by limiting the amount of information they distribute: eliminate the junk. Managers must consider how much corporate-level information should be sent to distributed team members and how to translate it into meaningful data in cross-cultural situations.

Graphic flow diagrams and process maps help any team make sense of information sharing, but they are absolutely essential for global teams. This design work should ideally be done in face-to-face meetings with plenty of space for large graphic displays (Sibbet, 1993). Eventually, technology could make a significant impact with improved simultaneous group graphics, group editing, and file sharing. Some of these products are already on the market, but few of them are practical for global teamwork in their present forms. Thus, the norm for many global teams is still the back-and-forth passing of information.

Making certain that information flows easily in both directions is a common problem. Managers often focus on getting their messages out to team members but fail to provide good channels for feedback and incoming communications. "Honor thy inbound," said an experienced global team leader. When teamwork processes require speed and coordination, the information channels must be open and accessible in both directions. Sharing information is another of those global challenges that demands drumbeat communications. Distributed teams need to set up regular communications on a formal basis. It does not happen spontaneously.

Organizational memory systems are tricky to design and maintain in a global environment, but they are well worth the effort in terms of making important contextual information available to all. Indeed, the entire challenge of sharing information in global teams is one of the more daunting problems managers encounter. But those who grapple with it and live to tell will stake out a clear competitive advantage, and their knowledge will have an important, long-term, cumulative impact.

GLOBAL TEAM BUILDING

The foregoing discussion of the key challenges posed by distance is meant to provide a broad, macro-level framework for grappling with the management of diverse and distant teams. But it is equally important to understand teamwork from the closer perspective of how teams actually evolve and learn to function—the phases of growth they must go through to get from wish to fulfillment. For culturally diverse and dispersed teams, especially, the process can be long and difficult. Without at least a conceptual road map, the process can easily end in failure.

Teams cannot function without a certain level of consistency and common understanding. Thus leaders must pay careful attention to group process—the complex dynamics that block or open the gates to productive teamwork. And for this we need a common frame of reference that allows us to evaluate the stages of team evolution, understand and prioritize the challenges and solutions, and foresee the predictable problems and devise ways of avoiding them. A graphic model illustrating the common course of team development can be an invaluable tool for the leader and the team.

Some caution is in order, however. Certain cultures do not respond as well as others to abstract models. Thus it is a good idea to supplement such models with more familiar metaphors of group collaboration, such as the family metaphor, which is universally understood. This is especially useful early in a team's existence.

The Drexler/Sibbet Team Performance Model (see Figure 5.2), developed by Allen Drexler and David Sibbet (1993), is useful because it addresses not only the task concerns of teams but the social issues as well. And, furthermore, it addresses the special considerations of distance and diversity at each phase of a team's evolution.

The model illustrates seven primary stages in team development, each representing a set of concerns that team members face as they work together, regardless of geographical separation or cultural differences. There is much behavioral science research suggesting that social concerns must be addressed before people are willing to advance to more complex issues such as team commitment and process implementation. This holds true for most national and ethnic cultures we have worked with. In real life, teams move through the various stages at different speeds and repeat some in varying ways, going back to reclaim knowledge that may have been skipped but is essential for later stages. Each stage builds on the others in an inclusive way. For example, building trust and goal/role clarification are integral to good implementation.

The model is robust in the sense that it can be applied to many different types of teams—management, technical, cross-functional, R&D—by including unique practices: the activities a team does to handle work processes and recurring team issues. One key role of the team leader is to make the process visible and to work with the team to select a number of "best practices" that support the team's work for each stage. This is the key to supporting distant and cross-cultural teamwork. The practices that may work for same-time/same-place and monocultural teams are often not appropriate when distance and diversity are involved.

The model illustrates the basic pattern of team dynamics—a continuous cycling between freedom (periods with many choices) and constraint (periods of bottom-line requirements). The basic direction of team process is always toward constraint in the formative phases of team evolution and toward freedom as constraints are mastered. Teams cycle back toward constraint, as new realities enter the process, and

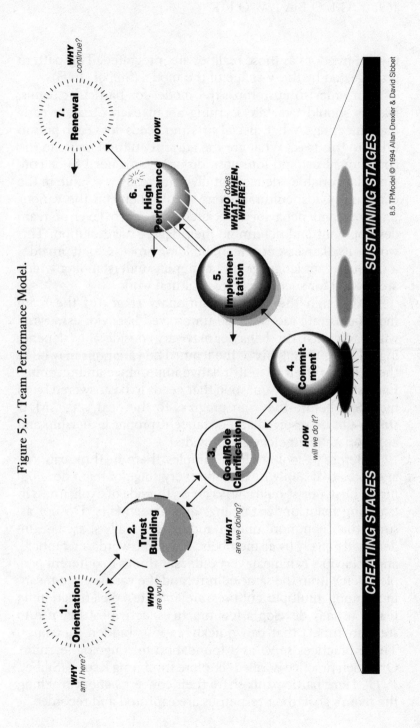

Figure 5.2. Team Performance Model.

WHY
am I here?

1.
Orientation

WHO
are you?

2.
Trust
Building

WHAT
are we doing?

3.
Goal/Role
Clarification

HOW
will we do it?

4.
Commit-
ment

5.
Implemen-
tation

WHO *does*
WHAT, WHEN,
WHERE?

6.
High
Performance

wow!

7.
Renewal

WHY
continue?

CREATING STAGES

SUSTAINING STAGES

8.5 TPModel © 1994 Allan Drexler & David Sibbet

toward freedom as those realities are integrated. This pattern is suggested by the V-shape of the model (Sibbet, 1993).

In order to customize the model for particular teams, leaders should facilitate learning about each other in early team meetings. What special gifts and needs does each person bring to this task? What are the current cultural issues in the company? First and foremost, distant teams need to be convinced through evidence that diversity really is a value in the company. Cross-cultural teams should focus on the various practices and behavior associated with each level of team development and determine their degree of resolution. This work is itself an essential team-building process, for it provides a unique team language and common understanding which are so vital for successful cross-cultural work.

Although the seven evolutionary stages of the team model illustrate resolved and unresolved behavior associated with each stage, this behavior may vary considerably, depending on the cultural mix of the team. The variations may be in the behavior itself or in its relative importance and meaning. Each stage has a key question that needs to be answered by all members before they can progress to the next stage. Most stages can be resolved at a distance if proper leadership and appropriate technology are provided.

Before we look at a few examples, there are three cautionary notes that apply to virtually every stage of team development. First, one should always err on the side of explicitness in exposing team understandings and agreements. Do not assume that "common" understandings are really shared or understood equally by all members. The same words, metaphors, and behaviors can mean very different things to different people, even within the same culture, and the variations in meaning among multiple cultures are infinite. Well-functioning teams usually develop a few practices (activities they use to stay "in tune") that can quickly expose hidden meanings. These practices serve as a foundation for ongoing learning. One such practice is called "Explore Inhibiting Issues" (Sibbet, 1993). Here participants share their concerns about reaching the team's goal; their responses are captured and recorded.

Second, remember that there is no "best way" of team management. Many American managers have received their education and training in a management paradigm that promotes the idea that there is always a universal best way of doing things. If there is a best way, it is usually a new "third way" that has to be invented anew for every team.

Third, since the selection of groupware tools invariably includes cultural assumptions about how people best communicate and often don't equally support good communication from all the cultures involved, people who don't share those assumptions will be shortchanged and resistant. Letting the resistance surface and looking for ways to adapt the tools, as imperfect as they are, is part of the leadership challenge.

We turn now to some of the key considerations for each stage of global team development and performance. The macro-level distance challenges discussed earlier will be alluded to at the stages where they are most likely to be encountered. Keep in mind, too, that the stages of team performance may be resolved in different quadrants of the 4-Square Map depending on the cultural groups involved.

Stage 1: Orientation

At the beginning of any group process, the key questions are always "Why am I here?" followed by "Why are they here?" and "What are we supposed to do?" In other words, teams at the outset have to focus on why they have come together and what is their purpose.

Cultural information from team members is a critical part of the orientation stage for cross-cultural teams, especially global teams. Personal fit and membership are seldom resolved until each person has some internal grasp of how he or she is similar to and different from others. Distributed teams should be given information about each culture on the team. Discussions should focus on how specific cultural differences can be overcome — as well as leveraged — given the added complexity of distance.

Above all, explicitness is a virtue. It is better to provide too much information than not enough, and it is better to state everything openly and repeatedly than to assume apparent understandings. Special effort should be given to:

- Providing enough cultural and personal information that basic knowledge about everyone is readily available

- Linking the team's purpose to the overall context of corporate vision and strategy

- Explaining in detail why this team was formed and why each member was selected, and providing the information in all primary languages

- Establishing the team's means of communication, including languages, and deciding when and how they will be used

If necessary, orientation can be done at a distance for most global teams. An e-mail system that can handle graphics and text works well. Graphics capability is especially important, as teams need visual aids, such as the Team Performance Model and corporate strategy models, to relate to the global vision. Also, global teams often suffer from an absence of context. This shortcoming can be effectively addressed with orientation videos designed to present the full background of the corporate vision and strategy and the team's place in it. These videos should be accompanied by printed or electronic text, in all primary languages, explicitly stating the team's purpose. Discussion regarding purpose, membership, and personal fit can be exchanged via e-mail.

Stage 2: Building Trust

"Who are you?" This is the basic question to be resolved in stage 2. Once team members know the basic purpose and mandate of the team and their own role in it, they need to know how the others fit and how they are supposed to relate to one another. "How much risk am I taking with these people?"

"What do they expect of me?" And most of all, "Can I trust them?"

Trust behaviors vary from culture to culture. The overt, spontaneous behavior and forthrightness so indicative of trust in the United States would be out of character in Japan or other high-context cultures, where trust is embedded in the network of workplace relationships. Unless this phase is successfully navigated, subsequent team developments are prone to breakdown. Key considerations include:

- Demonstrating respect for individuals at all times. In most cultures, personal respect is a deeply held value, and it is important to practice it in culturally acceptable ways for each member.

- Keeping alert for misunderstandings. They are inevitable given the different cultures and languages.

- Mapping the team's hierarchy of values. Clashes over basic assumptions and values can rapidly break down trust.

- Learning each culture's spoken and unspoken cues for signifying trust and distrust.

Face-to-face meetings are virtually irreplaceable for building interpersonal bonds. Voice mail and video conferencing can provide ongoing support for maintaining trust because they convey some of the emotional context and interaction impossible in text-only technology like e-mail. But face-to-face meetings are usually essential to establish trust in the first place. If travel resources for geographically dispersed teams are limited, they should be invested in this early stage. Many American teams mistakenly shortchange this phase and rush toward the implementation stages on the unexamined assumption that trust can be taken for granted.

Cross-cultural, multilingual teams in face-to-face meetings often benefit from computer support in brainstorming, as it permits anonymity and makes life easier for members working in a second language. Formal, computer-aided meetings should be balanced, of course, by informal personal and social time for getting to know (and trust) each other as people, not just teammates. "High-tech and high-touch," as the Naisbitt slogan goes.

Stage 3: Goal/Role Clarification

After everyone knows who and why, they need to know what. "Exactly what is it we're supposed to accomplish as a team?" "What am I responsible for?"

This stage of teamwork can be completed at different times and different places, depending on the task and the culture. For example, American distributed teams perform best if they negotiate roles face to face, since American culture values the ability to control one's own activities and time. In contrast, Mexicans are better able to handle role assignments at a distance—so long as it is absolutely clear what they are supposed to do.

It is essential to define the boundaries around roles and responsibilities, ever mindful of the special influence of such cultural variables as power/equality issues. Key considerations include:

- Clarifying the meaning of key terms for all cultures and languages.

- Exploring what constitutes the freedom to act within a role or responsibility. What kind of conditions support role and goal realization for each culture? What are the usual cultural boundaries of these roles?

- Paying special attention to defining subteam roles. They are a valuable implementing unit of teamwork, and they must be recognized up front.

- Being explicit about authority roles. Different cultures operate within different authority boundaries.

The roles/goals stage can usually be handled from a distance with two to three sequential steps. Suggested roles and responsibilities can be drafted and circulated by e-mail (one that can attach files with graphics is best). Visual graphics showing relationships is better than long narratives. These electronic communications should be followed by individual phone discussions to cover all clarifications; ratified agreements can then be sent by e-mail. This type of iteration is important because people often need to mull things over or check them out with their colleagues or managers before responding and negotiating.

If the early orientation and trust-building phases are successful, the goal/role clarification and commitment stages are less likely to require face-to-face encounters. However, immediate and constant feedback is important to clarify what is being considered, requested, agreed to, or rejected. Are you agreeing to do what I think you are agreeing to do? Lots of cross-checking is essential to confirm agreements and sharpen understanding in the goal clarification stage, so clarity and immediacy of communications is vital.

Stage 4: Commitment

With who, why, and what behind us, we next have to ask: "How do we proceed?" "How do we organize ourselves to carry out our goals?" "How do we share this vision with one another over time and distance and cultures?" "How do we develop the needed resources, including budgets?"

Shared vision, which must be reached in the commitment stage, connotes too much commonality for some cultures, as in Costa Rica, where individual variation is highly valued. Other behavior, like decision making, varies greatly among cultures in both style and process. Some common ground or at least explicit agreements must be forged at this stage if these differences are to be resolved.

Teams need to find a metaphor for their shared vision. This can be facilitated by creating a "context map" of all local sites showing how the team's purpose fits into larger corporate strategies and goals. Other key tactics include:

- Using a blend of decision-making styles that includes everyone in all key decisions.

- Determining which local site has the best resources for each team task.

- Clarifying time commitments—always a challenge, but failure to address it can sabotage teamwork.

- Giving people time to discuss commitments at their local sites.

- Avoiding documenting commitments until consensus is achieved. Formal documents are taken very seriously in many cultures. If the team is using text-based communications, it's a good idea to agree on a "look" or format for in-progress versus finalized documents.

Commitments demand a fast pace of interaction. Thus video and audio conferencing (with some shared-screen capability if possible) for certain same-time/different-place meetings is usually critical and worth the effort. Even if it means some team members have to work odd hours, most people would prefer this to travel.

Commitment is typically the most constraining point in the early life of a team. Thus a same-time/different-place medium (like conference calling, video teleconferencing, or image sharing on computer screens during an audio conference) is valuable so that all participants can give and receive immediate responses. Am I getting through? Does your response mean what I think it means? Can we confirm that this is the way we are agreeing to go forward?

Stage 5: Implementation

Now that things are moving, the question becomes: "Who does what, when, and where?" Having grappled with the turning-point decisions in the prior commitment stage, the team now must resolve all the new realities of actually working together if it is to move back toward freedom.

Action chains differ radically among cultures. Agreements about how things get done may be interpreted very differently in different cultural contexts — from viewing action as a straight line from beginning to end to seeing it as one that loops back and forth. Even the value associated with completion of a task differs greatly. Exploring these underlying cultural differences early and reconciling them between high- and low-context cultures saves time and frustration down the line. Key considerations include:

- Setting up an informal communication system. People have to be free to talk informally with one another, even if only electronically, to get the proper lubrication for information flow. Good relationships and open access to communications are the key to information flow and innovations.

- Ensuring "anytime" accessibility to leaders. Members have to feel they can make contact with leaders and other team members whenever they need to.

- Defining a process for iterations and working on shared documents.

- Setting the goals but letting members fill in the steps in culturally acceptable ways and according to local conditions.

- Setting group milestones and reporting systems, but avoiding detailed action plans unless absolutely necessary. Detailed plans should serve as guidelines, not prescriptions.

Audio and computer-conferencing capability is critical. Products like Lotus Notes can be a great support if set up in a customized fashion to support the team's task. Screen-sharing capabilities are useful too. People need ways to keep in touch frequently to share progress, test ideas, get help, build a data base. Access to the leader can be enhanced through fax, 24-hour voice mail, and e-mail.

Stage 6: High Performance

By now, the questions have been resolved and the team process is moving toward freedom on high gear. Intuitive understandings have replaced conceptual frameworks. This is a particularly difficult stage to reach at a distance and across cultures. Not only do language barriers and electronic protocols interfere with the need for synergism and intuitive communications, but cultural values associated with high-level performance vary immensely. Every cross-cultural team needs to define this stage for itself.

The combination of caring relationships and a challenging performance goal creates the best engine for high performance. Considerations include:

- Avoiding unrealistic expectations. High performance is unusual on all but veteran global teams.

- Providing performance-based support in a "just-in-time," on-line mode.

- Offering group-oriented rewards.

To get high performance there must be a system of flexible communications in place, preferably including voice mail, phone, and desktop video. These all provide avenues for both factual and expressive communications—classic high-tech/high-touch. Teams need access to learning materials and performance-based supports, at least in terms of coaching. Teams working in full-implementation and high-performance mode are like the fast-break stage of a basketball game: a dazzling blend of speed, instinct, and determination.

Face-to-face communications are rarely possible in the high-performance stage, especially for dispersed teams, because things are moving too fast. Information systems at this stage should always support the need for speed and flexibility, not work against it. At the present time, e-mail is the most useful support—especially if team members are working at a distance.

Groupware, if it is to be successful at this stage, must

support flexibility as new needs arise — for they are apt to arise quickly and unpredictably. Ironically, the more aligned and high performing a team is, the more it can utilize simpler means of communications like phone and fax. Great teams communicate nonverbally. There is little need for explicit communications, because they anticipate each other.

Indeed, intuitive communications often become the guiding medium, as each team member foresees the needs and reactions of others in advance of conscious requests and problems. In Japan, this sixth sense is called a "feeling presence" — the feeling a group of workers gets as they work intimately as a team in a crowded room, for example. The trick, of course, is to use electronic media in ways that facilitate a similar sense of team presence while members are working at a distance. For some teams, video provides an added social dimension and may help distant team members stay in synch with each other. For other teams, regular use of e-mail or voice mail keeps them in touch while everyone is still moving rapidly.

Stage 7: Renewal

High performance can't last forever. Members get tired, they move on to other teams, new members join, goals change. People start asking, "Why continue?"

Why, indeed, except to pass on the invaluable team and organizational knowledge they have acquired. Or if there are organizational reasons to continue as a team — perhaps on a new mission — it's often valuable at this stage to get together if only to celebrate the end and the beginning. In fact, any old reason to get together on a positive note is a good one. Because of distance, most global teams need to revisit earlier stages of team development again and again to clarify and reinforce shared understandings. Remember that:

- Celebrations of even small achievements keep members emotionally connected and convey a sense of progress and team identity. Face-to-face meetings and video conferencing are good technology choices for milestone renewals, which keep members moving forward and feeling optimistic about the team.

- Reports of each member's activities and performance should be dispatched by team leaders to the member's supervisor, especially before performance review periods. Keeping a data base of the team's history is helpful to new members who may be joining.

- Ongoing team learning systems, including a group memory or archive system, should be established.

Renewal is a periodic process of reexamining the basics of a team: where it has been, where it is now, where it is going. At times, renewal involves an acceptance that activities are over. (This stage may even involve a period of grieving if team members are disappointed in having to move on.) At other times, renewal involves a recommitment to a direction that may have grown less clear over time. Renewal is a reflective activity. It is important but usually not urgent. Hence it is often postponed far too long.

Good teamwork is not possible without intercultural learning at each stage of the Team Performance Model. Leaders and teams who use both the Intercultural Learning Model and the Team Performance Model will begin to develop an appreciation of their supportive, interactive relationship. Teams do not just happen, nor are they built mechanically like houses or other fixed structures. Teams are fluid and alive. They must be nurtured and grown, with great care and effort. Groupware, if it is to be successful, must intimately serve this very human process.

RULES OF THUMB
FOR GLOBAL TEAMS

The following strategies apply to all global team challenges. If practiced on a day-to-day basis, they contribute significantly to successful teamwork.

- *Create a communications drumbeat.* Continuity and an underlying pace and rhythm are the heartbeats of global teamwork. As one team leader told us: "The magic is in the routine." Said another: "Be obsessive with detail." A daily, weekly, or at least regular routine is critical. When the routine fails, information cannot flow and details get lost. Leadership should come in a steady stream, not in geyser bursts.

- *Use cultural guides liberally.* Realizing that you need help is a strength, not a weakness, in the global environment. When interactions among colleagues from different cultural backgrounds come to a grinding halt, get technical assistance from a translator, cultural "guide," or other expert. Knowing when to pull in expert resources is essential.

- *Build trust.* A key rule for building trust is to take time for relationships. This can be especially hard for managers with a cultural proclivity to get on with implementation. But successful team leaders take seriously the responsibility for creating the human "glue" of teams: a deeply held sense of purpose, high trust, and commitment. These values will carry the group through many unforeseen events.

- *Redesign work processes for the global environment.* How work processes are designed and perceived must be shaped by the cultural dimensions of language, context, time, power/equality, and information flow. Global teamwork often means linking and sequencing subordinate tasks among different locations. The team leader must facilitate the process of exposing different perceptions and help the team find a "third way" to work. Otherwise, some members will withdraw and others will dominate — resulting in low productivity and a lot of friction.

- *Manage with milestones.* It is critical to set up milestones for all phases of work. These must be clearly understood and honored by all members. The milestones should be established jointly—with everyone's cultural reality taken into account—so that each member can adapt specific action plans to local conditions without undermining the team's goals. The milestones should function as the team's mutual navigational system.

- *Be creative with technology.* Technological infrastructures vary considerably in sophistication across the span of a global team. This means that all members must be involved in creatively adapting the tools to their own specific needs and limitations.

- *Be fluent with cross-cultural management practices.* Fluency means being able to respond appropriately to a variety of cultural demands. Managers and leaders must be capable of switching from authoritarian-style to consensus-style supervision, for instance, or from direct to indirect feedback, depending on which style works with which member.

- *Create "third way" strategies.* It is increasingly clear that the old ways of working are culture-bound and will have to give way to new mindsets that reject the "our way/ your way" orientation. Finding the "best way" in the global team environment means crafting new and unique "third ways," which we explore in some depth in Part Two of the book.

PART TWO

Think Globally, Act Globally: Globalwork in Action

SIX

Creating the
Global Workspace:
Culture Clash and Confusion
on the Pacific Rim

In the global workspace, all the business competencies described in Chapters Two through Five come into play in a day's work. In this chapter, we discuss cross-cultural, team, and leadership competencies, as well as forms of technology that support them, within the context of a fictional business scenario involving a United States–China joint venture.

Of course, any such scenario can only be a snapshot of the current period in China, due to rapid social changes there. For example, as China incorporates market-oriented policies into its system, the focus on money and investment has increased. Those in business will notice that although time (as a commodity) has traditionally been less valued than human relationships, this is slowly changing. As younger people look outside and emulate some aspects of Western culture, it may seem that China is undergoing fundamental changes, but it is too soon to say which of these changes are temporary and which permanent. Most will probably not touch the deepest layers of Chinese culture.

Richard Safire stares out the window of the 747 at the thick cloud cover below. He knows the details of the proposed joint venture plan in his portfolio backward and forward. As a global business manager it makes perfect sense to him that his company is decentralizing to take advantage of offshore production opportunities with two new joint ventures. Yet he knows that when the plane descends into the clouds over Guang Zhou, China, things will not seem so clear cut.

The e-mail messages from Guang Zhou in advance of the trip had been so sketchy—very few of the questions about staffing and production goals had been addressed and those that had were extremely vague and not useful. Even the agenda was not confirmed—only the location of meetings and a list of key participants. Safire begins to feel that his Chinese colleague Lin-Chen Wu does not consider the joint venture a priority, and he feels frustrated about not having enough information to adequately prepare for his meetings.

Don Simonetti, president of Westwind Foods, had beamed when he said to Safire, "I'm really confident that you can present our plan and get feedback about coordination from Lin-Chen Wu and his group at the new joint venture. In fact, you should consider asking Wu to help you manage the process with our suppliers in East Asia as a timesaving measure. When you get back, let's move right into finalizing our implementation plan."

Westwind Foods, a large specialty foods manufacturer and distributor, is positioning itself to introduce a high-end line of Asian and European foods. They had established a joint-venture agreement with Royal Garden Enterprises, a state-owned food manufacturer in Guang Zhou known for its expertise in packaging, to produce several products and help solve some of the worldwide packaging issues for North America and France.

Lin-Chen Wu, a general manager with Royal Garden Enterprises, is competent in international business English and handles many of their American transactions. Wu had spent the day before reviewing the plan he had received from Seattle ten days earlier and tried to construct a picture of Richard Safire's place in the company relative to other people he knew. It was hard to tell—all the e-mail messages talk about "global teams" and "working together" and "giving honest feedback," which doesn't help him assess the pecking order of the relationship.

At 8:30 A.M., Lin-Chen Wu goes to the airport with his Foreign Affairs Department head, Mr. Li, to meet Richard Safire, chauffeured by the company driver. Wu greets Safire at the gate—it is their first face-to-face meeting, although they have exchanged faxes and e-mail for almost six months since the start of joint venture negotiations. Wu says, "I am very glad to meet you, Mr. Safire. I have heard that you work very closely with Mr. Simonetti."

"Well, yes. I met with Simonetti just yesterday. He is looking forward to getting down to brass tacks with this joint venture," responds Safire. Wu nods as the disjointed image of the brass tacks colloquialism floats by.

Richard Safire is a bit surprised by the size of the welcoming contingent, because he had planned to slip into his hotel unobtrusively and collect his thoughts. He wonders how long the welcome formalities will take. When the group reaches the car, there is an awkward moment as Wu and Li, waiting for Safire to slip into the back seat for a formal conversation with Wu, watch Safire open the door next to the driver. There is a palpable sense of discomfort in the back seat as Mr. Li takes the seat beside Mr. Wu, the place reserved for their special guest.

At the hotel, Safire tries to thank Wu and Li and slip away to his room, but they follow him upstairs, anxious to get acquainted and begin discussing the meetings of the next few days. "Would you like tea, Mr. Safire?" asks Li.

"Uh, no thanks, I'm fine," Safire responds, preoccupied with the search for a jack compatible with his laptop computer.

After a moment of hesitation, Li goes on to pour tea for everyone and sits down at the table. (Safire thinks it odd that no one understood his refusal of tea.)

Lin-Chen Wu describes his history with Royal Garden Enterprises, acknowledging his mentors within the company, as does Li. Although Safire knows it takes time to get down to business in China, he asks if they can turn their attention to the agenda—"so I can have some time alone," he thinks to himself. Wu outlines the next day's schedule, with a visit to the head offices in the morning and a top management meeting with the president, Mr. Zhao, and the vice presidents and general managers in the afternoon. The second day's schedule is to include a plant tour in the morning. The third day begins with a joint meeting of the top management plus all twelve department heads. "What do you have in mind for the specific meeting outcomes tomorrow?" Safire asks, still wondering how to prepare for his presentation.

"We hope to introduce our management group and begin our work relationship," replies Wu.

Safire begins to think he is not understanding the

encoded communication he is receiving—what kind of meeting did Wu really have planned? Or could it possibly be a get-acquainted meeting? He is too tired to pursue it any further and asks Lin-Chen Wu to arrange for an interpreter (since he knows it would be too awkward for Wu to interpret) before bidding him goodbye.

Safire is alone in his room by 11 A.M. He notices that his global time zone clock said it was 7:30 P.M.—yesterday—in Seattle. He calls home to sing happy birthday to his daughter on her ninth birthday. It's the second in a row he's missed. "No, sweetie. I'm not in Paris, I'm in Guang Zhou—at least I'm supposed to be." He speaks briefly with his wife, Vessna, who is still mystified by the fact that he couldn't rearrange his schedule to be in town for their daughter's birthday. "I'm really sorry, Vess. You know how this joint venture work is."

As Safire slumps into a chair, he realizes how little he knows about joint venture work. He worries that there hasn't been any groundwork done for his visit. Unfortunately, no one is there to tell him that his Chinese counterparts want to leave the agenda open ended in order to create the all-important space in which a meeting can unfold. He doesn't know that Wu has very similar long-term goals, but is trying to begin his journey toward them by establishing a solid relationship between Safire and his organization first.

The next afternoon, as Safire is escorted to the meeting room he is surprised at the banner announcing his arrival, the arrangement of the room with namecards all around, and the fact that everyone stands and applauds as he enters the room to take his seat beside Mr. Zhao, president of Royal Garden Enterprises. He feels flattered and somewhat uncomfortable with the pomp and formality and notices that Wu is sitting two rows away. Tea is served to everyone, and Mr. Zhao asks Safire about his trip and *his family back in Seattle. Safire feels the helplessness and frustration build in his body as he tries to think of a way to open the meeting. Then the president stands up to address the group. The interpreter begins, "We are honored to have Mr. Safire with us from Westwind Foods, as an emissary for Mr. Simonetti in this noble undertaking of our joint venture project. We feel fortunate indeed that the 'royal garden' we cultivate will send its fruits to other parts of the world." After more background about events leading up to the joint venture and Mr. Zhao's encouragement to everyone to voice their thoughts freely, it is Richard Safire's turn.*

He launches into his presentation without an acknowledgment of the leadership group and the extensive preparation done for his visit—something a cultural guide could have told him about. He discusses the interdependent tasks of Guang Zhou and the Asian suppliers in his best international business English—free of colloquialisms and American expressions. Pausing to wait for the interpreter, he feels flat and constrained, but the managers seem attentive and it helps to have color overheads of the key concepts and proposed timetable. "Are there any questions?" he asks at the conclusion. No questions, but much applause. An awkward silence follows. The top managers know that even though Mr. Zhao has asked for input, their suggestions are not completely welcome. After the meeting, everyone files out in order of their position in the company.

On the way back to the hotel Richard Safire has that strange, vague feeling he often has when doing business abroad, that a gap is opening. He turns to Lin-Chen Wu: "Mr. Wu, what is your assessment of the meeting this afternoon? Why the silence after my presentation?"

"Perhaps people were being cautious. Mr. Zhao

does not like comments on his projects—certaintly not public comments," replies Wu.

"Oh, I see. Could you tell what people thought of the presentation?" asks Safire.

"Well, I think the top managers were not yet ready to respond to specific plans. First meetings are often more general in nature."

"Then how will I get a response to the proposed plans to take back to Simonetti?" asks Safire.

"I will have to talk to them after you leave."

"Well, I'm really going to need you to push this through, then. Otherwise we will get behind our schedule," concludes Safire.

"Mr. Safire," Lin-Chen Wu asks, "May I stop to see my sister on our way to the hotel?"

"Sure. Will there still be time to plan for our last meeting?"

"Oh yes, of course." The stop, it turned out, is a family party for Wu's oldest sister, who is visiting from Zhong Shan and has just turned sixty—an auspicious event in China and an important life milestone. The restaurant is full of relatives and friends. Soon the courses begin to arrive—soups, chicken, pork, fishes on platters, and vegetables with intoxicating smells. Safire is annoyed that the party has come up unexpectedly on the night before a big meeting but soon finds himself engaged in a conversation with Wu's sister using sign language and his thirty words of Mandarin. The irony of the birthday situation is not lost on him.

After dinner, Richard Safire asks Lin-Chen Wu what Wu can do to speed the process within Royal Garden. Safire is worried that the large joint meeting might not result in any substantive discussions—exactly what Wu seemed to be predicting. Wu offers to communicate Mr.

Simonetti's interests to the other general managers but says that the process of agreeing on a business direction takes time. After their meeting, Wu feels off balance. He wants to find a way to tell Safire that Mr. Zhao is the person to influence, but he feels that perhaps it would be overstepping his role to tell Safire what to do, considering Safire's seniority.

On Day Three, the joint management meeting with Mr. Zhao, the two vice presidents, four general managers, and twelve department heads exhibit even more formality than at the earlier meeting. Richard Safire is again escorted to the head table beside Mr. Zhao. After tea and some informal conversation, Mr. Zhao opens the meeting with a presentation on Royal Garden. "We are proud to have five plants in the province employing almost three thousand people," Richard Safire hears Zhao say. The staffing list he had tried to obtain prior to his visit is recited in detail—numbers of managers, food processing workers, packaging workers, truckers. The quantitative stream of facts and figures, however, bears no relationship to the qualitative development plan Safire is about to present. Richard Safire continues anyway, laying out the global plan for decentralization and the focusing on activities in East Asia.

After the applause dies down, Safire knows that no one will respond but out of frustration asks for feedback anyway. The interpreter gives the responses literally—"It is a well-constructed plan" and "It is worthy of further study"—knowing full well that the embedded message is, "We cannot comment in public before our leadership." In a moment of supreme anxiety and frustration, Safire blurts out something else to fill the silence: "Then I would like to make a proposal for implementation. Mr. Simonetti has suggested that your group take a larger role in the corporate supplier relationships in East Asia because he trusts *your experience. One thought was that Mr. Wu could lead this effort."* After the interpreter finishes there is a stunned silence in the room. Richard Safire has the same feeling in the pit of his stomach, but it is impossible to ignore this time. Wu has a panicked look on his face, and Mr. Zhao looks distracted. Finally, Mr. Zhao speaks, *"We can consider Mr. Simonetti's suggestion."* Wu knows that Mr. Zhao is shocked and offended at the proposal and that the president has no intention of accepting it.

In the car on the way to the airport, Safire is steaming and upset, because he cannot believe he is leaving with practically nothing accomplished. *"What will I tell Simonetti? What did I do wrong?"* Lin-Chen Wu pauses and then explains that the proposal has put him in a very difficult situation because he is not in line to take on management of this project. Mr. Wong, vice president and Wu's superior, should have been asked behind the scenes. Wu can neither ask to be relieved of the assignment because Mr. Simonetti made the request nor ask for help within Royal Garden, because it would draw resources away from his superior, Mr. Wong. Patching up the damage will take at least a month and will leave the joint venture in a vulnerable situation. As a result, the Chinese part of the project will lag a month or more behind the U.S. and French groups.

Back in Seattle, Richard Safire writes a lengthy report on the trip and e-mails it to Lin-Chen Wu for comments, in an attempt to make some sense of everything. Wu responds to confirm receipt immediately but does not comment because he sees e-mail messages as formal documents that should reflect consensus on policies. In lieu of much communication from Guang Zhou, Safire begins to play back his trip to see how he could have made his colleague lose face as well as undermine his own assignment from top management. At the same time, Wu is

*reflecting on how he could have let things get out of hand
and how he had failed Safire as a guide.*

Richard Safire and Lin-Chen Wu's work *is* the global work-space. The megatheater of global business is as simple, and painful, as one person struggling to reconcile a child's birthday and a major presentation in a city where the business cues are baffling. And Lin-Chen Wu's experience of feeling off balance while doing business with a foreign colleague working awkwardly against the grain is repeated every day in a thousand different places. In the end, globalwork requires adaptation from all cultural perspectives: no one will have the comfort of being completely "at home" or "in balance."

In this chapter we track the efforts of Richard Safire, Lin-Chen Wu, and other managers who are working to create global collaborative spaces each day. We will view these experiences through the five cultural lenses: language, context, time, power/equality, and information flow (as introduced in Chapter Two). While traversing the open seas of culture, these "lenses" can serve as navigational guides for global business. The examples presented here are informed by the business processes, teamwork issues, and technology cited by our study participants. As Figure 6.1 illustrates, the fact that our examples can be seen through more than one lens demonstrates the holographic nature of culture: one facet comes to reflect the whole experience. In sum, "The potential of culture to confound and surprise us—and through us to surprise and confound others—is staggering" (Storti, 1990, p. 19).

LANGUAGE

As a global nomad, Richard Safire finds that the intricacies of language permeate his work at every level—from forms of address to corporate communications, from formal meetings

Figure 6.1. The Holographic Nature of Cultural Lenses.

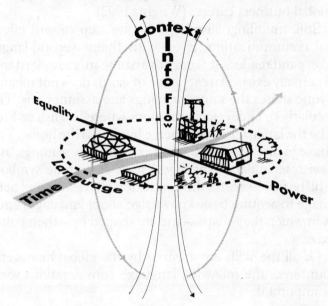

to family dinners. The bridging of languages will always be a challenge. And painful experiences like Richard Safire's will continue to be the norm because cross-cultural communication is far more than the literal translation of words. It requires the ability to translate cultures and, like the work of a poetry translator, the aim is to evoke a response as rich and textured as the original experience. This means being able to anticipate the impact of one's words in another culture — an art form still to be attained for global managers. Even the translation of silence is important.

Fortunately for Safire, his native language has become the closest thing to a global language. While it is the mother tongue of 300–450 million people, it is spoken with varying degrees of facility by up to one-third of the world's population, especially in Africa, in India, and throughout the Pacific. People who are trilingual in English, Spanish, and French (which is not exceptional in certain countries) are relatively at home in more than a hundred countries. This is certainly the best argument yet for making language training a high priority for global business careers (Wright, 1992).

Still, multilingualism is only one step toward effective global communication. Even with fluent second-language speakers and readers, it is easy to assume more understanding than actually exists. An exchange of words does not mean that everyone shares the same meanings and assumptions. This is particularly so in developing nations where English or French may be the language of commerce but not in the home. Teams will have to discover methods for confirming meanings, as well as devise secondary "languages" such as graphic symbols. It will still be necessary for those who don't have a second or third language to acquire basic knowledge about languages and the ways in which they shape — and are shaped by — their culture's worldview.

Of all the skills emphasized by the global managers we encountered, the following language considerations seemed most important.

Corporate Communications

Westwind Foods never made an explicit agreement with its joint venture partner for a corporate language; in essence, it made a unilateral decision to use English. This gave top management the distinct disadvantage of not being forced to look beyond its own viewpoint and, moreover, not always getting clear feedback. However, companies that assume all cultures are "equal" will find themselves having to select an official business language that becomes the voice of the corporate vision.

In addition to a corporate language, it is also important to have multilingual communications to get the word out. This will be much more than a cultural accommodation as knowledge workers become a valuable asset. As a global manager, Lin-Chen Wu was faced with questions from his manufacturing group about a complex production development plan in his second language that he had received only ten days before. Almost no time had been allowed for clarifying meanings.

Major corporate communications like restructuring plans, visions, and implementation strategies should be published in the official language as well as major secondary languages with plenty of lead time to synchronize interpretations and incorporate feedback. If this seems like an excessive investment, imagine receiving a fifty-page corporate vision from your parent company in Saudi Arabia — and how many conversations and meetings it would take (in Arabic) to be fluent enough in its concepts and assumptions to lead your Midwestern division with it.

Imagery often communicates when words alone are inadequate. One manager kicked off a redesign project at a distance with a video of herself and the key players explaining the new directions. This approach has much more impact than documents in high-context cultures like Kenya. Diagrams, illustrations, and entire graphic visions like that of National Semiconductor (described in the next chapter), with the addition of translated text, have proved very effective. Corporate publications, likewise, should be translated into as many languages as possible within the constraints of budget and space.

Critical Meetings/Presentations/Conferences

Richard Safire was unable to give his presentation in Mandarin since he had only begun his language study. He might have gained more trust from colleagues, however, had he given a portion of his presentation in Chinese. Every global manager should have some degree of foreign language competency as part of the business's long-term strategy of appropriately investing in specific managers. Multilingualism must become a corporate value — particularly for American businesses, like Westwind Foods, where language training is rare.

The use of professional interpreters is an inadequate substitute for multilingual global managers. Lin-Chen Wu was at a disadvantage without an interpreter who could translate into his or her native language. The staff interpreter gave an accurate translation of words, but he failed to translate the cues — so that Safire erroneously read certain expressions of interest as signs of approval. Later, Wu had to brief Safire on the import of the meetings.

In cultures where it is appropriate, a professional (native English-speaking) interpreter, one with a compatible style, accent, and status, would be helpful, provided a relationship has been established in advance to clarify needs and assumptions. This approach might have saved Safire and his company the breakdown that resulted.

One study participant told us how he attempted to approach a touchy issue diplomatically by saying, "Let's be careful to not sweep this under the rug" during a Korean-American project negotiation — only to have it translated literally, causing a bizarre communications breakdown. A business unit manager from the United Kingdom told us of insisting that a business colleague translate for a meeting from a genuine interest in "teaming," not realizing that translation is considered a low-status occupation in Thailand. Their promising relationship never recovered from the Thai colleague's having lost face.

The following list (adapted from Wederspahn, 1991, p. 2) presents strategies for working with interpreters:

- Give the interpreter the written text (at least an outline) and a glossary of terms beforehand and review them together before the event.

- Speak slowly and group your sentences around single topics.

- Avoid slang, jargon, colloquial expressions, and puns.

- Use metaphors and analogies only if you know they are commonly understood within the local culture. Avoid military terms. They are offensive to most cultures.

- Use specific, quantifiable terms whenever possible.

- Use charts and other visual aids.

- Monitor the listener's facial and other nonverbal expressions for signs of confusion or misunderstanding.

- Talk to the person, not the interpreter.

In meetings, speaking simply and directly, even though it may feel less sophisticated, works well—particularly when supported with translated overhead transparencies like those Safire used. In one conference in the Netherlands, a live graphic "recording" of the proceedings acted as the glue for a discussion in French, Spanish, English, and Dutch. Translators can also write on a large graphic, turning it into a linguistic meetingplace.

Research has shown that the use of networked computers in face-to-face meetings greatly improves effectiveness—particularly when multiple languages can be used (Gray, Olfman, and Park, 1988). Experiments have been done allowing participants to work in their primary languages, to think and make group contributions, followed by translations for the group at large. One group decision support system, Group Systems, although designed primarily for use in English, has an editing function that allows menus and commands to be entered in other languages compatible with a keyboard. Any user-friendly group decision support system will have to address the issue of multiple languages and presentations for instructions as well as user participation. Over the next ten to fifteen years, communication tools—from e-mail to group decision support systems—will be supported by computer-assisted translation services.

Team Tasks

Multilingual teams, like those developed between Royal Garden and Westwind, can establish language protocols in advance to avoid awkwardly defaulting to one language. Later in the year, the Guang Zhou and Seattle offices agreed that phone calls, which were infrequent but important, would be interpreted with the help of the AT&T Language Line. Critical text messages were sent in the sender's native language and translators were arranged for both locations to get the most accurate reading of the messages. Some languages lend themselves to business transactions more than others — which makes it hard for those who speak less direct languages, like Japanese, to express themselves to team members. The daily challenge is staying aware of the balance and interplay of languages so the burden of translation, and hence being off-balance in a second language, is spread evenly.

Asynchronous communication media are useful because they alleviate the pressure that nonnative speakers feel face-to-face in real-time conversations by phone and video conference. They give participants a chance to compose thoughtful responses. Richard Safire made sure that he began a rhythm of e-mail and fax messages as soon as the subsidiary relationship developed with Royal Garden. He could have gone further by structuring an e-mail or fax exchange to plan the meeting and presentation or by using a computer conference to encourage wider participation and more depth in gathering feedback from team members in France. Both Safire and Wu agreed that setting goals and strategies in advance of the meeting would have helped. Global managers who can design and facilitate inclusive processes like these in electronic workspaces will contribute to the expanding base of global team practices.

For functional teams that span the globe, professional languages can also be a communications link. The shared meaning implicit in scientific terms during well-facilitated technical discussions, for example, can constitute a base upon which to build trust for more difficult conversations about goals and team processes.

Perhaps one of technology's most important contributions will be in language translation. Strides are being made already in the form of the AT&T Language Line, which offers interpreters twenty-four hours a day in more than 140 languages as well as text translation services. On-line electronic message translation services will someday be a boon to productivity, too, particularly for high-performance teams engaged in creative thinking where the gap between first and second languages can make a huge difference. Human interpreters will still be needed, of course, to provide the nuances of communication and subtle meaning required for complete understanding.

Products/Labeling

Strategic choices about marketing and new products are shaped by regional field reports, newspapers, technical reports, and relationships with other business people in the area. It is hard to scan, study, and interpret this varied information through someone else's filter. Nothing substitutes for complete language facility in each market, so that product names and imagery can respond to the culture of local consumers. This is one reason for Westwind's China–France joint venture.

On one end of the spectrum was the infamous attempt to sell the Chevy Nova in Latin America, even though "*No va*" means "won't go" in Spanish. On the other is a global consumer goods company committed to global branding that spread its Chicago-based ice cream label worldwide — but let European manufacturers use a creamy color (which denotes quality in Europe) while maintaining a white ice cream for Americans who consider white as a sign of quality.

Personnel Evaluations

Language gives critical access to a culture. Without it one can never really know whether the data for personnel evaluations are accurate or even useful. Thus it's easy to misunderstand and make poor decisions about a person's performance. For example, our study participants spoke of being frustrated at having to evaluate English-speaking overseas managers without being able to speak to any of their staff members. Their only access to performance information was, alas, through the manager. The use of cultural "guides" (mentioned in Chapter Five) is helpful when managers feel isolated by language. Richard Safire could have worked with Lin-Chen Wu more fully to help him read cues and provide coaching to establish rapport with his new teammates.

CONTEXT

One of the great dramas of modern life is the global tension between high/low context cultures. It unfolds every day through the first truly global TV network — CNN — where the international news is often the struggle of two cultural dimensions trying to adapt to one another within the dizzying pace of global change. Today the high-context societies of Eastern Europe and the former Soviet Union are attempting to leapfrog their traditions and join the low-context race to the twenty-first century. But will they succeed without the reliable navigational aids that guide the low-context Western cultures? Russian entrepreneurs, for instance, are coming to Canada to set up supply businesses that sell goods back to Russia through personal contacts, because receptivity to Canadians is higher and trade restrictions lower than in the United States. The key link is the high-context personal contacts. It remains to be seen if these entrepreneurs can master the other aspects of Western-style business.

As we saw with Richard Safire, the need to adapt quickly to a lot of information pulls one toward a low-context approach. To explain the company's joint venture plan, he had to get down to business with as little interference as possible from "distracting and time-consuming" context in China. On the other hand, the need for long-term continuity required him to develop the kind of extensive personal networks that help high-context cultures filter and mediate the flood of information. Richard needed to slow down and take time to get "contexted" to work in Guang Zhou. Wu, on the other hand, needed to work at synchronizing with a low-context, egalitarian approach. He needed to see that as his colleagues didn't automatically know the structure of Chinese protocol, he might have been more explicit.

In our scenario, Richard Safire needed to make sound assessments of the discussions he had and the people he met. Yet he soon discovered that out of his usual context, the cues — tones of voice, verbal cues, gestures — were not recognizable. For this reason, the ability to suspend judgment and the accompanying, often visceral, automatic responses is a critical skill for global managers.

Even though managers like Richard Safire and Lin-Chen Wu naturally gravitate toward a solution compatible with their primary social culture, the challenge is to function effectively in both high and low contexts. These managers of the future will know that the persistent discomfort of working cross-culturally is simply a fact of global life — and will let the host culture set the tone as they seek creative and inclusive business processes.

The cultural dimension of context shapes behaviors and events in the workplace in thousands of different ways — some subtle and others shockingly apparent. The following selections highlight some of those context challenges that executives and managers told us were most different to adapt to or important process differences to anticipate and learn.

Family Events

Like it or not, a sixtieth birthday party became part of Safire's workday. From Lin-Chen Wu's perspective, however, a long day intruded on an important family milestone. It is a common low-context mistake to think contextual issues affect only the business sphere when in fact they usually encompass all of someone's life. This point was driven home to one of our study participants who returned to a project in Costa Rica to find that none of the scheduled deliverables had been completed due to a series of holidays and a birth in the family.

Context is a deceptively powerful frame: expansive enough to hold our image of the world, inherent enough to be perfectly transparent. According to cultural anthropologists Edward and Mildred Hall, the high and low context gaps are the hardest to bridge (Hall and Hall, 1989). As we saw in the docudrama, the cultural distance between China and the United States cannot be underestimated. Managers working in such situations must be committed to intercultural learning in order to survive, let alone achieve high performance.

Global teams need to remember that differences in the way team members balance work and family should not be swept aside or criticized. Teams that span high-context and low-context cultures must consider both work schedules and regular holiday and family events in order to develop an awareness of what is likely to happen when. They must also discover ways to handle unexpected events or delays.

Introductions

Executives in high-context cultures have probably learned a great deal about potential team members before meeting them face-to-face, as evidenced by Wu's research on his colleague. Safire, in contrast, wanted to use the face-to-face meeting itself as an occasion to establish a relationship and get work done. Such initial meetings can be extremely awkward when two or more sets of expectations are brought to the table. Following the host culture's pattern, with coaching from knowledgeable team members, generally yields the best results.

Strategic Planning

The entire planning process can run on two tracks that never seem to meet when high-context and low-context cultures attempt to plan together. In low-context cultures like the United States, the plan — the written, concrete document — is everything. In high-context cultures, it is merely the beginning of a long, evolving process in which key players line up networks of personal influence and support. Then the specific steps of a plan are expected to change, and change again, as the plan rolls forward, reflecting the networks of people supporting it.

Richard Safire did not know that the Chinese do not want to discuss strategic ideas until the power relationships are established. Both groups, therefore, proceeded unilaterally by their own cultural norms and reached a less than ideal result. Another scenario would have been a more open-ended plan that left space for forging a new relationship between Westwind and Royal Garden — the details to be determined by both parties — and including a clarification of roles and responsibilities for key players.

Although current strategic planning software can be used effectively by both high-context and low-context cultures, teams must consider many relationship issues prior to crafting information into a strategic plan. Groupware tools that support decision making must be employed carefully, for high-context cultures such as Japan build consensus privately. The Japanese do not like to conduct debate publicly or in a distributed event such as an audio conference. And high-context cultures like China that prefer harmony over problem solving may find electronic ranking and voting on controversial issues an unsatisfactory way of reaching agreement. One technology that probably will appeal to high-context, collectively oriented cultures — such as Thailand and most of Asia — are shared-screen technologies for collaborative tasks like design. The simultaneous collaboration on shared computer screens mirrors a group work process that is preferred to individual work.

Another consideration is the amount of uncertainty/avoidance a culture has — a cultural dimension studied by Geert Hofstede (1984) — in relation to context. The early use and adoption of technology is not always predictable and thus might tend to be avoided in cultures such as Japan, Korea, and Mexico where people prefer to use well-tried methods. In countries such as the United Kingdom, Singapore, and Sweden, however, team members might feel more comfortable in experimental situations that pose the possibility of snags.

Hiring and Promotions

Personal networks of influence dominate the hiring process in high-context cultures — often to an extent that looks like cronyism to low-context managers. Richard Safire, who would have gone out of his way to avoid having personal considerations influence hiring decisions, learned to accept the influx of new team members in China who at times seemed to be a stream of friends and relatives. Adding a new member to the team had been a loaded situation until some baseline criteria were settled. Lin-Chen Wu learned that his Seattle teammates needed background information in order to rationalize his recommendations to their superiors. This format developed from an exercise during which team members told one another what it meant to add a new member and how they preferred going about it.

Project Reports

Low-context Germans may take great pains to prepare a clear, detailed written report about everything involved. High-context Brazilians may want to talk about it informally and look at a graphic overview that documents the highlights. Imagine a mixed team deciding how to complete a report and then dividing up the workload: neither could ever satisfy the others' needs. One alternative is to establish standard reporting formats shaped in a way that blends cultures so that no documentation preference rules by default. A mix of text and graphics with a strong sense of informational presentation, accessibility, and content would be a starting point.

Until recently, computer technologies have been biased in favor of low-context cultures by focusing on text-based information. This is because software is often designed by members of low-context cultures. The advent of desktop video is beginning to alter the balance, as people now have the ability to see and talk to others at their workstations. A good rule of thumb is to use technology to support specific processes within a given business activity. Consider how the process would be conducted in a high-context or low-context culture—along with the types and amount of information each would want. Electronic meeting support, for example, would not have helped much at the Guang Zhou meeting, because people didn't know one another and lacked a basis for trust.

Performance Reviews

The need to preserve face is a dominant motive in high-context approaches to performance reviews (and work in general). Thus nonverbal and indirect communications are the norm: giving a person a low-status assignment, for example, or leaving them out of a meeting. In contrast, low-context cultures prefer to collect objective performance data and confront the person directly and discuss the problems. One of the worst uses of technology is to give performance reviews solely in written form without delivering it in the context of a relationship. In many cultures such as France, the written word is powerful and formal, carrying a great deal of weight. In others, such as Costa Rica, it is always secondary to a personal communication.

Managing Conflict

Face is a common element of many Asian cultures, especially Japan and China. Face encompasses credibility, integrity, and the ability to function as a member of one's group or society. Unfortunately, the direct ways of low-context cultures can inadvertently cause a loss of face when explicitly negative messages publicly single out and shame someone. Loss of face can be a major humiliation that goes beyond the job both personally and professionally. Low-context business people need to slow down and must learn to send and receive information in more indirect and culturally acceptable ways. Likewise, high-context business people will need to consider private, indirect ways in which they can accept constructive feedback.

In the vignette, Lin-Chen Wu lost face because he was given a role that rightly belonged to someone else in the company—and thus conflicted directly with *his* role. Even worse, his respect for authority (in this case, Mr. Simonetti) prevented him from asking for a workable solution. If the situation had not had such dire consequences, Richard Safire might have thought it laughable that someone could become so stuck. Of course Wu did not think of himself as one person, but rather an integral part of the organism of Royal Garden Enterprises.

Because many Asian cultures regard criticism of someone's ideas as a personal attack, the use of electronic brainstorming or publicly recorded flip charts about controversial issues is almost impossible. The whole idea of getting a group together to thrash something out will be culturally uncomfortable to many team members. Likewise, handling conflict at a distance requires a mastery of tools in the 4-Square Map of Groupware Options and an understanding of each tool's cross-cultural applications and range of expression (see Figure 6.2). Managers need to have a full repertoire of practices for managing conflicts and be skilled at selecting the best option for the mix of cultures and strategies. For example, managers should opt for voice and video communications—better at conveying concern, warmth, humor, and agitation—rather than document-based communications like e-mail and fax that are stripped down and abrupt, making team members guess at the emotional content. Remember that low-context cultures may send more information when problems arise whereas high-context cultures favoring harmony may send less than normal. Remember, too, which communication medium the receiving culture finds most comfortable.

Marketing and Advertising

The growing number of global consumers will mean more data and social/cultural contexts to track. A shared data base of key consumer preferences in different regions can help. When displayed in overlapping detail, this will also show where advertising needs may coincide. Such data bases might contain a category titled "Pitfalls"—including precautions against trends like using foreign words decoratively unless one knows the meanings. (This tip might have prevented a Japanese company from marketing t-shirts with lewd remarks in English to young people in its own country.)

The tension between leading consumer interests and following them is mirrored in the dynamic between local and global marketing initiatives. Companies can make it a practice to cultivate marketing suggestions locally and compare them to global activities. This can become a forum for seeking the best ideas.

Figure 6.2. The 4-Square Map of Groupware Options: Best Technologies for Global Teams.

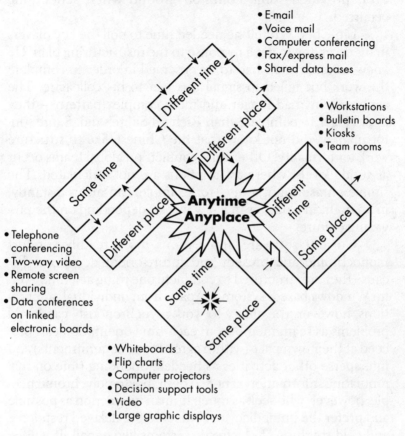

- E-mail
- Voice mail
- Computer conferencing
- Fax/express mail
- Shared data bases

- Workstations
- Bulletin boards
- Kiosks
- Team rooms

Different time

Different place

Same time

Different place

Anytime Anyplace

Different time

Same place

- Telephone conferencing
- Two-way video
- Remote screen sharing
- Data conferences on linked electronic boards

Same time

Same place

- Whiteboards
- Flip charts
- Computer projectors
- Decision support tools
- Video
- Large graphic displays

TIME

Different cultural orientations to time—polychronic versus monochronic, with varying orientations to past, present, and future—are often cited by global team members as one of the most common sources of confusion. Lin-Chen Wu's orientation was to the past: accomplishments and relationships developed over the years. His challenge was to juggle his company's cultural viewpoint with Richard Safire's, which was oriented to the near future. Their shared monochronic outlook, however, provided some common ground when scheduling occurred.

Lin-Chen Wu felt he needed time to poll the key players in his company to get a response to the restructuring plan. He knew certain rituals had to be observed in order to complete the work but failed to signal this fact to his colleague. The action chains had longer and more complex patterns—they took longer to complete than Richard Safire's did. Safire, unfortunately, did not know that the Chinese like to structure work for formality. Other time conflicts on global teams occur at subtle levels, where assumptions are not articulated. The simple phrase "right away," for example, can mean instantly, in an hour, in a day, or in a few weeks, depending on the prevailing culture.

Current software applications more readily support monochronic and present and future-oriented cultures because they are structured to complete one thing at a time even in Windows-based systems. Apart from individual applications, however, the ability to work asynchronously can avoid problems as team members in each time orientation can proceed at their own pace (within agreed time commitments) and intersperse other activities as needed. Spending time on manipulating information is not so desirable to polychronic people, however, who seek as much human interaction as possible and prefer the immediacy of contact to the delayed responses and cold rhythms of electronic systems like e-mail. It will be interesting to see which future-oriented cultures versus past-oriented cultures will easily abandon old ways of working in favor of new technologies.

The following business events and processes were among the most common and challenging in the global business arena.

Business Appointments

Monochronic Americans hate to waste time more than anything. As Richard Safire demonstrated in his insistence on getting to the point, time is a valuable resource to be hoarded and managed. This attitude toward time can be felt in the postures and urgency of our bodies—almost a physical impatience. Thus rigid adherence to schedules and appointments is valued highly. It is also a source of conflict when polychronic colleagues appear to treat time as something to be spent as opposed to saved. Waiting for a person you have an appointment with is insulting to Germans. But it is just part of life in Chile, where it is always assumed that the person had something very important and unexpected occur—which is worth waiting for. Most global corporations and teams will of necessity evolve a blend of time expectations and rules that will be right for the mix of cultures.

Results and Rewards

Future-time orientations affect the business environment in a pervasive and invisible manner. In many cultures people do not believe they control the future. Success by personal control and achievement makes no sense to them; in fact, it seems counterproductive. A past-oriented culture like that of China, on the other hand, is heavily influenced by historical relationships. This affects how people work together and determines what kind of performance reward systems will work.

Long-Term Planning

Different orientations to time can make the planning process a frightening roller coaster ride for everyone involved. In cultures where time is no object, schedules and flowcharts mean little. Goals are what count, and the steps required to reach them are expected to evolve out of one another. They are not set in stone from the outset, as some cultures like the English are wont to do. One compromise between detailed rigidity and leaving the result to fate is scenario-based planning, which develops several pathways and allows for adjustments midstream when changes demand them. Scenarios can be developed jointly in an interactive, storytelling fashion that serves both time orientations. It is best to concentrate on developing a high-level overview showing major goals and sub-goals that will keep all members moving in the same direction.

Working together over e-mail, or even in a collaborative data base, to complete detailed plans will not make sense to a polychronic worker who feels there are too many contingencies that could arise. There will be little interest in putting such intense effort into something whose details will probably change.

Meetings

Polychronic people seem to be able to do everything at once: conduct a meeting, take a phone call, chat with a passerby, eat, and switch subjects at the drop of a hat. In Paris, Richard Safire found that adjusting to these constant "interruptions" was extremely difficult for a highly focused person like himself. The team meetings often felt like a three-ring circus. Westwind learned that, in general, time had to be set aside for relationships in meetings with their French partners. Otherwise the meetings were not very productive.

Behavior in electronic meetings, whether video or audio, can also be affected by different time orientations. Because distributed meetings supported by video technology, for example, are scheduled in advance with rigid time constraints for the video conference room, it is wise to allow extra time for late starts. During the meeting, polychronic participants will probably feel constrained by having to take turns, which is contrary to their natural ease with interruptions. Same-time/same-place decision support tools, however, present no real obstacles to either end of the time continuum. In fact, polychronic workers relish living in a sea of information. Multiple lists of brainstormed ideas are not as overwhelming for them as they can be to monochronic people. In general, too, electronic meeting schedulers will be less attractive to cultures that favor impromptu meetings.

Office/Factory Hours

Whenever the time orientation is mixed in a workplace, as in a joint-venture plant, a local "time culture" must be jointly created. In the process, the work values and time orientations of everyone on site should be explicitly acknowledged. This can prevent misunderstandings about punctuality and reliability. Consider, for example, a Native American leaving work an hour early to meet an older relative who called to request an appointment during the day. The unannounced departure might be a surprise to a monochronic colleague but perfectly natural to another Native American who deeply respects that person's need to take care of personal business (without asking what it might be).

Sales Time

Customer relations can vary greatly according to time orientations. Polychronic salespeople will lavish time on customers, even when a sale isn't likely, because the long-term relationship is more important than the short-term transaction. For this reason, global sales and marketing strategies have to be customized to local conditions.

Most technology support for sales will be data collection and sales data transmission. These will be readily acceptable by both time orientations so long as polychronic salespeople have adequate time and support for building the relationship. Beautiful graphic and multimedia presentations will be welcome additions to sales calls, but they are no substitute for the sales process in polychronic cultures. Elaborate multimedia presentations will substitute for some of the relationship time in monochronic cultures but will have the opposite effect in polychronic cultures.

As time went on, Safire learned that the Chinese, who are polychronic, unlike Americans, needed a great deal of time to research and set up sales due to their past-time orientation. Wu learned that to the Americans, presentation and delivery (present-future orientation) are everything. He correspondingly spent more time on his presentation skills when dealing with headquarters.

POWER/EQUALITY

Despite the flattening of organizations in the United States and elsewhere, the vast majority of cultures remain very hierarchical. In the global environment, one must remain constantly aware of how various cultures assign different values to age and gender differences, handle promotions (merit or connections), treat relations between executives and subordinates, and value skills and professions.

Richard Safire began his work in Guang Zhou by scheduling tasks. Knowing that who you know is the first map to draw in Chinese culture might have saved his trip. If he had let Lin-Chen Wu, who shared Richard's ultimate goals, explain his role and diagram the power system, Richard might have known who to enroll to help with the East Asia units. In this case, the direct route to work was the most inefficient. In such cases global managers will need agreements on overall goals — on a large as well as small scale — and remain patient and open to different ways of achieving them.

Equality-conscious Westerners like Safire often forget that ascribing status and power on grounds other than pure merit seems to yield as many business successes as the egalitarian model — witness the business acumen of many Asian cultures. The problem in mixed-culture global teams lies more in offended sensibilities than in poor performance.

In hierarchical cultures that have wide gaps in power between workers at different levels, it will be hard to get people to use technology when it works across power levels. Electronic tools that create user anonymity in meetings will not be comprehensible in cultures where it is essential to know with whom one is communicating. Status dictates every aspect of interpersonal interactions — even the fact that there is an exchange happening at all. Similarly, voting and ranking tools that level the playing field by asking lower-status participants to share equally in a decision with those higher up can be very uncomfortable for both ends of the spectrum. Indeed, in many cultures it is disrespectful or even dangerous. The abuse of anonymity on computer conferencing in which disgruntled employees explosively express their anger toward management would never happen in cultures where authority is shown the utmost respect under all circumstances.

For those from egalitarian cultures, being ascribed a position in a hierarchical work situation can be perceived as a compromise of personal identity and integrity. These global workers need to feel comfortable putting on role "masks" that allow them to function in a new environment. Just as Shakespeare's characters assume temporary identities to move through society or speak their minds safely, global workers must be creative and flexible enough to work within the inherent logic of other cultures while maintaining self-confidence.

The business processes that follow were persistently difficult for exectuvies.

Communication Between Levels of Hierarchy

In cultures where status and power are assigned, there are often rigid lines of authority that cannot be jumped. This is particularly troublesome to the itinerant global worker who ultimately must depend on a "cultural guide" to reveal who talks to whom about what, when, and where. Americans and others who want to go straight to the top to resolve problems are often frustrated by having to deal with relatively powerless intermediaries.

The challenge is to map the lines of authority in order to see where "communication bridges" occur — and then use them appropriately. In our docudrama, for example, Lin-Chen Wu was fully prepared to act as the information output point for the managers at Royal Garden Enterprises. He could also have interpreted signs from the president for his colleague.

With data bases or collaborative electronic platforms that can be used by people at many levels within a network, there is always the question of information access and privacy. Because information flows along lines of power, it may be necessary to adapt tools like collaborative electronic "platforms" that combine a shared data base with e-mail and computer conferencing capabilities — in low-context, hierarchical cultures like Germany so that access is determined by one's grouping. This strategy would mirror the natural workflow and avoid inappropriate release of work being prepared for a "communication bridge."

For the most part, we found that executives were able to reconcile power and equality differences once they determined the rules and flow of power. But it was always uncomfortable and continued to be a struggle. The validity of input was often questionable when people from strongly hierarchical cultures were asked to participate on an equal footing in group situations. On the other hand, executives from more egalitarian cultures found many common practices just as uncomfortable: speaking one way privately and another way in team meetings, reluctance to state opinions publicly, and going along with a plan just because a superior endorsed it.

Debating Business Options

The give and take of discussing options openly, "playing the devil's advocate," and openly disagreeing with anyone, anyplace, anytime is sorely missed by egalitarian global team members. Americans, in particular, often feel they are operating in a straitjacket — in sharp contrast to their usual freewheeling style. This is particularly annoying when the differences in status seem minor or the point of disagreement is trivial. But in many cultures, challenging one's superiors is simply not acceptable and certainly never in public. Richard Safire assumed that everyone at the joint management meeting should have an equal opportunity to comment on the plan he presented. And he was right. Unfortunately, he didn't truly understand that the feedback process needed to happen in private and over a period of time.

Team Assignments

For the most part people from cultures where status is ascribed are competent and well prepared for their roles. The system sees to it by supporting and educating them. Nonetheless, "undeserved" assignments are a source of irritation and sometimes even anger for egalitarians on global teams. In such instances it is important to focus on the integrity of the entire work system: even if the assignee may not be the perfect choice, the interdependence of the workplace as a whole will more than compensate. As evidenced in Lin-Chen Wu's case, when giving an assignment it is also important to avoid putting someone in an awkward situation that would hamper work.

Once team assignments are made, there is the question of delegating or defining the work. One of our study participants noted marked differences in the amount of direction needed by teams in the United States versus England. The English members looked to leadership and wanted much more guidance about the task; the Americans needed more independence and were offended if given too much instruction. The degree of direction needed will often depend on cultural norms about work and whether team tasks tend to be solo or group endeavors. The North American notion of team connotes a flat, egalitarian structure that may not translate well into other cultures — even ones with a collectivist tendency. Teams must define the term "team" for themselves and should agree on common goals. The extent to which other team members can be called upon for help is equally important. Using the cultural dimensions to become aware of these assumptions is one way to cope.

Negotiations

High-status cultural guides and interpreters are a must for negotiations. It is impossible to negotiate toward a goal unless you know where you are in the hierarchy, and well-placed cultural guides can help. Creating a mental map or "gameboard" will help keep the complex relationships straight. It is critical to know one's social and work status in relation to other negotiators. Basic homework about communication cues, decision-making norms in the culture, and the organization are key, as is an understanding about timing.

As we saw in the scenario, Richard Safire did use Lin-Chen Wu as a guide. But Safire also made the mistake of over-relying on Wu to open doors with top management that were beyond his control. Ultimately, this was not effective and put Safire's colleague in an uncomfortable position as an intermediary. Richard Safire also needed to explicitly cultivate a solid relationship with Mr. Zhao and his two vice presidents, as a way of building a common understanding of the business they wanted to create. This would have required some study of the correct communication channels and styles at Royal Garden, in order to communicate his hopes in a way that Mr. Zhao and the top management could grasp. Productively managing the interface with leadership and cultural guides is a key challenge.

Status Attainment

Americans and others from achievement-oriented societies feel extreme discomfort when they are assigned a high status and treated with deference and privilege that is not due them at home. But their preference for their own egalitarian system can be insulting to their hosts. This issue is particularly problematic when they wish to work closely and openly with subordinates who are unable to respond to their overtures due to their status. The subordinates would be put in an embarrassing situation by doing what is asked of them by a higher-status manager. It is difficult for Americans, for example, to understand that status can even precede identity for very high authorities. In Japan, company employees always refer to the company head as "Mr. President" rather than by his family name.

Performance Rewards

In cultures where status is assigned, a supervisor often does "nothing" in our eyes and yet receives all the rewards for a subordinate's work. This undeserved credit is experienced as offensive and wrong in an American's eyes, yet protocol demands they say nothing. In fact, the subordinate probably would not want to be singled out ahead of his or her supervisor—it could be an embarrassment. Roles in hierarchical systems are more interdependent than those in egalitarian systems. As a result, job "rewards" may be less individual and more diffuse. It is best to take your cues from those involved.

Figure 6.3. Decision-Making Styles.

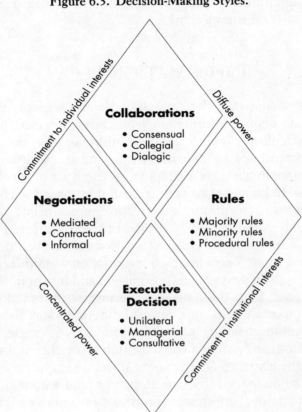

Decision Making

Decision-making processes vary greatly from culture to culture. Some workers look to authority figures to provide critical decisions; others depend on majority rule or broad consensus. The amount, type, and sequence of information needed for decision making are all issues affected by culture. Team leaders often facilitate an early discussion to map out decision-making preferences and styles.

Figure 6.3 displays a matrix of decision styles. Often cultures have strong preferences for one or two and apply them ubiquitously. Identifying differences and discussing them early on is important.

INFORMATION FLOW

Before diving into the flow, it is helpful to look at some culturally defined information "landscapes." For example, low-context cultures tend to think of information as documents and, increasingly, multimedia or video images. Shuttling them from place to place and manipulating them is a major element of work. In high-context cultures, information is a sea of goals, comments, perceptions, and relationships swirling through life—only some of which is quantifiable and linked to the workplace. The Royal Garden/Westwind team eventually had to invest time to decide which information was critical to the business, how it would be transmitted, and to whom. As they discovered, both the path and the rate of information flow were important. Guang Zhou had different ideas about how fast a communication, intended to produce a response, should move from one part of an organization to another and wanted to run the plan through the power structure to line up support. Information looped through numerous (and seemingly extraneous) approval and review processes far removed from the central pathway—many more critical events were required to release the right response than in Seattle. And although they never completely mastered the plan, the knowledge that the flows were different allowed both sides to avoid surprises and continue to function.

In the docudrama, Lin-Chen Wu was perplexed by the routing of the written joint venture plan to him. Had it been sent directly from Mr. Simonetti via Richard Safire? Had Safire given input—and if so, with how many others? Was Mr. Zhao notified at the same time? These unanswered questions made it hard to move the information through the system in Guang Zhou. For Wu it was most efficient to pass information through all the right channels to line up support; otherwise work could not proceed. For Safire it seemed most effective to limit the path of information to get a quicker response. The executive we talked to, who represented mainly low-context cultures, faced special difficulties with the following information flow challenges.

Indirect Flows

To monochronic people the information flowcharts of polychronic cultures often looked like doodles gone mad. To get from point A to point B, information often travels throughout the entire alphabet. The high-context Chinese had a people-intensive work process and were polychronic. In time, Safire understood why following the power/information flow was more effective than going straight to the point—because his tactics to shorten the flow upset the cultural logic and often landed him at zero. He soon realized that the links he needed to complete a task were like the vertebrae of a large, flexible dragon rather than a rigid-backed steer. Lin-Chen Wu understood that some changes would have to be made gradually. Thus he focused on gaining efficiency by grouping coordinating reviews and approvals.

Information Accessibility

Who gets access to what information and when? Westwind found that information sent to Royal Garden tended to follow fairly predicatable lines of authority—but would then spread out very far as it reached down through successive layers in the organization. Royal Garden found that although Westwind had its own version of hierarchy, the information remained self-enclosed and was not shared widely. Westwind eventually paid more attention to the information it sent, assuming it would be shared widely. Royal Garden, on the other hand, began to communicate and disseminate information more broadly, not depending on internal osmosis.

As relational data bases become the norm in businesses, there will be a cultural tug of war between those cultures who want access to everything and those who want to ensure privacy and security of information. Despite the arguments from the "business point of view," it is really an issue of culture, not business.

Documentation

Global team decisions include what information should flow by written channels, as well as what media and languages should be used. Information generally needs to flow in multiple languages, for written documents in one language never communicate completely to another language. Richard Safire was satisfied with the decision to send written documents of five pages or less in one's native language. Using only international business English would have meant composing with great care to ensure simple, culturally neutral communications. And given the deterioration of business writing skills at Westwind, anything else would have become a hazardous process.

Sometimes it helps to work with competent cultural guides to create a diagram of the information flow systems of all the team's cultures, including examples of action chains and human relationships. High-context cultures are less likely to document activities — which can create differing approaches to data-base management. Low-context team members often complain that they must personally contact members to get information they would expect to be documented in the team data base.

Cycle Times

Time efficiency is a design value for information technology supporting business, but it is not necessarily a value in every culture. Approaches to problem solving are linear and constraining for polychronic cultures because time is not considered a resource to be managed and moving between the two shortest points is not necessarily ideal. Richard Safire found that China's hierarchical work culture had implicit rituals that had to be figured into cycle times.

The more concrete the task, the more likely that monochronic time orientations can be accepted by all cultures.

Current workflow products currently support individual tasks and hence are easily used by both. Thus manufacturing processes can be sequenced and schedules adhered to by almost all cultures with proper training and orientation. In cycles such as time-to-market, however, polychronic cultures observe many more relationship loops and contingencies than monochronic cultures.

Procedures

Straightforward procedures like billing, accounts payable, and the processing of insurance claims can be adapted fairly easily by most cultures. But when procedures extend beyond simple, linked tasks and more elaborate and flexible processes are required, it is more difficult.

Even in the same language, misunderstanding can occur. One executive described a difference in the literalness with which team members read e-mail messages. This created a staff miscommunication on two sides of the Atlantic that eventually escalated to management and had to be handled explicitly.

Workflow

In the future great care will need to be taken in the design of workflow products because their use will be greatly affected by cultures. The whole notion of using computers to manage information flow is suspect in many cultures where total access to information flowing at all times from all directions is key to survival. Current workflow products, given the limits of technology, focus on very compartmentalized and vertical processes. Having "limited information" abstracting part of the whole environment is foreign to much of the world. Most software is biased toward completing a process no matter what. The commitment to complete action chains differs widely, and pursuing a project to completion just because it was started makes little sense to many people on the planet.

Workflow postponements, interruptions, and missed deadlines are a common feature in high-context cultures and extremely annoying to low-context workers. Projects should be designed with a fine balance between flexibility and on-time performance to accommodate both cultural proclivities. These criteria must be explicitly established among team members at the outset.

Making Commitments

Commitments can be seen as agreements to complete specific action chains. In most cultures, a task is not an isolated event but one that exists in a field of other activities. The task may need to be discarded in favor of other responsibilities that come to the fore. Westwind found that Lin-Chen Wu and his team could complete action chains within prescribed time periods—like that required to produce a draft package design—but had trouble coordinating work with the French, particularly for the fall season, because summer vacation and other events always intruded more than anticipated. The global management team had to discuss ways to avoid falling into monochronic versus polychronic manufacturing "camps."

Richard Safire quickly realized that he needed to recognize what a commitment looked like in Guang Zhou. During a phone conversation with Mr. Wong he answered "maybe" to a request to change the profit margin formula; only later, he realized that "maybe" means yes to the Chinese.

Information Overload

Due to the lack of adequate filtering mechanisms, information overload is a common complaint among global team members attempting to deal with a constant flow of data between corporate headquarters and distant outposts. Until good filtering systems are in place, this remains a problem best dealt with by central controls on the outflow of information. Richard Safire had no trouble sending data to Royal Garden because the Chinese, as a high-context culture, did not feel compelled to react to every bit of information.

Ideally, the varying practices of information flow in global teams can be mediated by an underlying management philosophy, such as total quality, supported by technology. These systems and tools could do much to level the workflow playing field and help create "third ways" of working.

WEAVING A THIRD WAY

In the day-to-day work of global teams, these five cultural dimensions will mix in more subtle and complex ways. Team members from a high-context, hierarchical, polychronic culture like Costa Rica may find themselves working with colleagues from a high-context, hierarchical, monochronic culture like Japan—and all that this combination entails for task completion and information flow—and discover their teammates have their own unique variations of their primary culture's outlook. Being fluent in the basic dimensions of culture will alow global managers to look upon their work as a process of weaving a third way, rather than a struggle to reconcile incompatible styles.

Lin-Chen Wu was relieved of his lead role in communicating with the East Asia vendors but stayed on the team with his boss, Mr. Wong. In reflecting on his first experience with Richard Safire, he was surprised at how much trust and status Westwind had accorded him—much more than he realized at the time. And even though he was now a junior team member, he wanted to return that consideration through his work. He also felt more confident in his dealings with Westwind and was now able to wear the mask that allowed him to play a different role than he did at Royal Garden.

Richard Safire took responsibility for the delay in implementing the restructuring, but he made a vow to use his failure to fuel his intercultural and team learning. Looking back, he coined a phrase: "The quickest route from A to B may not be a straight line if there is a cliff in between." He used this caveat to tell his story to other managers in the company and, as well, to elicit their own experiences. We'll examine more of Richard Safire and Lin-Chen Wu's learning in the following chapter about the ways in which global managers and teams can invent new ways to work together.

SEVEN

Global Vision:
Using Third-Way Strategies
for Collaborative Work

The struggles and cultural clashes experienced by Richard
Safire and Lin-Chen Wu in Chapter Six as they earnestly tried
to forge a productive global alliance for Westwind Foods and
Royal Garden Enterprises is a microcosm of the new global
workspace. It compels us to accept the fact that the old ways of
working are no longer adequate for today's business and that
we must learn new ways of working. In our multicultural world
neither "our way" nor "their way" serves at the organizational
or team level. We have a choice: clinging stubbornly to the one

217

way we know best while straddling the gap or choosing to jointly reinvent work and find "third ways" that have never existed before.

The second option is urged by Dr. Hanmin Liu, president of the United States–China Educational Institute of San Francisco and an expert on cross-cultural team creation and crossing the boundaries between China and the United States. He first introduced us to the term "third ways"—a metaphor to describe new, creative responses to the demands of work in diverse physical, cultural, and electronic workspaces. The ancient Greeks called such a place a *temenos*, a "sacred space within which special rules apply and in which extraordinary events are free to occur" (Nachmanovitch, 1990, p. 75). We think of this creative domain as a collaborative space. Stephen Nachmanovitch, in his book *Free Play* about the role of improvisation in life, gives a fitting description of such a space:

> We listen to each other. . . . We open each other's minds like an infinite series of Chinese boxes. A mysterious kind of information flows back and forth, quicker than any signal we might give by sight or sound. The work comes from neither one . . . nor the other, even though our own idiosyncrasies and styles, the symptoms of our original natures, still exert their natural pull. Nor does the work come from a compromise or halfway point (averages are always boring!), but from a third place that isn't necessarily like that either one of us would do individually. What comes is a revelation to both of us. There is a third, totally new style that pulls on us. It is as though we have become a group organism that has its own nature . . . from a unique and unpredictable place which is the group personality or group brain. [Nachmanovitch, 1990, p. 94].

What do these spaces look like and how could Safire and Wu have benefited from them?

CREATING
COLLABORATIVE SPACES

The new team from Westwind and Royal Garden did not know how to go about creating a collaborative space. They did eventually articulate the fact that all cultures in their global alliance were worthy of respect. And they did establish a few characteristic activities (similar to the GRIP model discussed later) and ground rules for their global teams that seemed to work. If they had gone farther, though, they might have added this to their description: a space where all cultures have equal importance, created by people gathered to explore new ways of working together.

It is important to remember that although we describe the ideal of the "collaborative space," the global managers we interviewed in the business and public sectors had, at best, experienced only moments of true cross-cultural collaboration. At present, this experience may not be continuously sustainable because third-way collaboration is so little understood. It is possible that artists and musicians have more extensive experience in this area.

In this chapter, we describe several tools and processes to promote collaboration, rather than the collaborative spaces themselves, which arise spontaneously under the right conditions.

In a truly collaborative space risk taking, experimentation, careful listening, intuition, building on others' ideas, and exploration are all cultivated as critical skills. If Safire and Wu had known about this approach, they might have begun with an opening dialogue to identify their cultural assumptions: social, professional, and corporate. Because past, present, and future converge on the space, it could have eased the tension between the past-oriented Chinese and the near-future-oriented Americans. Ideally, collaborative space can be created once, or it can be extended over a period of time—for example, as an activity within a project. It can take place in the same time/same place or, with practice, across time and distance.

The Westwind/Royal Garden team members found that respect for contributions from the other culture sparked ideas they might not otherwise have had. These attitudes, practiced over time, began to institutionalize the value of cross-cultural collaboration. Ethnocentrism, however, still remained a barrier because managers and others were naturally partial to their own countries' ways of working. They realized that developing cross-cultural competence, particularly among the managers, was an ongoing learning process. Figure 7.1 offers a conceptual model for seeing the relationship between collaborative spaces, global teams and team members, corporate culture, and the process of creating third ways within organizations.

Managers like those at Westwind lead teams that have lost some of the boundaries of centralized same-place/same-time teamwork—in which buildings, titles, and warm functional nests used to provide a universally consistent sense of identity and community. The challenge for their globally dispersed teams is to create their own boundaries which they can only hope will be supported by a strong corporate culture. What are the high-level markers that can give them a sense of virtual boundaries: a map of an invisible territory?

Without physical structures to act as boundaries, relationships are critical to continuity and effectiveness. Larry Hirschhorn and Thomas Gilmore describe four psychological boundaries—authority, task, identity, and politics (Hirschhorn and Gilmore, 1992)—that must be enacted continuously by managers and team members in global networked organizations. Each boundary is common to all work experiences and each, particularly authority and politics, is colored by culture. Richard Safire and Lin-Chen Wu eventually came to think of the joint venture as two grafted fruit trees—that is, growing distinct products while sharing resources. This became an important identity for their team and provided continuity in spite of geographical distance.

Figure 7.1. Cultural Collaboration.

THIRD-WAY STRATEGIES
FOR INDIVIDUALS

Richard Safire and Lin-Chen Wu survived their initial encounter and the disappointment of not achieving their desired result "my way." Although Richard barely made it past stage 1 (anticipate similarity) in Guang Zhou, his next trip to Paris encompassed both stage 1 and stage 2 of the Intercultural Learning Model (see Figure 7.2). He was shocked by his French teammates' ridicule of his cross-cultural inadequacy, even though he tried to be sensitive to the French way of working. As a result, he slowly developed a way of watching and listening for cues and monitoring his reactions. This practice eventually allowed him to open to other cultures and pursue learning (stages 4 and 5).

Lin-Chen Wu experienced the shock of stage 2 when Richard Safire blurted out his suggestion for Wu in the joint management meeting. He spent almost two months sorting out the work-related implications as he struggled to explain what had happened (stage 3). It was so hard to accept the Americans' apparent lack of respect for superiors that Wu looped back to stage 1 on occasion. Finally he realized that his colleagues had misinterpreted his ability to function in English in the role of spokesperson. And although this exaggerated authority made him uncomfortable, Wu committed to acting as a cultural guide—helping make explicit the relationship-building protocols he knew so well and was astonished to find were not universal. He, too, eventually experienced the opening of stages 4 and 5. And in the process he noticed the reflexive quality of his cross-cultural encounters: the more he came to understand others, the better he knew himself and his own culture.

The individual (cultural) learning that Richard Safire and Lin-Chen Wu experienced as they cycled through a seemingly endless series of difficult encounters is at the heart of productive work in a global environment. This learning required a choice and a commitment on the part of the Westwind/Royal Garden team—and not an easy one—because their basic human instinct was to pull back and remain in stage 2 or 3: unresolved.

Although these realizations may appear obvious to us as outsiders, this slow piecing together of understanding is quite typical of learning on global teams as they work to discover the inherent logic of other cultures. Cultures are revealed through team members bit by bit like a series of boxes. One team we met used a "Did I understand?" practice regularly to check their interpretations. The point at which a team becomes a "group organism" is a sign of high performance (stage 6 of the Team Performance Model) and individual learning (stage 5 of the Intercultural Learning Model).

Figure 7.2. Intercultural Learning Model: Global Learning Process.

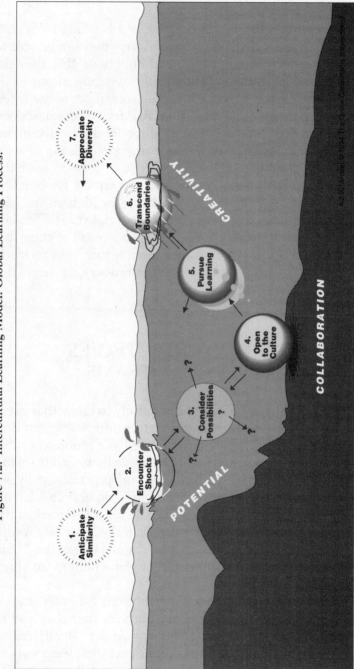

Remember that Richard Safire and Lin-Chen Wu may take time to apply their learning, and they may not be able to learn from every situation. We can only hope that they develop fast learning curves. If their joint venture improves its orientation programs and adds certain tools (such as the Intercultural Learning Model and the GRIP framework described later in the chapter), it could produce food products more efficiently and, ideally, develop its learning muscles in all areas in order to capitalize on the knowledge of workers over the long run. Cross-cultural experiences are critical for building this competence: there was no substitute for Richard and Lin-Chen discovering what worked and what didn't. The "collaborative spaces" they slowly developed as a result of their first encounters, as well as their commitment to intercultural learning, eventually gave rise to several third-way strategies for teams.

THIRD-WAY STRATEGIES FOR GLOBAL TEAMS

It would have helped Richard immensely to know that every team has certain needs, mandates, and culturally determined expectations that can only be addressed as a group when the team forms. In retrospect, he began to see how each team has to collaboratively design its third-way work processes or, by not doing so, make the decision (conscious or not) to limit its effectiveness. The choice to collaborate reflects stage 4 of the Intercultural Learning Model—where individuals take a turn toward learning—and is also part of stages 4 to 6 of the Team Performance Model: commitment, implementation, and high performance.

Team members come to the team with culturally shaped preconceptions and historical perspectives that they use to interpret and carry out the team's work unless an alternative interpretation is created. The Chinese members were wary of U.S. "cultural imperialism," for example, and the attempt to rush through the details of the restructuring plan made it even harder to establish trust and develop a partnership. One global team told us that training in cross-cultural communication and structured reading is very helpful at this point to learn how to validate others' approaches.

The Westwind/Royal Garden teams eventually stumbled on scenario building as a third-way alternative to the planning preferred by the American team members and the strategizing preferred by the Chinese. The packaging and distribution teams, for example, met during electronic conferences to discuss varied points of view by telling how they would handle various challenges. This forum began to resemble a neutral place where they could suggest alternatives while avoiding direct controversy. Because of the asynchronicity, the Chinese members had time to explain their scenarios fully before discussing them with the team at large. The team found that these new work understandings kept people from reverting to culture-bound interpretations—which would have been a severe handicap because they were jointly developing packaging designs for production in China and distribution in three continents. After two or three promising scenarios emerged, a "straw proposal" process was used to facilitate further buy-in.

Even as learning occurred, there was continuous dialogue and a trial-and-error effort to blend possibilities. At first Lin-Chen Wu did not grasp that it is impossible (and unnecessary) to find third ways for everything. It took him some time to make strategic recommendations to his group in China, focusing on opportunities with the most potential for increasing the team's effectiveness and profitability. For example, it served no purpose for Wu's superior to spend his time in Seattle revising their method for producing hoisin sauce—that work process was totally under the control of the team in China. He did, however, need to spend time on third-way approaches to strategic planning and benchmarking.

Just being on a team with very different cultures is a challenge, as we saw in the vignette. Cultures that value individualism, for example, such as the U.S. Westwind team, may find it difficult to participate fully with team members from cultures like Wu's that value collectivism. As they entered the strategic alliance, Wu's creative energy was spent assimilating corporate expectations and methodologies that felt foreign to him and his team in Guang Zhou. This intense focus on adjusting to the parent company's mindset prevented the Royal Garden group from contributing their unique business perspectives. Later, after more attention had been given to establishing ground rules that took all cultures into consideration, target business processes, new product designs, and marketing strategies were crafted collaboratively. The resulting business processes and strategies were guidelines, rather than prescriptions, that allowed local sites to develop the specifics in the course of their daily work.

One of the "three steps forward and one step back" involved timing. The top managers were a little too hasty in asking people on both sides of the Pacific to immediately relate to one another in new ways. People felt threatened—as if they were being asked to give up their primary culture to participate. Trust broke down, creating a domino effect on other stages of team process and hurting productivity. They found that everyone needed time to learn the skill of creating new cultural interpretations. Occasionally, the "mysterious information" referred to by Nachmanovitch would inexplicably flow among team members—when their timing for monthly reports was perfect or when team members intuitively sensed a logjam developing and acted to prevent it. On the few occasions it happened, everyone felt they were at stage 6 of transcending boundaries.

One practice that Safire did not discover but could have used was the tactic of reframing problems as opportunities. The activity sets up a creative problem-solving process that allows people to contribute using either intuitive or analytical thought to transform impossibility thinking into possibility thinking. Encouraging a diversity of ideas helps team members relinquish strongly held positions and avoid conflict. Because negativity and the expression of harsh feelings are not part of Chinese business culture, this practice could have added a positive spin to several awkward discussions. Structured problem-solving strategies can become collaborative spaces as well.

To support the development of third-way strategies, Hanmin Liu has cross-cultural team members create a physical representation of their collaborative space as a "culture laboratory" in the form of a three-dimensional structure early in the process. This act engages each person physically and activates a relationship at the most fundamental learning level, thus enabling other work at higher levels of intellectual understanding (Liu and others, 1992, p. 8).

The GRIP model can be a collaborative space in which team members explore their views of *goals* (results needed to achieve purposes), *relationships* (building relationships, maintaining trust and good communications), *information* (available resources including money, technology, time), and *processes* (work procedures and training to complete tasks). Common understanding in these areas allows a team to get a GRIP on its work together at a high level. If Richard Safire and Lin-Chen Wu had had this tool, they might have asked the product design, packaging, and distribution teams, for example, to create a global team GRIP at the outset as a high-level strategy. This process could have bonded members together as they work at a distance and in their own local environments.

The GRIP model shown in Figure 7.3 is one we imagine a Westwind/Royal Garden team could have created. Graphic displays can be used to illustrate all four quadrants of the GRIP model. Goals can be drawn out as a vision map or target, pulling the team's attention forward from the present reality. Relationship and stakeholder maps allow everyone to see their networks displayed graphically. Information and resources can be mapped and linked with geographical sites. Procedures and processes can be drawn as diagrams and a process map for the team's work. A visual "process map" like this, collaboratively developed by the team, can be instrumental in keeping the team aligned and managing the work toward desired results while continuing to work at a distance.

Another graphic tool that offers a space in which to

collaborate is the gameplan (O'Hara-Devereaux and Pardini, 1993). As shown in Figure 7.4, one large sheet of paper summarizes key understandings necessary to begin work. By integrating a portrait of the team with a clear statement of results, major phases, work tasks, critical success factors, and obstacles, members have an opportunity to orient themselves and monitor critical elements of the work plan. The large gameplan can be reduced, copied, and distributed to all team members. The Westwind/Royal Garden venture's top management could have used the gameplan as a way to bring forth high-level understandings on a shared whiteboard on which

Figure 7.3. GRIP Model Diagram.

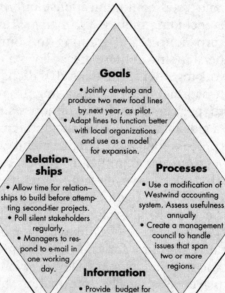

Goals
• Jointly develop and produce two new food lines by next year, as pilot.
• Adapt lines to function better with local organizations and use as a model for expansion.

Relation-ships
• Allow time for relation-ships to build before attempting second-tier projects.
• Poll silent stakeholders regularly.
• Managers to respond to e-mail in one working day.

Processes
• Use a modification of Westwind accounting system. Assess usefulness annually
• Create a management council to handle issues that span two or more regions.

Information
• Provide budget for translators so key information can be transmitted in English and Mandarin.
• Continue to operate in DOS over Internet.

Figure 7.4. Graphic Gameplan Diagram.

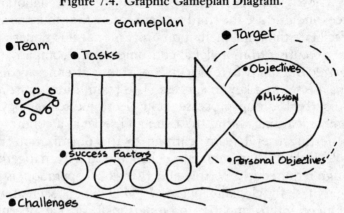

the graphic gameplan's outline was drawn. People could then interactively draw on the map and see one another's contributions.

In general, technology can be helpful if used cautiously and supported with orientation and training that makes cultural biases explicit. Companies should develop guidelines for global team start-ups and discuss their technology infrastructures and suggest the best practices for technology use. Here are some rules of thumb that have emerged from our research:

- Create an electronic form and use it consistently to announce a team start-up. Include the team's global purpose, members, locations, and scope of work. Attach a graphic framework like GRIP to the team start-up document. Include a required response request.

- Set up an electronic support system for the team's work.

- Explain how technology can be used in the team's GRIP map.

- Make sure the technical choices are culturally and geographically appropriate.

- Develop a regular drumbeat of audio conferences to support the work if it will require rapid iterations of designs or consensus decisions.

Global managers must not only create collaborative spaces and nurture the third-way approach, they must be able to facilitate the implementation process once it is under way. One executive from a global consumer goods company emphasized the ability to follow up consistently after new goals or plans are set as a key to success. The team leader must also employ both group processes and electronic technology to promote learning within the team and serve as a conduit for transferring useful team learning to the organization as a whole. Helping team members collaborate and learn together, though required in any truly effective global operation, is not an easy task for global managers. It takes patience, creativity, and a continuing appetite to be personally at one's learning edge. Facilitating these team processes and mastering collaborative media will clearly be a core competency for global managers. (See Chapter Four.) The managers and teams who are most adept at blending their core cultures with new cultural improvisations will most likely be the leaders in their organizations.

THIRD-WAY STRATEGIES FOR GLOBAL ORGANIZATIONS

Richard Safire and Lin-Chen Wu felt that if the challenges facing their team were like high peaks, the obstacles their organizations faced were entire mountain ranges. Not only were there several teams spanning the United States, China, and France that needed to coordinate their work, but the different communication standards within the electronic infrastructure often made it extremely difficult to communicate. Certainly there was a wide disparity between their financial systems, which had grown up over the decades before computing became widespread. And there was the anomaly of the Chinese practice of keeping bookkeeping logs hand-copied from the electronic spreadsheets.

Safire had many more opportunities to peer thoughtfully

from many more airplane windows. Gradually he began to realize that people and technology connected via networks — rather than buildings and hierarchies — would be the links for Westwind and its partners to do their work. He had few ideas about exactly how to support them. But he knew it would look very different from any corporate culture he had known.

For one thing, the traditional relationship between West-wind's company culture and the United States, where it was founded and rooted, was starting to stretch. He thought of cases like Benetton, an Italian firm, which became a virtual corporation with a tiny corporate headquarters and a web of contractual relationships worldwide, completely altering its connection to Italian culture. And the high-tech firms originating in Asia, Europe, and North America are so busy creating alliances and systems composed of dozens of globally produced parts that they hardly fit the traditional lenses. In another example, Mars, Inc., one of the world's largest private firms, is technically American, with headquarters in McLean, Virginia, but it is dominated by British management and has decentralized operations in three continents that in some cases have more loyalty to the company than their country.

It slowly dawned on Lin-Chen Wu that his "way" of wanting to know the exact hierarchy of Safire's firm before he negotiated wasn't going to work any better as an overall strategy than someone else's "way" of wanting a quick deal. He saw all of Royal Garden Enterprises — not just himself or his team — having to enter some kind of "collaborative space" and learn the art of the third way. But not having experienced it, he could only hope he would recognize it when it happened. So what kind of strategies were starting to work for other companies and what stood in their way? And was it even possible to create a shared culture the way it might be with smaller teams? Would "culture" develop in the same way given the diversity and distance to be spanned, he wondered?

Some new kind of culture will be created. Borrowing Edgar Schein's definition in *Organizational Culture and Leadership,* culture is any set of assumptions and habits of relationship that become implicit and systematic (Schein, 1991).

This happens whenever people relate to one another repeatedly — whether at a distance or face-to-face. But the cultures created in the global workspace may not feel similar or in fact be compatible. Bridging cultures are starting to evolve: corporate cultures that are rooted in the horizontal soils of common processes and professional languages, global brands, and general principles and visions, rather than the deep ground of national and social cultures or the culturally specific day-to-day activities at each site.

Westwind and Royal Garden had a vague idea that valuing respect and cooperation and staying open to varied cultural perspectives would be beneficial. They continued to search for some way of getting the best performance from people with infinitely different social cultural ways of working together. Although the joint venture would have benefited greatly from a graphic vision like that created by National Semiconductor (as we will see), they settled on several banner projects like the introduction of upscale pre-prepared Chinese meal components in order to pull their people together. The individual and team learning pursued by Safire and Wu translated into organizational learning as they modeled it for others and explained their discoveries. Through this process they both showed how learning is not only assimilating and acting on information: it means incorporating it in a way that informs wider and wider spans of activity and awareness. This process required them to find the kernel of knowledge applicable to as many other situations as possible.

One of their critical learning strategies that produced innovation was putting together cross-business-unit subteams as R&D "laboratories" to pull off the new upscale foods project. Selecting the right people turned out to be critical, for no amount of restructuring could result in organizational learning unless supported by solid personal relationships. This meant selecting members with a record of learning and coaching others. In addition, each unit's strengths and weaknesses, as well as the vital role it played, were determined and made visible to everyone by the nomadic managers with the most knowledge of the far-flung workers. The teams' experience was then documented on a standard form and distributed throughout the joint venture.

It is much easier to talk about creating third ways and changing a corporate culture than actually doing it. Many of the global companies we interviewed were still grappling with this challenge despite years of multinational experience. But without an effort to create a shared global culture there will be nothing to hold a diverse group together as they try to move forward. Sudden reversions to cultural nearsightedness as a coping mechanism during difficult times may seem to work, but usually they yield poor results in the long run.

As we noted in Chapter Two, all cultures learn to change in response to their environment. Historically, however, they have done so only slowly. The rate of change is related to the need for survival. The rapidly changing environment of global business means that the global corporate cultural layer will experience ongoing development and renewal, and the process of cultivating third ways will have to become the organizational norm.

SHARING GLOBAL VISION AS A THIRD-WAY STRATEGY

When asked to single out the internal factor that contributes most to team and organizational learning, most of the executives we questioned had this response: creating a common vision with input from all quarters. Richard Safire and Lin-Chen Wu eventually came to this understanding as well. From several books describing the role of global corporate visions, this is what they learned. Every global organization needs to create a unique layer of culture by clearly articulating a shared vision and communicating it to every manager and employee. Each manager's perceptions and behavior must emanate from this expression of the company's purpose and values. One crucial value is the equality of all cultures represented by the customers and workforce.

As it creates this first layer of corporate culture, the organization models its acceptance of diverse viewpoints by including major stakeholders and key managers from various countries in the vision's development. A vision that truly reflects the wealth of the organization's human assets acts as a "global glue" for operating units that often look quite different from one another.

Many companies invest heavily in global branding and identity as a force for integration. Mars, Inc., with its Mars bars, Snickers, and Wiskas brands, is one example. The soft drink companies are another. But global branding alone does not create a true global organization. In addition to these efforts Mars' owners have articulated a set of five principles that are posted in every facility and cited in business plans and training worldwide. They were kept general to invite constant reinterpretation by local organizations. Common office layouts, shared business practices, rotations, and heavy promotion from within have combined with these five principles to create a distinctive global culture that in many cases is stronger than other allegiances. Mars is somewhat unique — it is one of the world's largest family-owned businesses, which gives it a great deal of cultural continuity.

Apple Computer is another corporation that has used a shared vision and common identity to pull together its diverse operations. Not only is Apple's logo world famous, but they consciously promote their overall mission of bringing computer power within the reach of everyone. Apple does this in global campaigns that are as important to keeping the company creative and proud of itself as they are to convince customers of the quality of Apple's products. But Apple went further and operationally balanced its corporate-wide focus by consciously creating a "glocal" business culture — one that operates globally but acts locally. Their approach was to partner with local organizations and even have shared ownership. In this way they penetrated Japan with the Kanji Mac. A similar strategy led to extensive business in France and other parts of Europe. Interestingly, their maintenance of proprietary ownership of the central ROM chip allowed them to be more flexible in creating partnerships to generate software applications.

How can a large, global enterprise create a shared vision that is focused yet open? How can it reflect a variety of perspectives and languages and demonstrate that everyone plays an important role? Graphics and multimedia are emerging as promising tools in this regard because graphics complement the spoken and written word, providing a way to double-check meanings. Graphic communications are in fact the root language of systems thinking—a key to managing organizations and global networks.

Many technologies are emerging that support the use of graphic language: two-way video with data capture, data conferencing with shared screens, and the now ubiquitous faxes, which are getting bigger and more integrated with printers. Embedded in such interactive media is the opportunity for collaborative graphic processes that can elaborate general corporate visions and strategies with local inputs and ideas— literally letting everyone in the world see what is happening and giving them some say in how it all evolves.

A convincing graphic vision can become a corporate icon, a shared cultural symbol, and a key management tool. While even graphic language can be culture-bound, there is a growing body of shared imagery that is understood across cultures, facilitated by the increased use of international signage and comic books. The engineering and design communities are also creating common languages for illustrating workflow and technical procedures. When these well-known icons and pictographs are combined with archetypal backgrounds resembling landscapes, journeys, city maps, and vehicles, they create a bridging language for working cross-culturally with the entire workforce.

Another indication of this potential is the growth of companies like Learning Materials International (LMI) in Scandinavia and Advantage and Root Learning in the United States. These companies are taking corporate initiatives and creating graphic "work maps" that function like gameboards. Information is broken up into cards that are then fitted into highly visual backgrounds or text/graphic "maps" during team-based, interactive learning sessions. LMI used this method to train all Volvo employees about new models of cars. Root Learning has used the method to help employees at Lilly Pharmaceuticals understand complex markets, new processes, and overall strategies. These techniques are allowing companies to reach the operational level, such as line managers and factory floors.

National Semiconductor is using a large graphic (3 feet by 14 feet) to promote global integration and an understanding of its vision that can be discussed by everyone. Hanging a big graphic vision on the wall and inviting discussion encourages the local interpretations that bring it to life. It can be cascaded easily through various media and combined with interactive workshops and communication sessions. Large graphic images seem less formal than written documents and are not as readily associated with political or cultural biases. If a vision evolves with feedback from local sites, it can eventually display enough elements that a wide range of people can see their relationship to it—literally seeing themselves working together.

This process of participating in the vision increases awareness that cross-cultural strategic alliances and joint ventures are a good idea. People need to see and understand the concept's relevance to their own personal roles and responsibilities. Only then will they be capable of overcoming the discomfort of multicultural work environments. As more and more organizations become network-based, distributed, and multicultural, these integrating frameworks will become essential tools for communication—as we see in the case of National Semiconductor Corporation.

In 1991, National Semiconductor realized that it was not going to survive long without radically changing both the philosophy and practice of its business. The board hired Gil Amelio and gave him a mandate to transform the company. Amelio explained: "I inherited a company that was out of date, that was out of step with the market. My mission, in addition to diagnosis, was to transform the company and instill the professionalism to be a winner. . . . The cultural transformation was the most difficult" (Siegmann, 1993, p. D5).

Two years later, National was named one of the comeback companies of the year by the business press when it made a dramatic $250 million earnings swing. Sales grew by 12 percent. The company's market value jumped about 40 percent. Much of the credit was given to slimming down the menu of products, streamlining operations by cutting thousands of jobs and closing certain manufacturing sites, and breaking up centralized management. Even more work was being done to transform National into a truly successful global company. "The thing you can do the fastest is restructure, close factories, etc.," Amelio said upon National's being named the comeback company. "Those get you from the brink of disaster to a company that's viable. So, now we're viable but we are a long way from being a great company" (Siegmann, 1993, p. D5). This was the message he had been communicating through a parallel global visioning process begun in late 1991.

As the turnaround began, Amelio and his top managers held several off-site meetings to set a "vision and vector" for National Semiconductor. Out of this process came a white paper articulating a new corporate vision: the transformation of a low-cost, high-volume provider of hundreds of different commodity chips and "jellybean" electronic components into a truly upscale company allied with sophisticated customers to produce complete solutions in analog communication systems, and personal computing systems. The company at the time had 28,000 employees in operations as far flung as Greenock, Scotland. There were facilities in Israel, in Mallaca, Malaysia, in Singapore and Hong Kong, in Penang, Malaysia, in South Portland, Maine, in Arlington, Texas, and Salt Lake City, and in Santa Clara, California, the corporate headquarters. Getting the vision to every corner of this enterprise was a truly global challenge. And the thirty-page, all-text white paper alone would clearly not do the job.

A team of corporate staff was charged with creating a "Leading Change" program to develop the vision with the top five hundred managers in week-long programs and then communicate it to all employees. The Design Team, as they came to call themselves, included Kevin Wheeler (Human Resources Development), Michael Burns (Management Development), Pat Case (Employee Communications), David Kirjassoff (Quality Performance), Bob Miles (consultant to the Management Committee), and eventually Richard Feller (Organizational Excellence)—a position that was created to coordinate the change after the process started. Additional consultants and finance representatives rounded out the Design Team.

Kevin Wheeler, who had worked for National for thirteen years and had lived and worked in Asia, was very knowledgeable about cross-cultural communications. In earlier, less developmentally oriented times, he and Michael Burns had constituted the entire staff for such efforts. Wheeler knew that good communication of the company's global vision would be a key to making it an operational reality in the diverse NSC sites.

How could this message be sent forth in a form that people from varied national, ethnic, and functional cultures could understand and contribute to? The cultural change being contemplated was dramatic. There would be lots of resistance and a great need for involvement. National Semiconductor was changing from an ethnocentric U.S. organization—one whose global locations' sole purpose was to support the central business bottom line—to a truly global company with an equidistant cultural perspective among North America, Asia, and Europe. The old culture was a can-do, competitive culture where winning was everything and there was little desire to build long-term relationships either inside or outside the company. To compete in the upscaling semiconductor markets, they needed to become a true learning organization—one that would listen to the customer, aspire to continuous quality improvement, and contribute to the community.

Kevin Wheeler and Michael Burns happened to attend a graphic facilitation workshop with Graphic Guides Inc. (now Grove Consultants International) earlier in 1991. Now the idea of creating a graphic vision to support the Leading Change program took hold. They invited David Sibbet, founder of Graphic Guides and a senior consultant specializing in visioning, to help them. Over several weeks in early 1992, in a session that involved the Design Team and other key managers, a large, integrated graphic vision emerged in several versions. This vision would be built around a Star Trek metaphor — one that a large number of people at high-tech National would understand.

The vision was more than just a projection of a desirable goal. It was a graphic interface to a whole system of assumptions that would underlie the new organization: company beliefs and values, critical business issues in the immediate path of change, images of the organizational structure, and a depiction of major stages in the overall change process. After the vision was discussed with the Management Committee in a special off-site meeting, they insisted on adding a history section noting early accomplishments and milestones that signaled a key change in direction for National. By the first Leading Change program, most of top management had agreed on the vision's content. The process provided a focused way to let everyone "own" the white paper and its assumptions.

The week-long program itself was structured around the vision graphic and began with a top manager's explanation. After several days of examining other companies' change processes and new financial tools, small teams evaluated the vision for problems and virtues. (They used small adhesive notes on large photo images of the vision.) The teams then talked about what the vision would mean for their units and divisions. They prepared special presentations of their ideas for Amelio and presented them on the last day.

In parallel, the Employee Communications department, now headed by Mark Levin, produced a corporate-wide vision communication that included a videotape announcing the process to all employees. Company business planning began to incorporate the vision through Michael Burns's effort. It was reproduced on a large "goal alignment" poster that was used as a working framework for all departments. Although National Semiconductor is a vast global corporation, its links to distant sites mirror the relationships in certain joint ventures. The vision was used to establish working alliances with strategic partners and served as a framework for exploring where and how they would work together.

Quite soon it became clear that the graphic vision was stimulating widespread attention and excitement. People had posted small color versions all over the company and were arguing furiously about every little graphic. "More people," said teams from Leading Change. "Show the world." The vision began to go through versions 3.0, 4.0, 4.1. The changes were visible and clearly benefited from the Leading Change workshops.

In the original vision, a spaceship was being assembled. In early 1993, groups around the world began to insist that the spaceship needed to take off. Leading Change workshops from Singapore and Penang redrew the graphics, attached them to foam backgrounds, and stuck them to the vision. "Redo the vision," Gil Amelio and the Management Committee said in the spring of 1993. By fall, version 5.0 depicted the starship National taking off. Focus markets and other learnings were reflected in the new version. The vision had become such an icon that great care had to be taken to keep all the elements on which there was general agreement.

A remarkable aspect of this process was the ripple effect of the methodology. All of National's divisions and many departments are now creating their own graphic visions to complement the corporate vision. A cadre of facilitators within National has been trained by Graphic Guides and helps with the process. David Sibbet himself, creator of the graphic visioning process at National, has created at least a dozen. "This is the first company I know of that has a GUI [graphic user interface] on its overall strategic process," Sibbet said recently. The visions are being used to provide a larger context for redesign efforts, backdrops for communication sessions, and management team building.

The Design Team, now formalized as the Organizational Excellence Planning Committee led by Richard Feller, began planning for a dissemination to the entire organization in the spring of 1993. Human resource managers from Europe and Asia were networked into the process, and some of the tough issues of global communication began to surface. The large number of Asian operators needed a much different approach than the units in the United States. They needed more team involvement in the communications; they needed direct experience. Relations with supervisors and hierarchies were sufficiently different that a completely customized design would be needed for Asia, making sure the supervisors played a key role. Scotland, given its independent culture, would need direct involvement in the design process. So would South Portland, a wholly owned and somewhat independent subsidiary.

Ideas for using "work maps" emerged. Greater use of the rapidly evolving National Semiconductor internal network was proposed. Plans were developed for having a narrated video vision along with the new poster graphic. While all the challenges are still in the process of being met, there is no doubt that National has succeeded in getting many of its sites to think about the overall company vision. Will it be enough? Certainly not alone. The business decisions need to be right. Uncertainties abound with the global recession. But learning continues.

What are the lessons for global visioning? We can begin with these:

- The process of creating visions is just as important as the vision itself. Agreeing on visions and values creates bonds between senior managers that can withstand the inherent volatility of plans in an innovative business environment. The secret is keeping the process visible, explicit, and accessible.

- A corporate vision can stimulate related visions from different business units.

- The use of key words and simple graphics depicting real things, integrated within an archetypal graphic landscape, allows for understanding by many cultures.

- The vision should be a living communication, just as the corporate culture is living. It should reflect new ideas and changing views of the environment. Its framework must be open enough to accept a diversity of interpretations while maintaining its overall integrity.

- Top management's participation in creating and commitment to the vision—in the behavior they model—is critical.

After their reading, Richard Safire and Lin-Chen Wu concluded that a graphic vision for the joint venture would certainly have allowed for more discussion and involvement in the direction-setting process throughout both their companies. And it might have saved some time as top management searched for a way to structure its planning. The presence of a vision would not have affected the intensity of intercultural learning that occurred—nor would that have been the vision's purpose. Yet they felt it would have been helpful for the players to see the cultures coming together graphically in several collaborative spaces: a reminder of the common ground that must be created and recreated for work to take place.

Although Richard Safire and Lin-Chen Wu often regretted that their offices lay separated by the Pacific Ocean—knowing that closer proximity would solve so many problems of time and distance—the next chapter shows us that proximity isn't everything. Although the United States and Mexico share a border and several time zones, culture is still a powerful force in the lives of business teams.

RULES OF THUMB FOR FOSTERING THIRD-WAY APPROACHES

Creating third ways is all about choices. In business situations that call for a third-way approach, the attitude of creating common ground must be pervasive. Here are some guidelines:

- *Level the playing field.* A team cannot come to grips with its work if its members do not have equal access. This is the foremost concern of a global manager.

- *Be who you are.* Authenticity is your most important asset. Too many managers try to please everybody and become paralyzed and confused by adopting multiple personalities.

- *Be explicit about the action chains you propose to use.* People will behave according to how they have worked in the past. They can't really imagine how it might be done differently. Putting the process on the table allows the group to accept, modify, or replace action chains.

- *Maintain a degree of formality in meetings.* All cultures can participate if there is some commonly understood structure to meetings. Since every culture has its unique ways of conducting meetings, it is crucial to provide a few ground rules about outcomes, agenda, and roles that are culturally sensitive. This approach will go a long way toward ensuring effective meetings.

- *Don't express undue urgency about specific pieces of information.* Because most cultures are high-context rather than low-context, don't get unduly concerned about one information event. In an age when there's an abundance of information every day, it's important to see information in its wider perspective.

- *Don't rely too much on technology support.* Trust is the glue of the global workspace — and technology doesn't do much to create relationships. Software designs may be culturally biased, and a good application in one culture may not make sense to another. They must be used cautiously in globalwork.

- *Concentrate on good electronic networks and data bases so that people can choose the information they access at a given time.* Different cultures vary dramatically in how much information they want (and can use) and when they want it. Ease of access and quantity of information needed—these are key considerations. Work toward getting the information system culturally accessible to all in this regard.

EIGHT

Learning New Rules of Thumb: Partnering with Mexico

As this book was being written, the fate of the North American Free Trade Agreement (NAFTA), the object of fierce and bitter (and largely uninformed) bipartisan debate in Congress and the American public, hung in the balance. Congress did find the wisdom to ratify the agreement — thereby creating the largest, richest, free-trade region on earth, with 363 million people and a regional gross domestic product of $6.3 trillion.

Even if NAFTA had been defeated, the North American market of Canada and the United States and Mexico would have been a reality that no amount of nationalist anxiety or protectionist ideology can overcome. The level of cross-border trade within the region will continue its recent, rapid expansion. The intermingling of businesses, peoples, cultures, and languages will continue apace. Indeed, there is little reason to doubt that, with or without NAFTA, the North American market will continue to expand southward through bilateral and multilateral trade agreements until it reaches from the Yukon to Tierra del Fuego and includes virtually all of the Americas. The logic of economic integration and regional coexistence is too compelling for any other outcome. As Clint Smith, author of *The Disappearing Border* and a former U.S. embassy official in Mexico, has noted: "Conformity is unenforceable and pluralism is inevitable" (Smith, 1992, p. 32).

Already, even before NAFTA makes its mark, the pieces of the pan-American economic puzzle are falling together along the four critical fault lines outlined in Chapter One: emerging middle-class markets; the regionalization and globalization of business; the fragmentation and diversification of the workforce; and the expansion of knowledge and information services as regional products. Consider, for example, the present and potential size of the consumer market. The three NAFTA nations alone represent a middle class of some 69 million households today, projected to reach 104 million by the year 2010 (World Bank, 1993). While the vast majority of these households are in the United States, where wages and incomes are 10 times those of Mexico, NAFTA's growth is clearly south of the Rio Grande, where the Mexican middle class is expected to double between 1990 and 2010. The real promise, though, lies still further south. There are already more middle-class households in all of Latin America than in the market areas of China, Japan, Eastern Europe, or all the Asian Tiger countries—and they will more than double over the next two decades, riding a projected 4.4 percent annual growth rate for the region (World Bank, 1993).

The presence of foreign business interests and capital in Latin America is still relatively slight, but it is growing rapidly in countries like Mexico, Chile, and Argentina, which have made serious efforts to open their economies to regionalization and globalization. The Inter-American Development

Bank estimates that $50 billion in capital poured into all of Latin America in 1992, three times the 1990 level ("Public Services, Private Pesos: Infrastructure in Latin America," 1993, p. 40). Mexico, even prior to NAFTA, had already earned the International Monetary Fund distinction as the number one developing nation in attracting foreign investment—and was among the top ten worldwide. Between 1988 and 1993 the economic reforms implemented by President Carlos Salinas de Gortari had attracted $31.4 billion (Smith, 1993).

The same reforms that have attracted foreign capital to Latin America are attracting Latin countries to one another. Chile and Mexico reached a quasi-free-trade pact in 1991 (exempting a short list of products) that boosted trade by 42 percent in two years. Mexico and Bolivia have been seeking a NAFTA-type arrangement. Mexico, Colombia, and Venezuela (the Group of Three) were expected to conclude a free-trade pact by the end of 1993. Mexico, Costa Rica, and four other Central American nations are moving in the same direction. Already, by 1992, trade within the Central American countries alone had roughly doubled to $1.8 billion since 1986. While most of these countries remain badly underdeveloped and relatively untouched by deep economic or political reform, together they represent a market of 30 million people and $32 billion—almost as large as the robust Chilean market.

For most of Latin America, of course, open trade relations with Mexico represent the spring of the region's economic springboard. And for Mexico, free trade with its northern neighbors is the key to making the greater pan-American vision a reality. As Roberto Salinas Leon, an economist at the Center for Free Enterprise Research in Mexico City, has observed: "Clearly, a goal of Mexico is to function as an economic bridge or intermediary between Latin America and North America, as Mexico will be both Latin American and North American" (Scott, 1993, p. 14).

Any number of wildcard-type scenarios could slow down or upset this regionalization bandwagon. If Mexican wages fail to rise along with increasing productivity, the much-feared migration of jobs from the United States and Canada to a low-wage Mexico could become such that Americans would rebel against free-trade pacts. Conversely, higher productivity in the United States and Canada might undermine Mexico's ability to catch up internationally in a range of advanced industries, thus short-circuiting the growth of the Mexican middle class. Also, Latin America's political and economic reforms are largely untested and fragile, and some countries might easily revert to closed systems. The infrastructure throughout Latin America is still primitive by U.S. standards, and upgrading the transportation, electrical, telecommunications, sewage and water treatment, education, health, and other essential services to the standards required for hemispheric business operations will involve formidable costs and require a vast cadre of top-flight engineers, scientists, and technicians. Indeed, the lack of modern infrastructure could be the Achilles' heel of North American regionalization—although it is a weakness that is more apt to cause a limp than a breakdown.

In fact, there are other infrastructural challenges in the region that may be even more daunting than Latin America's dirt roads or postal shortcomings. These are the political, cultural, linguistic, legal, environmental, and economic gaps that exist between each of the separate pieces of the puzzle— the boundaries over which business leaders in each nation will have to build their own bridges. These bridges will have to accommodate, integrate, and leverage the sometimes extraordinary variations among the three countries in skills, organizational structures, information technology, and motivations for collaboration.

This bridge-building challenge to business is the real test of NAFTA—even more than Washington's acrimonious debate in the fall of 1993. In all likelihood, politicians cannot stop the inevitable process of economic integration throughout the region. But business leaders in Canada, the United States, and Mexico—and all over the world—can make or break the promise of regionalization through their own commitment or lack thereof. They have an enormous, almost unprecedented, task before them: constructing a business infrastructure across the great distances and the perplexing cultural, technical, and organizational borders of the Americas. This and the next two chapters explore these challenges in some depth, focusing especially on the cultural and technical implications and possible strategies for successful business collaboration.

MEXICO LOOKS NORTH

The following vignette was developed from a story we heard while talking to managers working in regional Mexican-U.S. teams. It highlights some of the common cultural clashes across this border.

"This orientation manual may have worked OK at the new division in Des Moines, but I'm afraid it's going to be disaster in Vera Cruz," lamented Guadalupe, the human relations manager at the Mexico City regional headquarters as she flipped quickly through the four-inch-thick document that had just arrived from New York. She and her assistant, Alfredo, were expected to have the new Vera Cruz branch up and running within two weeks. And now New York was flooding them with detailed, step-by-step, do-it-this-way directives. If they couldn't get out from under the documentation, they knew they'd never get around to figuring how to actually manage the task at hand.

"I told them last week to let us handle it ourselves, but the message never seems to get through," said Alfredo.

"Well, somehow we have to get past these 'Dear Team' faxes from headquarters," said Guadalupe. "I wish they'd come down here once in a while. Maybe if we could sit and talk they'd understand we can do this without their legal briefs and their constant, condescending, detailed instructions. Look at this," she said, proffering a letter. "This is the third warning I've had from the legal department

about offering bribes. They seem to think that's all we do. Of course they expect me to travel all the way to New York for a meeting. Last year they actually scheduled our meeting for May 5. I told them I'd have to postpone it until July 4," she chuckled.

"This year it's set for the same week as my daughter's quinceañera," said Alfredo. "No way I can get away then. If New York wants to work twenty-four hours a day, let them. We've got an office to open in Vera Cruz with a staff that would laugh us out of town if they ever read this manual—which, thank goodness, they'd never do anyway."

"Look," said Guadalupe, chucking the manual into the wastebasket, "Let's just do it basically the same way we handled the branch in Monterrey, which worked out fine. And then when it's all done we can tell New York we did it their way and write it all up just as if we were following a plan. It's a waste of time, but that's the way they like it so that's the way we'll do it. Let's get some lunch."

Everyday Cultural Barriers

Let's take a look at a few of the common cultural barriers raised in this almost-real-life scene—barriers that are part of the everyday life of business teams spanning the Mexican-U.S. border.

No Se Habla Español. It has long been accepted that if Mexicans want to communicate with Americans and Canadians, they will have to use English. This is part of the old paternalism, and it does not sit comfortably with Mexicans, especially now that they command increasing status in the world. As English has become the language of global business, most top Mexican business people and professionals speak it well. But the exclusive use of English communicates a lack of respect between the three countries. To be perceived as a serious player in the Mexican market, one should learn to speak Spanish when doing business in Mexico. Even a minimum effort at learning and using the language will be valuable in demonstrating a commitment to the business partnership.

The exclusive use of English also puts even bilingual Mexicans at a constant disadvantage, since they must use a language that is less expressive than their own to communicate the unique Mexican perspective. This lopsided communication pattern—and the poor productivity that often results from it—will hurt both sides of any U.S.-Mexican joint ventures and partnerships. Smart American firms with business operations in Mexico will require fluency in both languages for all staff involved in regional work. Some executive search firms in the United States have already reported a recent doubling in the number of demands for multilingual managers (Ward, 1993).

Had Guadalupe's superior in New York been fluent in Spanish, a trusting relationship might have developed between the two offices. At the least, the Mexican employees would have felt more confident in their efforts to explain to their U.S. superiors why some things need to be handled differently in Mexico.

Write It in Triplicate.   Extensive documentation of business procedures and a legalistic approach, so common in the United States, strike Mexicans as inflexible, impersonal, obsessive, and ultimately insulting. The American custom of having an attorney present at most business meetings is interpreted as a sign of distrust. As Guadalupe's solution—just do it our way and then write it down—suggests, Mexicans are learning to adapt if only as an act of self-defense. U.S. managers and trainers need to adapt, as well, by recognizing the strengths of the more flexible and trustful Mexican system.

Traveling Is a Nuisance.   Strong family traditions in Mexico translate into a deep resistance to travel, even when it only requires overnight stays. Deep daily involvement in home and family is part of Mexico's extremely important quality of life. Celebrating religious and national holidays and crucial events like first holy communion, Independence Day (May 5), or fifteenth birthdays for girls (*quinceañeras*), as well as attending to each family member's saint's day, is an ingrained part of the culture. Mexican companies do not generally expect or pressure employees to travel. And they strongly support cultural practices that they believe enhance quality of life.

Relationships Are Everything.   Caring, interpersonal relationships, particularly one-on-one, are critical to Mexican workers. Alfredo and Guadalupe had little respect for their New York superior because there was virtually no personal rapport between them. The U.S. staff related to their Mexican counterparts as a group or division, not as real people with whom one could develop a trusting, personal relationship. This kind of distant, impersonal, "businesslike" relationship can leave Mexicans feeling vaguely disoriented and out of touch. As one Mexican manager observed: "Americans just want to talk about business. Mexicans just want to talk."

Leave Your Stereotypes at the Border.   Both Mexicans and Americans view one another through stereotypes that may contain a grain of truth—but not much more. Americans, for instance, often believe that nothing gets done in Mexico, especially anything involving the corrupt bureaucracy, with the dread *mordida* (bribe or, literally, "bite"). This may have been largely true in the past, but anticorruption campaigns in recent years have cleaned up the worst abuses. Today a bribe is more likely to get you a jail term than a favor.

Never Disagree.   Mexican business relations involve a degree of formality and politeness that makes it almost impossible to directly disagree with someone or say no. Thus Mexicans, like the Japanese, have learned to say no by saying "yes, but...." Only Americans are capable of saying "No way, José!"

Emerging from a Lost Decade

Fully realizing the opportunities of an open North American market requires, at the outset, cultivating a deeper understanding among Mexicans, Canadians, and Americans of how we live as individual men and women, workers, families, communities, and national citizens. How can we work together in such a way that we transcend our separate nationalisms to glimpse a larger, regional citizenship? How can we meld three national economies, one of which is significantly less developed than the other two, in a way that all will benefit? Where do we make our separate cultures work together instead of keeping us apart? What will we each have to give up and contribute to make it work?

These are not abstract problems. They are already confronting all three cultures in concrete, immediate terms. For the most part, we have had to devise strategies and solutions on the fly. But those who have anticipated the problems and begun working on the kinds of changes that will be necessary for dealing with them have a decided competitive edge in what promises to be an exciting and prosperous new century for the Americas.

Not surprisingly, the problems are most serious between Mexico and its two northern neighbors. The United States and Canada have enjoyed a free-trade agreement since 1989, and the peoples of the two countries are culturally as close as any two societies can be, despite some interesting differences (which we explore in the next chapter). Mexico, though, is as culturally distinct from American culture as Anglo-Canadian culture is similar. It is a rich, complex culture undergoing rapid and profound changes that will challenge even the most seasoned American and Canadian business leaders.

Compared to the revolutionary nature of the political, economic, and cultural changes now under way in Mexico, the "reinvention" of American business looks like a passing fad. Mexico really is reinventing itself—from top to bottom. A Third World nation is emerging from the "lost decade" of the 1980s into a vibrant and promising international economy in which it expects to participate and contribute as a full partner with its highly developed neighbors. It is a remarkable, exhilarating, frightening phenomenon.

But Mexico has no choice. If the future seems irresistible, the past was untenable. For four decades following World War II, Mexico's nominally socialist one-party system pursued the politically safe but economically flawed Third World development strategy of closed borders, subsidized industrialization, and import substitution—the theory being that growing industries must be protected at all costs until they mature enough to compete with the developed world. The flaw was that under the protective umbrella of the state, neither industry nor the social structures that depended on industrialization ever had the incentive to mature. What was ultimately protected was the very immaturity that the system was supposed to grow out of.

In the early 1980s, the masked inefficiencies of the market came up against the all-too obvious realities of external debt and the shock of plummeting oil prices. In 1982 Mexico shocked the international financial community by announcing that it could not service its $90 billion debt. Later in the year President Lopez Portillo nationalized the banking industry and devalued the peso. But the country's mammoth debt, still accounting for as much as 76 percent of GDP by the middle of the decade, was stifling the economy. And oil revenues continued their decline. No foreign exchange meant no purchasing imports to supply domestic industries with inputs for production, to import food such as basic grains, or to pay off the debt. These events were deeply troubling to virtually every sector of Mexican society—especially to middle-class professionals and business people, who either fled the country for the United States or Europe or stayed put and watched their earnings and savings erode. Inflation rose toward 159 percent annually in 1987.

The first sign of a significantly new direction—toward liberalization—came in 1986 when President Miguel de la Madrid joined Mexico to the General Agreement on Tariffs and Trade (GATT), the global body that promotes open trade.

De la Madrid also attempted to steer the country back on track with painful austerity programs, debt refinancing plans, and the beginning of privatization and cuts to government subsidies. President Salinas greatly accelerated the privatization campaign when he came to office in 1988, and by 1991 he had completed the process of converting the banks to private ownership and begun negotiations to expand the U.S.-Canada free-trade pact into NAFTA. Economic growth rates are now averaging 2 to 4 percent of GNP, and inflation by 1993 had plummeted to just under 10 percent. The international investment community has responded to these changes by increasing its participation in the capitalization of the Mexican stock exchange from just 3 percent in 1989 to 22 percent in May 1993. Total foreign direct investment has steadily soared from about $13 billion in 1984 to $35 billion in 1991, and exports nearly doubled from 1985 to 1990, according to figures from the U.S. International Trade Commission and the Mexican National Commission on Foreign Investment (Smith, 1992).

The lost decade, as many called it, is over. But the future remains only dimly visible. Mexicans know that, somehow, they must learn to defend their national and cultural sovereignty and once-protected domestic markets in the context of a highly competitive, cost-conscious regional North American economy. As Ernesto Martens, CEO of Vitro, a major Mexican player in the emerging North American market, has observed: "We don't want to lose our identity as a Mexican company with a unique culture and relationship with our employees, but we don't want to be battered in the world marketplace either" (Nichols, 1993, p. 164).

In general, the Mexican business community is confronting that challenge with confidence, but also with realistic concerns about the sustainability of their past achievement. Corporate leaders hope and believe that the formalization of the regional market will help stabilize the positive trends — in part because the new rules sharply constrain the traditionally broad latitude the presidency has over trade issues. (Salinas's term expires in 1994.)

Furthermore, most business leaders now recognize that it is to Mexico's great advantage (if to its past disadvantage) to be located next door to the largest market in the world—a market that for other developing countries involves high shipping and freight costs. With the extensive experience Mexico already has acquired in dealings with the United States it will be better able to read rapidly changing consumer demands and adapt them to the domestic market. In addition, Mexico's workforce has become highly productive (thanks in part to its very low wages).

The confidence of the private sector is further buttressed by the fact that many major Mexican enterprises already have a substantial presence north of the border, with extensive ties among the Mexican, U.S., and Canadian auto and energy companies and major retailers. Consider, for example, the number of familiar names among Mexico's leading multinationals: GM, Chrysler, Nestle, IBM, American Express, Anderson Clayton, Sears Roebuck, Xerox, Dupont. The possibilities for developing innovative marketing and production partnerships, transfer of knowledge about markets and technology, and R&D collaboration are excellent for such companies. Furthermore, the country's fastest-growing industries (see Table 8.1) include both manufacturing and service enterprises, reflecting the ongoing attempt to balance economic growth and shift away from exclusively manufactured exports.

All of these factors are positive signs for Mexico's integration into North America. Inevitably, there will be frequent setbacks and occasionally serious clashes along the way as each country struggles to adjust to the others. Many of the problems will be resolved through political and legal remedies. But smoothing out the bumps and bruises resulting from clashing cultures must be left to the ingenuity and vision of the three peoples themselves—individually as well as in teams, partnerships, alliances, and genuine North American corporations. This human dimension of the challenge must begin with at least a basic knowledge of our cultural roots and the common features and differences that define us.

Table 8.1. The Most Dynamic Industries in Mexico in 1992.

Industry	Number of Firms	Growth Rate (1991–1992)
1. Nitrates/fertilizers	1	39.1%
2. Wood products	2	35.8%
3. Insurance	8	27.1%
4. Construction	20	25.1%
5. Clothing/garments	4	23.4%
6. Professional services	7	20.2%
7. Cement	6	19.5%
8. Small appliances	6	17.5%
9. Tobacco	2	16.6%
10. Communications	4	14.0%

Source: Based on the Mexican top 500 firms in *Expansión*, August 18, 1993, p. 324.

CULTURAL BOUNDARIES: UNLOCKING THE MYSTERIES

The human borders between the United States, Canada, and Mexico are significant on every dimension, from physical to spiritual. In the following pages we will examine those differences and common features from the perspective of our five cultural lenses. But first, let us glance briefly at Mexico from a broader perspective, noting some of the key cultural contours that will be most relevant in the business context.

Stereotypes and Layers of Reality

The first thing any American visitor to Mexico notes is that few of the old stereotypes apply. That may be because many of those stereotypes are based, however incorrectly, not on Mexicans but on Hispanic Americans. The Hispanic population in the United States and Canada has its roots in a variety of Spanish-speaking countries, all of which have distinct cultures despite their common linguistic heritage. Also, most Hispanic immigrants to the United States came from the poorer, less skilled, and less educated classes who migrated north seeking better opportunities. In the United States they have developed distinct subcultures that are neither Mexican nor Puerto Rican nor Guatemalan, but a blend of the various native and American cultures. Mexicans, in fact, tend to view Mexican Americans as North Americans, not Mexicans.

Like most national cultures, the Mexican culture is a complex weave of historical forces. Pre-Cortesian civilizations (Aztec, Mayan, Zapotec, and others), conquest by the Spaniards, the battle for independence from Spain, the Mexican revolution, and the ongoing, inescapable relationship to the United States are only a few of the major events that reflect the evolution of Mexico as a national culture. (For more on the significance of U.S.-Mexican relationships, see Clint E. Smith's excellent *Disappearing Border*.)

The historical layers of psychological, religious, and philosophical elements of Mexican life are impressively explored by Mexican poet and philosopher Octavio Paz in *The Labyrinth of Solitude: Life and Thought in Mexico* (1961). As implied by Paz's title, uncovering each layer is like wandering through a labyrinth: challenging, frustrating, exciting, and deeply rewarding at every turn. Paz describes the differences between his own people and Anglo Americans in the following way:

> The North Americans are credulous and we are believers; they love fairy tales and detective stories and we love myths and legends. The Mexican tells lies because he delights in fantasy, or because he is desperate, or because he wants to rise above the sordid facts of his life; the North American does not tell lies, but he substitutes social truth for real truth, which is always disagreeable. We get drunk in order to confess; they get drunk in order to forget. They are optimists and we are nihilists — except that our nihilism is not intellectual but instinctive, and therefore irrefutable. We are suspicious and they are trusting. We are sorrowful and sarcastic and they are happy and full of jokes. North Americans want to understand and we want to contemplate. They are activists and

we are quietists; we enjoy our words and they enjoy their inventions. They believe in hygiene, health, work and contentment, but perhaps they have never experienced true joy, which is an intoxication, a whirlwind. In the hubbub of a fiesta night our voices explode into brilliant lights, and life and death mingle together, while their vitality becomes a fixed smile that denies old age and death but that changes life into motionless stone [Paz, 1961, pp. 23–24].

From Aztec Pyramids to Hierarchical Corporations

Hierarchy has played a prominent role in Mexican culture since pre-Cortesian days. The Aztec hierarchical priest society, cacique, and hacienda form of control evolved down through history to current forms of hierarchy still present in the countryside and in rural towns. The Mexican revolution institutionalized key structures at the apex of society and the economy—including the ruling Institutional Revolutionary Party (PRI), which has been virtually synonymous with government since 1929, labor unions (the powerful Confederation of Mexican Workers, which is closely linked to the PRI), and state-owned industrial giants such as PEMEX, the largest organization in Mexico. The hierarchical order of government, society, and the business sector is further strengthened by a paternalistic family structure and the Catholic church.

Religion and Spirituality as Guiding Forces

The divine is a major driving force in Mexican culture, thought, and behavior. "The Mexican is a religious being and his experience of the divine is completely genuine," writes Paz. "But who is his God? The ancient earth-gods or Christ?" As Paz notes, Roman Catholicism has been superimposed on the "ineradicable presence of indigenous myths," creating the dynamic forces of contemporary Mexican spirituality (Paz, 1961, p. 106).

As Ernesto Martens, the CEO of Vitro, stated in a recent interview: "Our workers use the most advanced German technology under the watchful eye of Our Lady of Guadalupe.

And here in our corporate headquarters, you see the heavy dark woods and whitewashed walls that were common in eighteenth-century Mexico, but our mindset is twentieth-century capitalism" (Nichols, 1993, p. 164).

The Family as Central Institution

The family reflects the hierarchy and power relationships set forth in the Catholic church and provides the values that young Mexicans take with them to school, to university, and into the workplace. The father is the central authority figure: he is respected by all members of the family and his power is unquestioned. The mother is the key figure for affection, care, strength, and security: she is role model for her daughters and nurturer for her sons. The extended family, with its *compadres* and *amistades* (godfathers, godmothers, and close family relationships), serves as a unit for protection and community rather than active support. The family is there as a base for solace, emotional stability, and a sense of belonging and orientation.

Four Regional Variations

The geographical diversity of Mexico has helped shape four regional subcultures relevant to the business sector. The central area surrounding Mexico City and including Guadalajara has been the major business, financial, and government center of the republic. Since pre-Cortesian times, the region that is now Mexico City has exerted a powerful, centralizing pull on outlying provinces. Today, one out of four Mexicans lives in Mexico City, which has become a labyrinth of its own with its massive state bureaucracy, multiple layers of power, and circuitous communication channels.

The northern region, including Monterrey as the major city, with approximately 5 million people, is characterized by rugged mountains and the dry Sonoran desert, conditions that Mexicans believe are responsible for the *norteños'* fierce and aggressive style. Midday meals start an hour earlier in Monterrey than in Mexico City, which is significant given the importance of this meal as an occasion for establishing and nurturing business relationships — and the problems the time difference causes in terms of scheduling meetings and reaching associates by phone. The north has a somewhat stronger orientation to the United States, but it is unquestionably Mexican.

The border region, known as *La frontera,* including Tijuana, Mexicali, Ciudad Juarez, El Paso, Laredo, Nuevo Laredo, Matamoros, and Brownsville, has given rise to a completely distinct business and social culture, a U.S.-Mexican blend. There is a strong atmosphere of dynamism and innovation that carriers over into the many *maquiladora* joint-venture plants producing goods for export to the U.S. market. The workforce is young, transient, and poor, which has been a source of social problems as well as opportunities.

The south and southeastern region of Mexico is hot, humid, tropical, lowland terrain. The population is largely employed in subsistence agriculture. Mexicans have described the south as a place where it's easier to make your own living from the land and thus less oriented toward business and nonagricultural activities. Because the rich land would always provide, there was never the need to look for new ways to sustain the family.

A Young and Eager Workforce

"We take more risks," said a 32-year-old executive at a multinational computer firm, "because unlike you we have nothing to lose — no pensions, no job security. And most Mexican managers have no history of success or failure and its consequences." Mexico is an extraordinarily young country compared to its northern neighbors. Half of its people are fifteen years old or less.

A select cadre of young Mexicans has been well educated in both Mexican and foreign universities and professional schools over the last decade and a half. These young graduates are posted, or rapidly promoted, to high-level posts in many Mexican multinational and large national companies. They have little work experience but are schooled in modern business practices, making them highly valued. The hope is that they will be the engine that pulls Mexico forward into a more competitive global position.

This growing cohort of young executives clashes frequently with older, more experienced managers who have had less education and foreign exposure and find it shocking to have "children" disagree with them—worse yet, to have the young people's views prevail. Mexican managers often complain that the generation gap is one of their major difficulties— all the more because respect for elders is a highly esteemed value in Mexico. Given the graying of the American and Canadian workforces, and the generally older age of senior executives in these countries, some clashes are bound to erupt in U.S.-Mexican or Canadian-Mexican business relations. Will sixty-year-old American executives with decades of experience be able to negotiate on equal terms with thirty-year-old Mexican MBA graduates? Will they have any choice?

Sexism as an Institution

Mexican women are expected to stop working when they marry and absolutely must quit when they have children. While the proportion of women in the workforce has risen over the last twenty years, it still lags far behind most developed economies. Also, it is still unusual to find women in positions of authority. Most women in business are employed as support personnel, either clerical or administrative, although a growing number are finding their way into areas such as corporate communications, human resources, and training.

The overall paternalism of Mexican culture carriers over into male/female business relations. It would be highly unusual, for example, for a Mexican businesswoman to give a plenary session at a conference, even if she had done the work. Her male colleague or boss would take the honors. Although there are laws against sex discrimination in the workplace, they are largely ignored because women have not yet made sexism a major issue. They expect to play secondary and support roles and show deference to men, even when they occupy higher positions. The relatively few women in senior positions are expected to act in a formal manner and dress elegantly for all business affairs.

American businesswomen find it uncomfortable and at times almost impossible to assume leadership roles in joint U.S.-Mexican projects. Mexican executives are not apt to seek out female partners and may be uncomfortable when they have to develop close business relationships with women. Americans' directness and task focus seems particularly strange to Mexicans when it comes from women.

As more women graduate from professional programs, there will be a greater supply of adequately trained and eager professional women entering companies. This may be one asset that Mexican companies would do well to exploit in developing closer business relations with U.S. companies, where women are more prominent in positions of responsibility. The 1990s may be to Mexico what the 1970s were to U.S. business when women entered the corporate workplace in large numbers. This trend will, of course, be shaped profoundly by other social values such as the importance of the family. It is clear, however, that women will have a larger place in the corporate setting in the future.

Class and Race

Racism is not an issue in the Mexican workplace — in large part because there are so few people of color in the workforce. The corporate corridors, particularly, are relatively homogeneous. The large indigenous population in Mexico works primarily in agriculture and lives very traditional, rural lives. In some Latin countries, such as Costa Rica or Panama, the various skin shades of white and brown are valued differently. But most Mexicans proudly insist that *"somos Mexicanos — todos comemos chilis y frijoles"*: We are all Mexicans — we all eat chilis and beans — a common expression meaning we are all equal. Others are equally adamant that Mexican society is very class-conscious and that Spanish, mixed-blood, and native Indian variations in skin tone and hair color are closely related to class.

HOW MEXICAN CULTURE
SHAPES THE WORKPLACE

The key to successful business with Mexican corporations is understanding the common ways in which the Mexican workplace is the product of the underlying social culture. Once again, we will scan the environment through the five cultural lenses of language, context, time, equality/power, and information flow.

Language

It is not possible to know Mexico without speaking Spanish. This fact will have business consequences that are both subtle and highly visible to all. Despite the fact that most Mexicans who participate in regional business speak English, an English-only speaker will never have the same access to Mexican business opportunities as one who speaks Spanish.

Mexicans, like all Spanish-speakers, seem "wordy" to Americans. It does take about 25 percent more words to express the same idea in Spanish than in English. This means that business communications are normally lengthier and far more formal. The personal greetings and respectful sayings — like "let me take this opportunity to greet you" — before discussing business in a memo or letter are an important part of culturally correct communications. Because Mexicans esteem relationships, communications tend to be filled with niceties and relationship-building phrases. To Americans and Canadians, it often seems difficult to "get to the point."

Mexicans also customize the relative formality of their language according to the age or status of the person they are addressing — unlike Americans but similar to French Canadians. This practice is most noticeable in the use of a formal and informal second-person pronoun: *tú* for children and close relations, *usted* for superiors, older people, and strangers.

Mexicans often speak metaphorically and use lots of vernacular sayings, even in the business world. The use of *la picardía* — little jokes, comical anecdotes, or funny sayings —

and double-entendres is common. They are used frequently between men to build trust and add enjoyment to the work relationship. These little word games are extremely difficult to translate into another language, and they virtually disappear when Mexicans have to use English.

Mexicans correctly believe that Americans' reluctance to learn Spanish is a reflection of the unequal business relationship between the two countries. As the Mexican market grows in importance to U.S. trade, they will expect and demand a more bilingual environment. As they see it, pride and respect for Mexico are at stake, as well as their ability to participate fully in regional business, since translation is never an adequate substitute for fluent bilingualism, especially in technical or creative communications.

Besides, having a good grasp of Spanish will provide U.S. business managers in Mexico with an invaluable tool to unlock the complex Mexican culture. It is essential for developing a trusting, long-term relationship with Mexican business partners. At the very least, U.S. managers should make an effort to show some knowledge of Spanish out of respect to their Mexican counterparts. As one Mexican professional noted, "We have a language, too!"

Communication technologies that help people express themselves clearly in their second language or in modes other than their primary language will help cross-cultural workers. These tools will vary for different individuals and for different teams. Some may decide that text-based e-mail messages are the best way to express concepts clearly in a second language because each message can be prepared ahead of time and edited for clarity. Fax communications, which are common in Mexico, also may be useful when there is time to compose messages and add graphics or other images to express the idea. Voice mail, on the other hand, may be particularly difficult in this situation, especially for people with weak verbal skills. Video conferencing may be helpful, although costly, for high-level, remote meetings because visual presence may ease the tensions of communicating in a second language and nonverbal cues can be used.

Context

"Look in most Mexican executives' wallets and you will find a picture of the Virgin of Guadalupe," said a senior manager of a Mexico City–based transnational. "We are very religious, not so much in terms of going to church, but in terms of the importance of a relationship with God."

The high-context Mexican culture assigns the highest possible value to belief in God, family, and respect for the individual. Spiritual values permeate all aspects of life. In contrast, low-context Americans and Anglo-Canadians may attend church regularly, but spiritual values tend to be compartmentalized and isolated from business practices. High-context and low-context cultures like Mexico and the United States and Canada are apt to encounter difficult challenges in establishing good business interfaces. Differences in basic values, assumptions, and beliefs result in persistent discomfort in relationships.

In business, respect for the individual is demonstrated by polite and carefully constructed communications. It is also demonstrated by respecting each person's opinion and way of doing things. This works against teamwork in the American sense of completely shared goals and processes. Moreover, Mexican companies tend to hire lots of people and keep everybody employed despite the admitted need for efficiency. Although layoffs are relatively uncommon, the trend to competitiveness is bound to result in some "downsizing."

The most productive relationships are between individuals, not groups, as in Japan. In contrast to the United States, where loyalty to the team or the organization (an objective entity) can be very strong, loyalty in Mexico is more likely to develop among individuals and team members, not institutions. This difference has significant implications for developing motivation to reach goals, as well as for rewards. The personal relations context also results in hiring and promotion practices that favor friends and friends of friends. Companies do much to support family relationships and quality of life. For instance, employees are rarely expected to travel if doing so interferes with family affairs. Outsiders will find it difficult to break into the inner circle of family and business relationships, but once you do you are completely accepted. This is the basis of achievement and promotion.

Objective information that is isolated from the context of relationships is not as highly valued in Mexico as in the United States. Indeed, many find it difficult to establish productive business relations on the basis of such information. For information to be meaningful it must be personalized. For these reasons, technologies that provide open access to information may be difficult to introduce into Mexican teams, whose members are not accustomed to such accessibility. It may be hard for those in supervisory positions to give up control over information and equally hard for those unaccustomed to having it to use it effectively. More equitable use (or appropriate allocation) of information will have to be developed in teams so that they can integrate the use of software, shared data bases, shared-screen technology, computer conferencing systems, and groupware systems such as Lotus Notes.

As in other high-context cultures, great care is taken by Mexicans to create a proper environment for conducting business—including attention to such details as furniture, art, flowers, seating arrangements, and refreshments, even in temporary workspaces. Meetings are considered more important for building relationships than for doing work. Fixed agendas, therefore, are not of much use.

The influence of religion and history in Mexican culture has also contributed to a sense of fatalism that contrasts starkly with the American and Canadian sense of personal control. The current economic stability and the willingness by government and corporate leaders to pursue personal visions may be bringing some degree of change in this area, but it will be a slow evolution.

Time

"Mexicans work to live, not live to work, like their American counterparts," commented a Mexican senior technologist. Like other polychronic people, Mexicans are able to handle numerous, simultaneous activities—from socializing to listening to music to conducting serious business affairs—unlike their monochronic and more linear northern neighbors. This difference in orientation to time and history is reflected perfectly in Mexico City's Plaza de Tres Culturas (Plaza of Three Cultures), which exhibits pre-Columbian, Spanish Colonial, and modern-day architecture layered and integrated in one location. All three time periods exist at once as reminders of the influence, contribution, and presence of each generation of Mexico's history. The past is very much present, and it pervades most activities and ways of thinking—including relations with the United States.

Commitments to complete a transaction on schedule are common, but not commonly met. Nothing having to do with time is carved in stone. This attitude reflects the relativity of events and timing, as well as the contingency of activities, rather than irresponsibility, as some outsiders may believe. It could be explained as an ingrained sense of flexibility related to tradition, inefficient systems, unreliable infrastructure, and a fairly uncertain environment. As communication systems improve and the environment becomes more stable, time commitments may become more predictable.

Time is important to Mexicans, but not as a vital resource to be managed. Since time is allocated on the basis of relationships, the priorities go to spending time on activities that please one's superiors, being with family or friends, or celebrating religious holidays. Time efficiency has not been a part of corporate life.

Profoundly different orientations to time will cause plenty of friction in transnational business. The Mexican attachment to the past, for example, will make it difficult to establish relationships based on trust with North American partners. And the relatively rigid management of time in the United States and Canada will clash with Mexicans' orientation toward flexibility and contingency. Expectations that new communications technology will increase the speed and efficiency of information management may fall far short, for technology alone will not change the Mexican orientation toward time.

The Mexican's comfort with integrating past, present, and future means there will be differences in how the role of long-range planing is understood. For instance, Mexico's short-term orientation results in a lack of investment in corporate R&D. This tendency is related in part to Mexico's economic history, where foreign debt payments, massive devaluations, arbitrary and unaccountable government, a protected market, and costly capital made it difficult (or unnecessary for those in the protected domestic market) to plan for even the near term, let alone the long term. Surviving the 1980s has engendered a feeling of urgency among Mexican businesses. Mexicans are in a hurry to get things done, and they tend to believe research doesn't deliver benefits quickly enough. The short-term view of planning is beginning to be critically examined, however, thanks in part to the relative stability that is expected to result from the recent decade of reforms and regional integration.

Power/Equality

Mexicans tend to be extremely status conscious, as are most Latin Americans. Status is related to family, school, wealth, and authority, and once attained it tends to be permanent. Inequality between the sexes is a widely accepted norm.

Lines of authority are almost religiously observed, and *jefes,* or people in high authority, are not expected to admit errors. Indeed, it is uncommon for anyone in a position of authority even to ask questions, since lack of information implies a lack of authority. This, of course, leads to a lack of clarity in work roles and implementation strategies, which in turn contributes to poor productivity and inefficiency. Another result is the tendency of *echando la culpa*—putting the blame elsewhere. Mexican corporate offices reflect this orientation to power through a kind of symbolic opulence that far exceeds that of executives of similar power in either Canada

or the United States. Many offices are ostentatiously deco-
rated with museum-quality art.

The introduction of technologies that increase direct
communications between lower-level workers and top management inevitably upsets the hierarchical rules of communication and results in discomfort among managers and frustration among workers when the technology is short-circuited.
The use of such technology will have to involve a clarification
of roles, position, and authority if it is not to completely blur
the lines of power.

The relative corporate egalitarianism of the United
States and Canada tends to be accepted by Mexican managers, but not really understood. At a time when American
corporate structures are flattening and delegation of autonomy to lower levels is the trend, Mexico's hierarchical organizations are increasingly out of step with global trends and are
almost certain to become a barrier to productive joint ventures. The large holding companies are moving slowly toward
flatter, more decentralized structures, but the cultural barriers
remain formidable.

Information Flow

Information travels in circuitous routes in Mexico. Indi-
rectness is part of the way Mexicans show respect for the
individual and authority, and it often results from the fear of
being wrong. Information may be closely held because it is a
source of power; it may be kept deliberately ambiguous because it may be incorrect.

Similarly, action chains have many steps and tend to be
indirect. The polychronic time orientation adds to a penchant
for communicating around things rather than confronting
them directly. To preserve individual relationships and maintain loyalty to a co-worker, direct criticism or presentation of
embarrassing information is uncommon. The value of relationships takes priority over the efficiency of information flow
and access.

Information flow is also directly related to power and

equality characteristics — meaning that information tends to flow along strict lines of authority. Almost all information flows top to bottom. Because Mexico is an oral culture, a lot of information moves with little documentation, frequently by word of mouth. As a senior manager at a large Mexican multinational noted: "We put all information in brief visual form. Mexicans are more visual, so graphic information is used a lot. Reports are like annotated viewgraph reports and audiovisual communications."

Mexican executives are beginning to acknowledge that they need to streamline business processes and simplify their tedious and complex administrative procedures. Because Mexicans have few documented business processes, they often try to borrow procedures that have been successful in the United States or Canada but turn out to be inappropriate to Mexican culture. The need to add workflow technology, as well as to document and improve their own culturally appropriate processes, is one of the greatest business challenges.

Despite some well-meaning reforms, the Mexican governmental bureaucracy remains a formidable barrier to getting important information. The time-consuming process of developing relationships within the government ministries is frustrating to the fast-paced, information-oriented, North American executive. Mexican businesses have learned to go around the bureaucracy with their people network, but this option is not available to most outsiders.

WORK BOUNDARIES: NATIONAL PRIDE MEETS REGIONAL IMPERATIVES

As we have seen, the patterns of the primary social culture are visible in the workplace in every one of the five cultural dimensions. Mexicans are extremely proud of their national culture, and one of their deepest concerns about the regionalization and globalization of their economy is that it will compromise those values and practices that are uniquely Mexican.

Yet Mexicans, by and large, do not question the absolute necessity for regionalization and global competitiveness. They recognize that companies must transform themselves to adapt to the business reality of open markets, fierce competition from foreigners, new distribution channels, new consumer markets, new cost structures, and creative ways of using partnerships and alliances in the regional economy. These changes will require the workforce at all levels to adapt old and deeply embedded work cultures, both corporate and functional, to new visions and goals. The adaptations are certain to be difficult and even painful.

The biggest cultural shift, which is already well under way, parallels the national economy's fundamental change in course from centralized state controls and protectionism to privatization and greater market responsiveness. The "competitive crisis" of the 1990s is distinctly different from the crisis of 1982, and the major national and multinational corporations are responding by openly encouraging appropriate shifts in both the explicit and implicit corporate cultures.

In making these cultural shifts, many Mexican corporations find themselves undergoing challenges not unlike those of the major U.S. defense corporations, which operated for nearly half a century in a largely noncompetitive, guaranteed-profit environment. For these defense firms, survival in the more openly competitive civilian market requires a radical shift of the corporate mindset that challenges all the old habits, beliefs, and assumptions. One Mexican executive at a large holding company told us how he had been personally "shocked" when his organization purchased an American company and compared the relative production costs in Mexico and the United States for the same processes. The labor-intensive and structurally complex tasks so pervasive in Mexican business resulted in far greater inefficiencies and higher operating costs for the Mexican company than for the U.S. company.

Fortunately, the government and private sector are working closely together to promote a greater sense of competitiveness in Mexican corporate cultures. In many companies there is a major emphasis on total quality (*calidad total*), which has become a buzzword in corporate corridors and is the subject of countless newspaper articles. Also, there is wide recognition that Mexican business culture needs to adopt a long-term perspective that values R&D efforts and quality improvements. Key industries like textiles, food production, and oil will lose out to global competition unless they quickly update their technology and product quality. And unless both business and the government focus more attention and resources on long-range infrastructure improvements, Mexico will have trouble attracting the level of foreign investment needed to nurture and sustain globally competitive enterprises.

"We have to overcome the fact that Mexico has never really had a scientific or technical tradition," said one executive of a Monterrey-based multinational. With just 10 researchers per 100,000 inhabitants, he noted, Mexico ranks poorly in its number of engineers, scientists, and technical specialists, even compared to other developing countries. (Brazil boasts 25 per 100,000.) "It may take generations to develop a deep appreciation for long-range research and planning," he added, "but we have to start now by building up training programs and a cadre of research-minded managers." The government appears to recognize the need, too, having dramatically boosted spending on a major campaign to attract foreign (especially ex-Soviet) specialists to Mexico, as well as to induce Mexican specialists who fled the country in the 1980s to return home.

Developing a broad pool of scientific and technical research talent may take time, but it should not require a radical cultural shift, since education is already highly valued in Mexican business. Many high-level Mexican executives have completed graduate studies in the best American universities. They are usually selected and sponsored by corporations with full scholarships and are given a top management position upon return. Middle-level managers and those from divisions with less status, such as human resources, attend Mexican universities, also sponsored and selected by business with full scholarships. As was the case in the United States until recent years, the most valued business functions in Mexico have traditionally been those involved with finance, almost to the exclusion of all others. The cultural shift required to put a higher value on functions closer to the customer level, such as sales and marketing, will inevitably scramble the rigid hierarchical orders of Mexican business, which will literally be upsetting from top to bottom.

Nonetheless, if there is one clear lesson from opening up the domestic economy and competing with U.S. and other foreign companies it is that Mexican businesses will have to learn to read the consumer better. Consumer demand in Mexico is shifting rapidly as the vast population of young workers is exposed to new products and life-styles. A planning executive in Mexico City noted that in just two years the market for chicken shifted from demand for live birds to a soaring demand for processed, fast-food chicken products. Likewise, the customer-driven demand for refrigerated trucks, transportation systems, and quicker distribution channels is staggering. For many Mexican companies, learning to spot and respond quickly to such demands requires an almost complete makeover of corporate culture. As one Mexican investment executive commented, "In the past, Mexican companies didn't have to sell—consumers purchased. Now the consumer is calling the shots and business is scrambling to figure out how to respond."

All of these new demands will benefit from the fact that the work ethic in Mexico is very strong—from the smallest enterprise to the largest firm. Mexican workers take a great deal of pride in their work and adapt easily to new situations. So long as they feel valued as individuals, they participate with great commitment. American managers with experience in Mexico consider them fast learners and very creative at getting around problems—an impression that is borne out in any number of studies attesting to the high productivity of the Mexican workforce. This is not to suggest that all the hurdles of regionalism will be easily overcome. Cultural habits of paternalism, rigid hierarchy, male dominance, and favoritism in hiring and promotions, for instance, will continue to set Mexico apart—and at a disadvantage to—the United States and Canada. But Mexicans themselves are now acknowledging these cultural barriers, and that is the first step to overcoming them.

Finally, it must be noted that many aspects of the Mexican work culture should result in competitive advantages. We have already cited the strong work ethic of the young workforce. To this advantage we should add their strong spiritual orientation and their deep roots in family and community, which provide exceptional stability and support for facing the challenges and ego-shattering shocks of working at a distance and across cultures—especially cultures that have historically been regarded as dominant. The extensive social and professional relationships that Mexicans cultivate will serve them well in facing the difficulties inherent in dispersed work environments, where personal relations and trust are so important to effective communications. And their relative comfort with uncertainty and contingency, characteristic of their polychronic time orientation, will be especially helpful in managing the far-flung, cross-cultural networks characteristic of regional enterprises.

On balance, then, Mexico may in fact bring as many cultural advantages as disadvantages to the challenges represented by regionalization. But the challenges they face are immediate and fundamental, and they will require profound shifts in corporate culture. Among them:

- *Quality and competitiveness:* As a high-context and polychronic culture, Mexicans will find the sequential, linear, information-intensive processes involved in implementing total quality mysterious and perplexing. They will need to adapt third-way workflow patterns that are consistent with U.S. and Canadian practices without abandoning their own values.

- *Efficiency and time utilization:* The Mexican use of time and information flow is characterized by circuitous processes. The aversion to questioning others, particularly superiors, to clarify uncertainties results in inefficient work processes.

- *Technological adaptation:* Mexicans may resist using technology in place of the traditional person-to-person information flows. But once they become familiar with electronic communications, they should be able to extend their traditional networking capabilities with the emerging groupware tools.

- *Merit promotions:* Adapting to a merit-promotion system may be particularly difficult for a culture in which family and friendship networks have long been the key to survival and advancement. This is also true for performance reviews, which are inconsistent with the type of favoritism practiced in Mexican enterprises.

Many American business people have found working with Mexicans an especially rich and fulfilling experience. But it can also be extremely frustrating. The quality of the relationship depends ultimately on how much cultural knowledge and sensitivity both sides bring to the experience. The following strategies for U.S.-Mexican collaboration may seem obvious, but the most obvious strategies are often the most overlooked or forgotten.

- *Nurture personal relationships.* Take a few minutes a day to talk with Mexican colleagues about family and friends and other personal subjects. Get used to taking frequent, long, and leisurely lunches that do not revolve around work-related conversations. Begin telephone calls with a personal address rather than getting right down to business. Rushing into business is considered rude.

- *Humanize the workplace.* Help establish a work environment in which high-context Mexicans feel at ease—

maybe by adding some personal touches to the typically stark and functional American workplace.

- *Show respect publicly.* Avoid public criticisms or disagreements that could cause a loss of face. Make an effort to express disagreement in ways that show respect for other points of view.

- *Demonstrate interest in the culture.* This can be done in a variety of ways — from learning basic conversational Spanish to learning about important religious holidays and key cultural and historical figures, such as artists and revolutionary heroes.

- *Accept gender differences.* The women's equality movement in the United States and Canada has not made much of a dent in Mexican society or business. But until Mexicans themselves challenge their own norms on sexual equality, Americans would do well to accept them as they are.

- *Observe quitting time.* Even among executives, evenings tend to be reserved for family and friends, not business. Confine power meals to breakfast or lunch, not dinner. Adjust to the separate rhythms of the day — and the night.

REGIONAL TEAM ISSUES

"The concept and practice of teams is not part of our culture," said a Mexican senior organizational team consultant. He continued: "The relationship is between the boss and each team member, not the whole team. The boss has sessions individually with each member of the team. This shows respect for the individual and maintains their status."

Mexican social culture is built around one-to-one relationships and respect for the individual, which makes the very concept of teamwork somewhat antithetical. Yet the large holding companies, larger national Mexican companies, and *maquiladoras* are deliberately encouraging a shift to American-style teams in keeping with the deep Mexican interest in total quality. Despite this effort, there is little common ground between Mexico and its two northern neighbors in terms of the preferred styles of teamwork. Both Americans and Canadians are comfortable with delegation of responsibilities and egalitarian team communication processes that encourage open questioning and confrontation. Decision making is based on objective data, not relationships. Self-managed teams are common. Team leadership is often rotated.

None of this comes naturally to Mexicans, given their preference for hierarchical and one-on-one relationships. Typically, team members spend time nurturing their relationships with the boss, not each other. And Mexicans rarely seek clarification of goals or roles through open questioning, which signifies a lack of knowledge. Similarly, team meetings in Mexico are for creating and sustaining relationships first and foremost — not for getting task work done, as in the United States. Creating some common ground and a third way for regional teamwork, therefore, will be one of the greatest management challenges.

Resolving these challenges depends on the cultivation of a breed of team leaders willing and able to steep themselves in cultural learning, including bilingual fluency. Although not all team members necessarily have to learn the language of the other culture, the leader must. This point cannot be over-emphasized. American leaders must also focus on forming authentic relationships with Mexican team members, be capable of switching from high to low context at a moment's notice, and learn to move between authoritarian and egalitarian management styles. As Eva Kras (1989) has noted, Mexican management styles tend to be basically autocratic, theoretical, personal, noncompetitive, and flexible with regard to time. The American style, by way of contrast, emphasizes delegation of responsibilities, pragmaticism and action, performance-based promotions, pleasure in competition, and firm commitments to deadlines and workflow agreements. Finding third ways between such widely divergent styles is the ultimate test of leadership.

Mexican Teams: From Orientation to Renewal

During our research in Mexico we met with a great variety of U.S.-Mexican teams and explored their problems at each stage of the Team Performance Model discussed in Chapter Five. The following observations regarding each stage represent the views of most teams we observed. Figure 8.1 illustrates the best places and times for Mexican teams in their stages of performance. Mexican business teams focus intensely on Stage 3, because clarifying individual responsibility is of paramount importance. In Stage 4, each person puts his or her own twist to the team's shared vision.

Orientation.   "What's important to me is to know exactly what you want me to do," explained a Mexican team member. The concept of orienting to a common team purpose and vision—the first stage of team development in the United States—is a secondary concern to Mexicans, who want an early resolution of the role clarification process. Concrete information about each team member's individual responsibility creates trust and orientation. Many Mexicans are very uneasy until this issue is resolved. A team's vision and purpose are normally articulated by the *jefe*, or chief.

   Other orientation issues involved differences toward time: Would the team work on American time or Mexican time? What were the official hours? Americans usually worked from 8 to 5 while Mexicans preferred to come later and work later. What religious holidays would be observed? Of particular concern was Easter week, traditionally celebrated throughout Latin America. Exploring these questions helped both Mexican and American team members figure out how well they were going to fit together.

Building Trust.   "Having clear lines of authority spelled out gives the team trust," commented one team member. High-

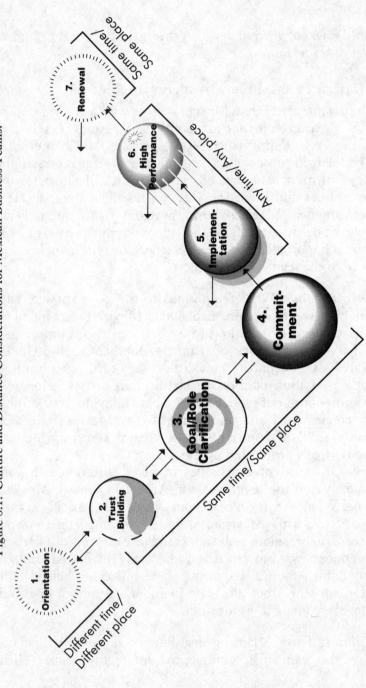

Figure 8.1. Culture and Distance Considerations for Mexican Business Teams.

context cultures in general, and Mexico's in particular, have woven trust into the very structure of both the social and work cultures through the central role played by personal relationships. Thus the issue is not a pressing concern in the early development of teams, which are merely smaller networks of personal relationships.

Of greater concern is the need to get the roles clear so the trust between leader and team member is not damaged by a failure to perform the assigned task. For Mexicans, trust is deepened by sharing personal values about the importance of family and religion, in contrast to the American need for sharing information about task-related skills.

One of the most common trust difference we found was the Mexicans' desire to have the team leader spend time with the team, even for just ten minutes a day. This need for more personal contact is often misinterpreted by American team leaders as a desire for more supervision.

Goal/Role Clarification. Of all the stages of the team model, role clarity is one of the hardest to resolve. Mexicans have a deep need to please superiors, but they are reluctant to seek clarifications because questions imply lack of information, which implies lack of status. The result is a lot of misunderstanding and anxiety that ultimately result in the circuitous work processes at stage 5.

Commitment. Confidence in the team leader's vision is the basis for commitment. Trying to create a "shared vision" that goes beyond mere cooperation is almost counterproductive; it violates one of the pillars of Mexican culture: respect for the individual. A completely shared vision would signify that the team members were automatons without individual differences. Part of the resistance also comes from a tendency to creatively adapt existing situations to new needs rather than designing entirely new approaches. This may be partly a reflection of low self-esteem in business endeavors in contrast to the high self-confidence of Americans.

Americans want to spend time making sure everybody is

100 percent in alignment on vision and get resources allocated beforehand. Mexicans want to agree with the overall direction and be left to their own devices.

Implementation.   Putting team plans into action often suffers from lack of clarity in roles and work processes. If questions aren't asked to clear up uncertainties, work proceeds on a trial-and-error basis. Since Mexicans will try to make things work even when they are unclear about goals and processes, implementation can become cumbersome and inefficient, with many more people involved than necessary, and deadlines often slip. This is not to say that the quality of implementation is not high but that efficiency is often sacrificed. Lack of commitment also surfaces during implementation time, which is especially noticeable when work requirements interfere with quality-of-life concerns.

Team leaders cannot abandon their involvement and supervision during implementation. Because asking questions is not part of the culture, the leader needs to check in frequently and keep an active motivation campaign going. Time management is challenging, as well. Mexicans will work long hours but not necessarily efficiently.

High Performance.   Leaders of Mexican teams often get all the rewards for the team's work whether they are involved or not. This dampens the will to do one's personal best and work toward high performance. Mexican workers will perform at high levels when they are trying to please supervisors or prove their productive value in relation to non-Mexican partners, however, such as Japanese or Americans.

Renewal.   Mexicans are not prone to do follow-up analysis and reviews. At the end of a team project, celebrations are common, with prizes and lavish praise, but they are designed for social entertainment, not self-reflection and team improvement. Whether or not a team stays together is entirely up to the leader, not the members.

Strategies for Team Facilitation

Of the many strategies that Mexican-U.S. teams were using, these are some that team leaders and managers told us were key to apply.

- *Learn to speak Spanish.* You cannot guide a regional team through all its ups and downs if you're not fluent in both languages.

- *Do not confuse the need for contact with a need for supervision.* Americans often frame Mexicans' desire for more involvement as a need for more supervision. Usually it is a need for a direct relationship with the superior.

- *Learn to accept uncommon respect for authority.* Mexicans treat foreign superiors and elders with the same elevated respect they show Mexicans. Americans who feel ill at ease with such attention need to learn to relax and enjoy it.

- *Spend more time defining individual roles.* Orientation and work processes are totally dependent on whether team members are clear about their individual roles.

- *Emphasize follow-up and documentation processes.* Do not assume that tasks will be documented or that they will be tracked throughout their progress. Managers must be explicit about recording activities and checking up on work. If done well, this effort can give managers a chance to spend more time with team members and show personal involvement in their work, building more trust and confidence among team members.

- *Make leisure time a team value.* Mexicans work to live and Americans live to work. Make sure there is leisure time to get to know people.

INFORMATION TECHNOLOGY
IN MEXICO

A variety of forces are shaping the future of information technology in organizations in Mexico, and in many ways they mirror similar forces in other emerging market economies, such as those in Eastern Europe. Many are internal—coming from the changing demographics of the Mexican workforce, the maturation of medium and large companies, the entry of young college-trained professionals into Mexican business, government reforms encouraging increased productivity, quality, and efficiency, and organizational restructuring. Other forces are external—including the increasing pressure of global competition, the transfer of technology through joint ventures and alliances with foreign firms, and educational partnerships between Mexican and foreign institutions.

One of the key factors behind Mexico's telecommunications revolution is the restructuring of organizations. Although Mexico's multinational and large national firms may never become as horizontal and networked as U.S. corporations, they are becoming more distributed through the process of downsizing, joint ventures and partnerships, outsourcing, and use of contract labor. The result, as in the United States, is a need to link decentralized corporate information resources both within Mexico and abroad: patents, R&D data, library resources, and, most important, people. Company executives told us they needed to have better information from plants in different locations so that headquarters can make decisions based on up-to-date, high-quality financial and operational data. As one manager stated, "We should be able to enter data into the system once, and not have to traverse the entire Mexican Republic in order to find it again."

While the largest Mexican companies have already integrated impressive information technologies into their organizational restructuring and operations processes, most medium-sized and smaller firms are only beginning to explore the opportunities. Small family-operated companies tend to view sophisticated information tools as too expensive and intrusive on traditionally labor-intensive ways of doing things. Nonetheless, with increasing regionalization and the already extensive business alliances and distributed firms radiating out from Mexico City to the United States, Europe, Japan, and

South America, the Mexican demand for improved information technology is large and rapidly growing.

Information Infrastructure

While the demand is there, however, the infrastructure is not. And even if personal computers had higher levels of penetration in Mexican companies (they are found mostly in the large companies), the communications infrastructure linking them is a constraining factor. This is an important hurdle for Mexican business. (The technology data in this section come from three U.S. Commerce Department reports cited in *Mexico Business Monthly*; see Flores, 1993a, 1993b, 1993c.)

Nearly one-third of Mexico's telecommunications capability is concentrated in Mexico City, and more than half is in Monterrey and Guadalajara. The telephone penetration level nationwide is a mere 7.7 lines per 100 inhabitants — compared to about 20 per 100 in most developed countries and 50 per 100 in the United States. Even with a projected annual growth of 13 percent, there will only be 11 lines per 100 inhabitants by 1995. The public telephone infrastructure is abysmal at 0.5 for each 1,000 inhabitants (and there's no official estimate of the number of out-of-order telephones). There is no surprise, then, at the business community's rapid adoption of cellular phones and its fascination with newer radio-based communication systems. The difficulty and delays in getting phone installation from TelMex, the national telephone company, have resulted in a boom in satellite-based and fiber-optic private networks and cellular communications. Today there are more than a thousand private data and shared-use networks in operation. These are now the norm for most business people.

Rapid expansion of the infrastructure is a high priority of the government's five-year plan. Not only does it call for progress in local line and long-distance digitalization, but a large, 13,500-kilometer fiber-optic network is scheduled for completion in 1993. This network will be the backbone of the national long-distance service. International services, meanwhile, are

**Table 8.2. Breakdown of the Mexican National
Long-Distance Telephone Network.**

	1990	1995
Trunk lines	330,041	700,000
Digital	55%	85%
Toll switches	137	250
Digital	41%	85%
Microwave network		54 routes
Channels	489,281	700,000
Digital	21%	50%
Fiber-optic length	4,134	5,935
Satellite channels		
(*Morelos*)	2,100	5,500

Local line level of digitalization
Total number of lines: 5.271 million
Analog: 71%   Digital: 29%
Total number of exchanges: 1,445
Exchange suppliers: Ericsson and Alcatel

Source: TelMex, Baring Securities.

struggling to keep up with a growth rate of 28 percent in
1992 — 90 percent of which were calls between Mexico, the
United States, and Canada.

A basic breakdown of the national long-distance network
is described in Table 8.2 and reflects the goal of the government and TelMex to improve the national infrastructure.

Fiber and Cable Systems.   The fiber-optic cable network,
scheduled to be completed in late 1993, will be the backbone
of TelMex's long-distance network. This network will link the
fifty-four largest cities. Additionally, TelMex has an "overlaid"
network that was merged with the telephone network in order
to gain experience in operations of fiber-optic cable. This
network provides high-speed services to corporate customers
in Mexico City, Guadalajara, and Monterrey.

In 1991, TelMex started offering Integrated Services Digital Network (ISDN) services to its major corporate customers. This network operates at a speed of 64 Kb per second and is capable of offering international links at 2 Mb per second. *Morelos I* and *II*, two geosynchronous satellites, were launched in 1985; each has twenty-two transponders. Two new satellites, planned for launch in November 1993 and February 1994, will replace *Morelos I* and *II* and support mobile telephony in addition to other forms of communication. Television and cable TV networks are operated in Mexico and dominated by Grupo Televisa and the government (which is selling its ownership of several channels). Uses are predominantly for entertainment and cultural programming.

Cellular, Pagers, and Other Devices.   Cellular service, available in Mexico since 1989, is divided into nine regions, each one assigned to a company. TelMex, however, was awarded a contract for all the country. In 1993 there were approximately 210,000 subscribers to cellular service; by 1994 there may be as many as 400,000. Cellular service was available to eighty-five cities in Mexico in 1993, with Mexico City accounting for 60 percent of total subscribers. The biggest obstacle to subscribers is the cost.

Paging is available in Mexico, but it's mostly used by doctors, not business people. This is not surprising given the preference for personal communications and because paging involves one-way communication. There is also a preference for voice rather than text. For example, a cellular call is preferred over an impersonal fax or e-mail message.

Fax machines are becoming more widely used for routine communications in business and universities. There are approximately 200,000 fax machines in Mexico, estimated to increase to 500,000 by 1995.

Given Mexico's comfort with cellular phones, the use of other personal communication devices may show similar successes. The potential market for Newton-type devices and other portable computing devices should find healthy niches in the Mexican market. Devices that link mobile managers to their desktop systems will also become useful as mobility within Mexico City and between that city and Monterrey becomes more constrained. This trend will be balanced with the Mexican's preference to stay local but work globally. The ability to transmit information to distant locations and gather information from various sites will be highly valued.

Use of Groupware

Groupware is still in its infancy in most Mexican corporations, both conceptually and in practice. It is likely to develop unevenly but rapidly, perhaps matching groupware use in the United States within a decade.

American firms in Mexico, including IBM, Hewlett-Packard, and General Motors, are leading the way in application of groupware, providing important exposure to the larger Mexican market. Mexican firms that have begun exploring the technology's potential have largely confined its use to middle management. It is virtually absent—along with almost all information technology—at the executive level, where secretaries and extensive personal support are still (and likely to remain) the norm.

Nonetheless, the business environment has become exceedingly complex and fast-paced, and the need for better, quicker communication is felt deeply. Mexican executives are keenly aware of the importance to their competitive position of gathering key information and human resources quickly, seamlessly, and efficiently.

Use of groupware in international teams is apt to be limited mainly to information sharing so long as bilingualism is a problem in the north. The use of technology for informal communications, for instance, is not likely when second languages have to be used. Even for bilingual Mexicans, English is not appealing for personal communications. Another factor affecting the future of groupware tools is the strong visual and oral orientation in Mexican culture. This inclination is likely to result in a bias toward tools that provide graphic interfaces and communication capabilities rather than text-based systems.

Tools: From Face-to-Face to Satellites

In this section we survey the status and availability of information technologies in Mexico. However, the use and adoption of technology will also be governed by cultural preferences. More than their U.S. counterparts, Mexicans will want to establish good personal relationships before extensively using fax and e-mail to conduct serious business. Face-to-face meetings and phone conversations will always be crucial, especially early in relationships and when important business is at hand.

Face-to-Face Meetings. This most basic tool in the groupware toolbox is still the most important method for sharing information and gaining trust and commitment on a team. And this is likely to remain true due to the high-context nature of Mexican culture.

The typical face-to-face team meeting features little more technological support than simple flip charts. Mexican executives told us, generally, that meetings are not very productive and there are too many of them. Most felt that the main problem with Mexican meetings was that they are too social due to cultural tendencies. They were not easily persuaded that electronic tools might resolve some of the problems.

Executive and board meetings, on the other hand, tend to be quite formal and involve little interaction. They take place in a very comfortable environment, sometimes supported by overhead projectors and, at rare times, videos. Most high-level decisions and communications take place in one-to-one relationships in a formal but more social setting, such as an executive office or an executive lunch room. Power breakfasts are common.

Telephone. As noted earlier, the telecommunications infrastructure in Mexico is still a barrier to good domestic and global communications. The phone system's inaccessibility and poor quality reinforce cultural preferences for face-to-face meetings. Indeed, it is unlikely that many business decisions at any level of consequence are decided by phone. Poor telecommunications also reinforce the Mexican reluctance to travel, since a high value is placed on maintaining frequent family contact.

Cellular Phones.   In the relative absence of a wired telecommunications infrastructure, cellular technology has enjoyed widespread popularity in Mexican business circles—especially in Mexico City and Monterrey, the two largest business centers, where gridlocked traffic makes face-to-face meetings particularly difficult.

Voice Mail.   The fate of this technology depends on improvements in the telephone infrastructure and shifts in cultural preferences for direct communication. So far, voice mail is more common in the homes of the younger generation of workers than in the workplace, where personal secretaries are still expected to answer the phone. As the infrastructure expands, generational change and workforce fragmentation will no doubt drive voice mail into the workplace.

Audio Conferencing.   This tool has great potential for growth in national companies, given infrastructure improvements, because of the trend to dispersed teamwork and the aversion to travel. In terms of multinational or global teamwork, it suffers the disadvantages attached to any bilingual, spoken communications. When used by global teams, the lingua franca is almost always English.

Computer Conferencing.   This technology is extremely limited, given the low base of computer installations and the poor communications infrastructure.

Fax.   The widespread popularity of fax technology in Mexico is limited only by the phone lines. It is used primarily for information transfer—sharing expenditure reports, budget analyses among dispersed offices, and logistical coordination. It is increasingly used to substitute for personal messengers, which have been a very common feature of business in Mexico. Due to increasing traffic congestion, personal messengers now take up to four hours to deliver documents in Mexico City. Fax will serve as a technological foundation for both national and multinational distributed work.

E-Mail. In firms well equipped with networked computer systems, e-mail is used much as it is in the United States — though less so for informal communications, which Mexicans prefer to conduct face to face. Some managers are beginning to view e-mail as a good tool for group coordination — helping define roles and generate trust throughout the more dispersed workforce. For global team members who travel a lot (one of the teams we studied traveled 150 to 180 days a year), e-mail is their main connection with one another and headquarters. As the infrastructure is developed more fully, e-mail will be commonplace for information sharing and coordination within Mexico. International use will remain somewhat limited by language barriers.

Audio-Supported Screen Sharing. This technology is very experimental at the moment. Some of the advanced technology companies, such as Hewlett-Packard and IBM, are using it for resolving technical problems and troubleshooting.

File Transfers. Regional, private networks and satellites are used to share financial information and hard data. Many business managers told us they think of file transfers only for hard data or other important information-sharing functions, not for discursive communications.

Group Decision Support Systems (GDSS). There are two GDSS rooms equipped with Ventana GroupSystems, one in Monterrey and one in Mexico City. There is a close consulting relationship between these academic institutions and the Mexican business community. The GDSS in Mexico City was installed specifically for helping businesses to expand nationally and internationally. The use of the room, which was installed in 1991, is actively marketed and its use is growing. Its initial business use has been for planning meetings, strategic development tasks, and problem solving, and it has been recognized as a great success.

Satellite Network.   Mexican businesses envision a global network connecting them to clients and suppliers for shipment data, billing and payment information, and the latest market trends. Most companies say they would take advantage of such a system once the infrastructure is in place.

Video Conferencing.   Video is available in some multinational holding companies, like Vitro, with installations in both Monterrey and Mexico City. Where it's available, it is used extensively because it reduces the need to travel. We learned of no regional links, but they are sure to develop. Indeed, video conferencing will probably come to be preferred over audio once it is improved, given the potential for more visual and personal exchanges, which are culturally important.

As we have seen, then, the greatest groupware challenge is the lack of a good telecommunications infrastructure. This, however, could improve quickly — certainly by the end of the decade — and it will be forced to do so by the demands of NAFTA. Thus the basic groupware tools should be fairly common in Mexico by the year 2000, though their primary use may still be limited to information sharing and coordination due to cultural and language barriers. Most creative work will continue to be done face to face.

Greater training and education about technology and teamwork are clearly needed. Even then, widespread use of new technology may come only with a gradual, generational change. One important factor working in information technology's favor is the deep cultural resistance to travel.

RULES OF THUMB
AND PITFALLS

The following rules of thumb and pitfalls apply for Americans and Anglophone Canadians doing business with Mexico.

Rules of Thumb

- *Maintain an equidistant perspective on all three cultures.* Avoid, if possible, falling back on your own cultural assumptions and practices when things get tough. Mexicans are already wary of their northern neighbors because of past historical relationships, so it's wise to educate yourself as much as possible in Mexican history and culture. There is no excuse for neighbors and partners not investing the time to learn about each other.

- *Learn Spanish.* It is essential that at least team leaders speak both languages. Try to create teams with as many bilingual persons as possible.

- *Invest time.* Building the one-to-one relationships that are so important to Mexicans requires time and attention. These relationships are the cornerstone of the Mexican culture and keystones to effective business. In team relationships, getting the best Mexican participation requires taking the time and effort to show respect for each individual.

- *Attend to the niceties.* Minor gestures, such as flowers and refreshments, can make major impressions.

- *Use technology appropriately.* Mexicans readily adapt to technology for information sharing and coordination, but personal, creative, and qualitative communications still depend mainly on face-to-face encounters.

Pitfalls

- Do not mistake Mexican culture for Mexican-American culture.
- Do not assume that Mexicans are comfortable using English.

- Do not inadvertently cross lines of authority. These are rigidly observed in Mexico, and violations cause serious embarrassment.

- Do not lose sight of the different interpretations of equality and power. Mexicans place a high value on status and class.

- Do not use technology in lieu of personal contact unless there are clear and mutually agreed reasons.

- Do not depend on Mexicans to travel as frequently as Americans. The home is the center of their lives.

NINE

Overcoming Differences and Sameness: Collaborating with Canada

If the Mexican challenge in the economic integration of North America is that of a culture and an economy that are in many ways profoundly different from those of its neighbors to the north, Canada's challenge is in some ways just the opposite. Its culture and economy are, at least superficially, almost indistinguishable from those of the United States. And therein lies Canada's special dilemma: how to preserve those aspects of its culture that define it as uniquely Canadian in the face of a predominant American culture that sees only an extension of itself north of the border—the "attic of America," as one writer

295

put it. It is a dilemma that many Canadians understand all too well, as the following scene suggests.

On the flight to Washington for the IABC conference, Sharon K., a marketing manager for an Ottawa-based telecommunications firm, spotted her friend Pierre from Montreal and sat in the adjoining seat. Pierre, as it happened, was going to the same meeting and introduced her to a colleague across the aisle, Mustafa, who was traveling with him. Sharon greeted him and apologized for her poor French, but Mustafa reassured her it was not a problem. Sharon was dying to know what Pierre thought about the upcoming federal election, but she knew better than to discuss politics with business colleagues, especially from Quebec, so they just chatted about mutual friends.

"This will be my first IABC conference," said Pierre. "What have they been like in the past?"

"They give you a good update on what's going on in the U.S.," said Sharon, "but the international perspective is weak. I've been on the board of directors for years but I haven't been able to affect the program in any major way. They organized a session on telecommunications in Canada last year and then had someone from AT&T coordinate it!"

Pierre laughed. "Yeah, my boss came back last year fuming. He said that no one in the trade show would talk to him when they found out he was from Canada. He had a hard enough time getting Canadians to talk to him."

From Dulles Airport they shared a cab to the hotel and met later at the reception. Sharon spotted Ishi, a representative from Japan Telecommunications Inc., whom she had met the previous year. "You may not remember me," she began, "but. . . ." Ishi gave her a big smile, bowed, and shook her hand. Sharon brought him over to meet her friends.

In the midst of their conversation, up walked Sam, a consultant from Houston who had recently bid on a contract with Sharon's firm. He marched over and grabbed Sharon's hand as if she were a long-lost friend. "Am I glad to see you," he enthused, still holding her hand. "When can we get to work on that project of yours? There's really not a lot of time, you know, and we've got real heavy demands right now. I was hoping we could spend some time here taking care of the preliminaries."

Sharon felt more than a little uncomfortable. In fact, the deal was far from firm. Her supervisor had been slightly put off by Sam's aggressive manner and was leaning toward a Canadian competitor who seemed much more willing to listen to what the company needed. She smiled at Sam and said, "Um . . . I'm sure we'll have a chance to talk about that later, but let me introduce you to my friend from Quebec."

"Mustafa?" said Sam, looking at the name tag. "What kind of name is that? Doesn't sound French to me." But before Mustafa could answer, Sam spotted another hot prospect across the room. "Excuse me, folks, I've just got to talk to Ted. I'll catch you later."

"What was that?" asked Pierre, laughing.

"Americans," said Sharon.

Later, in the conference hall, Pierre and Sharon found a seat together and looked over the agenda. "I asked one of the organizers last week why there were no Canadians on the program," said Sharon. "He said Canadians are no different from Americans except they pay more taxes."

Pierre shrugged. "I'm used to that. But I'm surprised there are no women on the program. I mean, look at this audience. It's got to be 30 or 40 percent female."

The program had noted that the opening address would examine telecommunications and competitive advantage, which Sharon was looking forward to. But she paled when she saw the speaker approach the podium, wearing a blue general's uniform. The conference committee had selected a Desert Storm hero to discuss the use of telecommunications in the U.S. armed forces. Sharon sighed and feigned interest as he droned on about how new technology was full of "killer applications" for training and communications with aerospace contractors.

After that evening's dinner, a well-known Washington comedy troupe, the Capital Steps, provided entertainment. Most of the audience was in stitches over a series of skits about American politicians and the elections, with plentiful references to Clarence Thomas and William Kennedy Smith. In the middle of it, Sharon turned to Ishi and Pierre and suggested it might be nice to move to the lobby bar for a drink. Pierre shrugged. Ishi said he was having a hard time understanding the jokes but he'd wait till the end.

At the end of the evening the group walked back to their hotel together. "What did you think of the entertainment?" asked Sharon, rolling her eyes. "I understood about half of it," said Ishi.

"Oh well, you know Americans," laughed Pierre. "They talk a lot about globalization, but they just don't get it, do they?"

Any discussion of Canadian cultural identity must begin with the observation that Canadians have always defined themselves primarily in relation to a powerful other, whether it was England, France, or the United States. This proclivity has resulted in what some observers view as a deep-seated sense of insecurity—a cultural condition that has found political expression in Canada's continuing constitutional crises, which have become almost a national pastime. In terms of national identification, this orientation to a powerful outsider has resulted in a "more-or-less" kind of cultural relativism: Canadians see themselves as more polite, more tolerant, more socially aware, more thoughtful, and more compassionate than Americans and, conversely, less racist, less loud, less militaristic, less crass, and less easygoing, relaxed, or confident than Americans. How they might view themselves without the American mirror is open to question.

Canada's seeming obsession with the United States stems, in large part, not from the differences between the two countries but from their undeniable sameness, which has been greatly reinforced by increasingly strong north-south trade ties. The vast majority of Canadians live within 100 miles of the U.S. border. Many work for subsidiaries of large American companies. They watch American television, read American books, follow American politics and social issues, and participate fully in American popular culture. In fact, Canadians probably spend a good deal more time thinking about the United States than Americans spend thinking about Canada and the rest of the world combined. But they think, especially, about how they are different from Americans and how to sustain those differences.

Let's take a brief look at some of the key cultural barriers as they emerged in the opening scene:

- *American insensitivity to Canadian differences:* It is a serious error to think of Canadians as quasi-Americans. This habit is tremendously annoying to Canadians, who properly insist on being recognized as members of a unique culture. The potential for good business relationships will suffer unless the three major cultures, American, Anglo-Canadian, and French-Canadian, achieve a more balanced perspective on one another. And Americans—more than Canadians—must get used to the idea that there are genuine cultural differences between the two nations. Canadians, for instance, are more apt to be impressed by a peacekeeping hero from Operation Provide Comfort in Somalia than by a war hero from Desert Storm. And they may take offense at the military metaphors that permeate American dialogue.

■ *Canadian stereotypes of Americans*: Canadians have their own stereotypes about Americans, such as the notion that all Americans, like Sam, are aggressive and pushy about business deals. Like most stereotypes, they may contain a grain of truth; but like all stereotypes they are frequent obstacles to productive business relations.

■ *Gender roles*: Feminism is more institutionalized in Canada than in the United States. There is more commitment to ensuring that women are well represented on committees, conferences, and so forth, particularly in any dealings with the government.

■ *Linguistic politics*: In dealings with Francophones, it is wise to at least make an effort to speak French, particularly in Quebec. Knowing French is a vital skill if you're dealing with government organizations and most major businesses in Quebec; it is less important in dealing with subsidiaries of American companies or Anglo-Canadian companies outside Quebec.

■ A *nation of two cultures*: The differences between English and French Canadians may be even more significant than the differences between English Canadians and Americans. These differences are a source of frequent friction between the two communities.

■ A *cultural competitive edge*: The experience of living in the shadow of the American elephant, combined with the reality of Canadian bilingualism and multiculturalism, has tended to sensitize Canadians to the need for cultural learning and toleration, which should serve as a major advantage in the global economy.

■ *Competing on its own terms*: The assumption that Canada always follows the American lead is a source of perpetual annoyance to Canadians. In fact, Canadians are world leaders in certain aspects of telecommunications. Northern Telecom, for instance, beat AT&T into the Japanese market. Canadians may not brag about their accomplishments—a standard joke is that Canadians won't recognize other Canadians until they've made it in the United States—but they do not take well to being patronized.

CULTURAL BOUNDARIES

"The Stern Daughter of the Voice of God"—that's how the late U.S. Secretary of State, Dean Acheson, half Canadian himself, once described Canada in a moment of slightly bitter wit.

In some ways, the description is an apt summation of the core values that have shaped Canada's history and national culture. It is a tradition that prides itself above all on patience, tolerance, consensual politics, peace, and compromise. Without such qualities, this bicultural, multiethnic nation could never have come together even in the federal form that exists today. And without the persistence of these qualities, the nation could well be overtaken by the growing forces of separatism, cultural intolerance, political exclusion, and the complete breakdown of the shared values that Canada will need in the age of globalization. The nation could become what some advocates of Canada's breakup claim it always has been: an artificial administrative entity with no psychological or cultural reality. That eventuality, however, is still overshadowed by a history that provides a great deal of common ground in basic cultural values. As usual in Canada, they are most often defined against the measure of the colossus to the south.

What are Canada's shared values? They are not really so hard to find as many Canadians might insist. Consider its national symbol, the beaver—chubby, industrious, herbivorous—in comparison to that of the United States, the bald eagle—soaring, majestic, and predatory. Such symbols speak volumes.

What are Canadians best known for on the international stage? Multinational peacekeeping, the invention of former prime minister Lester Pearson, is still the main venue for Canadian geopolitical activism. Compare that role to America's superpower global military forces, proud to claim the title of the world's mightiest warriors. Canadians remain content to spend just 2 percent of GDP on defense, less than half the rate in the United States. And Canadian military spending equals just 13 percent of health and education spending versus 32 percent in the United States.

Glance at the comparative history of Western settlement. In Canada, an initial force of no more than two hundred and fifty Mounties peaceably brought law and order to more than a million square miles of western and northern Canada. At the same time, Indian nations of the American West were being terminated and forced into exile by the U.S. Army. The Canadian aversion to violence is still evident in comparative crime statistics between roughly comparable U.S. and Canadian cities. In Toronto, a city of about 2.5 million, with fifty-five nationalities, the rate of violent crime in 1988 was 1,163 crimes per 100,000 residents. The rate in Detroit, across the American border, was more than twice as high at 2,375 per 100,000. Urban murder rates are typically around one-tenth of those in U.S. cities, and far fewer involve the use of guns.

Canadian culture, of course, is more than shared values, for the nation is far from monolithic. It remains officially bicultural and bilingual, reflecting its French and British founders, and there is growing recognition of the role of the First Nations, or Native Canadians. Postwar immigration increased the level of ethnic diversity, and today there is formal recognition of "multiculturalism" at federal and provincial levels. The one-quarter of the population that is Francophone, concentrated in the province of Quebec, wages an even greater struggle to maintain its own cultural identity vis-à-vis Anglophone Canada than the English-speaking population does vis-à-vis the United States.

Given that one out of three Canadian business school graduates is Francophone, this internal cultural struggle finds significant expression in a divergence of Canadian business views about regionalization. The new Quebecois business generation may be less interested in politics and independence than its elders, but it is also confident that Quebec can compete in international markets. French-speaking Quebecers were generally more enthusiastic about the 1989 U.S.-Canadian free-trade pact than Anglophones, perhaps because they are less fearful of domination by American culture. In effect, the Quebecois tend to view their relationship to the rest of Canada much as the rest of Canada views its relation to the United States.

The Changing Face of Canadians

In many ways, the profile of the "average Canadian" is changing at least as rapidly as that of its American counterpart. Major cities have recently witnessed a significant growth in immigrant populations, particularly in visible minorities. Federal and provincial government programs have been created to address multicultural issues beyond the traditional French-English bilingualism. In many cities, publicly funded education is available for courses in "heritage" languages such as Chinese and Japanese. And support for aboriginal self-government has grown significantly in recent years, although Canada's historical treatment of its native people is a continuing source of national embarrassment. Among the major trends shaping and reshaping Canadian society, the following developments are certain to have far-reaching impacts on how Canadians see themselves and are seen by others.

Graying Baby Boomers.   In terms of age characteristics, Canada, like the United States, is a graying nation with a low birthrate. Even predominantly Catholic Quebec has seen a dramatic lowering of the birthrate in recent decades—indeed, some view it as another cultural threat, given the higher birthrates of immigrant populations.

Canada may also be entering a period of generational shift, similar to the ascendancy of the Baby Boomers in the

United States as symbolized by the Clinton presidency. It probably is no coincidence that just months after Bill Clinton took office, the Canadian political spotlight focused on Defense Minister Kim Campbell, the woman who was slated to succeed Prime Minister Brian Mulroney at age forty-six, exactly the same age as Clinton when he became president.

Gains by Women.   Kim Campbell's sudden (though brief) political ascendancy was indicative too of another significant wrinkle in the social fabric: the increasing role of women. A self-avowed feminist (though criticized by many feminist organizations), Campbell is only one of a growing number of powerful female politicians. Indeed, almost 50 percent of the candidates running under the New Democratic Party banner in the fall of 1993 were women. Two of the three major parties were led by women in that election: Campbell, who led the Conservative Party (politically similar to conservative or moderate U.S. Democrats), and Audrey McLaughlin, fifty-seven, head of the socialist New Democrats. With the 1993 election of Liberal Party leader Jean Chrétien as prime minister, Sheila Copps—the party's forty-one-year-old deputy leader—is poised to assume a top leadership post.

To a degree, the trend toward gender equality is more advanced in Canada than in the United States. Canada had a higher proportion of women in Parliament in 1987 than the U.S. Congress did in 1992. U.S. feminist leader Gloria Steinem recently remarked that she had once considered applying for refugee status in Canada. Today, that option might actually be possible. A number of recent court decisions have granted refugee status to women based on persecution due to gender.

Affirmative action programs for women and government-supported compulsory paid maternity leave (fourteen weeks), supplemented by an optional nine months' unpaid leave for father or mother, put Canada well ahead of the United States in this area. Government agencies and universities all have gender-neutral language guidelines, although these are less common in the private sector. Employment equity law, advertising guidelines, and sexual harassment regulations are all more advanced in Canada than in the United States.

Women have also made significant, if uneven, progress in the professions. This trend should continue given that most of the business schools, law schools, and medical schools are now 50 percent female, although engineering schools lag behind at about 18 percent.

Nonetheless, gender issues are creating backlash and resentment. While female participation in the workforce is comparable to that of the United States (44.3 versus 45.2 percent in 1986–1989), the gender-based wage gap is similar, too, and demands for comparable pay have not fared well in the recessionary environment.

Liberalism with a Canadian Accent.   As in the ethnic, generational, and gender aspects of Canadian culture, Canadian politics are also "more or less" similar to American traditions — in this case, somewhat more liberal. In most of the country, the Canadian tradition puts less emphasis than Americans do on unbridled individual liberties and more emphasis on the role of government. The Canadian constitution, in fact, enshrines "Peace, Order, and Good Government." Although no one likes higher taxes, Canadians pay them and accept more government intervention in the interests of public safety, health, and welfare.

Populist conservatism is now enjoying growing appeal among a large segment of the population. Even so, it is fair to say that liberalism never became a dirty word in Canada, as it did in the United States during the 1980s. More than half the Canadian population lives in provinces that are at least nominally "socialist," and the country's generous, state-controlled universal health care and education systems are sources of great national pride.

Likewise, Canadians are less concerned than Americans about the much greater extent of direct foreign investment in their country. Nor do Canadians typically share American antagonisms to foreign-owned companies, despite the high rate of U.S. ownership. The share of mining and manufacturing industries, by sales volume, under foreign (mainly U.S.) control reached nearly 50 percent even before ratification of the U.S.-Canada free-trade pact. More than one-quarter of all nonfinancial corporations, measured by sales, are under foreign control. And the Canadian auto industry is 90 percent U.S.-owned. It may be that Canada's long experience with American economic dominance has, at least in some ways, made Canadians better prepared to deal with the realities of both regional and global economic integration.

Diversity Within. The flip side of Canada's common ground is a sea of ethnic diversity, rooted in the past and fed by trends in the present. A quick glance at the cultural differences among Canada's major regions suggests the great range of that diversity, as well as the extent to which it mirrors America's own diversity.

Alberta and the prairie provinces, for instance, tend to identify with the politically conservative, individualistic, resource-rich regions in America's intermountain states. The American "sagebrush rebellion" of the early 1980s found a sympathetic echo in this region, where sentiment runs strong against Ottawa's paternalistic federal bureaucracy. The prairies' deep-rooted alienation from the centers of political and financial power has recently given rise to a new regional political party, the Reform Party, whose popularity has spread with the slogan "The West Want In"—meaning it wants finally to be treated as equals by Ontario and Quebec.

Vancouver, British Columbia, is viewed as having more in common with the trendy, relaxed life-style of California than with other Canadian provinces, and its extensive trade and immigration ties around the Pacific Rim give it a more Asian than European orientation. Indeed, more than 20 percent of its 1.5 million people are immigrants from Hong Kong or China, and Asia buys one-third of all the province's exports. Even the Bank of British Columbia is now a subsidiary of the Hong Kong–Shanghai Bank.

Given the way British Columbia has led Canada's economic growth in recent years, many are beginning to view it as the tail that wags the Canadian dog. Many Vancouver business leaders see themselves in the middle of a global economy, the same distance from Tokyo as from London. And because the kind of economy that is emerging is so different from what they have experienced in the past, they see themselves as leaders, not followers.

The Atlantic Maritime provinces — 2.3 million people in four provinces — enjoy a northern New England-type reputation for down-to-earth, traditional values. Although they include Canada's poorest provinces, they tend to view themselves as stable, intimate, settled, and comfortable with their extensive social services. More than 90 percent of the people of the Maritimes were born in the region, making it by far the most homogeneous part of Canada. The Maritimes also have strong ties to Britain. St. John's, capital of Newfoundland, prides itself on being halfway between Toronto and Ireland. Its culture remains a blend of the old and new worlds. Even the distinct Newfoundlanders' accents echo their English or Gaelic heritage.

The big, industrial heartland of Ontario is the province everyone loves to hate — the largest, richest province and the nation's political and financial center. The Toronto–Ottawa nexus is to the rest of Canada what the New York–Washington corridor is to the rest of the United States. And everyone in Ontario loves to hate Toronto, the big-city, workaholic, WASPish, insensitive, worldly center of the province.

Cultural Separatism: Quebec.   The one instance of regional diversity that really has no American counterpart is Quebec, the big and powerful French-speaking province whose struggle to protect its French culture has been at the center of the ongoing constitutional crisis. Quebec's uniqueness in relation to the rest of Canada makes the rest of Canada look blandly uniform. Although the political battle for Quebec separatism is a relatively recent phenomenon, the cultural struggle has been going on for more than two hundred years, since the founding of Canada.

The current threat to Canadian unity is rooted in the historic conflicts between the French and the English. In response to "the Quiet Revolution" of the 1960s, there was an effort to counter emergent Quebec nationalism by advocating broader recognition of French Canadians throughout the country through policies to promote bilingualism and biculturalism. This drive to include French Canadians in federal governance and positions of power has succeeded to such an extent that it is now unthinkable that a Canadian prime minister would not be bilingual. Nevertheless, outside the province of Quebec—and outside government—there are few genuinely bilingual Anglophones. The imposition of bilingualism throughout the country has created backlash in some quarters, and at least one political party—the Reform Party—formally advocates its abolition.

Quebec nationalists remain unimpressed by the rest of the country's relative acceptance of bilingualism and biculturalism. Their focus is on preserving French in Quebec rather than in other parts of the country—and, increasingly, they view Quebec's independence as the only way to accomplish it. After all, they note, Francophones may represent 25 percent of the population of Canada, but 90 percent of them live in Quebec, which is undergoing declining fertility rates and high rates of emigration to other provinces.

The lack of true bilingualism in Anglophone Canada and the passion for the preservation of French in Quebec and other outposts of Francophone Canada has contributed to the persistence of cultural stereotypes, which are sometimes reinforced in English and French TV programming. (Quebecers naturally prefer their own television.) The French view the English-speakers as straight, unimaginative, rule-bound slaves of the Protestant work ethic—a view that is partially borne out in surveys showing an Anglophone devotion to the grindstone, in contrast to the traditional French joie de vivre. Anglophones, on the other hand, view the French as flighty, undisciplined, inefficient, independent, and hedonistic.

In many ways, Quebecers do share important cultural traits with their European Latin and Catholic cousins, but they insist on a unique identity as Quebecois. As Brother Jean-Paul Desbiens, a key figure in Quebec's cultural revolution of the 1960s, has written: "The Quebecois is not quite a Latin and not quite an Anglo-Saxon; he is a mixture of the two, and the facility for mixing we have borrowed from the Americans" (Desbiens, 1992, p. 30). Their unique identity, he argues, derives from five elements: Catholicism, French culture, British parliamentary government, American dynamism, and the sense of being a minority. "For the majority of Quebecois," he writes, "Canada is a boarding house where we find it hard to feel at home."

Like other Latin cultures, the Quebecois tend to have large families, and they value big group festivities. They drink and smoke more than their Anglophone neighbors, maintain large circles of close friends, enjoy fashionable clothing, and make frequent outings to friends' homes and restaurants. They are expressive and intimate in social interactions, and the men are said to be more at ease around the opposite sex.

All in all—with the exception of Quebec—Canada and the United States may have more in common than any two nations on earth. Indeed, the cultural similarities between the two countries should prove to be sources of extraordinary economic strength. But that power will be all the greater and the more satisfying to everyone if the differences, small and large, are recognized and respected.

Canada Through the Five Cultural Lenses

All the most fundamental cultural similarities and differences that define the overall Canadian relationship to the United States, as well as the multicultural relationships within Canada, also show up in business relations. Once again, it is useful to examine the contours of these relationships through the five cultural lenses that we have applied to other cultures in previous chapters.

Language. The struggle to preserve French is at the center of Canada's present political crisis. How this issue is ultimately resolved will play a major role in determining whether Canada remains whole or breaks apart into two or more separate but economically linked states.

The roughly 7-million-strong Francophone population, concentrated in Quebec, has recently strengthened its language protections — to the great consternation of Anglophones and others. Quebec's language laws now virtually prohibit the use of English in public signage or the workplace. All children — excepting families in which both parents have been educated in English — must be educated in French. This stipulation is having a tremendous effect in strengthening the use of French in Quebec and reversing the effects of English domination. The 1986 census showed that 58 percent of Quebec Anglophones under the age of twenty-five were bilingual, compared to 19 percent of Francophones in the same age group (Dodge, 1992). New immigrants to Quebec must be schooled in French, and companies wishing to operate there must have a competency in French, even though a large portion of the population is Anglophone. There is growing opposition to bilingualism in some parts of Canada, but there is also much support for it — particularly in large urban centers such as Toronto. Most English Canadians are not bilingual, but many send their children to public-supported French immersion schools.

Within Quebec itself a fairly broad range of linguistic diversity is evident: from backwoods French to the street vernacular to high French, which is considered pretentious. The type of French one speaks can have a good deal of influence over one's political or business prospects. Although Quebec French is a distinct dialect of the language of the mother country and has been influenced by English, it nonetheless has far more in common with other Romance languages, such as Spanish, than with English. Both languages differ from English in the use of gendered nouns and both formal and informal second-person pronouns. Both languages are also richer in expressiveness than English, though they may lack the economy of English.

Throughout Canada, English, of course, remains by far

the dominant language, though it is giving way to bilingualism. Canadian government offices are officially bilingual, and many areas of Ontario and the Maritime provinces are designated bilingual.

Canadian English, unlike that in the United States, is spoken with a uniform accent across all regions, excepting Newfoundland, where the Gaelic heritage is still audible. Canadian English differs from American English only in very minor ways, such as a preference for British spellings. Typically, English word processing programs have Canadian dictionary options.

In working with Francophones, it is important to show sensitivity to the language issue and to try to speak French rather than assuming that business will be conducted in English. Often, bilingual Francophones will switch to English, without being asked to, if they see evidence of one's willingness to try speaking French, however poorly. The way in which language issues are handled in the workplace depends on a wide range of factors. Within Quebec, French is the normal language of business. Concessions are sometimes made for Anglophones, however, depending on the organization and the people involved.

In other parts of the country, government agencies and national associations are more likely to require full bilingualism in meetings than are corporations based outside of Quebec. For example, the federal government has formal policies stating that participants in meetings or teleconferences may speak in either French or English. All formal proceedings of government are translated, and all materials are available in both official languages. In some meetings, participants do speak in either language. More often, meetings are conducted in English only because, generally, Francophones are more skilled in English than Anglophones are in French. This practice is a constant source of irritation, particularly among the younger generation of Francophones. As one government manager pointed out, "We can be in a meeting where everyone is French and bilingual except for one unilingual

English speaker. What happens? All the Francophones speak English."

The language issue presents serious dilemmas when implementing group technologies, especially audio conferencing. For instance, simultaneous translation is very complicated to provide for satellite conferences because a separate channel must be dedicated for French and one for English. Also, providing for French on e-mail and group meeting facilities involves bilingual interfaces and ensuring that the system can support French vocabulary, including the accents. French without accent marks may be intelligible to Anglophones, but to Francophones it looks misspelled. All technical discussion and user documentation must be translated, as well, which is often more difficult than one would assume.

In terms of the relevance of language to regionalization, Canada's bilingual executives should have an important edge over their unilingual American counterparts in dealings with Mexican business, even if they don't speak Spanish. They already know the difficulties of bilingual communication and some strategies for overcoming them. And it is generally easier for a French-speaker to learn Spanish than for an English-only speaker. Since most French-Canadian business people speak English, Americans will find few language barriers to working in the French sector, especially if they show a sensitivity to the issue.

Context. High-context Francophones tend to show greater satisfaction with their work and lower turnover rates than low-context Anglophones. They prefer supervised, discrete tasks and greater direction. Documentation and information management are much more important to the Anglophones, due to their low-context orientation. Building and managing relationships is a key Francophone work activity. Like Mexicans, French-speakers tend to see more circumscribed horizons and are more reluctant to relocate from their French language nests and close circles of family and friends in Quebec.

While all generalizations are dangerous, the following

observations about context differences between English and French Canadians are usually more accurate than not:

- Francophones tend to be more influenced than Anglophones by their social group—friends, colleagues, and especially family.

- Francophones have greater affiliation needs because of distinctive family and group ties and because they are an ethnic minority.

- Anglophones place greater emphasis on individual competence and position.

- Francophones are more concerned about personal relationships. They want to know personal details about people: your family, friends, schools, and so on.

- Francophones tend to prefer to do business in casual, informal settings, as over a beer or a meal, and they'll often conclude a deal with a handshake.

- Anglophones are more formalistic. They tend to want to do business in office settings and prefer detailed, written contracts.

- Francophones are more likely to do a favor for someone out of personal loyalty than because they want to please a superior.

All the general differences between high-context and low-context cultures can guide Americans when dealing with French Canadians. The relationship with English Canada will be easier because of the greater similarities, but there are key differences Americans need to remember. In general, Americans are much less formal and reserved and come across as friendly but superficial to Canadians. The individuality and sense of competitiveness in Americans is more extreme than in most Canadians. And the very characteristics that are considered advantages in the United States—confidence and aggressiveness—may be disadvantages in international environ-

Table 9.1. Cultural Time Matrix.

	Mexico	USA	English Canada	French Canada
Task management	■ Polychronic	■ Monochronic	■ Monochronic	■ Polychronic
Time value	■ State of being	■ A commodity	■ A commodity	■ A state of being
Influences on present	■ Past	■ Future	■ Near future	■ Past
Orientation	■ Short-term	■ Short-term	■ Medium-term	■ Medium- to long-term

ments. Conversely, while Canadians may seem lower key and more restrained in an American context, these very characteristics may give Canadians a competitive edge in international environments.

The context should always be considered in implementing group technologies. Personal contact is more important to Francophones, for example, so more effort must be put into initial orientation meetings before resorting to such things as teleconferencing. Also subtle differences in the role of the written word in French and English Canada may mean that real-time communications such as audio and video conferencing or voice mail may be easier to implement than e-mail in Francophone environments.

Time. On the time dimension French Canadians tend to resemble their Mexican neighbors just as Americans resemble English Canadians. Table 9.1 presents a comparison of the three countries in the cultural aspects of time. Here is a list of important English versus French Canadian differences:

- French Canadians are more relaxed about deadlines. English Canadians, like Americans, regard time as a resource to be carefully managed.

- The French-speakers tend to be oriented more to the past than English-speakers, who are basically present- and future-oriented.

- The French are better able to adapt to frequent changes in plans and schedules. Their work and leisure lives tend to be more integrated than the English community, who tend to separate their business lives from family and friends.

There will be few problems between English Canadians and Americans on the time dimension. Both are monochronic and sequential-oriented. Canadians, however, are generally oriented to a longer-term view than Americans.

With regard to implementation of group technologies, the key differences are between English and French speakers. While there are always individual differences, Anglophones, particularly in Toronto, are more likely to want to be reachable anytime-anywhere and are more likely to want to be able to work around the clock. French-speaking Montrealers may want to work in the home, but only because doing so allows more leisure or family time. The sense of urgency that drives the demand for certain technologies, such as teleconferencing, may be felt less acutely in some parts of the country than others. Firms implementing e-mail across cultural lines need to establish clear guidelines so that people check their mail with similar frequency.

Power/Equality. Francophones bring a bit of their love for anarchy to the workplace — there's a strong tendency to respect everyone's right to his or her own form of individuality. English Canadians are more like the British in their respect for hierarchy and lines of authority. Money is likely to confer more status for Anglophones; professional, artistic, or literary achievements mean more to Francophones.

The choice over which language to use is often perceived as a power struggle. And because of broader political battles between Quebec and the rest of Canada, authority questions frequently acquire a political cast. These problems are less severe at the top management level, but they are pervasive in most business relationships.

Fairly minor power differences in the U.S.-Canadian relationship are similarly magnified by the historical perception of American domination and superiority. Many Canadians told us that Americans are too aggressive and insensitive, that they "don't take us seriously," that they "assume their way is the right way, or in fact, the only way." On the surface, Americans, with their informal, first-name approach to most relationships, seem more egalitarian than Canadians, at least within an environment of very similar cultures. In the workplace, English Canadians show greater respect and deference toward authority than Americans, and they follow hierarchical communication channels more readily. Canadians may well have a more difficult time dismantling their hierarchical business structures to engage more successfully in globalwork.

In their use of group technologies, Francophones may be more inclined than English Canadians to use systems like e-mail to jump hierarchical boundaries. There have been several documented cases, for example, of workers and middle managers not adopting video conferencing because the facilities were located in the executive floors and hence out of bounds. Companies implementing group technologies must consider the extent to which they want to encourage access or restrain it. Similarly, in promoting group technologies in English-speaking companies, great emphasis must be placed on having senior management set an example. And while top-down approaches to system design and implementation are unlikely to work in any environment, this is likely to be even more critical in a French-Canadian setting.

Information Flow.   French Canadians and English Canadians follow the classic patterns of high-context and low-context cultures for information flow. The Francophone lives contentedly in a sea of information kept current by a web of relationships; workflows are more circuitous and action chains more easily broken. The Anglophone's workflows are sequential and efficient, but information overload is a constant concern. In turbulent business times, Francophones could have an easier time adapting and flexing with the changes.

Few workflow problems should be expected between

Anglophones and Americans. Both prefer extensive text documentation and have similar approaches to linking and sequencing tasks. The one area of difference is that Canadians are more guarded about giving information than Americans, a habit that could produce some friction.

Technology applications for information sharing are very similar between the two countries. America's less expensive infrastructure gives it a short-lived edge in usage — the average telephone line in the United States, for example, carries twice as much traffic as Canadian lines, even though Canada has a slightly higher level of telephone line penetration. The problem for Canadians is not so much one of providing greater access to more information but finding ways to control information overload. While workers want access to the right information in the right forms (imaging and video conferencing have been constrained, for example, by telecommunication costs), more and more managers are complaining about not being able to get through their regular mail, trade publications, e-mail, and voice mail in a day. There is a tremendous need, then, for improved information management.

The Challenge to Canadian Work Cultures

Canadian work cultures are struggling to adapt to the same organizational changes that are reshaping the American workplace: corporate flattening, downsizing, middle-management layoffs, outsourcing, and a shift to customer service and revenue-generation functions. This shift has been particularly difficult in Canada because of the historical role of a relatively paternalistic and activist government — a government that has helped protect Canadian businesses from the sharpest edges of global or regional competition.

In the late 1980s there was growing concern about Canada's long-term competitiveness as unit labor costs were growing faster than in any other of the so-called Group of Seven major industrialized countries while productivity was falling. The MacDonald Royal Commission recommended free trade as a way of bringing about restructuring and adjustment in a manufacturing sector in which costs were too high for too small a market. Thus while the U.S.-Canada free-trade pact and NAFTA were sold to Canadians as a way of opening new foreign markets, many believe it was equally important for forcing Canadian business to become more efficient.

Unlike Americans, who overwhelmingly supported the lowering of U.S.-Canadian trade barriers, the majority of Canadians opposed the agreement. Given the disappearance of many manufacturing jobs in the recession that followed, the solid opposition to free trade expanded during the debate over NAFTA, which passed Parliament only because Canada's system of bloc voting on key economic and social issues enables the government to defy public opinion polls.

While most of the business and political elite supported NAFTA and regard globalization as an inevitability, they have not persuaded the greater public that closer U.S. and Mexican ties are in their best interests. In addition to blaming free trade for the southern migration of Canadian jobs, many Canadians fear that open competition with U.S. companies, to say nothing of Mexico's, will result in the weakening of Canada's generous social welfare system, which is one of the significant ways in which Canada distinguishes itself from the United States. As Canadian novelist Margaret Atwood says, "We would like to think we're about to get the best of both worlds — Canadian stability and a more caring society, as well as U.S. markets. But what if instead we get their crime rate, their health programs and gun laws, and they get our markets, or what's left of them?" (Hurtig, 1991, p. 256). While everyone agrees that some jobs have migrated south as a result of free trade, there are differences of opinion regarding the extent to which the global recession has made this inevitable. Proponents complain that "free trade is blamed for every sparrow that falls from the sky."

At least some of those Canadian sparrows have been spared, thanks to "Canadian content" guidelines in trade agreements on publishing and broadcasting and other "cultural vehicles." Even the Conservative Party, which is credited with reversing eighty years of Canadian economic protectionism by winning approval of the U.S.-Canada trade agreement and negotiating the NAFTA accord, has maintained that certain infrastructure institutions are not open to trade negotiation—such as telecommunications carriers, which must maintain 80 percent Canadian ownership. Even so, more than 60 percent of all Canadian reading material is imported, mostly from the United States and France, and there is serious concern in some quarters about direct satellite broadcasting and a "Death Star" satellite system that will deliver hundreds of American cable TV channels to Canadian homes.

While the Conservative-led governments of recent years have moved Canada well along the path of privatization, many "crown companies" still exist and the government still plays a major role in setting industrial policy. Government and business partnerships will thus continue to be a prominent feature of the economic landscape. For example, the Ontario government has announced a telecommunications strategy that ties major provincial economic policies to a series of infrastructure and industry initiatives. And both the province and the federal government have plans for networks that parallel the U.S. National Research and Education Network.

In the global marketplace, Canada's performance remains competitive, but increasing concern has been expressed from a number of fronts about its vulnerability. According to economist Michael Porter (1991), Canada is at an economic crossroads: it has achieved one of the world's highest standards of living, along with a generous and socially progressive welfare state, but the source of its economic prosperity is at risk. Canada's rich natural resource endowments, its proximity to the United States, and its history of insulation from international competition have been major contributors to the country's success thus far. But industry is now undergoing rapid structural change and is showing signs of strain in adapting to an increasingly competitive environment. Porter focuses on low productivity growth, high unit labor costs, unemployment, and a lag in investments in upgrading skills and technology. Canadian research spending, for instance, has been about one-third that of Germany, Japan, and South Korea.

While domestic-owned companies are the leaders in revenues and profits, foreign-owned firms lead in exports—the source of greatest growth. Those firms are heavily dominated by autos and, especially, natural resources, which accounted for 46 percent of Canada's total exports in 1989. Porter (1991) notes that Canada has few internationally competitive machinery or service industries, and there is a deteriorating trade balance outside the resource sector.

Given the decline of certain sectors in the Canadian economy due to the recession and the loss of jobs to lower-cost producers in other countries, Canadian leaders are attempting to capitalize on the country's strengths. Historically the country has been an exporter of forestry products, wheat, metals, and energy products. Over half of Canada's machinery and equipment is imported. Increasingly attention is focusing on the high-tech information economy sectors as the source of national competitive advantage for the nation's well-educated workforce. Telecommunications, for example, employs more than 300,000 Canadians, which is more than the number of people working in traditional industries such as automobiles, banking, and pulp and paper.

Part of the strategy for global success must be to capitalize on these strengths while increasing the sophistication of the natural resource sector, reducing economic barriers, and promoting education and R&D. Canadian subsidiaries are looking actively for global markets for products and services. And governments at both the provincial and federal levels are working to enhance training and R&D and to promote improvements in the telecommunications infrastructure. Northern Telecom—an $8 billion (U.S.) company and, until recently, one of Canada's most successful corporations—has cited international markets as the key to its success. Spar Aerospace, Newbridge, and Lavalin are among many other Canadian high-tech companies with an international presence.

One of Canada's greatest strengths in meeting the challenges of globalization is the nation's highly educated and technologically sophisticated workforce. It'll be useful to elaborate on similarities and differences between Canadian and U.S. workers.

The Canadian and American worker look more alike than not—excepting the fact that 37 percent of Canadian workers belong to labor unions—well above the U.S. level. As a result, there is less discrepancy between high and low income earners than in the United States, and there are also more frequent strikes.

In terms of training, Canadians rely more heavily on public postsecondary educational institutions and spend less time in corporate training programs, so they owe their professional identities more to their universities than to their employers. This means that functional turf battles are not quite so strong as in the United States.

Similarly, Canadian corporate cultures are not significantly different from those in the United States. The differences that do exist are ones of degree more than substance and, moreover, are shaped by Canadians' somewhat more distrustful view of the private sector. Also, Canada's economic development has tended to favor large, family-owned business enterprises, while Americans have favored the small business sector. As a result, a higher proportion of Canadians work in these paternalistic oligopolies, where there is generally a greater sense of protection.

Most Canadian companies, like American firms, have a corporate culture that values individual over group performance and competition over collaboration, although this tendency may be more muted in Canada. Inevitably the tensions between the French and English communities come into play in the corporate culture. French workers resent taking orders from English managers, especially when working across distances. French branches of English companies prefer to develop their own solutions to local problems.

In the interface between Canada's French- and English-speaking cultures, workers have acquired invaluable experience in negotiating cross-cultural boundaries. This experience should serve them well in the imposing cultural challenges of the regional and global workplace.

Strategies for Cultural Learning

Here are some strategies suggested by Canadian executives:

- Canadians are offended by an aggressive approach. Plan extra time to discuss things in a civil manner, over a period of time.

- Canadians appreciate a recognition of their regional differences — beyond the obvious French-English divisions.

- Feminism is more advanced in Canada than in the United States. Expect to work closely with many female decision makers.

- Map the lines of authority in companies you are working with and respect them.

- Plan to accommodate Canada's need for consensus in decision making.

- Maintain some formality in relationships. The casual American approach can be more of a hindrance than a help in making Canadians open up.

- Show sensitivity to the language issue. The extent to which one must operate in both languages varies substantially from organization to organization. Within Quebec and the federal government, a knowledge of French is crucial.

- Recognize the linguistic realities when developing electronic communication protocols. Electronic systems must support the French language with appropriate accents, for instance.

- Understand the ways in which differences in cultural values — family, relationship, authority — translate into the workplace.

- Canadians are less direct than Americans, so learn to read between the lines.

CANADIAN TEAMWORK
AND TECHNOLOGY

As with everything else in Canada, the English- and French-speaking business teams have their own unique ways of supporting team process. The Anglophones may resemble Americans, but the small yet distinct cultural differences about trust, competitiveness, and respect for authority reveal themselves in teamwork. In the context of North American regionalization, the French Canadians have much in common with Mexicans: both are driven in teamwork by the high value placed on interpersonal relationships. In the following look at how two Canadian teams negotiated the various phases of the Team Performance Model, we try to give a flavor of the major strengths and weaknesses that Canadians bring to the challenge of regional teamwork.

In general, the average Canadian employee is working far harder and with more fear for his survival than in the past. While recognizing the need to make better use of staff and work through more responsive multidisciplinary teams, this environment is more conducive to survival-of-the-fittest competition than it is to collaborative models. Most organizations, of course, pay little more than lip service to collaboration. Most workers and managers do not know how to get out of the traditionally adversarial business relationships and into team learning and group brainstorming.

Groupware has been a help, but Canadians have had less access than Americans to information technologies due to the higher costs. A 1992 study for the federal Department of Communications (DOC) found that fewer Canadian than American companies reported using the entire range of communication technologies available, with the exception of cellular (Anguo & Cukier, 1992). Companies still rely on traditional voice networks: WATs, 800 services, and tie lines. Fewer Canadian firms use T-1 lines (dedicated phone lines capable of transmitting voice and data at high speeds) than American companies of similar size, the DOC study revealed. Regulatory changes and the introduction of long-distance competition have begun to make new digital services, such as Centrex Data (a more sophisticated service: switched 56 kilobits per second), available only in the past two years. Despite this lag, most Canadian companies recognize that telecommunications is critical to their competitive advantage and are building the necessary infrastructure for a broader range of applications. They emphasize better network connectivity in particular, because most professional workers in Canada now have access to personal computers, and an increasing number of them are networked.

Face-to-face meetings remain important for exchanging information, but Canadians still need to improve their skills in conducting effective meetings. Companies that invest thousands of dollars to bring people together often overlook the fact that the participants are the most important resource. It is not uncommon, especially in government, for meeting organizers to gather as many as three hundred people from all over the country, at government expense, and then provide no facilitation: no well-thought-out outcome and agendas, no good ways to get participation from the audience, and little thought to follow-up.

Simple meeting support tools, such as PC projector systems and electronic whiteboards, are available. A handful of corporate and academic sites have even installed sophisticated meeting support rooms on an experimental basis. But most meetings in Canada still rely primarily on low-tech tools like flip charts and overhead projectors.

Team Model Review

Here we focus on two Canadian teams that we studied in depth. Both reveal common cultural responses to team development as plotted on the Team Performance Model (Figure 9.1). English Canadians and French Canadians will both have many trust issues that continuously color team functions

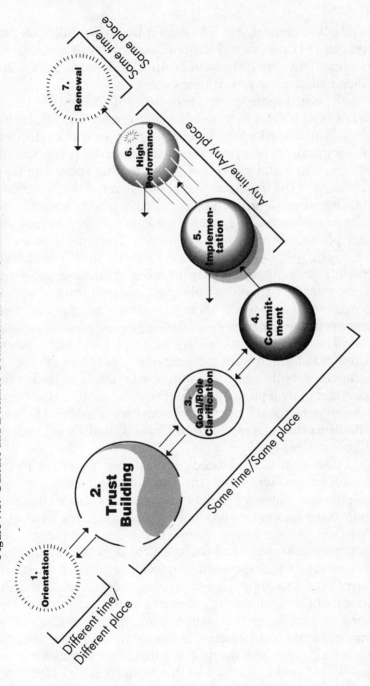

Figure 9.1. Culture and Distance Considerations for Canadian Business Teams.

in all subsequent stages. The Anglophones are culturally mistrustful and cautious and are particularly wary of business; the Francophones are distrustful of Anglophones in general, and Canadians are wary of Americans.

The first team, from a firm we'll call Western Financial Services, is a cross-functional team composed of fifteen English Canadians located in one western province. All were senior managers of a dispersed financial services organization; all were living and working within one time zone. The team consisted of the managers, a regional director, and functional staff members representing sales, asset quality control, and human resources. They met once a month face to face and used phone, fax, and e-mail in between. They had been a team for over a year and had invested heavily in a formal team training program when they first began to have problems. They provide a good example of a dispersed team in a small geographical area working on marketing strategies and work process improvements.

The second team, which we'll call Canadian Consolidated, was formed from merging four companies in order to compete in both local and international markets. Each company had its own product line, but because each company had a different regional focus they seldom competed head to head. The firms that merged to form Consolidated varied tremendously in size.

Canadian Consolidated's central staff worked with the product managers from the individual divisions, which roughly corresponded to the old companies. Once each year there was a face-to-face product manager's meeting that lasted two days. This meeting reviewed the state of the market, technological trends, and the status of projects in individual companies. It was also used to develop a plan for the subsequent year. In addition, the team used audio teleconferencing on a monthly basis to exchange information and make decisions on specific projects — new marketing strategies, for instance, or product launches. Some of these teleconferences were well organized: agenda and topics for discussion were distributed well in advance so that team members could consult locally before participating in the conference call. In other cases, however, this was not done.

When Consolidated was originally created, the internal information systems were overhauled to ensure that everyone could communicate. All members of the team had access to e-mail and had sufficient computer literacy to exchange messages requesting or offering information. This skill proved useful given the differences in time zones. Electronic mail was used principally as an alternative to memos or phone calls or to distribute agendas. There was less use of it for group information exchange, polling, or decision making. There was, however, no use at all of computer conferencing.

Orientation Stage.   The Western Financial Services team had a clear purpose: increase market share. Since they were within one company with a defined service role, they were able to complete the orientation stage at a distance through a well-written memo by the leader. Everyone could easily feel membership and see their personal fit. Canadian Consolidated, however, with its membership from multiple companies, never resolved the orientation stage. Each division's team members felt their principal loyalty to their division's purpose — the national perspective ranked a distant second. Little time or effort was invested in orienting new members to the team or its organizational objectives. The team was continuously plagued with trying to maintain its identity, a common challenge posed by distance.

Building Trust.   During the first few months of the Western Financial team's existence, the team leader sensed a withholding of spontaneity that he felt would never be resolved on its own because of the distances between members. Thus in this early stage he had the team go through intensive team-building exercises using a family metaphor. This was the turning point. It provided the team with a framework and common language that they frequently used as future problems arose. It allowed the leader to raise and resolve sensitive issues at a distance. And it also helped develop an appreciation of the different functional points of view. The team resolved to help each other despite the distances, and they also committed themselves to airing and resolving conflicts on the spot. The telephone was to be their medium for discussing sensitive issues. To avoid miscommunication, they agreed not to use the impersonal e-mail system. They were unanimous in their assessment that the bonds they developed could not have come about without the team-building exercises and without well-run, fully participative, face-to-face meetings.

Canadian Consolidated, on the other hand, experienced chronic pain during the trust-building phase. Some members felt that the largest division—based in Toronto where the Consolidated headquarters were located—enjoyed more influence than it deserved. One former team member noted that the other divisions often banded together to counter Toronto's influence. Most of the Consolidated group agreed that the face-to-face meeting was important for building relationships. "That is where you really learned who you could trust," said one team member. Some felt that the teleconferences were useful, though somewhat guarded. All felt that the best forum for discussing these trust issues was a face-to-face meeting over a beer. Trust was further complicated by the language issue. The team language was English, and few concessions were made even to French-speaking members with less than adequate English skills. The only exception to the English-only rule was when Consolidated's central staff people were working directly with French-speaking members on projects for the Quebec market. Technology clearly had a positive effect on this team by promoting frequent communications between the once-a-year meetings.

Goal/Role Clarification. The Western Financial team's team-building sessions helped them to develop a set of shared assumptions about goals and strategies centered on increasing market share. Roles were decided in the team's monthly, two-day, face-to-face meetings. The members' interdependency mainly revolved around the management of information—a common challenge compounded by distance. Different members took responsibility for tracking, developing, and filtering information. A critical leader role was filtering and prioritizing corporate information as well as translating it from "administrivia" so that it was palatable to dispersed sites.

On the Consolidated team, roles were decided between the constituent companies rather than between individuals. Smaller divisions tended to be more independent and innovative — often because they had only one or two principal customers to be concerned with or because it was easier to implement solutions on a small scale. At the same time, some of the smaller companies regretted there was not more collaboration on large-scale projects — such as joint advertising campaigns — that they could not initiate on their own.

Consolidated team members openly recognized the difficulty of putting aside their division roles to represent the interests of the cross-Canada team. The team relied heavily on audio conferencing for decision making and used e-mail for routine information exchange. The extent to which the participants felt engaged depended largely on the character of the team leader. In some cases, the leader acted as a "first among equals"; in other cases, members felt deprived of any significant role in decision making.

Commitment. The Western Financial Services team had little trouble arriving at a shared vision or coming to terms with resource allocation. The consensus-oriented decision-making process, however, proved troublesome. This was a critical problem, since experience had shown that implementation can be undermined when consensus is lacking. The members felt that face-to-face meetings were far preferable to audio conferences for working out the decision-making process at this stage.

Decision-making processes were a major stumbling block for the Consolidated team, as well. Most members indicated that the commitment to consultation appeared to vary with the leadership — which made the system as a whole untrustworthy. Some leaders appeared to consult extensively on most issues, even using subcommittees to ensure discussion. This strategy made it easier to reach consensus when a decision had to be made by the whole group. But at other times, it was felt, the decision had already been made and the consultation was only window dressing. Not surprisingly, the team leaders who put the greatest effort into consultation with dispersed divisions had an easier time achieving consensus — largely because the members were better informed and believed they had contributed to the decision. These leaders made extensive use of audio- and video-conferencing technology as an important adjunct to face-to-face meetings to build rapport with distant sites.

Implementation.   For the Western Financial Services team, the greatest implementation challenge was maintaining disciplined execution of the team plan at each distributed site. The leader spent most of his time between meetings coaching the sites by phone and e-mail. During the monthly face-to-face meetings they made extensive use of flip charts for keeping track of breakthroughs, action items, and lists of things they couldn't do. They also kept electronic meeting notes. To keep in contact, all members were equipped with e-mail facilities at home. They also made extensive use of audio conferencing to share progress. The other notable support for good implementation was the team's information management system. Thanks to agreements, filtering systems, and rapid circulation of key information, they never felt constrained by lack of information or information overload.

The Consolidated team reflected few of the differences between French and English Canada, since the largest division included both Quebec and Ontario but had only one representative. Within that division, there was recognition that implementation strategies that work well in English Canada may not work in Quebec. In general, the Quebecois were felt to be more creative and independent. Thus the monthly audio conferences were a way of sharing implementation ideas, not to nail down one strategy or get consensus. Some members noted, ironically, that the teleconferences were not as fruitful as they should have been. As agendas and materials were not distributed in advance, they didn't have time to prepare their responses. In Quebec the French members made efforts to meet face to face periodically. Formal lunches, complete with wine, offered frequent occasions to discuss major product developments or marketing planning.

High Performance.   The Western Financial Services team periodically reached the high-performance stage both together and at a distance. They attributed this success to the early team-building work, as well as the availability of the same technology at each site. Also, they were encouraged to use the technology to maintain communication, resolve conflicts, and rethink decisions during implementation. Phone and e-mail were the two technologies most valuable to support this stage.

Though groups at the provincial level may have achieved it on occasion, the Consolidated team never reached high performance at the national level.

Renewal.   The Western Financial team leader paid continuous attention to celebrating all the small successes of the team. This ongoing approach to renewal seemed better suited to the team than periodic acknowledgments or team reviews.

At Consolidated there was no specific strategy for renewal. The members simply attended to it along the way. The most dramatic renewal came after the firm went through a fundamental reorganization aimed at centralizing decision making and strengthening the corporate culture through an energetic marketing campaign that raised the company's profile. This campaign has had significant payoffs internally as well, as employees are now identifying with the new company rather than their individual divisions. Also, an ambitious orientation and training program is encouraging employees to identify more strongly with Consolidated than with their separate divisions (which have been renamed).

Strategies for Team Facilitation

The following tips and strategies about teaming in Canada were suggested by Canadian executives:

- Team-building exercises are a profitable investment even for teams that are relatively close geographically—especially if the exercises provide both a language and a framework that can be used during the life of the team.

- Nuances of communication may be lost with electronic support tools. Well-established feedback mechanisms are critical to connect distant members to the leader and each other in order to clarify questions fast.

- When controversial decisions are communicated to distant sites, don't assume there is agreement just because no one voices opposition. Build in a response system, such as audio conferences.

- Team leaders using electronic support tools must work even harder to build trust. Some face-to-face contact is always needed, especially for diverse teams. If your team meets only once a year, use a good portion of that time to build bonds. Don't make the mistake of focusing only on tasks.

- Where reward structures are tied to group performance, differences in language and culture become less divisive.

- Group memory is always an issue—even more so in an organization where staff are moved through roles. Who knows what?

- Reduce reinventing the wheel and build a clear sense of the benefits of belonging to the team.

- Encourage sharing of gossip and ideas, and preserve memory of the best ideas.

Information Technology

Canadian teams do not use work support technology in ways that are substantially different from their American counterparts. Both need to pay greater attention to "soft" issues such as common goals, leadership, interaction and involvement, open communication, attention to process, and feedback. For both Canadian and American teams, the irony is that as technology becomes easier the organizational issues get tougher. Moreover, the sheer volume of work and information overload that many people face is leaving them less time for relationship building, which may be more critical in Canada than in the United States. In the end, face-to-face meetings may remain the most effective form of groupware for building the relationships and trust needed for effective teamwork.

Although Canada and the United States are similar in terms of market penetration of PCs and modems, there remain major differences in the availability and pricing of communication services. This, in turn, influences the application of communication technologies. In Canada there are approximately 4.3 million personal computers in business and another 1.3 million in homes (International Data Corp., 1991). The country actually has a higher percentage (51.4 percent) of digital switched lines than the United States but a lower level of utilization (U.S. Department of Commerce, 1991).

The 1992 Department of Communications study, which contrasted telecommunication users in Canada and the United States, revealed some interesting differences. In general, Canadian businesses lagged behind those in the states in their use of telecommunication technologies generally and group technologies in particular. Video conferencing in Canada, for example, lagged significantly behind the United States, where it accounts for about 50 percent of the teleconferencing market. In contrast, video accounts for less than 20 percent of the teleconferencing market in Canada, though audio conferencing is common. And while Canada is considered a world leader in distance education, most institutions rely on relatively simple group communications—either broadcast TV or print and audio conferences. Few Canadian companies use telecommunications to support training. The above information was reported by Anguo and Cukier (1992).

While the overall level of technology diffusion is uneven, some Canadian companies are considered world leaders in their use of telecommunications and group technologies. Royal Lepage, a real estate company working with Microtel Pacific Research, Northern Telecom, and others has developed a working, on-line multimedia real estate system, one of the first in the world. Ryerson Polytechnic University, working with Roeger Communications and IBM, is one of the first sites to test multimedia communications using the Packetized Automatic Routing Information System (PARIS) standard. And Canada's cellular penetration is one of the highest in the world. The following paragraphs review Canada's experience with other key groupware technologies.

Data Sharing.   Most large corporations support a wide range of text and even graphic file transfers between groups. Combined with the advent of shared data-base technology, different parts of a company now are able not only to gain access to up-to-date information—they can also share their best practices, even across international boundaries. Instead of reinventing the wheel, users throughout the organization can access a colleague's product specifications as needed. The impact of this kind of sharing in the organization depends, of course, on the extent to which people contribute as well as access information.

Workgroup Computing.   The rise of local-area networks has created a potential for true workgroup computing, which can eliminate unproductive, redundant activities and improve the quality of work, decisions, and communication flow. Many organizations, however, are still using networks only for sharing software data-base files and peripherals and for sending e-mail. Perhaps this is because computer users do not usually feel at ease with group computing until they have mastered simple applications such as word processing and spreadsheets.

Fax and E-Mail.   Facsimile use has exploded in Canada as most companies have stand-alone fax machines as well as networks for distribution of documents. E-mail has not fared so well. Though most companies have access to both private and public e-mail systems, many systems still cannot talk to each other. Many large organizations are only now getting staff on-line. In the academic community, there are between

50,000 and 100,000 users of Internet. Few use filters or e-mail management systems.

Computer Conferencing.   This technology is used mostly in the nonprofit and education sectors, although some corporate and government applications exist. Generally, users will not adopt computer conferencing until they are comfortable with e-mail, which is still not universally available.

Voice Mail.   Voice mail has taken Canada by storm. Together with interactive voice response, it is one of the fastest-growing technologies. As in the United States, many users no longer answer their phones or engage in conversations but use the technology to exchange messages.

Cellular.   Canada has the highest penetration of cellular technology in North America — perhaps because of the early move to duopoly with only two carriers allowed into the market. Also, the service is comparatively inexpensive, given the high cost of conventional services.

Screen Sharing.   Screen sharing is popular in specialized segments — particularly for developing collaborative systems and as a means of providing systems user support — but it is not reaching its potential. Again, this may be because screen sharing is a second-level electronic communications tool that will become more accessible once users have mastered e-mail.

Audio and Video Conferencing.   Surveys since 1985 report a steady growth both in numbers of companies using audio conferencing and in their extent of usage. More companies are using scheduled and ad hoc conference calls to link team members — some because they need to, others simply because such technology has become available. At the same time, there is evidence that at least some companies are beginning to use voice-messaging features, such as broadcast, to perform tasks they might previously have done through a series of phone calls or an audio conference.

Video conferencing has grown exponentially in recent years as higher-bandwidth service has become widespread. Most financial institutions and a wide range of other organizations are using video conferencing, often to link with team members in an American head office.

RULES OF THUMB
AND PITFALLS

NAFTA will live up to its promise only if these two neighbors take the time to drop their stereotypical views of each other, learn about the differences in their cultures, and move toward greater equality. Here are some rules of thumb and pitfalls that may be useful for building that relationship.

Rules of Thumb

- Respect cultural differences between English and French-speaking Canadians. A One Canada business strategy won't work.

- Americans must recognize that Canadians represent a unique culture, not merely an American suburb.

- Government intervention is not necessarily welcomed in Canada, but it is more accepted than in the United States. There is a broad range of government/industry interactions. Find out how the role of Canadian government may affect your business dealings in a positive or negative way.

- Remember that Canada has profound regional differences and that most of its regions resent the influence of Ottawa. What works in Quebec may not work elsewhere.

- Blend business processes to take both competitiveness and cooperation into account. Canadians are less overtly competitive than Americans and find the usual American focus on competition aggressive.

- Take into account the Canadians' relative distrust of the private sector. Give them lots of room to assure themselves the business deal is truly in the best interest of Canadians and all employees.

- Bilingualism is essential if you want to work in Quebec. Don't assume Francophones should speak English, even if they can.

- Learn to listen. Begin by collecting information about the group you are dealing with: rank, status, roles, and so on. Give them an opportunity to talk about themselves. Don't assume you know what they need or want. Canadians like to be consulted. And remember: it is not always obvious who will make decisions.

Pitfalls

- Don't underestimate the strength of unionized workers.

- Be sensitive to the implications of human and minority rights legislation.

- Avoid humor or examples about sex, violence, the military, and references to politics.

- Don't overestimate the similarities between Canada and the United States.

- Don't assume relationships exist; you have to build them.

- Don't assume that the white male in the room is always the decision maker.

- Don't assume that Canadians will necessarily admire and follow the American example.

TEN

The United Nation of America: An Outside-In View of Distance and Diversity Within the United States

Cultural diversity has never been a stranger to the United States, nor have the challenges of distance. In a sense, the entire history of this nation has been an exercise in the creation of a uniquely American salad bowl of cultures — and the expansion of that identity across distant geographical and ideological horizons.

The United States' historical experience with diversity should stand it in good stead for meeting the challenge it faces today: the adaptation to a new tide of cultural complexity and economic competition that are staggering in their potential for positive and/or negative impact. Challenges confront the nation from all levels of human diversity: physical, social, professional/functional, even spiritual. (This last we will leave for others to explore.) And the adaptations will likewise have to come from all levels of American society: from local to national, from public to private.

Diversity is not the only major challenge confronting the American business environment. Just yesterday, it seems, the United States had unrivaled economic power, strong labor unions, seemingly never-ending access to wealth for the middle class, and a choice of well-paying jobs for most workers. Now, the U.S. workforce from CEOs to factory workers is dazed and bewildered by the fundamental changes caused by the fault lines described in Chapter One. Fragmentation of the workforce is causing an insecurity crisis among middle and upper-class populations not seen since the days of the Great Depression. Wages for low-skilled work will continue to fall and new jobs requiring advanced technical skills will increase—a shift that will ripple through communities and families supported by old working environments and our school systems, which will need to prepare more of this generation with advanced knowledge and skills. It is no longer enough to have the will to work. You must also be well educated and possess good technical skills.

So far, most Americans don't really understand the irreversible trends caused by the global economy. We still debate protectionism and blame unfair trade practices of other countries. Yet the answers to creating new jobs and continuing our high standard of living lie within our borders. The changes have come fast, and the response to them will be slow. But the challenges need to be specifically addressed by government and business alike to develop the new choices and support the new values and programs that must replace those that no longer serve us.

The United States holds a leadership position among the other advanced economies in the development and use of technology in the workplace and is a pioneer in figuring out how to support work at a distance. The installed base of personal computers, e-mail systems, local area networks, and advanced network applications such as client server data bases and groupware still continues to outpace other countries, although Western Europe and Asia are instituting more technology development and use at a quicker pace. People in the United States tend to be enthusiastic about new technologies, but their optimistic character often leads them to see the benefits of new tools and ideas long before carefully considering what some of the untoward consequences could be — particularly over the long run. Some commentors such as Neil Postman are concerned that the United States has too quickly and comprehensively adopted computer technology and that Americans are coming to believe that technological innovation is synonymous with human progress — a hypothesis he rejects vehemently and considers dangerous to the well-being of the United States (Postman, 1992, p. 117). All things considered, it is likely that both large and small companies in the United States will continue to push the envelope of technology in their quest for continued efficiency and competitiveness. The culture of the United States workplace will increasingly evolve to incorporate values and behaviors around technology, and those unable or unwilling to acculturate will find themselves less desirable to the workforce.

The United States is leading the way in experimenting with new forms of working at a distance, from telecommuting to nomadic computing. The driving forces to explore this option originate from diverse sources. They include the need to create more responsive and flexible organizations, lower office space costs, increase productivity, move workers closer to customers and support mobility, attract skilled workers, and decrease environmental pollution — to name a few of the important ones. The rapid evolution in types, functionality, and installation of technology tools both drives and fuels the capacity to support a dispersed and distributed workforce. The rapid evolution of smaller and faster tools and the innovations in software will bring the promise of networked nomadic workers to a commonplace reality soon. Some are predicting the feasibility of nomadic video conferencing by the end of the century, although compelling uses are still elusive. It is forecast that about 40 percent of corporations with extensive fieldwork will automate these workers by the late 1990s.

Pilot projects are starting up in many of the large American companies to explore the issues and to discover the best strategies and tools and new corporate policies to support these anytime/anyplace workers and telecommuters. This future workspace, with all its fragmentation, requires a very different mind-set and set of practices than the traditional office. Questions such as who pays for the setup of the home office or the vehicle, maintains the tools, and provides insurance are key policy decisions. Will the early productivity gains reported by pioneering experiments be sustained over time, as the novelty wears off or as different types of workers telecommute? What are the criteria for selection of jobs and people to spin off and make mobile? What about career advancement for those working primarily remotely or part time? American businesses will discover some of the answers to these distant work challenges from the real pioneering experiences now underway.

The U.S. business community is essential in meeting these challenges, for the impacts on business already are monumental. The question is not whether we should deal with the challenges but how. How can the United States put its growing knowledge about diversity to best advantage—not only dealing with the diversity of our own citizens but learning to be supervised by foreign-born managers of the increasing number of foreign-owned businesses? How will we respond to the Indian manager, the Swedish manager, and the British manager with their different ways? How can we apply our cutting-edge communication technologies to the challenges of a workplace characterized by a babble of languages, cultures, conflicting worldviews, and differing attitudes about work itself? How can we make sense—and progress and profit—out of what looks to many like chaos?

More than most cultures, people in the United States have learned—intellectually at least—to place a high value on human diversity. We know that multiculturalism is enriching and synergistic: it adds up to more than the sum of its parts.

We know all this in our heads. Now we are trying to learn at a more visceral level. The challenge is intimidating, but the rewards are easily worth the struggle. In this chapter we explore the national dimensions of the distance and diversity of social and work cultures in the United States and how they relate to teamwork, indicating throughout some strategies for turning them to positive ends in the business environment.

THE UNITED STATES:
A MICROCOSM
OF GLOBAL DIVERSITY

Let's drop in for a visit at the headquarters of the hypothetical UNA Corporation, a U.S.-based energy firm that's in the midst of a process that is increasingly common in U.S. companies, large and small: learning to leverage diversity. UNA decided it had better examine seriously the problems and opportunities of diversity after receiving overwhelming evidence through a confidential employee survey that its workers felt prejudice was rife throughout the company. After an outside diversity consultant spent a week persuading top management officials that the process of analysis and change could only come from within the company, a series of small, representative, multicultural teams were formed within and across the major divisions to explore the issues and make recommendations to top management for the next step.

"No time for coffee," said Margaret, as she breezed past her secretary. "Somehow I've wound up as chair of this new diversity team, and they'll just sit around and gossip until I get there."

"So how come you always get stuck with these

things?" asked Rick, her secretary, handing her a list of urgent voice-mail messages.

"Just lucky, I guess. That's what everybody said when I got promoted. No, the truth is nobody else wanted it and somebody has to do it. Guess I'd better take a minute to glance at my e-mail before I go to the meeting."

Entering e-mail, she saw she had thirty-seven new messages since 5 P.M. the day before. She felt that nauseated feeling she had every morning now when she opened her mail. She knew there would be more messages than she could possibly respond to—and most of them would be worthless. Scrolling through the list she noted an urgent message from Bob about an important deadline he had missed yesterday. This can't wait, she decided, reaching for the phone.

Margaret winced and her shoulders tensed as the phone rang three times and Bob's electronic voice came over the line. Damn, she thought, you can never get anybody when it's crucial. Now we'll play electronic tag all day.

When she got to the meeting room, most of the team was waiting for her. By the way that they muffled a chuckle when she entered the room she guessed the conversation had been intended for male ears only. Anna, the bright young supervisor from operations, she noticed, wasn't there again. The only Latin American on the team, Anna was often assigned to swing shifts and had trouble making regular meetings.

Margaret took a seat next to Tony, who was still miffed about her promotion. "Let's get this going," he said, showing a little irritation at her late arrival. "Maybe if we hurry we can get through it before the chief drops in. It's impossible to talk openly about these things when he's here."

The meeting proceeded with a discussion of the evaluation tool. Supervisors from accounting and sales gave *their ideas, making some good points about the value of anonymity, and Margaret listened attentively. Then Mr. Wong, the liaison from Hong Kong, began to speak. Margaret noticed that some members' eyes were wandering toward the windows, and even her own notes were turning into funny faces. She'd known Henry Wong for years, and she valued his intelligence. But after all this time she still had trouble following his sometimes strange syntax and heavy accent. She strained to pay closer attention. . . .*

Margaret's first hour at the office on this inauspicious day illustrates a number of the more common diversity issues that U.S. businesses are struggling with every day:

■ *Negative gender and ethnic stereotypes:* The notion that successful women, especially women of color, are unfairly favored due to unwritten affirmative action goals is still a pervasive attitude — despite all the evidence to the contrary. In the actual case from which the illustration was drawn, "Margaret" is an MIT graduate in computer science. She was assigned to head the diversity team purely on the basis of her competence and interest in the subject. Nonetheless, like many women and minorities in the corporate workplace, she must constantly be on guard against assumptions of favoritism, and she senses that there is always an invisible wall — if not an invisible ceiling — between her and her male colleagues. Productivity on both sides of the wall suffers as a consequence.

■ *The persistence of old cultural values:* Top management's best intentions don't always have good results. In this case, the boss is a leader as well as a manager who has worked tirelessly to promote a deep appreciation of diversity. Though he believed it would demonstrate support if he joined the team and was an active participant, it had the opposite effect. Other members were not prepared to deal with him as an equal because the company's oft-repeated commitment to a more open, cross-function, cross-role style of communications was not yet believable to line managers accustomed to the hierarchical values. Such changes cannot happen overnight. Most employees will continue to operate under the old rules, values, rituals, and beliefs that worked for so long until it is unambiguously clear that top management has discarded them.

■ *Linguistic diversity*: Henry Wong speaks English with an accent and occasionally mixed syntax—a considerable achievement for a native Chinese speaker. But Henry's achievement meant nothing compared to his failure to speak impeccable English. Moreover, some accents are considered respectable and others are not. As more highly skilled foreign professionals participate in the U.S. workforce through temporary or permanent assignments, this issue is apt to become ever more serious.

■ *Information overload and unfriendly technology*: Groupware is designed to support communication, but at best it is unnatural and at worst it creates dysfunctional relationships. The minute someone needs urgent, two-way communication, as Margaret did, the popular store-and-forward electronic messaging systems begin to look more like obstacles than supports. These systems have also contributed to information gluts that are a particular problem in a low-context culture like the United States. Adapting to the technology available, learning what to use and when to use it—and, ultimately, demanding better tools—remains a major challenge of the diversified, distributed American workforce.

Each of these issues is just a small part of the changing nature of U.S. social and work cultures and how they deal with the stubborn persistence of stereotypes. These stereotypes stand in the way of genuine understanding and collaboration. And most people in the United States remain imprisoned by them to one degree or another.

The fact remains that stereotypes are not entirely without foundation. As a leader of a multicultural group in a large

U.S. company told us: "Stereotypes can't be applied un-
critically to individuals, but it is also a mistake to ignore their
basic cultural validity. The more one works internationally
within our company, the more one realizes — with some surprise — that people often live up to their stereotypes. It may
not be politically correct to acknowledge this, but it is reality."

Perhaps it is. But stereotypes are a narrow slice of reality
that distorts the larger and more meaningful picture. Many of
the ethnic minorities that we interviewed felt depersonalized
by the subtle and explicit remarks that lump all African Americans, or all Japanese, into one homogeneous category. They
want to be considered as individuals first and members of
ethnic groups second, if that.

It's important to help people become aware of their
prejudices and stereotypes and how they play out in the
workplace. People in the United States often try to abstract
the situation and ignore the person. While understanding
abstract differences between cultures is important, seeing how
these differences manifest themselves in individuals is vital.
Businesses need to provide everybody with basic diversity
training. But training programs vary greatly in quality, and
even the best of them provide only partial answers.

People in the United States have an honest tendency to
think they don't have these problems and that people know
how to learn interculturally because the United States is so
multiracial. This, however, is not necessarily the case.

The continued stereotyping will be increasingly harmful
in view of the fact that people of color and immigrants will
account for 43 percent of the new entrants to the workforce between 1985 and 2000 (Jamieson and O'Mara, 1991).
The lack of penetration of African Americans and Latin
Americans into the upper echelons of business is of particular concern, since changing attitudes in a corporate culture
starts at the top. The same applies to the ongoing trend of
women moving into the workforce and up the corporate ladder. It is one of the most significant shifts workers in the
United States have experienced over the last three decades.
Women will have accounted for two-thirds of new entrants to

the labor force between 1985 and 2000 (Jamieson and O'Mara, 1991), by which time they will constitute half the total workforce.

Family-oriented workplace supports and opportunities have not kept pace with these numbers. In fact, U.S. workers lag behind those in most other industrialized countries that have far more generous child-care provisions as well as family and maternity leave policies. Ironically, surveys of lower-echelon workers reveal a growing appreciation for female managers — especially those who have family responsibilities — because they are viewed as being more sympathetic to the needs of employees in two-income families. This view, however, still conflicts with the stereotype current among many executives that women with children are unable to focus on their work.

Predictably, the United States will narrow the gender gap in workforce equity more quickly when more women move into powerful executive and management positions — although there is clearly a chicken-and-egg problem here. While the number of women in management rose dramatically between 1975 and 1985, the total number is still small. The glass ceiling remains in many corporations.

In addition to gender and ethnic workforce diversity, it is increasingly important in an aging United States to pay attention to age as a diversity issue. Generation gaps are really culture gaps, and the U.S. workforce today is divided along generational fault lines: the over-fifty senior workforce, the huge cohort of Baby Boomers, and the younger, entry-level Baby Busters. Each has a distinct culture shaped by the different social experiences of their formative years: World War II and Korea for older workers, Vietnam and the social/cultural revolution of the 1960s for Baby Boomers, and the increasing pressures of economic competition for younger workers.

The values, behavior, and expectations of workers over fifty are very different than those of Baby Boomers who may be only a few years younger. Globalization, fragmentation, and other workplace trends are hardest to reconcile for older workers, whose cultural expectations include rewards for company loyalty and long-term employment. Older workers acculturated to large paternalistic organizations are now suddenly having to create a new life after layoffs they never imagined would happen. They have no skills for seeking work in the new smaller businesses and in any case will find these workspaces and their cultures quite foreign. They will need special support or their valuable skills and knowledge could be lost at a crucial time when the United States needs to reinvent work.

Boomers, who are having to cope with a change of rules in midcareer, will face a much more uncertain work life and retirement than they anticipated when they entered the workforce. And entry-level workers are not sure what to expect and are thus most open to riding the waves of opportunity and challenge.

These conflicts in value systems may be exacerbated by economic factors as U.S. society continues to age. Concerns about an era of economic warfare between generations are not misplaced. For fewer and fewer young workers (including a growing percentage of immigrants) will be financing the retirements of more and more elderly workers, who are predominantly white and relatively affluent. Such generational conflicts may add an ugly new dimension to the nation's increasing ethnic diversity.

Fortunately, people in the United States bring unique strengths to these challenges: the durability of their national identity and their historic sense of themselves as an exceptional people. Indeed, their high degree of internal mobility (close to half of all U.S. residents live outside the states in which they were born) has contributed to the enduring strength of a national culture in relation to the weakening influence of regional cultures. A growing level of shared understandings and values between Southerners, Midwesterners, New Englanders, and the people of the plains and the West have had the beneficial effect of creating a basis for a greater openness to the values of all "outsiders." But barriers have arisen. New immigrants increasingly are locating in a wider number of states but generally become residents of Texas,

California, Florida, and New York. Many communities are bilingual and English/Spanish bicultural, and more are being influenced by a wide range of Asian immigrants from Eastern and Southern Asia. As concerns about jobs and other economic insecurities become widespread anxieties, a tendency to blame the shift on overly liberal immigration policies and illegal foreign residents has led to increasing racial intolerance. People in the United States need to come to grips with the real source of economic shifts and not allow themselves to fall prey to myths and confuse the issues.

It hardly needs to be said, of course, that despite the increasing multicultural complexion of the United States, U.S. culture is still dominated by the values of its white, Anglo-Saxon, Protestant inhabitants' heritage. The image of the dominant culture in the United States ("mainstream America") as white is beginning to fray at the edges — most visibly in urban areas such as New York, Chicago, Miami, Houston, Los Angeles, and San Francisco, but increasingly in rural areas as well. In recent years, Spanish, Chinese, and Vietnamese-speaking communities, for example, have grown and their existing communities have become recognized more widely. Today "Americans" are less easily stereotyped than in the past. Yet there still exists a clear, dominant Northern European–American culture. Along with many nondominant cultures, it inhabits a complex web or race, culture, and economic class.

One of our assumptions is that all people living and working in the United States — are expressions of the U.S. social culture that underpins business in the United States. Unlike the members of more homogeneous national cultures we have discussed earlier, people in the United States comprise a complex mix of ethnic cultures and the dominant Northern European–American culture, which has strongly influenced the government and educational systems. And although the United States is made up mostly of immigrated cultures, any discussion of cultural diversity must carefully weigh the distinction between first-generation immigrant and U.S.-born members of ethnic cultures, so that "hyphenated" Americans (for example, Korean Americans, African Americans, Arab Americans) are not inadvertently put in the category of outsider or foreigner.

Perhaps one of the most interesting aspects of cultural diversity in the United States is the dynamic of dominant and nondominant or minority cultures. For those born into the dominant culture (or perhaps acculturated to it as newly arrived Northern European immigrants), the United States may be a place of many different kinds of people, but popular culture and social institutions constantly reinforce the dominant identity. For those born into minority cultures, living in the United States is an experience of constantly working "cross-culturally" — of experiencing culture shock and all the feelings and behaviors described by the Intercultural Learning Model. Certainly, Asian Americans, and Latin Americans, for example, make adaptations, and they may seem to mask the underlying cultural differences. But some U.S. residents live in two or more cultures, constantly having to communicate and work cross-culturally, while some live in only one. This is why we have been cautious about overgeneralizing about people in the United States unless we can be specific about whom we are referring to — my ethnic group, your ethnic group, or corporate America? Interestingly enough, it is much easier for white Northern European Americans to generalize about U.S. culture, because from the dominant perspective, the United States does seem much more cohesive and consistent than it does to those whose cultures are not yet built in to the existing social institutions.

Given how deeply embedded the white, Anglo-Saxon, Protestant values are in all national institutions, from law to education to government, they are likely to remain dominant for many years. Primary social cultures change very slowly even when under great external pressure. Recent events in Eastern Europe and China, for instance, testify to the staying power of long-held cultures. Ethnic subcultures can influence the dominant culture — as Californians and others have discovered through the incipient "Latinization" of border regions and certain cities — but it is a slow evolution (with frequent steps backwards) toward new values and new behavior.

In fact, people in the United States may be adapting better to cultural diversity in the global context than in the national one. The rapid development of the global economy has enabled them to view the unique values and behavior of international competitors such as Japan and Germany as positive characteristics worth emulating. Thus many U.S. companies have imported Japanese management styles, for instance, and adapted them to the U.S. workplace. The best hope is that the United States's experience and learning in the global context will help U.S. business cope better with the multicultural world within its own national borders.

This is one of the reasons why intercultural learning is key in the U.S. workplace — perhaps even more than in the global arena. As members of a heterogeneous culture, U.S. workers may combine aspects of several distinct cultures, making them difficult to "type." The practice of intercultural learning is one way of continually encountering new cultural situations, honestly reacting to them, and incorporating learning into one's work and personal life.

The workplace is a unique blend of individual and collective values and organizational structures. This may be one reason for the United States's reputation for innovation in business and science: the juxtaposition of so many perspectives and value systems generates a creative tension. America's tendency to be an early adopter of technology, especially groupware technology, could offer a third-way space for more collaboration between cultures. Many workgroup computing technologies require groups to formally address and decide how they will work together and use the tools to support achieving their purpose. Since using these tools is new for everyone, the playing field is somewhat level, requiring people to think outside the confines of how they usually work. Essentially, the United States is an ideal environment for third-way strategies, because so many differences and discontinuities exist that could use creative responses.

But in the United States corporate culture often exhibits the qualities of the dominant culture, making it difficult for those from other cultures to participate and contribute fully.

In order for corporate culture to achieve its potential of providing glue in our heterogeneous society, it will need to become more porous (that is, inclusive), attentive, and respectful of all cultures' ways of working. Employees will then not need to spend so much of their energy "adapting" themselves to corporate culture and can invest energy in contributing to innovation.

We forecast that the equidistance of all cultures will be a concept from global business that begins to take root in U.S. society out of necessity. A new understanding of a diverse workplace in the United States or elsewhere requires not only a recognition that many types of people work together—it means an understanding of the dominant social and corporate cultures in which they are asked to work. This will require a willingness to accept, value, and model deep respect for all cultures, inclusiveness, equidistance of all cultures, and the use of third-way strategies and intercultural learning.

HOW U.S. SOCIAL CULTURE PERMEATES THE WORKPLACE

If U.S. business is to adapt to the growing diversity of cultural values within and without its borders, it must first learn to recognize its own dominant social values—one of the most difficult challenges in cross-cultural learning. Once we understand ourselves we are halfway toward understanding how to bridge our differences with other cultures. As we have noted in earlier chapters, the dimensions of language, context, time, power/equality, and information flow all provide valuable lenses for cultural learning, whether applied to another culture or our own. They offer a neutral and objective way to look at primary cultural characteristics that may otherwise be invisible. It is important to use the five cultural lenses to see exactly how individuals in your team and organization embody the heterogeneous U.S. culture and to learn how to best work with them. Once they are brought into focus, we have the choice of living with them or attempting to transcend them and remold ourselves.

The following look at U.S. culture in the workplace, as seen through the refractions of the five cultural lenses, is not meant to be comprehensive but merely suggestive. The reality, of course, is infinitely more complex than the abstractions. We have included scales for each of the five dimensions and circled areas where we feel there is more emphasis in the United States.

Language

The dominant U.S. culture is expressed almost exclusively through English, and anyone whose speech deviates from standard English is recognized as being outside the dominant culture. Dominant U.S. culture is relatively intolerant of strong dialects, accented English, and other languages — as evidenced by the growing movement to have English declared a "national language." This intolerance is matched by the fact that many people in the United States are monolingual. At the same time, literacy rates continue to decline.

The business implications of these characteristics are serious, considering that the dominant English-speaking culture has always shared the workplace with a diversity of ethnic and linguistic groups. The cultural diversity only increases with workers from around the globe joining the U.S. workforce.

The new picture of the U.S. workplace includes both dominant and nondominant (or minority) cultures. Demographics are beginning to shift the balance away from the white Northern European–American culture in some areas of the United States. For example, in vast parts of cities such as Miami, New York, and Los Angeles, English is virtually a foreign language; doing business depends on one's ability to communicate in Spanish. The presence of these and other distinct linguistic and ethnic communities turns the tables on the traditionally dominant culture and makes bilingualism and multilingualism a necessity for effective business communication.

Many U.S. companies are beginning to recognize that, with limited-English-speaking as well as monolingual workers entering their ranks, it behooves them to support English as a Second Language (ESL) and foreign language courses. After all, businesses cannot afford to have poor communications with large portions of the workforce or marketplace. Some businesses have also taken the opportunity to institute basic literacy programs. While some companies have energetically promoted ESL, second language acquisition, and literacy programs, most have made only token efforts. These companies often complain the loudest when they are unable to hire literate, bilingual, and fluent English-speaking workers.

As more non–native English speakers move into the upper ranks of business, supervisors must learn to keep any linguistic biases they have in check. They should not automatically assume that colleagues who sometimes stumble over English syntax or misuse common allusions are uninformed. Indeed, they should encourage people who are struggling with the complexities of English to speak freely without fear of making mistakes or being constantly corrected. Supervisors should themselves make special efforts to listen carefully when communicating with non–native speakers and learn to accept that the content of communications is more critical than the quality of delivery. And supervisors must also make the effort to learn a second or even a third language, just as their colleagues may be.

New groupware and communication technologies can be either a help or a hindrance regarding linguistic diversity in the workplace. On the one hand, store-and-forward communications like e-mail allow users to take the time to compose their communications carefully and avoid embarrassing mistakes. On the other hand, most electronic communications put a very high premium on writing skills, with an emphasis on clarity and brevity, which are difficult to achieve without mastery of a language. Some executives told us that it was far easier to use the phone and voice mail with team members who have English as a second language after at least one face-to-face meeting. With such media, the receiver has time to read and reread or listen and relisten — without the demand of an instant response.

Context

The dominant U.S. culture is low-context. It values objective data over information that is embedded in a larger context of meaning. It prefers communications that are "clean" — meaning direct and isolated from the social milieu.

In the global arena, U.S. residents are known for their spirit of individualism and a basic aversion to working on teams and committees. They seem to like being in control of events — the opposite of more fatalistic cultures — and tend to believe that all things are possible. They are thought of as strongly supporting freedom of choice, privacy, and self-determination — all qualities that could be helpful in fostering tolerance and greater acceptance of diversity.

If this is the dominant culture's face to the world, it is important to remember that nondominant groups may only share some of these values — for example, Native Americans' respect for the individual or the Japanese American sense of privacy. In some instances, nondominant cultures have adapted to dominant values, effectively masking differences.

Emotional control is another expression of low-context U.S. culture — particularly among men, who may be animated in their communications but are rarely emotional. High-context Americans, who are tied to a more complex web of human and environmental relationships, often include those outside the dominant culture (see Table 10.1).

In the workplace, and especially on cross-cultural teams, clashes over context are inevitable. Some cultures will want more face-to-face relationships to develop trust. This need should be acknowledged and accommodated.

Recent immigrants — especially at the executive and senior technical levels — who come from high-context cultures may have trouble coping with the fast decision-making style of U.S. business. They are used to a consensus-seeking management approach and more extensive, if unstructured, information-sharing activities.

Table 10.1. Context Patterns of American Subcultures.

High	Medium	Medium Low	Low
Filipino	Greek	Canadian	German Swiss
Native American	French	English	German
African American	Italian		Scandinavian
Hispanic	Portuguese		
Japanese			
Arab	(Women)		(Men)
	(Rural)		(Urban)

One of the most disturbing context differences cited by workers is the obsession of many U.S. managers with quantitative or written information. Indeed, low-context Americans often seem cold and remote to colleagues from high-context cultures. While they tend to be friendly in a glib sort of way, these managers seldom want to form deeper relationships, especially across cultural boundaries. These fundamental conflicts set up formidable barriers to effective teamwork—especially in the early trust-building stage of team development.

Margaret's team in the scenario that introduced this chapter decided to take some time for building trust. They explored some of their cultural differences using the five cultural lenses and the Team Performance Model as tools to help them discuss their differences calmly. The most helpful lens was the high/low context scale, they said, because the ethnic groups and different functions were able to talk freely about what their context level meant to them.

The group members mapped themselves on the context scale and discussed their choices. Asian American members placed themselves in the low to middle of the context scale, African American members mapped themselves between low and medium high, and white team members placed themselves in the low to middle range. The lower-context members wanted to focus on task completion, while higher-context members wanted to understand the power/equality issues first. These higher-context people also preferred working in small groups rather than on individual assignments. Interestingly, they doubted the validity of group work in computer-assisted meeting rooms, since they felt it promoted superficiality and lack of ownership of information. The team members preferred a team goal of open group discussion of hard issues.

Margaret's team conducted another team exercise: an intuitive diagnosis of their team process using the Team Performance Model (presented in Chapter Five). The shared models helped the team address technical and social differences. For instance, the white males on Margaret's team liked to focus on stages 3 to 5—roles/goals, commitment, and implementation—and had little patience for the orientation and trust stages. The women, however, and members of high-context cultures, wanted to spend time building trust in order to work together effectively. The team agreed to begin meetings with personal discussions and also planned a social event.

Clarifying roles and goals on a team is particularly important in view of the dominant American culture's individualism and its orientation to personal achievement. Because many people in the United States prefer to negotiate their roles actively, this is a difficult stage when distance is a factor. Members of many non-European cultures may themselves prefer roles to be divided up among team members based on a group decision. Technology can be helpful to this role clarification if the human communication issues have been worked out.

Margaret's team put their roles and subgoals in the discussion data bases—thus making them public. By annotating and discussing them electronically, they worked out any misunderstandings and forged links between each others' roles and subgoals. Thus the shared data bases were used extensively to explore the team's goals and build on each others' ideas early in the team's life.

Again, technology can help bridge the gaps—but it could also create even greater conflicts. Nothing can replace the regular face-to-face encounters demanded by many high-context U.S. subcultures, including those rooted in Latin and

Asian countries. But video conferencing, which is relatively inexpensive and accessible in the United States, can at least put a human face on distant communications. Supervisors and cross-cultural team leaders should be wary of extensive use of decision-making software that is not designed to tolerate a certain degree of ambiguity, intuitive thinking, and consensual process. The terse voice-mail preferences of white male supervisors may prevent high-context team members from using this mode—and thus prevent the flow of important information.

Technology—particularly groupware—will work only if it fits the participants' cultural context and supports appropriate ways of sending messages that elicit the right response. Most software is developed by low-context Westerners like those in the dominant European American culture, who automatically program the technology with their cultural biases such as the value of rationality, verifiability, objective measures of efficiency and productivity, and a preference for problem solving over acceptance of nature and human events. Members of the predominant U.S. culture feel they have a right to use and manipulate natural forces and human institutions as objects. Other cultures prefer less linear and direct approaches to problem solving and value a more harmonious contact with nature and people. Their measures of efficiency take "soft" variables into consideration. The following list summarizes some important cultural considerations we have adapted from Dennis Goulet (1977, p. 48).

Western Cultural Traits Built into Technology

- A procedure and manner of problem solving, based on the application of logic in a linear manner.

- A hierarchical and vertical framework of organizational authority in the decision-making process.

- Individual initiative in taking action, viewed as integral and essential to the proper application of technology.

- Time and tasks viewed as integrated into a linear schedule, and significant to the timely achievement of technological goals.

- Individual performance receives and deserves individual reward and/or punishment.

- Pre-emptive action is necessary to prevent technological problems.

- Questioning, conflict, and confrontation are valued and critical to learning and applying technology.

- Personal self-worth and social status are primarily determined through one's work and material achievement by using technology.

- Self-determinism rather than fatalism is the modus operandi of working behavior to make technology work.

Time

The dominant U.S. business culture views time as a monochronic, sequential reality—a perspective that leads to short-term thinking and a focus on the present and near future. "Time is money" describes it well. Everything is done in a hurry. Results are expected *now*. Decision making is fast and based on objective data. This sequential linear reality is built into the function of most business computing. Faster processing speeds are contributing to an even faster-paced business culture.

While minority cultures may tolerate or even admire these values, they don't necessarily share them. Latin Americans, Middle Easterners, and recent immigrants from the Mediterranean countries, for instance, may be polychronic and see time as a state of being rather than a resource to be managed. Asians tend to view the past and future as coequal in importance to the present, and thus they are more at ease with long-term planning, research, and investment. Asian Americans may share some of these characteristics.

Although U.S. business may adapt somewhat to longer-term perspectives, this is one cultural characteristic that is likely to persist, despite the existence of polychronic ethnic minorities. The biggest clashes will involve differences in sequential versus synchronic time. Polychronic people prefer doing many things at once and have a high tolerance for the kinds of interruptions that can be extremely disconcerting to members of the dominant culture. Monochronic Americans find it hard to understand, for instance, how a busy supervisor can talk to her kids on the phone and complete job tasks at the same time.

Monochronic supervisors have a difficult time appreciating the efficiency of polychronic employees. They must remember that polychronic workers may be more productive over the long term because of the ease with which they work on multiple tasks simultaneously. Likewise, foreign executives working in the United States often have a hard time with the American obsession with short-term gains to the detriment of long-term growth and direction.

Most of today's information technology is best suited to monochronic, present-oriented users who treat time as a valuable commodity. Group scheduling, project management, strict agendas, and the ranking of programs can impose unnatural and uncomfortable—and unproductive—constraints on polychronic workers who are not bound by the rigid sequentiality of the business culture. U.S. managers of cross-cultural teams must be particularly sensitive to the cultural drawbacks of such programs and keep the pressure on software developers to design more flexible formats.

Power/Equality

For all the talk about the rat race of the U.S. workplace, the United States is in fact much less status and power-oriented than most cultures. Equality, fairness, and an aversion to social class distinctions are strong and deeply held U.S. values. People in the United States find it normal to hold work positions of varying degrees of status and power during their work lives. For the most part, they value themselves for who they are and what they accomplish as individuals, not according to ascribed status. But saluting the value that "all people are created equal" is one thing. Living it is quite another. At odds with these values is a strong vertical economic structure. If in fact all people were accorded equal opportunity, people in the United States would not be going through the tense gender, ethnic, and racial upheavals that are so characteristic of our times. The power/equality landscape is a combination of hierarchical situations such as that in the corporate United States, superimposed on a flat, egalitarian base. Nondominant cultures that favor hierarchical relationships can constitute some of the "skyscrapers" on this landscape as well.

As the percentage of citizens of color increases, and as their political, educational, and economic attainments grow, they will doubtless demand and get greater equality. In some regions, if not throughout the nation, this process of cultural change will involve a dramatic shift on the part of the dominant culture as new ethnic pluralities or majorities challenge the traditional notion of integration: all cultures must adapt to the dominant culture. When a minority becomes a majority, as they have in some regions, they may well begin to ask who should be integrated into what. The resulting cultures, in such cases, may represent genuine blends of values and practices — an entirely new, "third way" culture — as opposed to the absorption of either one into the other.

As far as the U.S. workplace is concerned, there is no greater arena for potential culture clashes than the power/equality dimension. It has implications in every facet of organizational life — from equal pay for equal work to equal access to higher positions. Since the dominant culture has shaped the values and practices of U.S. corporations, its stereotypes are reflected in the corporate culture. Thus we will continue to see broad social conflicts such as gender and racial inequality reflected in the workplace, framed there in terms of affirmative action, hiring quotas, promotion policies, and equal pay for equal work. Perhaps the most stubborn source of social conflict will be the ignorance we have about one another's culture in the workplace — and the actions that stem from that ignorance. There is no easy way through this process, and American business has until very recently been negligent in facing up to it. The progress achieved so far has mostly been driven by government regulatory prodding against a stubborn status quo.

Ironically, the commitment to equality that is needed to bring minority cultures into full participation in the U.S. work-force is a value that some of those cultures themselves find it difficult to take advantage of. Many cultures bring a high degree of status consciousness to the workplace and expect more formality than people in the United States are ac-customed to in dealings between subordinates and superiors. Many immigrant workers remain rooted in cultures where legal notions of worker rights, minority rights, or racial and gender discrimination are not taken seriously. Mexico, for example, actually has stronger labor-rights laws than the United States, but few people expect them to be upheld.

Power and equality issues come to the fore on multi-cultural teams in the United States as Margaret's team at UNA began to see. All of the minority members experienced the same problem with "personal fit" — an important issue of the orientation stage in the life of a team. They feel they were selected for their ethnicity rather than personal competence. This was particularly true for the more junior and younger members. This problem seldom gets completely resolved in business because, as on this team, companies trying to balance racial input often target a predetermined cultural mix. Al-though members resolved some of their suspicions simply by discussing them openly, doubt and uncertainty persisted.

"We have a lot of caution," said a white female on the team. "I don't think we should have to be so cautious. We should be able to say anything, and as a team we should be able to address what anyone says — even the chief." Caution was certainly a hallmark of Margaret's team. They had spent no time getting to know each other. They were almost strangers. People get to know each other best by learning about their lives outside of work, but distance and lack of time made this difficult for Margaret's team. Building a personal data base about the team can bring people closer and help them discover common interests. Personal conversation at the beginning of each meeting can be useful — and may soon become unnecessary if spontaneous communications develop.

People on the team generally felt too intimidated by the boss's presence to speak freely. Added to that was a palpable sense of caution about being politically correct and using the proper terms for other ethnic groups. Do you say "black" or "African American"? "Hispanic" or "Latino"? Team members had an opportunity to explain to one another what these terms meant to them, which released enough of the charge to open solid lines of communication.

The fear of offending was by far the strongest cross-cultural barrier to free-flowing communications. There was a strong companywide fear of retaliation for speaking openly — and particularly criticizing middle and upper-level management. Everybody knew that crossing your manager would result in a poor performance rating: "You get a label, maybe not today or tomorrow, but it happens." The depth of this problem was underscored when the team was reluctant to reveal its true feelings even in an anonymous computer-supported work session. Members later acknowledged they felt so threatened that they erased and changed the opinions they had originally expressed — even though UNA is a very progressive company.

There's no denying that top-level bosses can have a stultifying impact on teams when they participate as members. Ethnic minorities frequently have deep feelings of respect and fear of top managers — who are often white males — and may go along with decisions even when they know problems are likely. Margaret should have managed senior management's participation and maintained a degree of balance. You can't leave it up to the team — or the well-meaning but intrusive top manager. But Margaret was not in fact that sympathetic to her younger colleagues. She herself was much older and part of senior management. From her perspective there is so much more opportunity now than twenty years ago it is hard to understand today's concerns.

The more diversity on a team, the more potential for conflict. Not only had Margaret's team ignored the power/ equality differences, but several team members were not fully engaged in their shared work and valuable insights had been lost. Clearly, cultural misunderstandings and conflicts over questions of equality, which have long troubled the U.S. workplace, can only be expected to grow more intense as new waves of immigrants find their way into the mainstream economy. Every culture brings its own view of equality, but not all views carry equal weight. If the dominant U.S. culture is committed to preserving its own notion of equality, it will have to redouble efforts to make it a reality in the workplace.

New information technologies have both broad and narrow implications with regard to workplace equality. Even the use of common communication tools like e-mail and voice mail will be shaped by the cultures of the managers and team members. Some nondominant cultures in the United States are much less egalitarian than the dominant culture, and those members will not feel as free to send messages up the chain of command. Likewise foreign managers from more hierarchical cultures may not take well to direct and uninvited messages from subordinates.

Margaret's team scheduled a second meeting just to give people a chance to express their concerns—both on a decision support system through an anonymous electronic discussion and in open face-to-face dialogue. Both the electronic and face-to-face meeting were facilitated by a cross-cultural expert. Having both the tools and the facilitator allowed the team's members to expose assumptions in front of the group and have the topic dealt with openly and without personal attacks. Just using the electronic tools would not have been satisfying, the team reported, because confronting the issues involved more than putting information on the table. This meeting modeled, in a safe setting, the openness needed to handle the tough ethnic and functional issues that might arise in the later stages of teamwork.

As noted earlier, decentralized technologies have put access to information—the ultimate source of power—in the hands of individual workers, thus altering the traditional balance of workplace power. But so long as some cultures in U.S. business are treated as less equal than others, their access to the power of information will be limited. Yet different cultures react differently to the level playing field of decentralized information technology. Some will be quick to take full advantage of the opportunities; others may view such opportunities as destabilizing and the technology as threatening and awkward. Decision-making supports, especially, may have to be adapted for third-way alternatives between top-down processes and two-way processes.

Information Flow

Information in the United States is highly compartmentalized and jealously guarded. Great attention is devoted to restricting access to information, guarding privacy, and putting all information in written form. Typically, the flow of information follows the shortest line between two points. And this straight-line efficiency is almost as important culturally as the quality of the information itself.

Also, the compulsion to complete action chains—finishing a job at any cost—is characteristic of U.S. business culture. Midcourse reviews and changes are tolerated, but only as inconveniences, not opportunities. And since information tends to be compartmentalized and restricted, data that should logically alter an action chain may not alert people until it's too late. On the one hand, excessive time is spent deciding who should get sensitive information; on the other hand, managers tend to overload workers with extraneous information. Action chains also vary by function. Engineers, for example, like to get straight to the point and consider mostly objective data, whereas human resource people can culturally understand the value of looping ideas through a group and considering soft variables. And then there are action chains that appear to be established but are never fully realized. In the case of Margaret's team, the company's stated goal of improving relationships between all groups of people in UNA was thwarted by unresolved team issues like trust and commitment. "If people don't share their thoughts and hold their bigotries inside, you won't have implementation," commented a senior management member of the team.

As the team members discussed commitment of resources and implementation, they kept returning to trust and cultural diversity concerns as a barrier to the kind of shared vision they really needed. "What do we really have in common?" they frequently asked one another. Another underlying feeling that rarely surfaced was a concern about the true meaning of equality and how strongly team members believed in it. And hovering over these questions were other issues, such as the availability of time and resources to do the job. If the company was so committed to respect for individuals and cultures and cross-functional teamwork, why were they having so much trouble getting the time to work on it? Struggling with these corporate culture concerns often put the diversity issue on the back burner and paralyzed action chains.

The dominant culture's information-flow practices parallel its low-context practices. It requires overloads of data because it does not cultivate the information-rich webs of human relationships characteristic of high-context cultures. Low-context Americans tend to rely exclusively on objective data rather than trust in the subjective information available from an array of informal sources.

One of the main implications for the workplace is that a great amount of patience and learning time should be devoted particularly to helping non-native Americans adapt to the closely linked and sequenced information-flow practices of American work culture. Gantt charts, for instance, may have more meaning to low-context Americans than high-context Americans. A lot of workflow and project management software is designed by and for low-context Americans and may be difficult for others to adapt to.

On Margaret's team the failure to resolve how team members were to work together meant that a long time was spent deciding what processes to use. At times they would use a workflow support system to discuss useful approaches. But because the decision-making process was unclear, work proceeded slowly. Moreover, some members were unsure how to use the workflow system to its full advantage. No comprehensive plan had been developed. There was also some resistance to using technology in place of resolving intercultural problems. Not using it became a way of showing resistance.

Team members did a fair amount of suspicious imagining about each other outside of meetings—worrying about what people were really doing and fretting about an unequal sharing of the workload. One shift worker who didn't have access to all the technology that would have supported his distant participation felt that people were not interested in his participation.

Most workflow products in use thus far are confined to narrow operational procedures that focus on such things as insurance claims management or accounts payable. In these cases, teams work in tandem—rather than working in real time to collaborate on larger business processes like product development or total quality. But these products are coming in the next three to five years and should be designed with multicultural users in mind. Most likely, complex business processes will be supported by combination applications rather than one product.

Cultural conflicts over workflow are not limited to different ethnic groups. They may appear even between men and women—as in the different gender approaches to meetings. The masculine "let's get to the point and vote on it" orientation to meetings is inconsistent with the needs of many women and high-context cultures whose approach to decision making is more oblique and contextual. The speed and directness of U.S. decision making can be disconcerting to some people, including those in the United States itself, and it may preclude their full participation.

As the workforce becomes more diversified, alternative ways of managing information and work processes must eventually emerge. This trend will show up in less insistence on writing everything down, for example, and in freer access to information. And as organizations flatten out and decentralize, information will have to become more diffuse and flow to more decision-making nodes—which will break down old habits of centralization. Products such as palmtop computers to support sales and inventory management in the field will become commonplace. So long as technology is recognized as only one aspect of process support and people are well oriented, it should be accepted by most of America's cultures.

HOW U.S. WORK CULTURES CREATE THEIR OWN BOUNDARIES

The unique attributes of the primary social culture are not the only ways that culture shapes the U.S. workplace. Work cultures—corporate, professional, and functional—play almost as great a role as primary culture in making the American workplace a special and, to many, very strange environment. Let's drop in on one such environment by way of another scenario: a large, national marketing firm headquartered in Dallas with branch offices from coast to coast.

At Dallas headquarters, Jack picked up the phone to call Bruce in the New York office. He wanted to prod him once again for the financials. "This is the second time he's missed a deadline," Jack muttered to himself, glancing again at the e-mail note from his manager. Headed "Urgent," it set a drop-dead date for final reports on noon Friday.

"What is it with Bruce?" he wondered to himself, as he listened to the second ring. "He gives me nothing but lame excuses two months in a row—and now he messages me that he'll be late again because his local manager's on his case about some other project. Don't these bozos ever talk to one another?"

The phone rang the third time. "Come on, come on," said Jack. "Pick it up!" *He knew he couldn't finish his financials until Bruce sent him the profit-and-loss data from software sales, and his manager was going to be furious if he was late again this month.*

He glanced at his watch. 9:15 A.M. *11:15 in New York. Finally, on the fifth ring, an answer:* "This is Bruce Johnson. Sorry I'm not at my desk right now. I'm in meetings until four this afternoon. Please leave a message and I'll call back when I can."

Jack's first feelings were anger and frustration, but he quickly resolved not to accept defeat. He wasn't going to let Bruce slip out of it this time by hiding behind his voice mail. Anyway, Jack's manager had told him to "do whatever you have to do" *to get the report in.*

"Bruce, Jack in accounting here," *he said to Bruce's voice mail.* "In Dallas. Just got your message about wanting to slip the financial deadline tomorrow. Wish I could help, buddy, but this month management needs these figures by Friday at 8:30 sharp. They've scheduled a big meeting and all the numbers have to be on the table. Best I can do is give you till 2:30 Thursday. That pushes me, but I can go ahead and wrap up the report from our other eight sites and add your figures in last. Thanks a bunch. I knew you could make the deadline."

Jack sat back, satisfied his strategy would work. Yes, Bruce would probably have to burn some midnight oil, he reflected. But so what? It's good for those undisciplined screwballs in sales to be forced to shape up once in a while.

Jack was pulled from his smug thoughts by a knock at the door. George from systems and Elliot from public relations came in for their scheduled team meeting on a divisionwide review of technological supports. Jack's manager had asked him for a special favor: sit in on the discussion and protect accounting's interests.

"So," began George, "I was just telling Elliot here that I think we need to take a second look at our client and LAN operating systems. If we get rid of everything but IPX and TCP/IP, that means we have to sacrifice native access to IBM LAN Server and possibly to Windows NT entirely. There might be a way to get around this with NFS, but I'm still working on it. What do you think, Jack?"

Jack and Elliot glanced at one another. Neither had any idea what George was talking about. Fifteen minutes later, after George had patiently explained his reasoning, both Jack and Elliot firmly assured him that they agreed entirely and there was no point in prolonging the meeting.

The first thing next morning, Jack's boss called him in: "Why is it nobody bothered to make sure our department gets some information about training and support for these new systems? That's what you were on the team for, Jack— to look out for us. And incidentally, I just got a call from New York. Sam, the regional manager, says he's got to have Bruce finish up a critical marketing analysis this week. This could be very big business for us, and Bruce is the top marketing guy, so I told him not to worry about our financials until next week. By the way, did I miss a meeting we were planning for tomorrow? Sam said something. . . ."

Strange? Not anymore. The kinds of issues and conflicts that poor Jack experienced in a single day are the everyday frustrations of people sorting out their place and role in a business environment undergoing tremendous flux. Let's take a look at a few of the major issues.

First: talking past one another. In the vertically structured organization, every division or department becomes a fiefdom unto itself and there's little concern for the organization at large. Jack's first allegiance was to the finance division: his first priority was meeting the division's goal of timely reports. He really didn't see Bruce as a team member, just a difficult colleague, and he had little interest in trying to find out why Bruce was late. Besides, he never had much sympathy for the sales division. They never seemed to take their reports very seriously, and they certainly didn't take deadlines seriously. Meanwhile, Bruce, in New York, felt much the same way about the bean counters in Dallas. Didn't they appreciate the fact that a potentially big deal was in the making? It seemed to Bruce that accounting cared more about last month's numbers than next month's deals.

Second: jargon. The specialized languages developed by different functions and professions have become a major barrier to cross-functional teamwork. This is particularly true of ultra-technical areas like information systems. The jargon associated with computer technology, for example, is not readily understood by most people in an organization. Even though Jack was in finance and was indeed computer literate, he felt lost whenever technology discussions left the realm of the English language. Instead of insisting on clarity or boning up on the techno-talk, both Jack and Elliot just nodded their heads and let George from systems have his way.

Third: different conceptual frameworks. Getting different functions to view problems from multiple perspectives is a challenge. George and Bruce had trouble accepting viewpoints alien to their own. This is particularly difficult between functions that have little in common: it's hard to get an engineer to view a problem in its full social context, just as an accountant may be less likely than a marketing manager to appreciate deals-in-the-making with the same enthusiasm they bring to yesterday's balance sheet. Compounding the cultural differences, there are often no incentives to work in new ways, since rewards are given by functional areas and based on their specific criteria. Jack's manager rewards Jack for Jack's performance, not Bruce's.

Fourth: pocket vetoes. Jack's manager committed a common error by intervening in the cross-functional process for setting deadlines and priorities after he had delegated authority to Jack. Cross-functional teams often fear the collusion of

Table 10.2. Corporate Culture Shifts in the United States.

Paternalism	⟶	Fraternalism
Male	⟶	Female
Authoritarianism	⟶	Democracy
Traditional Family	⟶	Blended Family
Hierarchy	⟶	Horizontal
Old Boy Network	⟶	Team

managers who come in with pocket vetoes rather than letting members sort out their own problems.

Work cultures have come to play an increasingly prominent role in the United States, perhaps in direct proportion to the weakening grip of intimate family and regional values that operate in more agrarian, less mobile societies. As a result, people in the United States, more than most peoples, really are what they do at work. It is how they define themselves.

Traditionally, the highest level of work culture in the United States is at the corporate level, where corporatewide values, practices, and symbols have evolved over time to give large enterprises a unique and defining vision and direction. UNA, for example, a large multinational energy company, had undertaken a major corporate cultural shift to improve productivity and maintain its competitive edge. The broad categories of cultural shifts being nurtured by UNA are similar to many of those described by the executives of large U.S. companies we talked to (see Table 10.2). It was not uncommon for them to use the family metaphor to describe the old corporate culture and liken it to a traditional family, where the father was all powerful and was responsible for taking care of the other members. The increasing numbers of women and minority subcultures entering the workforce appear to be forcing a discussion of the need for change at the top management level. However, the executives we spoke with were also impressed with how difficult it was for the workforce in general to trust the company enough to act on these newly espoused values and culture shifts despite the claims from the top. Culture changes of this magnitude will take a long time to truly be adopted throughout the organization, when the old culture is reinforced daily in timeworn business processes shaped by the previous culture.

Keen on developing a better team culture, UNA had instituted a top management team to model this cultural shift in power/equality for the rest of the organization. And as one top technology manager reports, they were struggling with the challenges:

> Team-based management is reducing the traditional power of management and placing accountability at much lower levels. Middle management's role is changing from direction/control to coaching/counseling, planning, and organizational restructuring. This causes concern and in some cases resistance. Team members are being required to assume more responsibility for traditional management functions such as budgeting and human resource planning while continuing to carry out the primary team objectives. In parallel to this, the status associated with management is being reduced. This combination results in unfulfilled expectations by all involved—I'm doing a manager's work, but where are the old perks that used to go along with it?

Within these high-level cultures, transcorporate cultures have also evolved around various professions and business functions. These skill-related cultures, visible through all five cultural lenses described in Chapter Two, are a valuable touchstone of personal identity. But they can also represent artificial boundaries within a single enterprise.

Most functions evolved over the last forty to fifty years in scientific management fields that developed in traditional hierarchical organizations. Certain professions tended to work in certain functions, and functions became vertically organized with little contact outside their departments. Management was by command and control, and administrative procedures grew more unwieldy as greater specialization demanded more administration for coordination and control. Corporations became little more than bureaucracies thinly disguised by successful corporate trimmings.

In his book *The Seamless Enterprise* (1992, pp. 6–7), Dan Dimancescu observes:

> A large majority of American—and indeed many European—corporations are still managed by top-down departmental accountability. The organizational labels are similar: engineering, finance, purchasing, sales, legal, and research and development. Many times plants, sales offices, and laboratories are geographically dispersed. In this "vertical" management style, individual tasks are often completed in one department or group and then handed off to the next without full appreciation of the whole process. Specialized groups often develop their own professional language, not readily understood by other departments. In other cases, cumbersome administrative procedures are instituted with the sole purpose of managing the transfer of work from one group to another. Organizational chimneys, or stovepipes, quickly develop their own narrow reward systems. The resulting allegiance to such departmental chimneys can work at cross purposes with the company's overall needs.

In contrast to the "stovepipe" orientation, cross-functional work is generally associated with "horizontal" activities or processes of enterprise-wide importance: quality assurance, personnel training, strategic planning. The focus is on how things get done, rather than on business results.

As corporations undergo enterprise-wide shifts to cross-functional work in response to competitive demands, functional cultures are experiencing tremendous stresses. In the past, for instance, business function's distance from the customer was a mark of status: the further from the customer, the higher the status. Thus financial number crunchers and legal eagles enjoyed greater status than salespeople. As we said earlier, any cultural changes are fundamental ones and come more slowly than other business decisions. Resistance and confusion can be expected and must be addressed. Changing a culture basically means making it in a new culture. The skill of intercultural learning will be key to highly productive cross-functional teams. As functions closer to the customer—like marketing and sales—gain in status and perceived power, those who have lost status can be expected to react negatively.

All that is changing in the horizontal leveling and distribution of corporate functions, which depends on cross-functional teams as a key source of innovation. "The whole point is to get diverse ideas, backgrounds, and experiences to interact," explained a manager in an energy firm that encourages cross-functional teaming. "This allows people to find out things they didn't know before. This diversity fosters a tremendous learning, yet it's a tremendous challenge to manage the diversity and accompanying conflict."

Yes, cross-functional teamwork implies an ability to bridge the often treacherous gaps between functional cultures. As the manager of a cross-functional team in a U.S. consumer products firm complained: "There is a lack of mutual respect among these different functions. There is generally a base of ignorance of what contributions each group brings. This is a very destructive attitude because there is a critical interdependence that exists, and no group can achieve success without the others."

Before cross-functional teams can be fully operational and productive, however, they must develop a common understanding of the entire process they are examining and see how it fits into the overall corporate picture. Team building will be difficult without a shared language to describe the work and monitor progress. Without such a language, each function will tend to slide back into old, addictive behavior patterns as implementation gets under way.

Orientation is difficult for cross-functional teams because they often can't see the reason for their existence. Their perspective may be the old, specialized way of working within one department or function. Since these teams exist primarily to improve processes, they must be empowered to work in a broad way that transcends narrow functional or departmental territories and to begin developing third-way strategies that go beyond cross-functional conflicts to address the real business issues. The human and technical knowledge they gain in the early stages of creating a team becomes the basis for their capacity to innovate.

In the docudrama, Jack certainly didn't feel he was on the same cross-functional team with Bruce. There was little to remind them they were a team. Had the company installed a groupware platform that included discussion in data bases, they could have had access to each other's projects — Bruce's big marketing analysis, for instance. This would have allowed them to review all the team's work, as well as related work, whenever they could check in with the team electronically. Dispersed teams need communication support other than the voice mail that Jack and Bruce had.

Meetings are often poorly designed for cross-functional teams. You can't overplan a cross-functional team meeting in the beginning of the team's life. Never assume that people really know each other's functional areas or what they can contribute. Get it out on the table as quickly as possible. People are most motivated to try out new ways at the beginning of a new team. Be sure to send out agendas in advance and get input from all functions. Provide technical materials in advance, too, so everybody has a chance to understand the input of other functions. The team leader will do well to design the meeting to meet the needs of the higher-context members, balancing the social discussion time with presentation of hard data and assuming that results are measurable for the low-context engineers.

As Jack and Bruce discovered, team members often imagine that others are undermining them when they're absent — especially when special pressures come into play like the financials Jack needed. Jack thought that Bruce was not carrying his weight in data gathering, the tedious time-consuming part of the team's work. It is easy to blame absent team members when things aren't working well — particularly if they come from a different functional area. Suspicion and dark imaginings can quickly fill a vacuum of communication. And distance will increase the likelihood of false accusations or misunderstandings. Complex technology like decision support tools is often counterproductive if it's used before a team has developed trust, for there's often little motivation to contribute. It's easier just to keep working at a low level of productivity without bothering to understand the overall process.

It's essential to keep all the multiple managers well oriented and engaged. Almost every cross-functional team we met had problems similar to Jack and Bruce — but worse. The prevailing feeling was that team members had not been briefed sufficiently by top management. Some were told they were spending too much time on one assignment; others were given competing priorities. And the middle managers who gave them the most criticism — and were also responsible for their performance reviews — were worried about their own jobs because of downsizing. Understanding these differences and this confusion can be helped by looking at them through the cultural lenses of information flow and power/equality. People working in one function area are acculturated to certain sets of behaviors and become confused (or experience culture shock) when thrown into cross-functional teams — practically virgin territory without an existing culture.

All this contributed significantly to the team's slow performance. Most people believed that top management was seriously committed to a cross-discipline approach to technology planning and support for users; but middle management, they thought, was much less committed. Ambivalence in the middle layer was common. Since they were the ones who evaluated individual performance, they tended to make the team's goals secondary to their own work.

Managers of cross-functional team members must be brought in right from the start and kept current with the team's goals and roles. Top management has to keep after middle managers to ensure they don't consciously or unconsciously impede work. When cross-functional teams have to contribute resources, time, money, and materials to the new vision from their own functional departments, lots of resistance results. These old culture/new culture clashes must be examined and thoroughly resolved. The team leader must be especially careful about exploring everyone's contributions. Otherwise, implementation will become a mess. And without thoughtful alignment it will be hard for members from different functions to juggle their relationships outside the team.

Implementation is the stage where the tendency to revert to old ways is strongest. Sometimes this impulse results from trying to do too much and attempting to manage too many new habits and practices at one time. Cross-functional work can be tremendously draining. Leaders must coach their teams to proceed at a pace they can maintain. The team leader needs to supply a drumbeat. Phone calls and voice mail, the more "human" technologies, were the best support — and for new teams they were needed often.

A common error is to set a modest goal on the premise that it's better to choose one that's easily attainable. Yet ambitious performance goals actually facilitate faster learning and the ability to transcend functional boundaries. People can learn quickly if they have to overcome difficult odds. The tendency to scale down goals is a step in the wrong direction.

A strong corporate vision that is shared across functions can help a lot. People need high-level shared frameworks to support their work. Senior managers can help cross-functional team leaders if they do their work of creating and communicating the company's vision and values everywhere. Such efforts keep the team oriented to its common higher purpose.

A strong driver for greater cross-functional management is the total quality management (TQM) movement. Behind the jargon (which is intense), quality programs operate as enterprise-wide management efforts, seeking to bridge the functional areas of an organization in order to create an orchestrated whole. The defining characteristics of quality programs — apart from continuous improvement and innovation — include a focus on customers, an enterprise-wide view, concurrence of actions, emphasis on process rather than outcomes, and a long-term orientation. It is a pitfall to focus on details and specific task work when a cross-functional team does not have overall, common understandings at the big picture level.

When people look at quality programs, however, they often see nothing more than repackaged common sense.

Quality does make sense, but enterprise-wide quality efforts are by no means common. Effective quality programs can be likened to a corporate superculture that is flexible enough to engage many functions and consistent enough to provide a common language for work spanning several functional areas. This makes TQM practitioners the pioneers of cross-functional management.

LESSONS
AND IMPLICATIONS

Diverse and cross-functional teams are hard to work with. Team leaders need strong facilitation skills—especially when working with teams made up of technical specialists or those that span the high-context and low-context functional cultures. Given current demographic and business trends, U.S. business teams will increasingly look like the UNA team. Margaret's team offers a dramatic illustration of how unresolved cultural issues—corporate, functional, and ethnic—move to the foreground at different stages of teamwork. Each issue has the power to impair good teamwork. Taken together, they constitute a formidable barrier to honest communications and better productivity.

In difficult times people's major concern is their job and its security—whatever their ethnic background. It is unlikely, therefore, that cultural issues can be addressed very effectively when the overall environment feels so unstable that any change is considered risky. In fact, workers who try to correct cultural biases are seen as troublemakers and thus candidates for pink slips during downsizing.

Learning is a big challenge for cross-functional and cross-cultural teams alike. Collaborative platforms are a key technology tool that supports the potential of these teams to learn. Margaret's team was using a group data base to work asynchronously on its task. Although it worked well for sharing information, communication, and coordination about the task, it's too early to tell just how much team and organizational learning was taking place. The team did use the Lotus Notes conferencing capability to address hot topics of a technical nature but only gingerly approached interlevel communication problems.

When teams do achieve high performance and look forward to rewards, what can they expect? At the present time, most U.S. companies encourage participation in cross-functional teams but still reward people within their own functional areas — as evaluated by peers and functional managers. And very often a person's career path will be different from his or her role on a cross-functional team. If, in addition, the individual rewards are inconsistent between teammates' functional areas, the business is sending the message that cross-functional work is less important than handling functional tasks.

There is a larger issue here for many companies: team reward systems in general. In most U.S. companies, people are encouraged to contribute on business teams, but they are rewarded for individual performance. This is part of the way the U.S. social culture penetrates the workplace. Even though successful teams form the backbone of quality programs and cross-functional work, team reward systems are unusual. It would be wrong to eliminate individual rewards — given the underlying social culture — but it should be possible to add team rewards to the mix.

Then there is the issue of negative rewards. If a cross-functional team fails, who takes responsibility? "It's not my department!" is not a very constructive answer, but it's one that is often given. Incentives, as well as negative rewards, may need to be devised in a way consistent with current reward systems. Once developed, there is the question of who is responsible for awarding them. Will authority revert to the stovepipe functions? Or will it be shared in a way that reflects the new cross-functional work?

Although multiple technologies were used extensively by the teams in the docudramas, the technology wasn't a major factor in resolving the human issues. Indeed, the electronic support may have allowed the teams to skirt the key ethnic, functional, and interlevel communication issues that needed to be thrashed out and resolved face to face. Face-to-face meetings are expensive but they do serve a purpose.

Teams should avoid the pitfall of trying to use technology to solve too many problems or inappropriate problems. So many tools are available that U.S. companies often purchase too many products and fail to use them to their full potential. To avoid this, goals should be resolved before deciding which technologies make the most sense for this team or that organization.

The United States has connectivity for many groupware and other technologies. This advantage should be exploited to its fullest potential but with caution. And because the United States has the most cutting-edge technology, it is too easy to revert to technological solutions. Technology is destined to play an increasingly greater role as distributed and diverse teams become the norm for U.S. corporations. Companies need to choose wisely, depending on their needs, and keeping it simple is always best. Make sure everybody has the same or easily compatible technology, and get agreement on how it will be used. Do not forget proper training and orientation.

Within a national context, communications enjoy the advantage of a common national identity and culture, which provides a context and buffer when things are not going well. Thus there are few valid excuses for mismanaging communication and information-sharing challenges. In the United States, especially, distributed teams should maximize their knowledge of tools and their use, building on the sophisticated and extensive infrastructure already in place.

The diverse teams we met were struggling to find effective strategies to maximize the value of cross-cultural teams. Interest in this subject, and in cross-cultural learning generally, is growing. But so too is the bewilderment over how to do it. Although the challenges of culturally diverse and distributed teams working within a single nation's boundaries may not be as great as those of transnational or global teams, the differences are largely ones of degree. The problems themselves are universal. The United States as a nation needs to learn from its global experiences at a deeper level—to openly and willingly change the dominant culture to reflect the nation's cultural diversity. The reward for such a movement toward real cultural equity and inclusion will be an enriched and truly creative society that can exhibit—much more than is possible today—the full potential of all its citizens. This is the challenge and the lesson from globalization.

RULES OF THUMB

Struggle is still the norm in the effort to develop strategies for meeting the cross-cultural and cross-functional challenges in the U.S. workplace. Among the approaches taken by scores of major corporations, the following are the most likely to yield positive results.

■ *Help people see the big picture.* Many U.S. workers feel disoriented enough by the new work arrangements created by the new global economy, let alone the changing faces in the workforce. In business environments where there is extreme turbulence, management needs to practice "helicopter thinking" for itself and all employees. Tell everybody your company's perspective on how these changes will improve your workspace in the long run and how you intend to manage them. Be careful to help all groups of employees see how the big picture affects them negatively and positively. No one cares about the big picture unless it reflects their reality.

■ *Address diversity concerns early and directly.* Companies should strive for racial and ethnic diversity in all types of teams, for cultural learning only takes place in real encounters. Cultural diversity issues that will affect teamwork should be explored at the time of the team's formation. These problems are always frustrating, but they just get worse over time. Dealing with them directly is the best strategy.

Workers should have regular forums where they can

explore personal, functional, gender, and ethnic differences. This type of session needs a skilled person to balance participation and keep it honest yet productive. Such forums are particularly helpful for cross-functional teams and somewhat more difficult with cross-ethnic groups.

People learn best when they're actively engaged. Unfortunately, most diversity training is encapsulated in one-time programs and there is little to show that it is being translated to behavior in the workplace itself. These programs are sometimes abstract, as well, and less connected to the work world than sessions that include a work-related goal. Try to integrate cultural learning into everyday activities. Exploring the contributions that each culture can make to a specific task—as well as openly discussing anticipated problems—can prevent serious miscommunications.

- *Define the learning boundaries.* Some diversity issues that appear in the workplace are the tip of the iceberg of a larger social problem—racism or sexism, for instance. These issues cannot be fully addressed in the workplace, no matter how hard one may try, so it's vital to set realistic limits. People get frustrated if they feel they have to solve all of society's ills in the context of their team. The team should list their key diversity challenges and then decide which ones they can productively address.

Do not, however, underestimate the impact of diversity on the workplace. All social cultures are not treated equally, and pretending they are will only induce a climate of distrust. And if your company is truly in cultural chaos with shifts in corporate culture, ethnic mix, and new cross-functional approaches, do not try to deal with all the diversity at once.

- *Create a cross-functional team culture.* Start by asking: "What if we had already been working together for five years? What would our collective culture be like?" Collaboratively invent values, rules, heroes, and behavior. Begin this process by treating other functional areas as different cultures with their own values, symbols, and behavior. Working across functional cultures can be even more difficult than working across ethnic or national boundaries. Start by assuming there is massive misunderstanding across functions—it's better to be surprised by shared perspectives than to assume alignment when there is none. Also assume, for the most part, that people don't recognize their own habits and practices within their functional areas of expertise. Help people imagine how both ethnic and functional diversity can serve as a source of innovative ideas.

It is easy to assume, erroneously, that functions in a corporation are more aligned than they actually are when it comes to corporate strategy, direction, and procedures. Often, each function is more like a separate company than part of a larger whole. Be careful not to ask for cross-functional work in a vertical corporate structure that has not shifted to new values and ways of working at the top. Don't be carried away with cross-functional team mania. It's quite easy to assume that you know about the culture of another functional area when you really do not. Be careful not to define people narrowly by functional stereotyping.

■ *Foster fluency in the corporate culture.* Fluency in the corporate culture can be essential to members of dispersed and diverse teams who need a common framework to help them maintain their corporate identity and unity. This "glue" is difficult to form during times of sweeping changes like those taking place today in many U.S. corporations. Some companies describe their new vision and the kind of culture they hope to create by communicating it widely throughout the company. The most successful efforts include dialogue at all levels and make the vision explicit and easily accessible through booklets, large graphics, strategy charts, and videos featuring top managers.

■ *Executives should set examples.* Top-level and middle managers must set the pace and demonstrate the company's commitment to dealing with cross-cultural and cross-functional learning. If they put themselves at risk by sharing their concerns and demonstrating resolution, others will follow. As multiple teams with multiple managers proliferate, coordination and a shared vision for all teams' work may be lacking at upper and middle management levels. If managers undermine each other, teams will follow suit.

- *Support better technology use.* People don't automatically know the best use of technology to support their work. The variety of technology choices in the U.S. business environment is staggering—and the options are growing. This bewildering variety needs to be managed with better orientation, and long-term support must become part of the corporate culture. Although technology has changed the very content and methods of working, many people still try to incorporate new technology into old ways of working. Encourage the use of computer conferencing and other collaborative tools as these applications become more widely installed and user friendly. They are particularly useful for cross-functional work, as they offer a neutral place for communicating diverse and sometimes contrary opinions.

- *Apply knowledge gained from global cross-cultural work to national teams.* U.S. business leaders who have crossed international boundaries in response to the pull of the global customer have begun to recognize cultural diversity at home and its potential—particularly for competitive innovations. This enlightenment of leadership is one of the keys to mining the cultural diversity that resides within U.S. business.

ELEVEN

Voyaging into Cyberspace:
The Anytime, Anyplace
Global Workspace

The future of distance and diversity in the workplace will be played out in an increasingly strange and mysterious world — the invisible but intense world of cyberspace. The popular press has already discovered and celebrated cyberspace in bizarre and breathless feature articles. These splashes of interest are serving an important conscious-raising function for business people, magnifying an important social phenomenon that has been developing quietly for more than two decades. Unfortunately, most popular press accounts of cyberspace emphasize the weirdness factor, which is definitely there and easy to write about. But the implications of cyberspace — for organizations, for individuals, and for society—are far more complex than superficial analysis allows. Globalwork is likely to change in profound ways as cyberspace develops. But when? And how?

Executives have a right to be confused. Most people have only recently adjusted to electronic mail, electronic data interchange, and worldwide telecommunications networks. From their perspective, cyberspace may look like a straightforward extension of these horseless carriage technologies. Cyberspace will not, however, be a straightforward extension of anything. Cyberspace represents a subtle but profound shift in the nature of communications as a medium and in our perception of distance. For most of this century, communications has been a conduit linking different physical locations. Now we are moving beyond communications as conduit to communications as a destination in its own right—a virtual space in which we will spend ever more of our business (and perhaps personal) lives.

Today's incarnation of cyberspace is hardly high-tech: it is little more than text, voice, and graphics over a variety of electronic networks. But bandwidth is booming and with it will come video and visually enhanced realities that could have major impacts on business and on life. This sea change in the way we work with computers and telecommunication devices is already turning the traditional mode of stand-alone computing on its head. In fact, the very notion of stand-alone anything will likely be a quaint oxymoron by decade's end. Globalwork will be redefined within this emerging electronic world.

The quiet progress of this revolution is clear in some little-noted statistics. The number of computer network nodes—personal computers linked into electronic networks—is growing more rapidly than the number of new computer sales due to the retrofitting of machines already installed. Network connectivity has ceased to be a nice option; it is an essential computer feature. One manufacturer estimates that this growth is occurring at the rate of a million new nodes per month. As of the end of 1993, there were tens of millions of private e-mail users, a threefold growth in only two years.

Public networks and bulletin board systems are growing even more rapidly. Traffic on Internet, the world's largest network of networks, is booming. Public networks are experiencing similar growth: there are now an estimated 50,000 public bulletin boards; more than 10 percent of the adult population of the United States uses some public bulletin board system. CompuServe claims over 1 million users; Prodigy claims 1.5 million customers.

Despite this rapid growth, most personal computers are still not networked, and most of current network traffic is for basic functions like sharing printers—not for exotic global collaboration. Overall, perhaps 45 percent of current personal computers are connected to networks in some way, and only about half of these have e-mail. Still, the rapid growth is significant, since e-mail is the primary point of departure for people and organizations about to beam up to cyberspace.

A new generation of ultraportable, ultrapowerful computing devices—personal information appliances—is being defined above all by what they connect us to, rather than what they process for us. This is the computer as connector and coordinator, not just processor. The processing revolution has ended, and an access revolution is rapidly gaining speed with often dramatic impacts, especially in the scientific community. Indeed, the basic modes of scholarly correspondence and debate are being reincarnated in electronic form, and the academic review process is being utterly transformed.

BEYOND E-MAIL

E-mail may be the port of entry, but the digital infrastructure opens up a sea of opportunities that go far beyond today's corporate electronic mail systems. Businesses are already discovering electronic networks for company-to-company connections, such as EDI (Electronic Data Interchange, a supplier/customer electronic exchange standard), to provide direct communications between remote computers coordinating vast business networks. And even intercompany networking is tame compared to what lies ahead in cyberspace.

Cyberspace is distance and diversity off the dials. The word is shorthand for a fundamental shift in how we view communications. In cyberspace, communications is not a connection between points A and B, but a virtual electronic space in which people at points A and B can come together in the same virtual space to meet colleagues, close deals, carry on idle conversations, and amuse themselves—in short, everything they do in the physical world today, as well as some things they can only do in virtual worlds.

The term *cyberspace* was coined by science-fiction writer William Gibson in his novel *Neuromancer* (1984), and it has quickly become a point of reference for what today's leading-edge designers and users hope to make available sooner rather than later. Though the term evokes science-fiction notions like "virtual reality" and direct mind-to-network links, manifestations of cyberspace actually exist today, built on nothing more than existing telephone and computer networks (particularly Internet) and simple, text-based interfaces.

The more exotic promises of cyberspace, however, are by no means farfetched, and they are already influencing cutting-edge technologies. After all, when it comes to turning computer technologies into products, reality often imitates art—particularly when the art is science fiction. Already, a growing army of digital visionaries is working to make real the cyberspace vision in its many variants. Just as the scientists building moon rockets in the 1960s were inspired by the Hugo Gernsback pulp novels of their childhood, a new digital generation is working to make their teenage dreams a reality—and they are reshaping the rest of reality in the process. Gibson's work prompted an entire new genre of science fiction, "cyberpunk," which is adding detail and direction to the cyberspace trend. Gibson's own description of cyberspace hints at what lies ahead. Cyberspace, he says, is "a consensual hallucination experienced daily by billions of legitimate operators.... A graphic representation of data abstracted from the banks of every computer in the human system. Unthinkable complexity. Lines of light ranged in the non-space of the mind, clusters and constellations of data" (Gibson, 1984, p. 51).

In the short term, the rise of this new digital medium will erase the "place" from workplace. We will take for granted an ever-increasing capability to conduct business from multiple locations, asymptotically approaching Stan Davis's vision of anytime/anyplace work (Davis, 1987). In the long run, the workplace is transforming into a workspace—a cyberspace with both physical and virtual dimensions. It will be a venue for both working and living, an environment that is essentially electronic, but with portals back into the physical world. Who we are and who we become in this new world will be up to each of us as individuals and as a society. The rules of work, business, and life will be redrawn in cyberspace. Even basic laws, like the U.S. Constitution, are likely to take on new meaning— or lack of meaning.

It will be a very strange world indeed, a world inhabited not only by electronic extensions to human presences but by electronic alter egos and life forms as well—alive and almost alive. Electronic communications, for instance, will no longer require human participation. "Communications" today implies humans talking to humans or (in the computer community) computers talking to computers. In the future, humans talking directly to humans will account for only a small proportion of network traffic, as will routine mechanical communications among machines. Much more important will be communications among "computerized agents" who exchange information with each other on behalf of their human masters.

The first hints of these long-term trends are already evident. For example, nearly two-thirds of the transpacific phone traffic between the United States and Japan is not people talking to people; most is accounted for by fax machines communicating with other machines. Add in e-mail and computer-conferencing traffic and the trend becomes even sharper.

The great majority of machines communicating on our behalf today, however, are blindly stupid. But the steady addition of intelligence will make them ever more autonomous and will extend the scope of their influence. And before we know it, cyberspace will evolve into what the French theologian Teilhard de Chardin called the "noösphere"—a thinking envelope among people, a generalized nervous system containing our accumulated experience and offering us further liberation from isolated human bodies. Cyberspace will be an environment we inhabit, as well as a home for our electronic alter egos and perhaps stranger entities yet. There will be ghosts in our machines, and the ghosts will be us.

EVOLVING TOWARD
CYBERSPACE
VIA ARPA AND MUDS

The road to cyberspace began at least twenty years ago when the first of the sophisticated computer networks, known as ARPAnet (Advanced Research Projects Agency Network, the predecessor of Internet), became fully operational in the early 1970s. In those early days, communities of users developed spontaneously, quite to the surprise of the systems designers and administrators. Originally ARPAnet was envisioned for use in data and program exchanges among Defense Department research sites. Such exchanges did occur, but the major use was for interpersonal communications. Back then, many people in the technical community thought that e-mail and computer conferencing over sophisticated computer networks was, essentially, a misuse of computer resources. Gradually, however, it became clear that interpersonal communications are the essence, not the by-product, of network links.

Early on, the Institute for the Future conducted a series of informal experiments on ARPAnet with groups of scientists in energy research, geology, and space exploration. At the fringes of this work, without official endorsement, the network was used to explore the idea of collaborative "fast thinking"— that is, individuals attempted to bond their own thoughts together and create ideas more quickly and of higher quality than would have been possible face to face. Other teams experimented with extrasensory and psychic research problems, crisis simulation, and other forms of role playing. None of this work was formally reported at the time, and official funds were not used to support it. But now what seemed like the twilight zone is resurfacing with new vigor and new possibilities.

One of the ways it's resurfacing is in the development of multiple-user dimensions (MUDs), which provide a useful glimpse into cyberspace. MUDs are a novel approach to computer conferencing that emphasizes intense, informal interactions among users in a mode that is reminiscent of psychodrama. Unlike traditional e-mail, it is a hallmark of MUDs that more than two users simultaneously interact in a manner approaching face-to-face conversations. The result is a shared social virtual environment: part interpersonal exchange, part psychodrama, and part something that has never been experienced before.

A big part of the MUDs' appeal comes from their ability to become whatever users want them to become. Participants don't just communicate: they can modify their shared virtual world by creating new spaces and even populating those spaces with new objects and other "life" forms. This feature dates back to the origin of MUDs in the early 1980s as "Multi-User Dungeons"—multiple-user versions of the then-popular Dungeons and Dragons fantasy games. Just as Dungeons and Dragons offered users magical powers, MUDs give their participants capabilities not possible in the real world.

You won't find dragons on most MUDs today, but a recent tour through one of the well-known MUDs, called "Lambda.moo," revealed everything from a cuckoo clock to a garrulous cockatoo, as well as half a dozen human visitors, all lounging in a living room modeled loosely on the living room in the home of Lambda.moo's creator, Pavel Curtis, a Xerox PARC researcher (Curtis, 1992). When one visitor departed, he didn't just walk out but disappeared in a puff of blue smoke.

Lambda.moo was constructed by Curtis to include an

Figure 11.1. Lambda.moo Cockatoo Prop.

easy-to-use programming language that participants can use to build "props" like the cuckoo clock and cockatoo. The cockatoo had been programmed by one "mudder" to randomly repeat snatches of conversations overheard in the living room. This eventually became annoying, so at the group's request, he programmed a "gag" that can be slipped over the cockatoo's beak, silencing the bird until it slips the gag off after about ten minutes (see Figure 11.1).

Another attribute defining a MUD is rather surprising in these days of multimedia: MUDs are text-based. They operate fully within the ASCII confines. Visitors to Lambda.moo's cyperspace do not don space-age virtual-reality goggles; they type in simple commands to interact with their world, and they read text descriptions on-screen. Typing "look deck," for example, yields a detailed description of the deck just outside the house. Mudders talk to each other using commands like "say" and "whisper," followed by a statement. Other mudders see the dialogue on their screens as "Curtis says, 'Did someone gag the cockatoo?'" This text orientation sounds like a hindrance compared to video or computer graphics, but the actual MUD experience is vivid in much the way a good novel is sometimes more vivid than a movie.

Curtis explains that Lambda.moo's text orientation is critical to fostering the user's ability to tailor and adapt the system, given the current state of technology. Describing, for instance, a cottage with the best of today's graphics systems can be a programmer's nightmare, and the results will be disappointing. Doing the same in text requires little more than typing a description like: "a cozy gingerbread cottage nestled beneath the snarling branches of an ancient oak tree."

Meanwhile, Curtis himself is building a prototype multimedia MUD that overcomes the text barrier by adding simultaneous two-way voice and slow-scan video. Participants can sit at their desk and converse while seeing the other participants in windows on their screens. The result is an entirely new form of video interaction, more structured than a video phone call, but less formal than a video conference. Curtis's work in this area builds on earlier work at Xerox by Adele Goldberg, Steve Kaufman, Mark Abel, and others at PARC who did early explorations of spontaneous video for drop-in meetings (rather than scheduled video teleconferences in conference rooms).

Imagine the following scenario. Each morning when I arrive in my office, I log into the MUD and enter my "virtual office," where I remain seated in a lounge for discussions with a larger group. The lounge might even have a water cooler as a quaint reminder of the old days. These virtual spaces could exist entirely in a cyberspace, or map onto actual locations in my office, enriching the interaction still further. The lounge could be the virtual twin of the actual lounge down the hall. People sitting in the actual lounge could interact with MUD visitors in the virtual lounge via a large-screen display, allowing meetings to be attended both physically and electronically.

MUDs can be downright addictive, judging from current activity on the Internet, where MUDs are popping up constantly. The Australian authorities, concerned about limited bandwidth in satellite traffic, even had to prohibit MUDs after the Internet traffic out of that country jumped by 25 percent within months of the MUDs becoming available. Meanwhile, the University of Massachusetts in Amherst banned MUDs because they used up too much computer time—and student study time. System administrators on the Internet are worried because MUDs tend to expand to fill all bandwidth and memory available, at the risk of crowding out other communications. Curtis reports that several Lambda.moo users routinely spend over four hours per day on the system, and at least one reached a point where he was doing nothing but "mudding" and sleeping. As a result, Curtis built a "safety lock" into the MUD: a user can tell the system to automatically disconnect after a certain interval (say, four hours) and not allow one to log in again until the next day. Internet already has a special conference for recovering MUD addicts.

Multimedia near-MUDs are already serving as recreational areas. The oldest is "Habitat," a virtual world created in the late 1980s at LucasFilm by Chip Morningstar and Randall Farmer. Instead of viewing simple text, Habitat's visitors encounter an animated cartoon world occupied by buildings, landscapes, and the like. Users appear as cartoon characters (you visit a "body shop" to design your own persona from an inventory of heads and body parts), and their typed-in conversations are inserted in bubbles over their heads like something from the Sunday funnies.

Habitat was released in simplified form as "Club Caribe" by America On-line in 1988, and a full-fledged version of Habitat exists on the NiftyServe system in Japan. Though the point of Habitat is recreation, it nonetheless offers a true multiple-user virtual world built around a spatial metaphor. Habitat is different from "pure" MUDs, however, since users are limited in their ability to adapt the environment to their own needs: Habitat dwellers cannot build their own spaces, or design cuckoo clocks, as in Lambda.moo.

The number of these multimedia almost-MUDs is increasing nearly as rapidly as MUDs themselves. The game company Sierra On-line has "Red Baron," a multiple-user World War I aerial dogfight game, as well as "LarryLand," a virtual Las Vegas complete with casinos, slot machines, and dancing girls. Visitors to LarryLand select their body and persona like visitors to Habitat, and then go off to play games, win "LarryBucks," and have lots of sleazy Las Vegas fun. MUD wrestling, anyone?

SCIENTISTS IN CYBERSPACE

While gamers continue to probe the limits of MUD construction, there will be major impacts in professional and business domains. For example, Xerox's Curtis is helping launch "Astro.moo," a MUD for astronomers seeking to maintain close collegial contact while spread all over the globe. As Curtis explains it: "You go to a conference and meet the five other people in the world who work in your specialty, you have a fantastic discussion, and then you don't see them for a year. Astro.moo is the answer for staying in touch." The result is a virtual astronomer community, an "invisible college" linked across time and space (Curtis, 1992, p. 3).

Of course, the astronomers will want to do more than chat. The programming language built into Astro.moo will allow its users to construct custom props such as a shared calculator that supports specialized discussions. The astronomers might use this to help in conversations about black holes, but the same feature could be useful to any community of specialists communicating via MUD, from automotive engineers to molecular biologists.

The Worm Community System (WCS) gives us a hint what professional MUDs might be like. The Worm Community is an invisible college with shared data bases and resources linking a global community of researchers who have devoted their careers to understanding the nematode worm *Caenorhabditis elegans*. This system supports researchers with a hypertext-like structure, maintaining a large pool of documents and research behind an e-mail/conferencing front end. Though it lacks the metaphors and dramatic qualities of a MUD, the result is an environment reinforcing the deep sense of community this group of researchers already feels. It has become an indispensable tool for them all. Clearly, founder Bruce Schatz's "WorldNet" aspirations are a visionary statement regarding scientists in cyberspace. And Schatz is not just writing about it, he is building it. His motto is this: "Today the worm, tomorrow the world" (National Research Council, 1993).

If cyberspace is already a reality in the scientific community, there also are indications that it is nudging its way into the world of business. Early ventures are underground or unofficial, but if current traffic demands created by MUDs in the research and university communities are any measure, it will be difficult to hide a business MUD in the corporate network. Official MUDs will probably require the approval of senior management — a fact that is likely both to retard their spread and to shape what kinds of uses will be pursued. MUDs are beyond the imagination of most of today's senior executives. Hence there's a real blindside potential for sabotage or at least playful anarchy.

As suggested in Chapter Three, senior exeutives and corporate lawyers are very nervous about corporate e-mail and conferencing systems. Obviously, there are corporate liability issues to consider, and the fact that e-mail files have been subpoenaed with increasing frequency by courts only makes lawyers more nervous. Retention limits on e-mail and strong "For Business Use Only" messages are the norm. Despite these obstacles, cyberspace represents some obvious advantages that businesses will eventually find attractive — such as building global communities and supporting workers without heavy dependence on expensive travel. Cyberspace offers great potential for global community building... if corporations can learn how to take advantage of the potentials and avoid the pitfalls.

We expect that topic-oriented MUDs and other forms of cautious cyberspace will begin surfacing within businesses sooner rather than later. In fact, the MUD metaphor represents a natural evolution of the computer conferences and bulletin boards that already go on within many companies.

Expect business MUDs to be less exotic than those described here. You won't find the in-your-face bizarreness of today's recreational MUDs. On the other hand, business MUDs will be more intense, more challenging, and probably more fun than today's boring e-mail systems. Just as some companies use bowling leagues, golf tournaments, and corporate outings as a way of building esprit de corps, so may business MUDs play similar roles for distributed teams in the future. For global and cross-cultural teams, such networks could become a vital source of bonding, learning, and support.

COMMUNITY ORGANIZING IN CYBERSPACE

There is a downside, however, of MUDs and other cyberspace environments: their power to pull employees away from their organizations with considerable centrifugal force. Given the business trends toward workforce fragmentation and weaker employee commitments to employers, cyberspace might look like a threat. Are there ways to develop the frontier of cyberspace so that it provides a kind of compromise or common culture for diverse and distant users?

One reason Curtis and Xerox are interested in MUDs is that they hope they can make it possible for people to be full social members of PARC's research community without having to be physically present at PARC more than a few days per month. The problem is the cost of Silicon Valley real estate, which makes it difficult for researchers in other states to accept jobs at places like PARC. If MUDs enable a "community at a distance," these researchers could live in inexpensive rural areas and make a lengthy commute once a month or so.

This application will be important for businesses like Xerox, but the use of MUDs in most businesses will depend on simpler applications. For instance, MUDs can fill a clear social need for community in an ever-more-fragmented world. As Howard Rheingold (editor of the *Whole Earth Review* and author of numerous books on computers) observes: "We all know more people than ever, and our identities are fragmented along multiple business and private persona. MUDs are a medium that fits well with this reality." The real test will come when cyberspace becomes a medium for work by normal people, not just those working at exotic think tanks. Consider the dispersed outsource webs described in Chapter One. How might these work teams be joined electronically to facilitate their work yet allow enough flexibility to be attractive to workers?

One of the more intriguing appeals of cyberspace may be the ability to pretend to be someone you are not. This could be simple fantasy—the "Trek.Muse" MUD allows users to become the characters in the "Star Trek" TV series—or it could be something more subtle. It is estimated, for instance, that over half of the "females" on underground bulletin boards are in fact males. Strange as this sounds, one researcher concludes that this is a healthy way for teenagers to explore their identities and understand what it's like to be a member of the opposite sex. MUDs are a way for people to adopt and explore multiple simultaneous personas. The ability to adopt different personas could be very useful in learning about different cultures and different perspectives—walking in the other person's moccasins, as the American Indian saying goes. The key will be in developing appropriate software to allow learning about different perspectives while still keeping track of who's on first and what's on second.

This raises yet another potential downside for business applications: the possibilities for disruption, spying, and even sabotage are staggering. There will be technological safeguards, such as electronic verification of the user's identity, but the potentials for abuse are at least as real as the prospects for positive innovation. A more subtle threat is the probability that these new cyberspace systems will greatly accelerate ongoing changes in corporate structures. The hierarchical, place-based corporation as we know it may be headed for the ash heap of history, and it is likely to be replaced by something more weblike and based on ecological rather than mechanistic models. MUDs would undoubtedly facilitate such a change.

Despite the drawbacks, MUDs are an ideal way for dispersed teams to build a sense of telecommunity, which is one of the central notions underlying the exploration of cyberspace. MUDs amount to community-on-demand, overcoming the tyranny of distance. In this sense, cyberspace harks back to the same urges that created the Greek agora and the medieval notion of the commons in England. It offers a social meeting ground that is safe and potentially rewarding, the "great good place." In this case, however, people will gather in a "great good space."

THE DEMONIC ZONE

There is another kind of space represented by the potentials of cyberspace that may or may not be so good. It is a space of great mystery. This is evident in one purist's definition of a MUD: he concludes that a MUD cannot be interesting "unless you can die." Habitat's designers recognized that "virtual death" is no laughing matter. They eliminated the ability to kill other avatars peopling their system. Imagine having your MUD alter ego killed off after you've devoted six months to building the character. Mudders have reported members experiencing genuine grief over such a death—and developing close personal bonds with other players who saved their virtual personality from death at the last second.

There is a demonic quality to the early forms of cyberspace that shows up in both the cyberpunk literature and many of the early MUDs. By "demonic" we don't necessarily mean evil, but rather something that is profoundly ambiguous—capable of good or evil. It is this ambiguity, or unpredictability, combined with power that makes demons seem so dangerous. Demons are border-dwellers, and it is from the subliminal nature of borders that they derive both their ambiguity and their power.

Demons are the shape-shifters of anthropological lore that live between worlds: between order and disorder. The Trickster coyote of American Indian legends is a demon. So too are Hermes, the demonic messenger of Greek mythology, and Daemon, the son of Zeus. Demons are thus inferior divinities (or superior humans) midway between the gods and humankind. The denizens of the bar scene in *Star Wars* were demons in a border zone. These ancient and modern mythic traditions teach us that demonic energy must be treated with caution, for it is often both exciting and full of surprise, as well as dangerous. Demons can't be ignored, for, as the foregoing examples suggest, they are also the wellsprings of creative energies. Cyberspace is an electronic frontier, a border between the real and virtual worlds. It thus is a promising zone for shades, shape-changers, and shape-makers of all varieties. Cyberspace is a demonic zone, and the terms used by its inhabitants—cyberpunks, edge-surfers, outlaws, heat-seekers—reflect this fact.

As the cyberpunk literature already indicates, all varieties of interaction are possible in cyberspace—including new forms of older human expressions that many will find disturbing. (There is even a magazine devoted to "teledildonics"—virtual sex in cyberspace.) Yet there is also much that is reassuring, for cyberspace allows new forms of human communication and a greater sense of community and continuity across great physical and social distances. Cyberspace constitutes an emergent parallel world whose cultural norms are still to be written. Above all, context will determine cultural norms, and context switching will be a critical cultural characteristic. It is likely that inhabitants of cyberspace will look to external icons as shorthand indicators of the cultural norms to be followed in this situation or that.

Cyberspace's nature as a "consensual hallucination" will make it a profoundly ambiguous and contextual environment. It will offer a proliferation of frames of reference but few fixed reference points. It is easy to imagine a situation where users have difficulty determining what is real—and serious risks creep into such situations. In fact, such experiences are already happening and the category of experience even has a label: the Ender's Game Scenario, conferred from the title of a science-fiction story that explored its implications (Card, 1985).

Hints of cyberspace are already available from similar zones. A pilot on an actual F-16 training flight, for example, was wearing a heads-up display to simulate night flight with vision restriction and infrared images. The pilot reported what happened: "I experienced...a failure. I removed my vision restricting device. . . . I descended into a valley, checked my gas, my timing, and pressed on towards the upcoming mountain ridge. Shortly thereafter, I got the scare of my life. I was not flying the airplane. I was waiting for it to fly itself over the ridge! I was lucky I recognized it early and was able to safely clear the rocks. But what had happened?" (Slocum, 1991, pp. 5–7). In this case, the pilot got confused about which reality he was in—about whether he or the computer was in control of the airplane. A human factors psychologist commented on this episode and its implications: "A similar incident could occur if a virtual reality (VR) system operator failed to distinguish between what was real and what was synthesized. VR systems must be implemented in such a manner that the user recognizes the potential for this type of incident. Research is needed to quantify and explain the effect" (Wells, 1992, pp. 1–3).

The research on transitions between boundaries in cyberspace is only just beginning. One consequence of such research might be the creation of new kinds of team skills such as "context surfing"—the ability to spin quickly through multiple points of reference in order to find the one most appropriate to the team's needs at a particular moment and then deliver that perspective back to the group. Will "perspective spinning" become a key business skill?

In any case, corporate cyberspace will not be a straightforward benevolent reincarnation of the paternalistic companies of the 1950s. Many executives look forward to the promise of electronic networks, but few are prepared for the gravity of the downside possibilities: the Pandora's Box aspect.

As Robert Reich, the new secretary of labor, once noted in *New Republic* magazine, "Many of the new technologies are themselves subversive. Computers and telecommunications equipment not only incite unorthodox ideas, they also allow them to be exchanged instantly. They inspire communities of dissent" (Perry, 1992, pp. 22–23). Cyberspace is no electronic heaven. It need not be an electronic hell, either. But it may borrow attributes of both simultaneously.

Teams will become an essential unit of organization in this emerging cyberworld, since distance will virtually disappear. Is a team that is distributed geographically but occupies the same location in cyberspace centralized or decentralized? Or is it both? Younger-generation "infonauts" who grow up in cyberspace will treat these questions as mildly idiotic, but older managers will find them troubling and confusing. In the end, the answers will be distinctions without a difference to anyone other than lawyers, as teams discover that they can function with full effectiveness in this strange new world.

There will be challenges, though, such as synchronization—maintaining alignment between the virtual and the actual realities. Cyberspace encourages people to reinvent themselves as virtual personas quite different from their physical presence, and the adoption of multiple simultaneous personas is already common. How will people cross between the two worlds without experiencing jarring personality shifts?

The opportunity for paradox is there, as well, as in any good border zone. What happens, for example, when multiple personas of the same person interact? What if one is the actual human and the others are semiautonomous agents? Working out cultural norms for acceptable and unacceptable behavior in this regard will be difficult and full of surprises. Moreover, once one has developed an effective and compelling cyberspace persona (such as the multiple-gender entity that disappeared in a cloud of smoke in Lambda.moo), the problem of projecting that persona into the physical world remains. How, for example, could it turn up at a board meeting?

But the subtlest problem of all may be determining where cyberspace stops and the physical world begins. Will the participants in one world always know when their actions are having an impact in the other? The U.S. military, for instance, is busy building a next-generation cyberspace successor to SimNet, a distributed system that allows tank commanders and others to fight virtual battles in a primitive cyberspace. On this future system it is likely that a soldier driving a real tank at, say, the Fort Irwin tank training ground will be able to interact electronically with a "virtual plane" flown by a jet jockey sitting in a simulator thousands of miles away. When the virtual jet fires and hits the tank, will the death be virtual or actual? Will the jet jockey ever know?

Another critical team issue will be the role of nonhuman team members. The semisentient ghosts apt to inhabit cyberspace are likely to be treated as team members for some purposes and as lifeless bits of software for others. How do team members distinguish between these situations? And when a ghost does something untoward (like filtering out an important message or routing it to someone who finds it offensive), who will be responsible?

Organizations are shaped above all by their channels of communication, and changing the channels inevitably changes the organization. Reliable postal systems yielded the monarchy model of management of the early 1800s, which gave way in the late 1800s to infant corporate hierarchies, which were made possible by the advent of the railroad, tele-graph, and emerging telephony. The information revolution eroded this command-and-control hierarchy and triggered the rise of the business team described by Peter Drucker as the new basic building block of organizational structures (Drucker, 1988).

Now the advent of cyberspace is pulverizing organiza-tional structures and traditions once again. Even simple e-mail systems have created conduits between widely disparate orga-nizational levels, as mail clerks correspond with CEOs and bands of techno-anarchists conspire to eliminate entire divi-sions within their companies. The stories are remarkable, even though most of them are only discussed in private. But PCs and e-mail merely flattened organizations; cyberspace will do much, much more. In the short run, it will add dizzying complexity to our horizontal organizations by creating seemingly endless numbers of links and networks. Old-style senior executives who try to flex their control over these organizations will learn the real meaning of digital anarchy.

MANAGING
THE UNMANAGEABLE

Some organizations are already trying to reimpose traditional hierarchical structures in cyberspace, but their efforts will fail. When you think of successful organizational adaptations to cyberspace, think of the fishnet. Fishnet organizations can be picked up at any node, and new structures will terrace out beneath them. Corporate effectiveness will depend on finding the right balance of links between nodes: too many and the sheer redundancy in channels will gridlock the organization; too few and the organization will be starved of information.

Organizations in cyberspace will be built on explicitly ecological models, and words like *symbiosis* will become the executive buzzwords of the turn of the century. These organizations will model themselves on that of organisms, puzzling over issues like coordination among "nodes" (either teams or individuals), definition of optimal web structures, and means of "grafting" effectively onto networks of external partners.

The very term *management* may be an early casualty of this new way of organizational thinking. Management implies the ability to see, comprehend, and control the full extent of one's organization — which will be impossible in full-fledged cyberorganizations. The number of internal links and interdependencies will be too complex to grasp in more than a summary way, while the range and intimacy of connections with external allies and partners will make it impossible to determine where one's own company stops and another begins. The organizations of the future won't be companies but organic entities defined above all by whom they cooperate with. Perhaps the term *management* will disappear, a quaint relic from the age of Taylorism unable to mutate to fit in a new cyberworld. At least, the idea of management as control will disappear in the clouds of uncertainty.

If rigid management is anathema to cyberspace, organizational learning via simulation is an almost inevitable byproduct. We are entering a world where just-in-time learning will mean going through the motions on simulators before trying the real thing in the real world. We will hone our experiential skills in the virtual worlds of cyberspace before playing for keeps on the competitive gameboard. Of course, simulated learning has been on the edge of success for more than two decades, but cyberspace may allow its full potential to finally be realized.

SimNet, the military system mentioned earlier, is a rather modest and almost obsolete simulation network that nonetheless has become a most effective platform for virtual wargaming by tankers. Tanker teams can drive their vehicles through vivid virtual terrains and face dogged enemy threats in a manner that allows them to explore all the confusing minutiae of actual conflict situations: fields of fire, radio coordination, artillery call-ins, even fratricide. Virtual death in SimNet is almost as cruel as the real thing, but the players survive to fight another day, much the wiser for their experience. The terrains they fight on are simulations of actual terrains, and the battles are modeled on actual battles from military history—one from the Gulf War, the Battle of 73 Easting, is especially popular, having been played for congressional audiences. And the military has plans for a far more capable network. DARPA's IDA Advanced Simulation Laboratory is hatching a Distributed Simulation Internet that will, by next decade, allow as many as ten thousand simulators to link remotely into a single virtual battlefield.

Elsewhere, other researchers are designing educational MUDs. Cambridge computer scientist Barry Kort has constructed "Micromuse," an educational MUD designed as a space colony in the twenty-fourth century. Its student visitors enter the MUD, find a place, build a room, and join the community. Its goal is to teach children about science and education. These early experiences could provide insights that will later be useful in corporate settings. For example, simulations could be used to explore complex situations that global teams are likely to encounter—before they experience them for real and before the pressures of a real business situation are upon them. Cross-cultural issues within the team could be a key topic to explore.

CYBERSPACE
FOR THE SENSES

Information technologies will become the circulatory and nervous systems of our emerging new cyberorganizations. Continuing a long tradition, new information tools will become ever more intimate complements to individuals and teams. What follows is a sampling from a much longer list of new technologies likely to appear on the organizational horizon over the next decade or so.

The cybernaut's dream is a direct brain-to computer link. Such a dream is unlikely to become a reality within any reasonable time frame, but less ambitious goals in this direction are possible as we continue to expand the range of computer input/output options. Three decades ago, man-machine communication was limited to punch cards, paper tape, and printouts. Two decades ago, screens and keyboards moved to the fore. Today you can choose from nearly as many options as you have senses, including stylus, touch-screen, speech, and sound. Scent remains problematic, but even that option is being explored at the outer fringes of entertainment-based virtual reality.

We have expanded the ways we interact with computers into a digital sensorium, and now researchers are beginning to explore more direct links bypassing the senses. Researchers at Fujitsu and elsewhere are working to detect brainwaves in a controversial effort to capture "silent speech," the mental states that stop just short of being voiced. Elsewhere re-searchers have constructed chips capable of interfacing be-tween computer systems and human nerves. Global workers are unlikely to have to have chip implants in order to perform their jobs, but the application of these devices in mental and physical rehabilitation work will have important implications.

Knowledge workers will take for granted that they'll be able to choose from a wide range of interface options — and always find the right option for a particular task. It will be a world not of input/output at all, but of electronic "body music" as humans and machines work in ever more intimate collab-oration to create new knowledge products. The global work-space will be characterized by such mind/machine harmo-nies — or dissonance.

Cyberspace will be largely inhabited by extrahuman in-telligences. In face, the bulk of "conversations" in cyberspace may be machine-to-machine and machine-to-human rather than human-to-human. True artificial life forms exhibiting a degree of sentience that is unquestionably "alive" will remain the stuff of science-fiction novels, but "virtual life forms" are here today in the form of ever more capable autonomous programs. Today's EDI systems, from program trading on electronic stock exchanges to the parts-moving systems of Detroit automakers, already depend on such programs.

Advances in the field of artificial life and elsewhere are creating even more effective and robust agents. As their robustness increases, we will entrust these electronic alter egos with greater and greater responsibilities. Already, e-mail mavens can avail themselves of mail "demons" performing garbage-collection filtering tasks — for example, automatically deleting any mail from sources identified by the recipient as offensive or unworthy of a response. And primitive agents are flying some of the weapons platforms that occupied center stage in the Gulf War, such as cruise missiles. The biggest surprises in agents may in fact come out of the defense sector, covering everything from fighter-pilot assistants to exotic, electronic warfare agents.

One thing is certain: people will question the intelligence

of agents even as they exhibit ever greater degrees of sentience. But whatever degree of skepticism we bring to them, the fact will remain that our systems will be inhabited by semiautonomous, semisentient virtual creatures. They will be electronic incarnations of the subliminal beings of folklore and mythology. Perhaps we will even call them "ghosts" in unconscious acknowledgment of their liminal status and propensity for occasionally whimsical and unpredictable behavior. And the media for displaying or experiencing the ghosts of cyberspace are becoming increasingly powerful.

Though hopelessly overhyped, virtual reality (VR) is finding application in a wide range of areas from arcade games to scientific visualization. The technology remains quite primitive—even the best cyberspaces available today offer little more than fuzzy colored polygons requiring the active imaginations of humans to turn them into virtual terrains. This is cyberspace with astigmatism. Without a doubt, though, the view will improve over the next two decades as our computers become more nimble and as novel viewing techniques like laser-based retinal scanning or headsets that can be worn like eyeglasses replace today's clunky stereo eye-phones. But even before crisp, holo-color, virtual cyberspaces emerge, many teams will have found today's fuzzy cyberworlds a convenient place to meet and work.

The most likely scenario is that the first such communities will emerge from scientific visualization applications. Virtual reality has found early application in areas such as biochemistry, where gloved and goggle-clad researchers hope to be able to build new compounds by tugging and pulling at the links and atoms of organic molecules suspended in virtual space. And what could be better than meeting a colleague in the same virtual space to explore the secrets of a molecule together? Scientists communicate through models already; VR allows them to meet inside of models instead of conference rooms. Such shared model building can be especially helpful when colleagues are working in labs on opposite sides of the earth.

This scenario is already possible. Shared cyberspaces

with near-adequate computer graphics are already available to teenagers in game arcades, while far more vivid, structured cyberspaces are proliferating in the military research and training sector. SimNet, the Pentagon's aging strategy simulation network, has pioneered more advanced remote training — and, as noted, a more capable system is waiting in the wings. Meanwhile, research scientists are beginning to sink their virtual heads into virtual molecules as part of system prototyping. The cost of developing such systems for the relatively small scientific research and defense market is likely to provide an early incentive to diffuse advanced VR systems into the consumer marketplace. And once the scientists begin to work in this environment, they are certain to use it for informal collegial meetings as well. From time to time, they will invite a "suit" — an executive colleague — into such a meeting, and thus VR will spread.

Today's ridiculous-looking wearable computers will mature into unobtrusive and essential information tools for mobile professionals. Knowledge workers — from artillery officers to utility repair workers, from couriers to ambulance technicians — will don information and communication devices that extend their skills and effectiveness: the information exoskeleton. The point here is not to forecast cybernetic fashion trends but to note that the computers which transport us into cyberspace will be designed to fit naturally into our workstyle and lifestyle.

Wearing your computer to work, and at home, may be a new status symbol — like wearing a beeper used to be. For some people (even a few executives), a meeting in a cyberspace — pumped into existence by monster supercomputers and gobs of optical-fiber bandwidth — will become a corporate perk of even greater status than hopping the Concorde for a meeting in Paris.

During the next decade, at least, the cost/performance ratios of such systems will close precipitously. But the vividness gap — the gap between virtual and real worlds — is so great that the systems will remain expensive as every ounce of spare cash is sunk back into improving the "reality" of the virtual worlds. Ten years from now, we will be longing for better resolution and goggles that don't tire our eyes after an hour or so. But more than a handful of professionals will take meetings in cyberspace for granted: ordinary and unremarkable parts of globalwork.

During this same period, we will have a much better sense of which media are best suited for which business and social tasks. We will learn that face-to-face communication may not be the ultimate in human exchange. And more media and more bandwidth—even if it produces holographic virtual images of people at other sites—may not be better in all cases. Perhaps more constrained media, such as text and audio, will prove richer for certain types of communication, just as the radio has discovered its real and lasting strengths in the age of television. For example, laboratory research conducted in the United Kingdom during the 1970s indicates that it is easier to detect lying via audio than via audio/video or face-to-face encounter (Short, Williams, and Christie, 1976). Especially as the quality of audio improves, we may come to prefer it for certain tasks, just as some of today's mudders prefer the ASCII text constraints to multimedia. Certainly it is appropriate to be cautious about which media are good for what. In cyberspace, the rules will change.

FROM HERE
TO THERE

The only way to really learn about cyberspace is to begin experiencing it by sending a few eager pioneers out to the frontier. As on any frontier, nobody is sure what they'll find. The explorers may not come back, or they may come back different people. Expect to be surprised, often. Do not assume that cyberspace is a simple extension of e-mail, telephone, fax, and other familiar media. It is much more, and it will be very different.

Electronic media have already suggested that the face-to-face encounter may not be the ultimate form of human communication for every situation, though most people are not willing to listen to this lesson. Cyberspace will introduce us to a new range of options, at least some of which may be superior to face-to-face—at least for certain tasks.

It is reasonable to assume that global organizations will have to develop new ways of managing people in cyberspace. The old ways are not likely to work, at least not in the ways that managers have come to expect. Traditional organizational control methods are likely to be counterproductive in cyberspace. In fact, it is dangerous to assume we know how to control much of anything in cyberspace. We do not.

Globalwork on the cyberspace frontier will take years to mature, but it is an exciting territory with many opportunities—as well as serious pitfalls. The cross-cultural work of today will provide a ground for creating new "third ways" of globalwork in cyberspace.

CONCLUSION

Global Living and Global Work: New Knowledge, Values, and Communities

We began this book by noting that the globalization of work and economic activity is opening up new worlds of opportunity for social and business interaction, productive cooperation, and personal and collective growth. We end it with a new appreciation for a lesson that we ourselves have learned in the course of writing this book. It is the realization that the key forces that define the successful global enterprise — dispersed, collaborative, mutually supporting networks of individuals and teams; a deep commitment to continual learning about technological and organizational innovation; and a broad and deepening sensitivity to the fundamental role played by cul-

l values, both our own and those of others — are the precur-
of not only a richer and wiser world but, more important, a
world in which wisdom itself will be the coin of the global
realm and a new sense of community will be the ultimate
product of globalwork.

The notion of wisdom as wealth and power is not new, of
course. It is a major theme in Plato's Socratic dialogues. But for
much of modern times, *Homo economicus* — the capitalist version of what Eastern Europeans once disparagingly called
Homo sovieticus — has been chasing wealth of more tangible
sorts: the wealth of personal consumption and possession. And
why not? After all, goods are the natural wealth of a manufacturing economy — cars, houses, TVs, refrigerators, toys of all
sorts, and, of course, the money to buy them.

But the manufacturing economy, along with all its elaborate organizational hierarchies and mechanical work processes, has given way, as we all know, to a radically restructured, decentralized information economy in which facts,
knowledge, and ideas, globally dispersed, are both the principal products and the sought-after rewards of economic life.
Facts and knowledge may not be equivalent to wisdom, but
they are clearly steps along the path.

Shumpei Kumon of the Center for Global Communications at the International University of Japan is one pioneer of
the new global landscape who has not been afraid or embar-
rassed to let his imagination point the way toward what we
might daringly call the wisdom economy. He writes of the
information economy's "informatization," meaning continuous technological innovation, as a process that "will lead to the
emergence and spread of a new type of social actor, that is,
intelprises who become players of what might be called the
wisdom game" (Turner and Kraut, 1992).

And what do tomorrow's "intelpreneurs" produce and
how are they rewarded? Obviously, they produce information
and knowledge, and, says Kumon, "by successfully sharing
their information, they demonstrate the value of the individual pieces of information . . . in terms of the social values of
truth, goodness and beauty. Their reward is wisdom, which is

the abstract and general ability to persuade or exert intellectual influence."

Kumon's intelprise, for all its idealistic echoes of Socrates, is not some futuristic concoction of a lofty imagination. It exists today, in the thousands, strung all along the fast lanes of the Internet's electronic global highway: exchanging, sharing, bartering, inventing, and reinventing in the cybernetic commons of "intelspace." But for all their heroic innovation, can anyone seriously claim that they have yet begun to produce anything so grand as wisdom"?

Probably not. For we have barely begun the journey toward the ultimate treasures of the global information economy. Indeed, we are not even sure which road or roads to take, except for our largely intuitive knowledge that we have to create those "third ways" between "my way" and "your way" that we have talked about throughout much of this book.

There are a few other signposts in which we can feel some confidence, too. We know from centuries of economic and social history that the societies which have produced the world's greatest wealth have combined, as economist Joel Kotkin (1993) has pointed out, a unifying sense of cultural values with two other key characteristics: geographical dispersal and a cosmopolitan passion and open-mindedness for technical and scientific progress. Think of those cultures that have dominated economic and political history at various times: the Greeks and Romans, the Spanish, the Dutch, the Native American empires of Meso-America, the Jews, the British North Americans, and today the Japanese and the Chinese. All of them have built their empires on the solid, if not eternal, foundations of shared culture, geographically dispersed networks held together by trust, and a voracious appetite for knowledge. Are not these the same foundations upon which today's global information enterprises must stand or fall? Let us look at them briefly, one by one.

First: common cultural values. We have devoted a significant portion of this book to the importance of culture in globalwork. But it could be that we have erred in overemphasizing culture as a challenge rather than an opportunity. If so, it is because the great opportunities of cross-cultural work—the innovation that arises from the convergence of fundamentally different perspectives and skills—can be mined only after long, hard, and often painful learning.

Indeed, if one looks only at the daily newspapers, there is more evidence of cross-cultural killing than cross-cultural collaboration. One morning as we were writing this book, for example, the front page of the *New York Times* (February 7, 1993) contained four separate news stories about ethnic violence: in India, in Germany, in Israel, in Somalia. Bosnia's "ethnic cleansing" did not even make the front page that day. Another recent article cites at least fifty spots around the world where ethnic or cultural violence is occurring as we write.

As businesses struggle to move forward toward a more multicultural paradigm, the resistance continues to build. Look at the monumental battles of recent years against regional and global free-trade accords, including the North American free-trade pact, the EC's Maastricht Treaty, the Uruguay Round of GATT, NAFTA, and all the proposed reincarnations of the Japanese-led Greater East Asian Co-Prosperity Sphere, now taking shape as APEC. The popular resistance to these vital, growth-engendering, global and regional trade zones is not, as some assert, a product of old-fashioned nationalism. For nationalism went out with the nation-state (or at least the weakening of the nation-state). The resistance is by and large cultural—a profound fear that the values and perspectives of one culture will dominate or dilute another. The French and the Canadians are fearful of American culture, not America. And Americans are fearful of the powerfully persistent quality of Hispanic and Asian cultures, not Mexico or Guatemala or China or Japan.

There is a good side to this, for at least it signals that globalization has made us more than ever aware of our cultural heritages. The downside is that the fear has blinded us to the rich possibilities for multicultural collaboration and invention. The irony is that until we undertake the hard work of cross-cultural learning, we cannot really understand much about ourselves. For the beginning of self-knowledge lies in seeing ourselves reflected in the cultural prism of others. We learn the strengths and the weaknesses of our own cultural myths and mores only when we look at them in relation to other cultural myths and mores. And until we really understand ourselves, we cannot begin to understand others.

Where do we begin? At the beginning, of course. We do not plunge into the depths of cross-cultural work without a life preserver. We learn to use the simple but robust conceptual frameworks and shared languages of such tools as the Intercultural Learning Model, and we develop new cultural competencies as we go, falling back on just-in-time access to knowledge as we need it. The process involves continuous learning, and there are no technological fixes. Indeed, our technical tools — reflecting, as they do, our own cultural biases — are often a greater hindrance than a help. The objective, in the end, is to capitalize on culture in two ways: first, by embracing our own primary and corporate cultures as a strategy for glue to hold us together with mutual trust in the geographically dispersed networks of global enterprise; second, by using the confidence gained from self-cultural knowledge as a key to unlock the richer treasures of multicultural collaboration. More simply put, we must be secure in our own culture to be productive in the multicultural world of global business.

Second: geographical dispersal. Nomadic cultures and globally dispersed businesses succeed because they go where the opportunity is. They don't sit at home and wait for the customers to come banging on their doors. It's a simple lesson, one that even bank robber Willy Sutton understood. And it is, by definition, a key characteristic of the successful global enterprise, just as it always has been a trait of the most successful societies.

Dispersal, of course, is not enough. Without the glue of common cultural values, the dispersed enterprise (or society) is nothing but fragments. Somehow, despite the vast distances and time zones, it must function as an organism, a system. That means enormous effort and skill must go toward the crucial elements touched on in Chapter Three: communication, collaboration, and coordination. These are the realms where technology does work, although it does not *do* the work. It merely provides an enabling edge. It makes things possible that otherwise would be impossible. Some day, perhaps, when groupware evolves into comprehensive, integrated systems that are more like a state of mind than a toolkit, technology will play a much greater role. But for the time being, the emphasis on learning should be more on the dynamics of the group than on the capabilities of the ware. The core technologies — phone, fax, voice mail, e-mail, LANs, and WANs — are of course indispensable to global teaming, but it is essential that we get them right before we push on to more elaborate, expensive, and exotic tools. In the meantime, collaboration and coordination depend on the human side of groupware: learning the conceptual frameworks of team process and development, along with human facilitation, graphic language, and cross-cultural learning.

And third: technical/scientific innovation and openness. As we have said over and over, technology is the great enabler of global enterprise. Along with cross-cultural learning and the skills and competencies that make for effective teamwork, it is a *sine qua non*. But the real promise of technology lies in the future of cyberspace, and it will only come to those organizations that have prepared themselves for its arrival.

That promise lies just beyond the horizon of communication, collaboration, and coordination. It comes at the juncture where all three meet in the attainment of that holy grail of globalwork: continuity. Continuity means balancing multiple forces such as work and leisure, work and home, oneself and one's view of reality. It means getting it all together — individuals, teams, tools, visions, goals, values — and keeping it running smoothly and productively over time, distance, and culture.

The office is already more process than place. Increasingly, global organizations will be defined more by their position on electronic networks than by the location of their office buildings. This modified concept of the office will introduce a new set of options and, in all likelihood, a new set of obstacles for some workers. Again and again we will ask ourselves: How can information systems provide a nucleus for organizational and personal continuity? How can they support relationship building, team growth, and maintenance of organizational cultures on a global scale?

We are intrigued by the vision of an all-purpose "continuity machine," which might yet evolve from today's groupware products. Increasingly, computers are used to provide balance in the face of uncertainty, not just certain answers. In the future, they must support puzzling, not just problem solving. The more mechanical applications of computers will give way to software that facilitates more fluid and more important activities and goals, like centering, balance, and the nurturing of community—all in the face of great discord and uncertainty.

In Japan, for example, the prefecture of Oita is committed to the creation of something called "gross national satisfaction" through the creation of an electronic community linking homes and offices. This is more a social experiment than a technological one in that economic structures and incentives are established to encourage the interdependence of people throughout the prefecture, some of whom are working from their homes, some in offices, some in between. The technology is a straightforward combination of simple electronic tools (like messaging and electronic shopping) that can be used from home or workplace. The vision is to connect the cultures and communities of the workplace, the home, and the recreation center for the benefit of the entire prefecture.

Farfetched? Not at all. Even the workaholic, fourteen-hour-day executives of Silicon Valley are whispering the hot new buzzword "community" and puzzling over how information systems can help create and sustain it. "Intelpreneurs" in Santa Monica, Berkeley, and other California cities, for instance, have equipped numerous coffeehouses around town with one or more tables with recessed computer screens and keyboards on which customers can chat with fellow caffe latte drinkers across town. Meanwhile, other efforts are under way to create "electronic marketplaces" where participants can communicate and transact business through electronic networks. And the notion of an "electronic democracy" through electronic townhalls is being played out with increasing frequency in the political arena.

Community on a global scale. Think of it: a cross-cultural, cross-functional, globally dispersed team, linked by a continuity machine, driven by a common enterprise vision, sharing in the common values of the emerging global culture, and producing out of their cultural, organizational, and technical richness and complexity a constant flow of wisdom. A true global cosmopolis in cyberspace.

This is the vision we have seen appearing like a shadow in the first rays of morning. We hope this book encourages all of us to join in making it real.

REFERENCES

Anguo, L., and Cukier, W. *Telecommunications and Business Competitiveness.* Canada Department of Communications, Apr. 1992.

Applegate, L. M. (Frito-Lay, Inc.). *A Strategic Transition (Consolidated).* Boston: Harvard Business School Press, 1992.

Applegate, L. M., Feld, C., and Jordan, M. "Managing in an Information Age: Transforming Frito-Lay for the 1990s." *Harvard Business School Working Paper Series,* May 1993.

"As Ethnic Wars Multiply, U.S. Strives for a Policy." *New York Times,* February 7, 1993, p. 1.

421

Bartlett, C. A., and Ghoshal, S. *Managing Across Borders: The Transnational Solution.* Boston: Harvard Business School Press, 1989.

Birkhead, E. "The Message Is the Medium." *LAN Computing,* May 1993, p. 14.

"The Canadian Crisis." In *Partners in Prosperity: 1990 Facts.* Ottawa: Prospectus Publications, 1990.

Card, O. S. *Ender's Game.* New York: Doherty, 1985.

Cohen, R. "Europeans Fear Unemployment Will Only Rise, *New York Times,* June 13, 1993, Sec. 1, p. 1.

Coleman, D., and Kaufman, M. (eds.). *Proceedings of Groupware '92.* San Mateo, Calif.: Morgan Kaufman, 1992.

"Communications." *Mexico Business Monthly,* February 1993, pp. 7–11.

Conference Board Survey 1993. Reported in Louis Uchitelle, "Strong Companies Joining Trend to Eliminate Jobs," *New York Times,* July 26, 1993, p. 1.

Copeland, L., and Griggs, L. *Going International: How to Make Friends and Deal Effectively in the Global Marketplace.* New York: Random House, 1985, p. 107.

Curtis, P. *Mudding: Social Phenomenon in Text-Based Virtual Reality.* No. CSL-92-4. Palo Alto Research Center, Xerox Corporation, April 1992.

Dalton, R. "Integrating Yesterday, Today and Tomorrow." *Groupware Integration News.* Menlo Park, Calif.: Institute for the Future, 1992.

Davis, S. M. *Future Perfect.* Reading, Mass.: Addison-Wesley, 1987.

Davis, S. M., and Davidson, W. H. *2020 Vision.* New York: Simon & Schuster, 1991.

de Chardin, T. *The Phenomenon of Man.* New York: Harper & Row, 1959.

Desbiens, J. "Attic of the U.S.A." In S. Sanders, J. Capua, and W. Alpert (eds.), *The Canadian Crisis.* New York: William M. Donner Foundation, 1992.

Dimancescu, D. *The Seamless Enterprise: Making Cross-Functional Management Work.* New York: Harper Business, 1992.

Dodge, W. (ed.). *Boundaries of Identity*. Toronto: Lester Publishings, 1992.

Drexler, A. B., and Sibbet, D. L. *The Drexler/Sibbet Team Performance Model*. Version 8.5. San Francisco: Graphic Guides, 1993.

Drucker, P. F. "The Coming of the New Organization." *Harvard Business Review*, January-February 1988, pp. 45–53.

Duffy, C. A. "Pondering Groupware's Future." *PC Week*, October 26, 1992, p. 32.

"East Asian Miracle." Editorial. *Far Eastern Economic Review*, October 21, 1993, p. 5.

Endrijonas, J. "Is Hand-Held Computing Part of Your Future?" *Bay Area Computer Currents*, September 21, 1993, p. 34.

Flores, J. "The Fiber Optic Transmission Equipment Market in Mexico." U.S. Commerce Department, American Embassy, Mexico City, September 1992. Cited in *Mexico Business Monthly*, February 1993a, pp. 7–11.

Flores, J. "The Telecommunications Equipment Market in Mexico." U.S. Commerce Department, American Embassy, Mexico City, January 1993. Cited in *Mexico Business Monthly*, February 1993b, pp. 7–11.

Flores, J. "The Cellular Telecommunications Equipment Market in Mexico." U.S. Commerce Department, American Embassy, Mexico City, February 1993. Cited in *Mexico Business Monthly*, February 1993c, pp. 7–11.

Fuchsberg, G. "Taking Control." *Wall Street Journal*. Executive Education Supplement, September 10, 1993.

Galbraith, J. R., Lawler, E. E., and Associates. *Organizing for the Future: The New Logic for Managing Complex Organizations*. San Francisco: Jossey-Bass, 1993.

Galinski, E., Bond, J. T., and Friedman, D. E. *The Changing Workforce*. New York: Families and Work Institute, 1993.

Gatewood, D. "Recent Layoffs Haven't Helped Companies, Survey Says." *Newsday*, September 23, 1993, p. 23.

Gibson, W. *Neuromancer*. West Bloomfield, Mich.: Phantasia Press, 1984.

Goulet, D. *The Uncertain Promise — Value Conflicts in Technology Transfer.* New York: North America, Inc., 1977.

Gray, P., Olfman, L., and Park, H. "The Interface Problem in International Group DSS." Paper presented for the task force on International Group Decision Support Systems at the 21st Hawaii International Conference in Systems Sciences, Honolulu, January 5–7, 1988.

Hall, E. T., and Hall, M. R. *Understanding Cultural Differences: Germans, French, and Americans.* Yarmouth, Maine: Intercultural Press, 1990.

Hampden-Turner, C. In P. Evans and others (eds.), *Human Resource Management in Intercultural Firms.* New York: St. Martin's Press, 1990a.

Hampden-Turner, C. *Creating Culture: From Discord to Harmony.* International Management Series. Reading, Mass.: Addison-Wesley, 1990b.

Henkoff, R. "Winning the New Career Game." *Fortune,* July 12, 1993, p. 46.

Hirschhorn, L. *Managing in the New Team Environment.* Reading, Mass.: Addison-Wesley, 1991.

Hirschhorn, L., and Gilmore, T. "The New Boundaries of the Boundaryless Company." *Harvard Business Review,* May–June 1992, pp. 104–115.

Hofstede, G. *Culture's Consequences: International Differences in Work-Related Values.* Cross-Cultural Research and Methodology Series, vol. 5. Newbury Park, Calif.: Sage, 1984.

Hofstede, G. *Cultures and Organizations: Software of the Mind.* London: McGraw-Hill, 1991.

Hurtig, M. *The Betrayal of Canada.* Toronto: Stoddart, 1991.

Institute for the Future. *Corporate Toolkit for the Nineties: Organizations, the Workforce, and Technology.* Corporate Associates Program, vol. 4, no. 2. Menlo Park, Calif.: Institute for the Future, 1993a.

Institute for the Future. *Global Opportunities: Searching for Markets and Working Across Borders.* Corporate Associates Program, vol. 4, no. 1. Menlo Park, Calif.: Institute for the Future, 1993b.

Institute for the Future. *Ten-Year Forecast*. Corporate Associates Program. Menlo Park, Calif.: Institute for the Future, 1993c.

Ishii, H. "Cross-Cultural Communication and Computer-Supported Cooperative Work." *Whole Earth Review*, Winter 1990, pp. 48–53.

Jamieson, D., and O'Mara, J. *Managing Workforce 2000: Gaining the Diversity Advantage*. San Francisco: Jossey-Bass, 1991.

Johansen, R. *Electronic Meetings: Technical Alternatives and Social Choices*. Reading, Mass.: Addison-Wesley, 1979.

Johansen, R. *Teleconferencing and Beyond: Communications in the Office of the Future*. New York: McGraw-Hill, 1984.

Johansen, R. *Groupware: Computer Support for Business Teams*. New York: Free Press, 1988.

Johansen, R., and others. *Leading Business Teams: How Teams Can Use Technology and Group Process Tools to Enhance Performance*. Addison-Wesley Series on Organizational Development. Reading, Mass.: Addison-Wesley, 1991.

Johnson-Lenz, P., and Johnson-Lenz, T. "Groupware: The Process and Impacts of Design Choices." In E. B. Kerr and S. R. Hiltz (eds.), *Computer-Mediated Communication Systems: Status and Evaluation*. New York: Academic Press, 1982.

Katzenbach, J. R., and Smith, D. K. *The Wisdom of Teams*. Boston: Harvard Business School Press, 1993.

Kiechel, W. "How We Will Work in the Year 2000." *Fortune*, May 17, 1993, p. 39.

Kotkin, J. *Tribes: How Race, Religion, and Identity Determine Success in the New Global Economy*. New York: Random House, 1993.

Kras, E. *Management in Two Cultures: Bridging the Gap Between US and Mexican Managers*. Yarmouth, Maine: Intercultural Press, 1989.

"Las 500 de Expansión, Fortune y the Financial Post." *Expansión*, August 18, 1993, p. 324.

Liu, H., and others. *Quantum Leap*. San Francisco: United States–China Educational Institute, Spring 1992.

Lottor, M., "Internet Growth (1981–1991); RFC 1296." *Network Working Group Request for Comments*. Menlo Park, Calif.: Network Information Systems Center, SRI International, Jan. 1992.

McCaig, N. M. *Global Nomad Quarterly*, Spring 1992, p. 2.

"Murdoch's Asian Bet." *Economist*, July 31–August 6, 1993, p. 13.

Nachmanovitch, S. *Free Play: The Power of Improvisation in Life and the Arts*. New York: Tarcher/Perigee, 1990.

Naik, G. "Beyond the Borders." *Wall Street Journal*, Executive Education Supplement, September 10, 1993.

National Research Council. *National Collaboratories: Applying Information Technology for Scientific Research*. Washington, D.C.: National Academy Press, 1993.

Nichols, N. A. "From Complacency to Competitiveness." *Harvard Business Review*, September–October 1993, p. 164.

Noble, B. P. "Dissecting the 90s Workplace." *New York Times*, September 19, 1993, p. 21.

OECD. Reported in "Musical Chairs." *Economist*, July 17, 1993b, p. 67.

O'Hara-Devereaux, M., and Pardini, R. L. "Seeing How to Work Together." *IABC Communication World*, March 1993, pp. 29–32.

Patiño, G. M. "Analisis Financiero de las 500." *Expansión*, August 18, 1993, pp. 321–339.

Paz, O. *The Labyrinth of Solitude: Life and Thought in Mexico*. New York: Grove Press, 1961.

Perry, T. S. "Electronic Mail: Pervasive and Persuasive." *IEEE Spectrum*, October 1992, vol. 29, no. 10, pp. 22–23.

Porter, M. *Canada at the Crossroads*. Council on National Issues, October 1991.

Postman, N. *Technology*. New York: Knopf, 1992.

Powers, J. "What's the World Coming To." *LAN Magazine*, May 1993, p. 38.

"Public Services, Private Pesos: Infrastructure in Latin America." *Economist*, July 17, 1993, p. 40.

Radwaniki, G., and Lutterwell, J. *The Will of a Nation*. Toronto: Stoddart, 1992.

Rao, A. "Team Spirit." *LAN Magazine*, March 1993, p. 109.

Read, R. "New Windows Big in Japan." *San Francisco Examiner*, October 3, 1993, p. E-10.

Reddy, B. W., and Jamison K. (eds.). *Team Building: Blueprints for Productivity and Satisfaction*. San Diego, Calif.: NTL Institute for Applied Behavioral Science and University Associates, 1988.

Rosall, J. "End-User Multimedia and Integrated Messaging Trends: Shifting Practices." In R. M. Baecker (ed.), *Groupware and Computer-Supported Cooperative Work*. San Mateo, Calif.: Morgan Kauffman, 1993.

Samovar, L. A., and Porter, R. E. (eds.). *Intercultural Communication: A Reader*. Sixth ed. Belmont, Calif.: Wadsworth, 1991.

Schein, E. H. *Organizational Culture and Leadership*. San Francisco: Jossey-Bass, 1991.

Scholtes, P. R., and others. *The Team Handbook: How to Use Teams to Improve Quality*. Madison, Wis.: Joiner Associates, 1988.

Scott, D. C. "Mexican Vision of Free Trade—NAFTA Is Only the Beginning." *Christian Science Monitor*, August 23, 1993, p. 14.

Scott, J. Quoted in "Talk of the Electronic Generation." *Los Angeles Times*, September 24, 1993, p. 1.

Sesit, M. R. "Flocking to the Frontier." *Wall Street Journal*, September 24, 1993, p. R4.

Shenon, P. "Missing Out on a Glittering Market: Southeast Asia's Economies Are Booming." *New York Times*, September 12, 1993, p. F6.

Short, J., Williams, E., and Christie, B. *The Social Psychology of Telecommunications*. London: Wiley, 1976.

Sibbet, D. *Graphic Guide to Facilitation, Principles and Practices*. San Francisco: Graphic Guides, 1993.

Siegmann, K. "National Semiconductor Wins 'Comeback' Honors," *San Francisco Chronicle*, April 19, 1993, p. D5.

Slocum, D. "The F-16 and LANTIRN." *Flying Safety*, April 1991, pp. 5–7.

Smith, C. E. *Disappearing Border: Mexico–United States Relations to the 1990s*. Stanford, Calif.: Stanford University Press, 1992.

Southerland, D. "Sprouting Start-Ups with a Mix of Academia, Austerity." *Washington Post*, August 24, 1993, p. C-1.

Storti, C. *The Art of Crossing Cultures*. Yarmouth, Maine: Intercultural Press, 1990.

Tan, B.C.Y., Watson, R. T., Wei, K. K., Raman, K. S., and Kerola, P. K. "National Culture and Group Support Systems: Examining the Situation Where Some People Are More Equal Than Others." IEEE, 1993.

Trompenaars, Fons. *Riding the Waves of Cultures: Understanding Cultural Diversity in Business*. London: Economist Books, 1993.

Turner, J., and Kraut, R. (eds.). "From Wealth to Wisdom: A Change in the Social Paradigm." *CSCW92: Sharing Perspectives*. ACM Press, 1992.

U.N. Population Fund. *State of the World, 1993*. New York: United Nations Publishing, 1993.

U.S. Bureau of Labor Statistics. *Current Population Survey, 1948–97*. Washington: GPO, 1992.

U.S. Bureau of Labor Statistics. *Handbook of Labor Statistics*. Washington: GPO, 1989.

U.S. Bureau of Labor Statistics. *Monthly Labor Review*. Washington: GPO, 1990.

U.S. Bureau of Labor Statistics. *Employment and Earnings*. Washington: GPO, 1991, 1992.

U.S. Bureau of Labor Statistics. Reported in Louis Uchitelle, "Strong Companies Joining Trend to Eliminate Jobs," *New York Times*, July 26, 1993, p. 1.

U.S. Department of Commerce. *Telecommunications in the Age of Information*. Washington: GPO, October 1991.

U.S. Small Business Administration. Small Business Database. Office of Advocacy, 1991.

Ward, L. B. "When a Deal Can Turn on a Phrase." *New York Times*, September 12, 1993, p. F7.

Wederspahn, G. M. "Don't Get Lost in the Translation." *Cultural Diversity at Work*, November 1991, p. 8.

Weisbord, M. R. *Productive Workplaces: Organizing and Managing for Dignity, Meaning, and Community*. San Francisco: Jossey-Bass, 1987.

Wells, M. J. "Virtual Reality: Technology, Experience, and Assumptions." *Human Factors Society Bulletin*, September 1992, pp. 1–3.

World Bank. *World Development Indicators*. Cited in Institute for the Future, *Global Opportunities*, Corporate Associates Program, vol. 4, no. 1, 1993, p. 2.

World Investment Report 1992: Transnational Corporations as Engines of Growth. Cited in Institute for the Future, *1993 Ten-Year Forecast*, pp. 9–10.

Wright, J. W. (ed.). *The Universal Almanac*. Kansas City, Mo.: Andrews & McMeel, 1992.

INDEX